Implementing and Supporting Microsoft Internet Explorer 4.0 Using the Microsoft Explorer Administration Kit (Exam 70-079)

MCSE Training Guide: Internet Explorer 4 (1-56205-889-4)

Chapter 1: Planning

Objective	Page Reference
In Corporate Administrator mode or Internet service provider mode, choose the appropriate installation of Internet Explorer 4.0, with or without Windows Desktop Update	*Choosing the Appropriate Internet Explorer Installation* see page 22
Develop custom installation strategies for Internet Explorer 4.0	*Custom Installation Strategies* see page 27
In Corporate Administrator mode, develop appropriate security strategies for using Internet Explorer 4.0 for various sites	*Developing Secure Internet Explorer Usage Strategies* see page 42
Public kiosks	*Public Kiosks* see page 51
End-user sites	*End-User Installations* see page 53
Business sites	*Business Installations* see page 54
Choose Active Desktop items and develop Active Channels	*Active Channels* see page 55
Develop strategies for replacing other Internet browsers	*Migration Issues* see page 62
Microsoft Internet Explorer 3.*x*	*Replacing Previous Versions of Internet Explorer* see page 63
Netscape Navigator	*Replacing Netscape Browser Products* see page 64
Develop strategies for replacing other Internet mail clients. Other mail clients include:	*Replacing Other Internet Mail and News Clients* see page 65
Internet Mail and News	*Replacing Other Internet Mail and News Clients* see page 65
Netscape Mail	*Replacing Other Internet Mail and News Clients* see page 65
Eudora	*Replacing Other Internet Mail and News Clients* see page 65
Choose the appropriate configuration strategy for Microsoft Outlook Express	*Choosing a Configuration Strategy for Microsoft Outlook Express* see page 66
Choose the appropriate configuration strategy for Microsoft NetMeeting. Elements include:	*Choosing a Configuration Strategy for Microsoft NetMeeting* see page 69
Settings	*Settings* see page 70
Restrictions	*Settings* see page 70
Choose the appropriate configurations for the NetMeeting client	*Choosing a Configuration Strategy for Microsoft NetMeeting Client* see page 74
Internet Locator Service (ILS) server connectivity	*Internet Locator Service* see page 74
IP connectivity	*IP Connectivity and Peer-to-Peer Networking* see page 75
Peer-to-peer networking	*IP Connectivity and Peer-to-Peer Networking* see page 75

Objective	Page Reference
Proxy server settings	*Proxy Settings* see page 75
Proxy client settings	*Proxy Settings* see page 75
In Corporate Administrator mode or Internet service provider mode, choose strategies for managing automatic configuration by using the IEAK Profile Manager	*Strategies for Managing Automatic Configuration Using the IEAK Profile Manager* see page 76
Microsoft JScript autoproxy	*Strategies for Managing Automatic Configuration Using the IEAK Profile Manager* see page 76
.ins files	*Strategies for Managing Automatic Configuration Using the IEAK Profile Manager* see page 76
.adm files	*Strategies for Managing Automatic Configuration Using the IEAK Profile Manager* see page 76
Develop a configuration plan for Active Setup components	*Strategies for Managing Automatic Configuration Using the IEAK Profile Manager* see page 76
Develop strategies for using the Internet Connection Wizard in Internet Server provider mode	*Developing Strategies for Using the Connection Manager Administration Kit* see page 81
Modem detection	*Developing Strategies for Using the Connection Manager Administration Kit* see page 81
Stack installation	*Developing Strategies for Using the Connection Manager Administration Kit* see page 81
Configuration of dial-up connections	*Developing Strategies for Using the Connection Manager Administration Kit* see page 81

Chapter 2: Installation and Configuration

Objective	Page Reference
Install and configure Internet Explorer 4.0, with or without the Windows Desktop Update, on computers that run various operating systems:	*Installing Internet Explorer 4.0* see page 111
Microsoft Windows 95	*Installing Internet Explorer 4.0 for Windows NT and Windows 95* see page 112
Microsoft Windows NT Server 4.0	*Installing Internet Explorer 4.0 for Windows 3.1, 3.11, Windows for Workgroups 3.11, and Windows NT 3.51* see page 116
Microsoft Windows NT Workstation 4.0	*Installing Internet Explorer 4.0 for Windows 3.1, 3.11, Windows for Workgroups 3.11, and Windows NT 3.51* see page 116
Microsoft Windows 3.*x*	*Installing Internet Explorer 4.0 for Windows 3.1, 3.11, Windows for Workgroups 3.11, and Windows NT 3.51* see page 116
Macintosh	*Installing Internet Explorer 4.0 for Macintosh* see page 119
Specify and customize Active Setup components	*Using the IEAK Wizard to Customize Active Setup Components* see page 127
Customize the browser	*Customizing the Browser* see page 144
Configure built-in and custom components of Internet Explorer 4.0 by using the IEAK wizard	*Configuring and Customizing Components* see page 157

continues

DAVID GULBRANSEN
KENRICK RAWLINGS

MCSE
TRAINING GUIDE

INTERNET EXPLORER 4

New Riders

MCSE Training Guide: Internet Explorer 4

International Standard Book Number: 0-56205-889-4

Library of Congress Catalog Card Number: 7-52064-05889-2

Printed in the United States of America

First Printing: June 1998

00 99 98 4 3 2 1

Trademarks

All terms mentioned in this book that are known to be trademarks or service marks have been appropriately capitalized. New Riders Publishing cannot attest to the accuracy of this information. Use of a term in this book should not be regarded as affecting the validity of any trademark or service mark.

Executive Editor *John Kane*
Acquisitions Editor *Steve Weiss*
Development Editor *Chris Zahn*
Managing Editor *Sarah Kearns*

Project Editor
Susan Ross Moore

Copy Editor
Alice Martina-Smith

Indexer
Bruce Clingaman

Technical Editors
James Cooper
Gerry High

Software Development Specialist
Jack Belbot

Production
Michael Henry
Linda Knose
Tim Osborn
Staci Somers
Mark Walchle

About the Author

David Gulbransen has been employed as an information systems professional for over eight years. He began his career with the Indiana University Departmental Support Lab as an analyst/manager, overseeing a consulting group responsible for advising university departments on technology deployment. After an appointment as the Computing Support Specialist for the School of Fine Arts, David left for a position as the Manager of Information Systems at Dimension X, a Java tools development company.

While there, he grew the information systems environment from a small UNIX-based shop, to a shared UNIX-NT environment serving customers as diverse as Fox Television, MCA Records, Intel, and Sun Microsystems. Upon the purchase of Dimension X in 1997 by Microsoft, David founded Vervet Logic, a software development company developing XML and Web tools for new media development. Some of his other titles include *Creating Web Applets with Java, The Netscape Server Survival Guide,* and *Special Edition Using Dynamic HTML.* David holds a BA in Computer Science and Theatre from Indiana University.

Kenrick Rawlings has been a professional software developer for over ten years, working extensively in client server applications and Internet/intranet distributed applications. He began his career at the Indiana University Departmental Support Lab as the lead PC specialist, and also served as the Departmental Computing Support Specialist for the Department of Physics. Ken was employed by Scopus Technologies as a software engineer, responsible for the migration of several core products from C++ to Java distributed applications. He recently left Scopus Technologies to co-found Vervet Logic, a software development company developing XML and Web tools for new media development. Some of Ken's other titles include *Creating Web Applets with Java,* and *Special Edition Using Dynamic HTML.* Ken holds a BS in computer science from Indiana University.

Acknowledgments

Thanks to all the wonderful people at New Riders who helped make this title go smoothly, especially Chris Zahn and Steve Weiss. Thanks also to Jim Causey, Luke Heidelberger, Steve Volan, and many others for input along the way. Thanks to Scott and Erin Cramer, Kim Spahr, Dusty Fisher, Sam, Heidi, Hee, and Jenn for keeping us sane during the writing process. Thanks for nothing to Stef. And finally thanks to our families, friends, and all the other people who are too numerous to list here; you know who you are.

Contents at a Glance

Table of Contents

Introduction

MCSE Training Guide: Internet Explorer 4 is designed for advanced end users, service technicians, and network administrators with the goal of certification as a Microsoft Certified Systems Engineer with the +Internet credential (MCSE+Internet). The Internet Explorer 4 exam (Exam #70-079: "Implementing and Supporting Microsoft Internet Explorer 4.0 by Using the Microsoft Internet Explorer Administration Kit") measures your ability to implement, administer, and troubleshoot information systems that incorporate the Microsoft Internet Explorer Administration Kit (IEAK).

Who Should Read This Book

This book is designed to help you meet these goals by preparing you for the Microsoft exam "Implementing and Supporting Microsoft Internet Explorer 4.0 by Using the Microsoft Internet Explorer Administration Kit" (Exam #70-079).

This book is your one-stop shop. Everything you need to know to pass the exam is here, and Microsoft has approved it as study material. You do not *have* to take a class in addition to buying this book to pass the exam. However, depending on your personal study habits or learning style, you might benefit from taking a class in addition to this book or buying this book in addition to attending a class.

This book also can help advanced users and administrators who are not studying for the exam but are looking for a single-volume reference on Internet Explorer 4.

How This Book Helps You

This book conducts you on a self-guided tour of all the areas covered by the IE4/IEAK exam and teaches you the specific skills you need to achieve your MCSE certification. You'll also find helpful hints, tips, real-world examples, exercises, and references to additional study materials. Specifically, this book is set up to help you in the following ways:

Objectives

- **Organization.** This book is organized by major exam topics and individual exam objectives. Every objective you need to know for the "Implementing and Supporting Microsoft Internet Explorer 4.0 by Using the Microsoft Internet Explorer Administration Kit" exam is covered in this book. We've included a margin icon, like the one in the margin here, to help you quickly locate these objectives as they are addressed in the chapters. The objectives information is also conveniently condensed in the tear card at the front of this book.

- **Time-management advice.** Quizzes appear at the beginning of each chapter to test your knowledge of the objectives contained within that chapter. If you already know the answers to some or all of these questions, you can make a time-management decision accordingly, adjusting the amount of time you spend on a given topic.

- **Extensive practice test options.** Plenty of questions appear at the end of each chapter to test your comprehension of material covered within that chapter. An answer list follows the questions so that you can check yourself. These review questions help you determine what you understand thoroughly and what topics require further review on your part.

You'll also have a chance to practice for the certification exams by using the TestPrep test engine on the CD-ROM that accompanies this book. The questions on the CD-ROM provide a more thorough and comprehensive look at what the certification exams are really like.

Note

> For a complete description of New Riders' newly developed test engine, please see Appendix D, "All About TestPrep."
>
> For a complete description of what you can find on the CD-ROM, see Appendix C, "What's on the CD-ROM."

For more information about the exam or the certification process, contact Microsoft:

Microsoft Education: 800-636-7544

Internet: `ftp://ftp.microsoft.com/Services/MSEdCert`

World Wide Web: `http://www.microsoft.com/train_cert/default.htm`

CompuServe Forum: `GO MSEDCERT`

Understanding What the IE4/IEAK (#70-079) Exam Covers

The "Implementing and Supporting Microsoft Internet Explorer 4.0 by Using the Microsoft Internet Explorer Administration Kit" exam (#70-079) covers the IIS 4.0 main topic areas represented by the conceptual groupings of the test objectives. Each chapter represents one of these main topic areas. The exam focuses on determining your skill in six major categories:

- Planning
- Installation and configuration
- Configuring and managing resource access
- Integration and interoperability
- Monitoring and optimization
- Troubleshooting

The "Implementing and Supporting Microsoft Internet Explorer 4.0 by Using the Microsoft Internet Explorer Administration Kit" certification exam uses these categories to measure your ability. Before taking the exam, you should be proficient in the job skills described in the following sections.

Planning

In corporate administrator mode or Internet service provider mode, choose the appropriate installation of Internet Explorer 4.0, with or without the Windows Desktop Update.

Develop custom installation strategies for Internet Explorer 4.0.

In corporate administrator mode, develop appropriate security strategies for using Internet Explorer 4.0 for various sites. Sites include the following:

- Public kiosks
- End-user sites
- Business sites

Choose active desktop items and develop active channels.

Develop strategies for replacing other Internet browsers. Other browsers include the following:

- Microsoft Internet Explorer 3.*x*
- Netscape Navigator

Develop strategies for replacing other Internet mail clients. Other mail clients include the following:

- Internet Mail and News
- Netscape Mail
- Eudora

Choose the appropriate configuration strategy for Microsoft Outlook Express.

Choose the appropriate configuration strategy for Microsoft NetMeeting. Elements include the following:

- Settings
- Restrictions

Choose the appropriate configurations for the NetMeeting client. Configurations include the following:

- Internet Locator Service (ILS) server connectivity
- IP connectivity
- Peer-to-peer networking
- Proxy server settings
- Proxy client settings

In corporate administrator mode or Internet service provider mode, choose strategies for managing automatic configuration by using the IEAK Profile Manager. Methods include the following:

- Microsoft JScript autoproxy
- INS files
- ADM files

Develop a configuration plan for active setup components.

Develop strategies for using the Internet Connection Wizard in Internet service provider mode. Elements include the following:

- Modem detection
- Stack installation
- Configuration of dial-up connections

Installation and Configuration

Install and configure Internet Explorer 4.0, with or without the Windows Desktop Update, on computers that run various operating systems. Operating systems include these:

- Microsoft Windows NT Server 4.0
- Microsoft Windows NT Workstation 4.0
- Microsoft Windows 3.*x*
- Microsoft Windows 95
- Macintosh

Specify and customize active setup components.

Customize the browser.

Configure built-in and custom components of Internet Explorer 4.0 by using the IEAK Wizard. Components include the following:

- Microsoft Outlook Express
- Microsoft NetMeeting

Configure channels, software distribution channels, and site subscriptions.

Configure Outlook Express for custom installations of Internet Explorer 4.0.

Configuring and Managing Resource Access

In corporate administrator mode, create and assign various levels of security for security zones.

In corporate administrator mode, manage proxy server support for custom installations of Internet Explorer 4.0.

Manage automatic configuration by using the IEAK Profile Manager. Methods include the following:

- JScript autoproxy
- INS files
- ADM files

Integration and Interoperability

In corporate administrator mode or Internet service provider mode, deploy a preconfigured version of Internet Explorer 4.0 by using the IEAK. Distribution methods include the following:

- Download
- CD-ROM
- Floppy disk

Replace other Internet browsers. Other browsers include the following:

- Microsoft Internet Explorer 3.*x*
- Netscape Navigator

Replace other Internet mail clients. Other mail clients include the following:

- Internet Mail and News
- Netscape Mail
- Eudora

Configure NetMeeting for various tasks. Tasks include the following:

- Multipoint application sharing
- Transferring files
- Video conferencing

Monitoring and Optimization

Customize active desktop items and active channels.

Use the IEAK Profile Manager to optimize network resources and components.

Set up schedules for automatic updates. Locations include the following:

- Site subscriptions
- Channels
- The active desktop

Optimize caching and performance.

Troubleshooting

Diagnose and resolve the deployment failure of a preconfigured version of Internet Explorer 4.0.

Diagnose and resolve problems related to the IEAK Wizard.

Diagnose and resolve connection failures of Outlook Express.

Diagnose and resolve connection failures of NetMeeting.

Diagnose and resolve failures of Webcasting. Types of Webcasting include the following:

- Site subscriptions
- Channels
- Active desktop items

Diagnose and resolve failures of caching.

Choose the appropriate tools for troubleshooting network connection failures. Tools for troubleshooting include these:

- IP configuration
- Ping
- Trace route
- Network Monitor
- nslookup

Hardware and Software Recommended for Preparation

As a self-paced study guide, *MCSE Training Guide: Internet Explorer 4* is meant to help you review concepts with which you already have training and hands-on experience. To make the most of the review, you should have as much background and experience as possible. The best way to do this is to combine studying with working on real networks, using the products on which you will be tested. The following sections give you a description of the minimum computer requirements you need to build a solid practice environment.

Computers

The minimum computer requirements that you need to ensure that you can study everything on which you'll be tested are one or more workstations running Windows 95 or Windows NT Workstation and two or more servers running Windows NT Server, all connected by a network.

Minimum Requirements for Workstations: Windows 95 and Windows NT Workstation

- Computer on the Microsoft Hardware Compatibility list
- 486DX 33MHz or better
- 16MB RAM
- 200MB hard disk

- 3.5-inch 1.44MB floppy drive
- VGA video adapter
- VGA monitor
- Mouse or equivalent pointing device
- Two-speed CD-ROM drive
- Network Interface Card (NIC)
- Presence on an existing network or use of a hub to create a test network
- Microsoft Windows 95 or Windows NT Workstation 4.0

Author's Recommendations

- 75MHz Pentium or better
- 32MB RAM
- 500MB hard disk

Servers: Windows NT Server

- Two computers on the Microsoft Hardware Compatibility list
- 486DX2 66MHz or better
- 32MB RAM
- 340MB hard disk
- 3.5-inch 1.44MB floppy drive
- VGA video adapter
- VGA monitor
- Mouse or equivalent pointing device
- Two-speed CD-ROM drive
- Network Interface Card (NIC)

- Presence on an existing network or use of a hub to create a test network
- Microsoft Windows NT Server 4.0

Author's Recommendations

- 75MHz Pentium or better
- 64MB RAM
- 500MB hard disk

Connections

An Internet connection is also required.

Tips for the Exam

Remember the following tips as you prepare for the certification exam:

- **Read all the material.** Microsoft has been known to include material not expressly specified in the objectives. This course has included additional information not required by the objectives in an effort to give you the best possible preparation for the examination and for real-world network experiences to come.
- **Complete the exercises in each chapter.** The exercises in each chapter help you gain experience using the Microsoft product. All Microsoft exams are experience-based and require you to have used the Microsoft product in a real networking environment. Exercises for each objective are placed at the end of each chapter.
- **Take each prechapter quiz to evaluate how well you know the topic of the chapter.** Each chapter opens with at least one short answer/essay question per exam objective covered in the chapter. At the end of the chapter, you will find the quiz answers and pointers to where in the chapter that specific objective is covered.

- **Complete all the questions in the "Review Questions" sections.** Complete the questions at the end of each chapter—they help you remember key points. The questions are simple, but be warned: Some questions require more than one answer.

- **Review the exam objectives.** Develop your own questions for each topic listed. If you can make and answer several questions for each topic, you should not find it difficult to pass the exam.

Note

Although this book is designed to prepare you to take and pass the "Implementing and Supporting Microsoft Internet Explorer 4.0 by Using the Microsoft Internet Explorer Administration Kit" certification exam, there are no guarantees. Read this book, work through the questions and exercises, and when you feel confident, take a practice assessment exam using the TestPrep test engine. This should tell you whether you are ready for the real thing.

When taking the actual certification exam, make sure that you answer all the questions before your time limit expires. Do not spend too much time on any one question. If you are unsure about an answer, answer the question as best you can and mark it for later review, when you have finished the rest of the questions.

Remember that the primary object is not to pass the exam—it is to understand the material. After you understand the material, passing the exam should be simple. Knowledge is a pyramid; to build upward, you need a solid foundation. The Microsoft Certified Systems Engineer programs are designed to ensure that you have that solid foundation.

Good luck!

New Riders Publishing

The staff of New Riders Publishing is committed to bringing you the very best in computer reference material. Each New Riders book is the result of months of work by authors and staff who research and refine the information contained within its covers.

As part of this commitment to you, the NRP reader, New Riders invites your input. Please let us know if you enjoy this book, if you have trouble with the information or examples presented, or if you have a suggestion for the next edition.

Please note, however, that New Riders staff cannot serve as a technical resource during your preparation for the Microsoft certification exams or for questions about software-related or hardware-related problems. Please refer instead to the documentation that accompanies IE4/IEAK or to the application's Help systems.

If you have a question or comment about any New Riders book, there are several ways to contact New Riders Publishing. We will respond to as many readers as we can. Your name, address, or phone number will never become part of a mailing list or be used for any purpose other than to help us continue to bring you the best books possible. You can write to us at the following address:

> New Riders Publishing
> Attn: Publisher
> 201 W. 103rd Street
> Indianapolis, IN 46290

If you prefer, you can fax New Riders Publishing at 317-817-7448.

You also can send email to New Riders at the following Internet address:

`certification@mcp.com`

NRP is an imprint of Macmillan Computer Publishing. To obtain a catalog or information, or to purchase any Macmillan Computer Publishing book, call 800-428-5331.

Thank you for selecting *MCSE Training Guide: Internet Explorer 4*!

Chapter 1

Planning

This chapter helps you prepare for the exam by covering the following objectives:

Objectives

- In Corporate Administrator mode or Internet Service Provider mode, choose the appropriate installation of Internet Explorer 4.0, with or without the Windows Desktop Update.
- Develop custom installation strategies for Internet Explorer 4.0.
- In Corporate Administrator mode, develop appropriate security strategies for using Internet Explorer 4.0 for various sites. Sites include:
  - Public kiosks
  - End-user sites
  - Business sites
- Choose Active Desktop items and develop Active Channels.
- Develop strategies for replacing other Internet browsers. Other browsers include:
  - Microsoft Internet Explorer 3.*x*
  - Netscape Navigator

continues

- Develop strategies for replacing other Internet mail clients. Other mail clients include:
    - Internet Mail and News
    - Netscape Mail
    - Eudora
- Choose the appropriate configuration strategy for Microsoft Outlook Express.
- Choose the appropriate configuration strategy for Microsoft NetMeeting. Elements include:
    - Settings
    - Restrictions
- Choose the appropriate configurations for the NetMeeting client. Configurations include:
    - Internet Locator Service (ILS) server connectivity
    - IP connectivity
    - Peer-to-peer networking
    - Proxy server settings
    - Proxy client settings
- In Corporate Administrator mode or Internet service provider mode, choose strategies for managing automatic configuration by using the IEAK Profile Manager. Methods include:
    - Microsoft JScript autoproxy
    - `INS` files
    - `.ADM` files
- Develop a configuration plan for Active Setup components.

continues

- Develop strategies for using the Internet Connection Wizard in Internet service provider mode. Elements include:
  - Modem detection
  - Stack installation
  - Configuration of dial-up connections

Test Yourself! Before reading this chapter, test yourself to determine how much study time you will need to devote to this section.

1. Identify the minimum installation requirements for the Internet Administration Kit Configuration Wizard.
2. Explain the differences in the components installed in the Standard, Enhanced, and Full installation options for Internet Explorer 4.0.
3. Identify and explain the differences between the three deployment roles available for the Internet Explorer Administration Kit.
4. What are the primary advantages of a network-based installation distribution, using the Active Setup Wizard?
5. Identify the four security zones and their applications.
6. Explain the major functionality of the Windows Desktop Update.
7. What are the primary upgrade concerns when transitioning from Netscape Navigator 3.0 to Internet Explorer 4.0?
8. For which email packages does Internet Explorer support a migration path? What settings are preserved for each client?
9. What are the primary advantages of the Active Setup Wizard?
10. What are appropriate uses for the Connection Manager Administration Kit?
11. What functionality does the IEAK Profile Manager add to the IEAK?
12. What features of Outlook Express can be customized using the IEAK?
13. What functionality is provided through OSD and CDF channels?
14. What are some of the primary concerns with an enterprise deployment of NetMeeting?

The answers to this prechapter quiz are located at the end of this chapter. Score your answers against those provided to determine your course of study for this chapter...

Test Objectives Overview

Adequate planning is the foundation of a successful deployment of any IS solution, and an Internet Explorer deployment is indeed a complex IS solution. Because of the flexibility Internet Explorer can provide and the various demands it places on hardware and network infrastructure, planning for deployment can be a very involved and detailed task.

The objectives for the Planning section of the "Implementing and Supporting the Microsoft Internet Explorer Administration Kit for Microsoft Internet Explorer 4.0" MCSE exam are designed to make sure that you understand the steps to be taken to plan for IE deployment. The exam objectives also ensure that you are familiar with the various customizable features and how those can be adapted to a variety of situations.

The objectives deal not only with the customization of Internet Explorer, but also the installation and customization of the various optional packages that can be deployed to make your Internet Explorer installation a more complete solution, including packages such as the Active Desktop, Outlook Express, and NetMeeting.

Many of the objectives in this chapter are more theory and less "hands-on" than the objectives in some of the later chapters. This chapter contains a lot of discussion about requirements for packages, appropriate applications, migration from older versions, and developing deployment strategies. Many of these types of objectives don't really have a direct exercise equivalent. However, at the end of the chapter are some exercises to help you work through planning issues. Some of these exercises are simple worksheets and checklists, but in spite of the fact that they don't necessarily include hardware, they are the foundation for much of the hands-on material you will find later in this book, and they are key to any successful rollout of Internet Explorer.

Here are the topics addressed in this chapter. Each is essential to proper planning for using Internet Explorer and the Internet Explorer Administration Kit:

- The Microsoft Planning Model
- Choosing the appropriate Internet Explorer installation
- Custom installation strategies
- Developing secure Internet Explorer usage strategies
- Active Channels
- The Windows Desktop Update
- Migration issues
- Choosing a configuration strategy for Microsoft Outlook Express
- Choosing a configuration strategy for Microsoft NetMeeting
- Choosing a configuration strategy for Microsoft NetMeeting client
- Strategies for managing automatic configuration using the IEAK Profile Manager
- Developing a configuration for Active Setup components
- Developing strategies for using the Connection Manager Administration Kit

The Microsoft Planning Model

Microsoft outlines the planning process in the following manner, based on information that must be determined to successfully implement Internet Explorer and make the most efficient use of IS department resources:

- **Assemble project teams.** Because the large-scale implementation of a product as complex as Internet Explorer is bound to involve many areas of your organization, it is often appropriate for the migration/installation of IE to be handled by teams. Typically, one project leader coordinates the activities of the teams, which may include planning teams that determine the necessary deployment plan; installation teams that perform the actual customization and installation; training teams that provide training to end users and develop documentation; and support teams that answer end users' questions and provide support during and after the rollout.

- **Identify technical requirements for deployment.** The project manager in conjunction with the project teams should determine the requirements for servers, workstations, network infrastructure, and so on. Successful deployment may be hindered by inadequate hardware, software conflicts, or other technical difficulties. Therefore, the complete technical requirements for the planned deployment should be drafted and compared to existing systems to ensure that all necessary technical requirements for IE4.0 and supporting software have been met.

- **Identify client/server configuration and end-user needs.** To determine which components of Internet Explorer should be installed, it is first necessary to determine how end users can take advantage of the various IE features. Once the useful features have been identified, the current client/server environment at the organization can also be evaluated to provide the most efficient solutions and to add any services that may be necessary.

- **Identify migration issues and compatibility issues.** For services that are being replaced or supplemented with Internet Explorer, organizations should be careful to consider the issues associated with migration from an older browser platform (such as IE3.0 or Netscape 3.0) to the latest version of Internet Explorer. Failure to adequately address migration issues can lead to problems with software interoperability, and potentially lost data.

- **Determine the best distribution strategy.** The IEAK provides a set of flexible options for distributing custom builds from floppy disks to network installations. It is necessary to determine the best distribution mechanism for your build in conjunction with the needs of your operation. The distribution mechanism impacts the custom build, so it is an area that should be addressed.

- **Determine your custom build configuration.** Once you have determined the needs of your organization, the needs of the end users, and the technical requirements, you should outline all the features to be implemented in your custom build. Developing a checklist at this stage can also help ensure that features are not overlooked at later stages.
- **Determine the deployment plan/schedule.** Finally, considering the technical requirements, custom build creation time, deployment time, and training, you should develop a plan and a schedule for your customized IE rollout. By using a schedule, you can help users acclimate to the new software and also make sure that each team has adequate time and resources to successfully achieve its goals.

Choosing the Appropriate Internet Explorer Installation

Objective

A number of considerations should play a role in determining the appropriate installation of Internet Explorer. You first must consider the requirements of Internet Explorer, in terms of hardware and network resources, to determine whether your current hardware base can support the installation you are considering. Next, you must determine the needs of your organization and of the end users who will be using Internet Explorer. By determining their needs and your hardware constraints, you should be able to select the implementation that is right for your organization.

Internet Explorer Requirements

Because of the customization possibilities of Internet Explorer, you have a number of considerations when evaluating whether a workstation can adequately support an installation. However, you should consider some minimum requirements when installing.

Here are the Microsoft requirements for Internet Explorer running under Windows 95:

- All Service Packs installed
- 486/66 processor or greater
- 8MB RAM (16MB with the Windows Desktop Update)
- 39MB disk space (Minimal install)
- 51MB disk space (Standard install)
- 64MB disk space (Full install)

Here are the Microsoft requirements for Internet Explorer running under Windows NT:

- Service Pack 3 required
- 486/66 processor or greater
- 16MB RAM (24MB with the Windows Desktop Upgrade)
- 39MB disk space (Minimal install)
- 51MB disk space (Standard install)
- 70MB disk space (Full install)

Most current machines meet these requirements without difficulty. However, for large corporate installations and ISP installations that are dealing with legacy systems or older systems, you should always consider these guidelines.

It is also important to note that although these minimum requirements are all that is absolutely necessary to install and run Internet Explorer, these are far from optimal machine specifications. Because Internet Explorer is a robust, complex application, performance increases dramatically with faster processors and more memory. Also keep in mind that you will want to have additional disk space available for the browser's cache.

Keeping these requirements in mind, you should be able to adequately determine which machines in your planned deployment can run Internet Explorer adequately, and plan upgrades for any machines that are insufficient.

Requirements for the Internet Explorer Administration Kit Configuration Wizard

When planning your deployment of Internet Explorer, you should also consider the requirements of systems you will be using for administrative and deployment purposes. Creating custom builds can be quite resource intensive, especially in disk resources when you are building a version to be distributed on floppy disks or CD-ROM.

The Internet Explorer Administration Kit is not really one application. Rather, it has two main components and some utilities:

- **The IEAK Configuration Wizard.** The IEAK Configuration Wizard is the application you use to create your custom build of Internet Explorer. The IEAK Configuration Wizard guides you step by step through the customizations you can make based on your deployment role.
- **The IEAK Profile Manager.** The IEAK Profile Manager is used to update or change the configuration after you have created a custom build with the IEAK Configuration Wizard. Using the Profile Manager, you can quickly change configuration information or update files for automatic browser updates.
- **IExpress Wizard.** The IExpress Wizard is a tool for aiding administrators in creating custom packages. It helps you collect installation information into cabinet files and assists with signing code.
- **The IEAK Resource Kit and Tools.** These components are actually a collection of utilities and command-line applications used by the main IEAK components. There may be

times when you need to use these tools separately, but generally, the main focus is on the IEAK Wizard and Profile Manager.

Here are the requirements for the IEAK Configuration Wizard:

- Internet Explorer 4.0 installed
- 486/66 processor or greater
- Windows 95 or Windows NT 4.0
- 8MB RAM (for Windows 95)
- 16MB RAM (for Windows NT)
- 40MB to 60MB disk space for installation
- 40MB to 100MB additional disk space per custom package
- Internet connectivity

Note

You must have Internet connectivity to run the IEAK Configuration Wizard.

A solid installation of Internet Explorer is essential if you are to correctly create custom builds with the IEAK Configuration Wizard. The wizard draws on your installation of IE 4.0 for many of the files it needs. The IEAK Configuration Wizard also requires a connection to the Internet if it is to run.

With these limits in mind, the single biggest other concern is disk space. Because you have to create all the installation files for the packages you are choosing for your custom build, the amount of disk space consumed by the IEAK Configuration Wizard can be quite extensive.

Note

The installer for IE and the IEAK Wizard have slightly different nomenclature when referring to the various installs you can perform. The IE terms are *Minimal*, *Standard*, and *Full*; the IEAK Wizard refers to *Standard*, *Enhanced*, and *Full*.

Here's a breakdown of the basic disk space requirements for various configuration options for the IEAK Wizard:

- **43MB Standard Installation.** The Standard installation includes Internet Explorer, Outlook Express, and ActiveMovie.
- **50MB Enhanced Installation.** The Enhanced installation includes Internet Explorer, Outlook Express, FrontPage Express, and ActiveMovie.
- **59MB Full Installation.** The Full installation includes Internet Explorer, Outlook Express, NetMeeting, FrontPage Express, Microsoft Wallet, NetShow, and ActiveMovie.

These disk space guidelines are not complete however. In addition to varying based on the packages you install, the disk requirements vary based on installation methods. For example, if you are creating a custom build that is going to be installed on floppy disks or CD-ROM, you will be creating the images and files for those media as well. If you are creating distributions for media such as CD-ROM, you can effectively double the amount of disk space required for your custom build.

Which Installation: Standard, Enhanced, or Full?

Internet Explorer offers three installation options for you to choose from: Standard, Enhanced, and Full. With each successive option, you provide end users with more services and options they can use in conjunction with Internet Explorer. Here's a rundown of the package variances:

- **Minimal Installation.** The Internet Explorer Minimal installation includes the core productivity applications of the Internet Explorer suite. This suite includes the Internet

Explorer Web browser and its feature set, Outlook Express (which provides client email services), and ActiveMovie (which can display and play back multimedia files encountered by users of the World Wide Web).

- **Standard Installation.** The Standard installation includes all the features of the Minimal installation and adds FrontPage Express, which allows the end user to create and manage site content from his or her own workstation.
- **Full Installation.** The Full installation includes all the features of the Standard and Enhanced installations and adds a host of other productivity tools. These tools include Microsoft Wallet (which allows the user to configure payment information for performing online purchases within a secure environment); NetShow (which is Microsoft's multicasting technology that allows viewers to participate in network broadcast events); and NetMeeting (which is conferencing software that allows voice, video, and data conferencing over the Internet).

Which installation you choose largely depends on the end-user requirements of your organization. Hardware issues aside, for many organizations, the Standard installation meets the majority of users' needs without adding too many confusing features to their browser configurations. However, if your end users have to perform site maintenance, or if they create content for the Web, the Enhanced installation provides the tools they need. Finally, in an information-rich environment, where end users perform online transactions, participate in network distributed training, or have applications for audio/video conferencing, the Full installation provides the most comprehensive feature set. It includes many advanced tools, such as NetMeeting, that can be used to expand the applications of your network.

Custom Installation Strategies

Objectives

When you work with Internet Explorer in conjunction with the Internet Explorer Administration Kit, you can configure nearly every aspect of the installation. You can determine whether users are presented with the choices for their own configurations or whether they are given no choices. The variety you can provide during the installation process is precisely what gives you the power to create customized builds and installers that meet the requirements of your end users.

Distribution Mechanisms

The Internet Explorer Administration Kit offers four mechanisms for distributing Internet Explorer:

- Internet
- Intranet
- Floppy disks
- CD-ROMs

Each of these distribution mechanisms can be used to distribute your custom build. However, some specific issues must be addressed regardless of the distribution mechanism you employ. There may not be one single method that fulfills all the requirements for your organization, and you may have to create several different installation mechanisms for your organization. The following sections describe some of the issues you must address with each of the four distribution mechanisms.

Internet

The Internet is probably a distribution mechanism with which you are already familiar. Chances are you have upgraded your own version of Internet Explorer by using a download site provided by Microsoft on the Internet. Internet connectivity is a very important part of using the IEAK, even if you choose not to use it as your distribution mechanism. The IEAK Wizard contacts Microsoft over the Internet to make sure that you have the most current components when you are creating your custom build. This check ensures that you are always using the latest components, complete with any bug fixes and security patches that may have been applied since your initial download.

Grabbing the files for distribution from Microsoft Internet sites is also one of the advantages to using the Internet as a distribution mechanism for your custom build. The IEAK allows you to select up to 10 sites from which you can download files, so that the Installer can optimize network performance for the download.

Of course, some issues are associated with using the Internet as your distribution method. For example, if you have a proxy server or corporate firewall in place, you must make sure that you properly create your custom package to deal with the increased security. You may encounter problems if you have many locations with difference security policies, or if you frequently make changes to the proxy servers or firewalls for additional security.

Security issues aside, Internet bandwidth should also be a concern when considering Internet distribution. Not all network connections are created equal, and at times it may not be a very efficient way to download installation files. For example, a user at your headquarters connected to the Internet by a T1 or greater line may find the download quite fast and installation may take only 20 minutes or so. However, a user at a remote office dialing in to the network, may find that downloading and installing over 28.8 bps modems is extremely time consuming and frustrating. For this reason, you should carefully examine the quality of connectivity of your users if you intend to distribute your IE installation over the Internet.

There are also some significant advantages to Internet distribution, including the fact that your file versions are maintained by Microsoft. Additionally, the installation process verifies the integrity of the downloaded files, making the possibility of your installation being tampered with relatively low.

The greatest advantage of distribution over the Internet is for organizations with Wide Area Networks or extremely diverse geographical settings. If your organization is spread out with offices around the world, the Internet may be the one common resource that reaches all your users.

If you are evaluating the Internet as a distribution method, keep these issues in mind. Even if you choose not to use the Internet as your primary distribution mechanism, there may be cases in which it can help you reach remote users.

Intranet

Like the Internet, your organization's intranet can also be a very useful tool for distributing Internet Explorer. Unlike the Internet, a secure intranet can help you eliminate any problematic issues with a firewall or proxy server, while still allowing widespread distribution throughout your organization. Similarly, if all the users you have to reach with your installer have access to your intranet, you can use the intranet for widespread distribution over a diverse geographic area.

However, like the Internet, not all your end users may have equal access to intranet resources. Perhaps your organization has telecommuters who will require this custom installation in their homes, but they dial in to the corporate network using 28.8 bps modems. Here again, bandwidth concerns may impact your decision to deploy IE over a network resource.

Floppy Disks

Perhaps the most accessible method of distribution is floppy disks. No matter what the location or the configuration of your end users' machines, they likely have access to a floppy disk drive. And because floppies are a physical media, they can be delivered to nearly any location on the globe, offering a widespread distribution area.

There are some significant drawbacks to floppy disk distribution however. The biggest drawback is that floppy disks do not have very large storage capacities. Performing a customized, Full installation using floppies can consume huge amounts of disks for distribution throughout your entire organization.

Floppy disks are also quite slow to reproduce and use and are more prone to failure than other media. You may have noticed that software vendors have largely moved away from floppies for mass distribution; this trend is continuing as CD-ROMs become a standard hardware feature. Regardless of these disadvantages, floppy distribution might be in order for very limited distribution in small organizations or for installation on older hardware. Floppy disks will probably not comprise your entire installation strategy, but they can play a role in ensuring complete distribution to your entire organization.

CD-ROMs

Because of their storage capacity and the widespread acceptance of CD-ROM drives as standard equipment, CD-ROM distribution offers an ideal distribution media for Internet Explorer. As CD-R drives become more accessible, even smaller organizations may decide to burn a few distribution CDs for the organization. Larger organizations that enjoy an economy of scale may find it cheap to produce a large number of CD-ROMs to distribute throughout the organization.

An entire custom build can easily fit on a CD-ROM, and the IEAK can create the build for the CD-ROM with all the necessary support files so that the entire installer can be transferred to CD very easily. Installation from CD-ROM is fast, efficient, and can be quite inexpensive. Creating customized CD-ROMs offers the best solution for most distribution needs.

Installation Options

In addition to selecting the distribution method you are going to employ, you must also consider several different installation options, such as which components will be installed, how they will be initially configured, and how you will address some of the security issues involved in deploying and using Internet Explorer. The following sections describe the installation options for which you must create a strategy.

Administrative Roles

The Internet Explorer Administration Kit has three deployment roles you can select when you initially launch the IEAK Wizard. Each of these roles has a unique set of options that allow you to customize Internet Explorer in a slightly different manner depending on the type of installation you are providing. Keep in mind that the role you choose must be in keeping with the licensing agreement you signed with Microsoft before downloading the IEAK. The three deployment roles for the IEAK are listed here:

- Content Provider/Developer
- Internet Service Provider
- Corporate Administrator

After you select the type of licensing agreement for the IEAK that fits your application, you will receive an email message with a 10-digit customization code that is used to authorize your IEAK installation. This code also determines the options available to you in the IEAK Wizard based on your license terms. If you have to create different installations for different applications within your organization, you can do so but you must acquire separate license agreements for each type of deployment you intend to produce.

Caution

Although the deployment features outlined in the following sections are available through the Internet Explorer Administration Kit, some of the options may not be available to you, depending on your licensing agreement. If you encounter a feature that is not available, but you want to use it, try applying for a new license under a different role. Also be sure that you review your license agreement carefully; terms, such as logo and trademark display, are often associated with public redistribution of Internet Explorer.

The **Content Provider/Developer deployment role** provides you with the following capabilities:

- **Customizing Setup Appearance.** Content Providers can change the appearance of the Setup Wizard by customizing the images displayed for auto-run CD-ROMs and the splash screens displayed during installation.
- **Bundling IE and Components.** Content Providers can create a single downloadable package that contains the IE browser and any custom components to make downloading and installation easier for end users.
- **Customizing Active Setup.** Content Providers can customize the sites used by Active Setup to download the latest files. When you customize the sites, you can point users at the servers that will be fastest and most reliable for them based on location and connectivity.
- **Custom Language Versions.** Content Providers can create custom foreign language versions for distribution.
- **Enable Internet Distribution.** Content Providers can enable channels and Internet distribution mechanisms to allow users to download installation files and receive updates using the Internet.
- **Customizing Browser Settings.** Content Providers can customize the default browser settings (such as the Start, Search, and Support pages) to point users at your resources. You can point the browser to the content being supplied.
- **Customizing Favorites.** Content Providers can customize the initial favorites configured in the user's browser, so that the user has instant easy access to any created content.
- **Customizing Channels.** Content Providers can add one channel but remove multiple channels from the channel bar. They can also build customized channels to provide software updates.

- **Customized Branding.** Content Providers can alter the splash screens, title bars, and logos to those of their organization or client organizations to create a custom-branded software application for a company or service.

For Internet Service Providers (ISPs) who want to distribute Internet Explorer to customers with accounts on their systems, Microsoft has created the ISP role. **The Internet Service Provider deployment role** provides you with the following capabilities:

- **Customizing Setup Appearance.** ISPs can change the appearance of the Setup Wizard by customizing the images displayed and by choosing the default installation (Standard, Enhanced, or Full) to be performed on the end user's machine.
- **Bundling IE and Components.** ISPs can create a single downloadable package that contains the IE browser and any custom components to make downloading and installation easier for end users.
- **Customizing Active Setup.** ISPs can customize the sites used by Active Setup to download the latest files. When you customize the sites, you can point your users at the servers that will be fastest and most reliable for them based on location.
- **Customized Scripting and Rollouts.** ISPs can use customized scripts to create new services or to install additional programs for customers.
- **Language Customization.** ISPs can select the default language for the installation of Internet Explorer and its support programs.
- **Customizing Browser Settings.** ISPs can customize the default browser settings (such as the Start, Search, and Support pages) to point users at Internet resources. You can point the browser initially to the ISP home page, to customer support pages, and so on.

- **Customizing Favorites.** ISPs can customize the initial favorites configured in your users' browsers, so that they have the resources you want them to have available immediately. You can point users to tutorial information about the ISP and services or to guides on using the Internet and its resources.
- **Customizing Channels.** ISPs can add one channel and remove multiple channels from the channel bar. They can also build customized channels to provide software updates.
- **Customized Branding.** ISPs can alter the splash screens, title bars, and logos to those of their organization to create a custom-branded software application.
- **Account Sign-Up.** Internet Service Providers can create a customized account sign-up mechanism that allows users to switch to your service or to create a new account on your service in conjunction with receiving your customized IE installation.
- **Serverless Distribution.** ISPs can also create installation versions for floppy disks and CD-ROMs that do not require an Internet connection or contact with servers for installation.

Note

Use of Internet Explorer for external distribution requires use of the Internet Explorer logo on your marketing, promotional, and packaging materials. Be sure to consult your license agreement for the specific terms of logo and trademark usage for Internet Explorer distribution.

The Corporate Administrator deployment role is designed for organizations that want to customize a version of Internet Explorer for distribution inside the organization. In this role, you create a custom version that is distributed internally and not to the general public.

As is true with the ISP role, you can control a number of customized settings when you use the IEAK in the **Corporate Administrator deployment role**, including the following:

- **Customizing Setup Appearance.** You can customize the Setup Wizard to specify the type of installation (Standard, Full, or Enhanced) to be performed.
- **Bundling IE and Components.** You can create a single downloadable package that contains the IE browser and any custom components that make downloading and installation easier for your users.
- **Customizing Active Setup.** You can customize the sites used by Active Setup to download the latest files. When you customize the sites, you can point your users at servers on your intranet for distribution.
- **Customized Scripting and Rollouts.** You can use customized scripts to create new services or install additional programs for your users.
- **Language Customization.** You can select the default language for the installation of Internet Explorer and its support programs.
- **Customizing Favorites.** You can customize the initial favorites configured in your users' browsers so that they have the resources you want them to have available immediately. You can point users to resources on your intranet, departmental servers, and so on.
- **Customizing Channels.** You can add and remove channels from the channel bar and configure which channels will appear on your corporate desktops.
- **Customized Branding.** You can alter the splash screens, title bars, and logos to those of your organization to create a custom-branded software application for your company.

- **Control the Windows Desktop Update.** You can control the Windows Desktop Update feature, which includes Active Desktop items, desktop toolbars, My Computer, and control panels. You can also specify which resources users can or cannot alter.
- **Create a Custom Desktop.** You can create customized desktops for your organization or departments and control which settings users can alter.
- **Create Software Distribution Channels.** You can create customized channels to perform software maintenance and upgrades for your organization's standard applications.
- **Manage Certificates.** You can preinstall organizational, site, and individual security certificates. You can also prevent users from installing new certificates or altering currently installed certificates.
- **Control Rating Settings.** You can control the Internet ratings settings to prevent users from accessing sites with certain rating types. You can also prevent users from altering ratings settings on their own.
- **Customize Signatures and Disclaimers.** You can create customized signatures for email and customized disclaimers for newsgroup postings that can protect your organization from public liability.
- **Configure Security Zones.** You can establish and control the security zone settings for the Internet Explorer browser.
- **Configure Proxy Settings.** You can configure the proxy settings for using applications in conjunction with a proxy server or from behind a corporate firewall.
- **Serverless Distribution.** ISPs can also create installation versions for floppy disks and CD-ROMs that do not require an Internet connection or contact with servers for installation.

The Corporate Administrator deployment role provides the widest range of customization and is specifically designed to allow you to configure important features such as access levels and security. This level of functionality is provided so that you can customize Internet Explorer and its support applications for the needs of your end users, without including features that are unnecessary or potential abuses of the Internet and its resources.

Version Control

The Internet Explorer Administration Kit features Automatic Version Synchronization (AVS) to make sure that your custom build always contains the most current version of the Internet Explorer components. By default, the AVS feature is enabled, and when you undertake the process of creating your custom build, the versions of the components you are including are checked against those at the Microsoft Web site. If there are discrepancies, the newest versions of the software are downloaded for inclusion in your custom package.

Keeping your software compatible with the most current versions is generally the best course of action. Doing so ensures that you have the latest versions that incorporate any new bug fixes or new security patches. However, if you are engaged in a complex deployment at your site and have conducted extensive compatibility testing, you may want to maintain the versions you have tested and not risk any incompatibilities by downloading new versions. If you do not want to synchronize your IE and component software to the latest version from Microsoft, be sure to disable AVS.

Component Installation Options

The IEAK allows nearly complete customization of the installation process your users will perform to install your customized build. In doing so, you can create an installer that forces users into a specific configuration or that gives them virtually any degree of flexibility you require.

Here's a rundown of the various aspects of the installation you can configure, and what impact the option has on the user's installation:

- **Silent Installation.** By configuring a silent installation, you can prevent the end user from altering any of the initial configuration settings you have chosen. This option allows you complete control over the configuration of the browser and components, without requiring any user input during the installation process. Although this option does not allow user customization, you can still configure the installation for the needs and requirements of the end user.

- **Up to 10 Custom Components.** Using the IEAK, you can specify up to 10 custom components to be installed in conjunction with the Standard, Enhanced, or Full installation options that already exist. You can use this option to install additional support components, plug-ins, and so on to add features to the Internet Explorer installation and to further tailor your IE custom package to your organization.

- **Up to 10 Download Sites.** You can select up to 10 different download sites from which the user can choose to retrieve Internet Explorer installation files and component files. Customizing the available site URLs allows you to point users to resources on your intranet or to Internet-based resources that are geographically convenient or that have superior network connectivity to your site. Pointing users to the appropriate download site can dramatically increase the efficiency of their installation.

- **Up to 10 Installation Options.** You can specify up to 10 different installation options from which users can choose during the installation process. These installation options can be used to create a single installation that allows slight configuration variations for different areas within your organization. For example, an engineering department may have slightly different requirements than the sales/marketing department. By allowing some degree of flexibility, you can create a single installer that is appropriate for several different applications.

- **Customized Install Options.** By using the IEAK, you can configure any combination of components to be included in each installation option. This gives you the complete freedom to specify exactly what each installation option should include from both the standard and custom components you have included in your customized build.
- **Specify Version Number and Identifier.** You can specify a version number and a configuration identifier for your custom build. This feature provides you with an internal mechanism for tracking the deployment of your custom IE build so that you can track any changes or revisions you make to custom installations. You can also use this information for creating client/server applications that use Internet Explorer as a Web client front-end.
- **Specify Installation Folder.** You can specify the exact location of the customized installation on the end user's hard drive. This can be useful if you exert control within your organization of machine configurations and have a specified location for internal or customized software installation.
- **Integrate the Windows Desktop Update.** The IEAK allows you to specify whether you want to include the Windows Desktop Upgrade in the installation. Including the Desktop Upgrade increases the requirements of the installation; however, it also gives you a wide range of control over the user's operating environment. The Desktop Upgrade allows you to control elements such as Active Desktop components, the channel bar, toolbar options, screen savers, and so on. The Desktop Upgrade is a powerful tool that allows you to control the level of shell integration used with IE and to exert control over the end user's working environment.

Look-and-Feel Configuration Options

You can set a number of appearance options using the IEAK to create a customized "look-and-feel" for your customized build of Internet Explorer. Each of these features allows administrators to give Internet Explorer the appearance of a customized application so that end users are aware that the program has been customized by your organization.

- **Customized Title Bar.** Administrators can choose the text to be displayed in the Internet Explorer title bar.
- **Customized Toolbar Background.** The IEAK allows administrators to customize the background that appears in the Internet Explorer toolbar. Keep in mind that the background should be light enough so that you can read the black text that will be placed over it.
- **Customized Logo and Animation.** The IEAK allows you to customize the Internet Explorer logo and the animation used when IE is contacting servers and downloading information.
- **Enable Automatic Browser Configuration.** Administrators can configure the default browser installation to search for automatic browser configuration files. When you specify that the browser use the Automatic Configuration feature, the IE browser checks the supplied URLs each time it is launched to see whether the configuration has changed. The URLs provided should point the browser to the location of any `.INS` files that contain Internet configuration settings, or any autoproxy (`.JS` or `.PAC` files) that contain proxy settings for the browser.

Security Issues

When creating or customizing any application based on retrieving and exchanging information over a network, there are a number of security issues that must be addressed; Internet Explorer is certainly no exception. Because IE allows users connectivity to resources available on the Internet, it has a number of built-in safety mechanisms that allow administrators to customize the security features of the browser. These mechanisms include the following:

- **Specify Site Certificate and Authenticode Settings.** Your organization can take advantage of site certificates and secure servers to exchange sensitive data over the Internet. You can also have external sites (such as vendor or client sites) that make use of certificates and Authenticode to verify the origin and integrity of information downloaded over the Internet. Authenticode is a method supported by Microsoft that allows developers to sign their programs with digital signatures.

The IEAK allows you to preinstall certificates and to configure Authenticode options for the end user so that there is no risk of a misconfiguration later. The IEAK also allows you to restrict the changes end users can make to security settings, thereby preventing users from accidentally compromising the security features of the browser and your network.

- **Specify Security Zones.** Internet Explorer supports several different security zones that specify varying levels of browser security for specific applications. Security zones include an Internet Zone, a Local Intranet Zone, a Trusted Sites Zone, and a Restricted Sites Zone. The specific applications of each zone are discussed in the next section, "Developing Secure Internet Explorer Usage Strategies."
- **Specify Content Ratings.** Internet Explorer also supports content filtering based on content rating systems such as the Recreational Software Advisory Council on the Internet (RSACi). These content ratings provide a way for administrators to filter out content that might be questionable for viewing in the workplace. More information about the specifics of the RSACi rating system can be found at `www.rsac.org`. Administrators should also be aware that no rating system is foolproof; although applying rating specifications may filter out *most* controversial content, there is no absolute guarantee that none will find its way into users' hands.

Developing Secure Internet Explorer Usage Strategies

Objectives

As is true with any network application, a number of security issues confront an installation of Internet Explorer. There are issues concerning downloading corrupted data, verifying that downloaded components and applications do not contain viruses, and authenticating that information is being provided by a reputable source. There is also the issue of securing data transmission between the client and the server so that your data does not fall into the wrong hands. Fortunately, Internet Explorer supports a wide range of security options that can be configured for your installation of Internet Explorer. The following sections explain the different options that are available, and their impact on security.

Internet Explorer Security Zones

Internet Explorer supports four default security zones that incorporate the various uses of Internet Explorer and create categories for various security settings. These zones are Internet, Local Intranet, Trusted Sites, and Restricted Sites. There is also a My Computer Zone that contains all the files on the user's local file system. However, the My Computer Zone is considered a trusted zone, for which the settings cannot be altered.

Each of the zones functions as a group for configuring the security settings that apply when you are browsing pages in that zone. The default security settings for the zones are shown in Table 1.1.

Table 1.1

Default Levels of Security for IE Security Zones

Zone	Setting
Internet Zone	Medium (Warn before running potentially damaging content)
Local Intranet Zone	Medium (Warn before running potentially damaging content)
Trusted Sites Zone	Low (Do not warn before running potentially damaging content)
Restricted Sites Zone	High (Exclude content that could damage your computer)

Internet Zone

The Internet Zone is designed for pages located on servers outside your organization and accessed through the Internet. Any site users access with a full URL (such as `www.microsoft.com`) are automatically considered part of the Internet Zone. The default security level for the Internet Zone is Medium, which provides some security features but allows a high degree of functionality, including scripting, Java, and ActiveX controls. If your organization is concerned about security issues resulting from the Internet, you may want to increase the security setting for the Internet Zone to High. However, doing so will likely affect the functionality of some pages, particularly those that make use of advanced technologies and scripting.

Local Intranet Zone

The Local Intranet Zone is designed to provide a security zone for use in conjunction with your local network resources that reside behind a proxy server or firewall. Because of the added level of security provided by the proxy server and firewall, you can generally place the security level for the Local Intranet Zone at Low.

The Local Intranet Zone is initially configured to include any hosts that have been set to bypass the proxy server. Administrators can also configure additional hosts to participate in the Local Intranet Zone. These hosts include the following:

- **All hosts bypassing the proxy server.** If your organization is using a proxy server, this setting places any site that does not use the proxy server into the Local Intranet Zone. However, if your site does not use a proxy server, this setting has no effect.

- **Local sites.** This option includes any site not already included in another zone and that is considered a "local" site. Local sites are those sites that do not use the complete domain name. For example, `http://mysite.wherever.com` is not considered a local site; `http://mysite` is considered a local site because the domain name is completed by the Domain Suffix Search Order specified in the Network Control Panel, under the TCP/IP Settings. Hosts that complete their domain names using this mechanism are part of the Local Intranet Zone.

- **Network paths (UNCs).** Any local network path (for example, `\\Server\myfiles\letter.doc`) can be included as a member of the Local Intranet Zone. Because these paths usually refer to local resources, enabling this option should not be a problem. However, if your site employs the Common Internet File System to serve Internet resources to your network so that they appear as local resources, you may want to consider disabling this option.

Trusted Sites Zone

The Trusted Sites Zone allows you to specify URLs for sites your organization considers to be highly secure. These types of sites might include client sites or vendor sites with whom you enjoy a trusted relationship. Trusted sites can also include sites that make use of HTTPS to provide encrypted data transmissions from the client to the server. In fact, Microsoft recommends that you use HTTPS with any sites you place in the Trusted Sites domain to ensure security. (This is a recommendation; it is not required.) The default level of security provided to the Trusted Sites Zone is Low.

Restricted Sites Zone

Just as the Trusted Sites Zone allows you to set security for sites you trust, the Restricted Sites Zone allows you to add the URLs of sites you consider a security risk. Sites placed in the Restricted Sites Zone have a High security setting and therefore may not function correctly. Keep in mind that simply placing a site in the Restricted Sites Zone is no guarantee of security. For example, if you place a particular shareware site in the restricted zone, but neglect to include any FTP mirrors to the site, users can bypass the restricted site and obtain the same potentially compromised data from another source.

Each of the zones has a default level of security, as shown in Table 1.2. The following sections take a look at each of these security options and describe how it impacts Internet Explorer functionality.

Table 1.2

Default Security Option Settings for IE Security Levels

Security Option	Low Default	Medium Default	High Default
Script ActiveX Controls Marked Safe for Scripting	Enabled	Enabled	Enabled
Run ActiveX Controls and Plug-ins	Enabled	Enabled	Disabled
Download Signed ActiveX Controls	Enabled	Prompt	Disabled
Download Unsigned ActiveX Controls	Prompt	Disabled	Disabled
Initialize and Script ActiveX Controls Not Marked as Safe	Prompt	Prompt	Disabled
Set Java Permissions	Low Security	High Safety	High Safety
Allow Active Scripting	Enabled	Enabled	Enabled
Script Java Applets	Enabled	Enabled	Disabled
Download Files	Enabled	Enabled	Disabled
Download Fonts	Enabled	Enabled	Prompt
Use Logon for User Authentication	Automatic logon with current user name and password	Automatic logon only in Intranet Zone	Prompt for user name and password
Submit Nonencrypted Form Data	Enabled	Prompt	Prompt
Launch Applications and Files in an IFrame	Enabled	Prompt	Disabled

Security Option	Low Default	Medium Default	High Default
Install Desktop Items	Enabled	Prompt	Disabled
Drag and Drop or Copy and Paste Files	Enabled	Enabled	Prompt
Set Software Channel Permissions	Low Safety	Medium Safety	High Safety

Internet Explorer Security Features

Although security zones allow you to group security settings by the type of site to which they apply, the security settings can still be controlled individually to provide the most robust security solution. Administrators have the option of configuring these security settings for each of the zones or for the entire browser. Administrators can also lock down security settings, preventing users from altering the security settings on their own.

ActiveX Settings

The ActiveX control settings determine the security features implemented for downloading, scripting, and running ActiveX controls. These settings are applied any time a user encounters an ActiveX component on a Web site. However, if the ActiveX control is being downloaded from a site other than the referring site, the default security is for the more restrictive of the two sites. For example, if a site in the Local Intranet Zone (with Low security) refers to an ActiveX control on an Internet Site (with Medium security), the ActiveX control is treated with the Medium security settings because those are higher.

- **Script ActiveX Controls Marked Safe for Scripting.** This option determines whether an ActiveX control that has been marked as safe for scripting can interact with scripts on the user's system.
- **Run ActiveX Controls and Plug-ins.** This option determines whether ActiveX controls and plug-ins can be run at all.

- **Download Signed ActiveX Controls.** This option allows users to download signed ActiveX controls from the zone and referring page. Enabling this option allows IE to download any controls without notifying the user; select Prompt to require approval from the user; select Deny to prohibit the downloading of signed ActiveX controls.
- **Download Unsigned ActiveX Controls.** This option allows the user to download ActiveX controls that are not signed. This is an extremely nonsecure option, and should generally not be enabled.
- **Initialize and Script ActiveX Controls Not Marked Safe.** This option determines whether an ActiveX control that is not marked as safe can be initialized or interact with scripts. There are three settings: Enable (allows all ActiveX controls to be initialized and scripted); Prompt (prompts the user for a decision to allow or refuse the ActiveX control); and Disable (refuses any ActiveX control not marked safe). If the option is set to Enable, it overrides the setting for the Script ActiveX Controls Marked Safe for Scripting option.

Java Permission Settings

The Java permission settings control how the IE browser downloads and runs Java applets from Web pages within the current zone. Similar to the way ActiveX control settings work, if the site referencing a Java applet is in a different zone than the applet itself, the more restrictive security setting of the two zones is used.

The options determine the level of security applied to signed applets without user notification, the permissions assigned to unsigned applets, and the permissions applied to scripts that interact with applets on the current page. The Java options are listed here:

- **Custom.** This option allows the administrator to specify the permissions granted using the Unsigned and Allowed Without Warning tabs.
- **Low Safety.** The Low Safety setting allows Java applets to perform all functions without any restrictions.

- **Medium Safety.** This option allows Java applets to run within their memory sandbox, provides access to local scratch disk space, and allows user-controlled file system access.

- **High Safety.** This options restricts Java applets to running within their memory sandbox.

- **Disable Java.** This option prevents Internet Explorer from running Java applets at all.

Scripting

With the increased functionality provided by many Web pages today, many sites employ various scripting mechanisms to automate features and user interfaces. These settings control how scripts are run in IE.

- **Active Scripting.** This option enables scripts to be run on pages within the current zone. It applies to scripting languages such as Microsoft JScript (ECMAScript) and Microsoft VBScripting Edition scripts.

- **Scripting of Java Applets.** This option allows Java applets to be scripted on pages within the current zone.

Downloads

The download options allow administrators to specify whether files and fonts can be downloaded to the client machine. However, unlike the ActiveX and Java options, the security level for download options is determined by the site that contains the link to the file, not by the actual site that will be providing the download.

- **File Download.** This option determines whether or not files can be downloaded to the local machine.

- **Font Download.** This option determines whether HTML fonts can be downloaded to correctly render special text.

User Authentication

For interaction with sites that use HTTP authentication, the following settings can be configured to determine the level of logon security provided:

- **Anonymous Logon.** If this option is selected, HTTP authentication is disabled. For Common Internet File System resources, only the guest account is enabled.
- **Prompt for User Name and Password.** This is the normal functionality for HTTP authentication. The user is prompted once for user name and password, and then this information is provided to the site silently for the remainder of the user's session at that site.
- **Automatic Logon Only in Intranet Zone.** This option allows the browser to retain user name/password information for sites within the Local Intranet Zone, and to provide automatic logon to intranet sites. Sites in other zones are still prompted.
- **Automatic Logon with Current User Name and Password.** This option provides automated logon using the Windows NT challenge/response approach for the current user information. If the information is not correct for the site, the user is prompted for the correct logon.

Other Security Settings

A number of other miscellaneous security settings can impact Internet Explorer and security within the various zones:

- **Submit Nonencrypted Form Data.** This option determines whether users can submit form data to a site if the site is not a secure site using Secure Socket Layers (SSL).
- **Launching Applications and Files from an IFrame.** This option determines whether users can launch applications and open files referenced from a directory within an IFrame.

- **Installation of Desktop Items.** This option determines whether users can download and install desktop components from the current zone.
- **Drag and Drop or Copy and Paste Files.** This option determines whether users can drag and drop or copy and paste files from a site in the zone to and from the local system.
- **Software Channel Permissions.** This option allows you to specify the level of security applied to software channels. There are three levels (low, medium, and high), each of which provides a different level of functionality. Low safety allows email notification, auto download, and auto installation. Medium safety allows email notification and auto download. High safety disables the features of software channels entirely.
- **Launch from Web View.** This option determines what can be launched from folders viewed as Web pages. These options include My Computer, Local Intranet, Trusted Sites, Internet, and Restricted Sites. However, the end user cannot modify these settings. They are available for configuration only in the IEAK.

Security Scenarios

All the security options provided for in Internet Explorer make it a very flexible browser for a variety of applications. By creating customized security settings for your custom builds, you can create a version of Internet Explorer for use in applications from end-user browsers to interfaces for a public kiosk. The following sections describe a few scenarios in which you might want to use Internet Explorer—and the security considerations that must be addressed in each of the specific situations.

Public Kiosks

Many organizations use public kiosks to provide information in a variety of applications. Kiosks can provide location information in a building lobby. They can provide product and company information at a trade show or conference. They can be a part of a traveling presentation. Regardless of their application, many organizations are finding that rather than using complex custom programmed multimedia applications for kiosks, Web pages using dynamic HTML can accomplish very sophisticated multimedia presentations.

Using Internet Explorer for public kiosk installations has some very practical advantages. Content can be authored in HTML and be mirrored on the local kiosk machine as well as the server. Updating channel content can be completed through software update channels, so that content at the kiosk is updated and fresh, and so that multiple kiosks can be updated quickly and easily.

However, there are some significant security concerns when using Internet Explorer in kiosk applications. In a kiosk, Internet Explorer is used by the general public. The machine may also be connected to your network (although it could operate in a standalone configuration as well).

Here are some other security issues to consider for kiosk applications:

- **Locking Down Settings.** Because of the high user turnover and the lack of control you can exert over who is using your kiosk, you will want to lock down the configuration of the browser so that users cannot alter the configuration settings in any way. If users have the ability to change the settings, they can potentially alter the performance of the kiosk—or worse, change the presentation entirely.

- **Installing Only Necessary Features.** To maximize kiosk performance and to limit the potential for abuse, the only IE components you install should be those directly necessary for your particular kiosk application. Installing superfluous applications is only an invitation to disaster.

- **Disabling Downloads, Channels, and Desktop Components.** Unless there is some specific application for downloads at your kiosk, you will want to disable the capability to download files and fonts. You will also likely want to consider disabling the capability to subscribe to channels and to download and install desktop components. Although kiosk users are ideally not able to reach outside sites for downloads, if they did manage to reach a download site, disabling these features can prevent abuse.

- **Java, Scripting, and ActiveX.** You will also want to consider disabling support for scripting, Java applets, and ActiveX (unless they are used in your kiosk content). Eliminating these features may increase performance slightly, but more importantly, it prevents kiosk users from downloading or running any nonsecure components on your kiosk.
- **Using the Windows Desktop Update.** A kiosk application is the perfect use for the Windows Desktop Update. With it, you can limit access to My Computer and customize the functionality of the toolbars so that users will have a difficult time bypassing your kiosk application.

Keeping these issues in mind, you can develop highly interactive kiosk applications using Web technologies and Internet Explorer and to present them in public safely and securely.

End-User Installations

The security issues associated with developing appropriate end-user installations depend greatly on the needs of the end user and of your organization. Generally speaking, you will want to configure as many Internet Explorer options as possible but without locking them down, so that users can change them as necessary.

Depending on your security policies, you will most likely want to allow a low to medium level of security for most end-user applications. You will probably want to allow users to download and run secure Java applets and ActiveX controls. You will also probably want to allow scripting. Downloading files and fonts are also core functionality of the Web for many users, so you will probably want to enable those features as well.

The best way to control security for end users is to develop a few choices for security during installation and allow the user to select from one of several levels of security that you have deemed appropriated. Generally, end users accept the settings administrators have chosen; however, end users also tend to respond poorly when they are restricted too much. By setting security options for them, but still allowing users to alter the settings, you are providing the best of both worlds.

Business Installations

There are a variety of business applications for Internet Explorer. IE can serve as any of the following:

- A standard browser for the Internet
- An access method for intranet resources
- A method of communication with clients and vendors
- A custom interface to in-house Web-based applications

Again, how you configure security greatly depends on the needs of your organization and your intended applications. You will likely want to configure as many of the settings as possible for corporate users. You will probably also want to optimize the security and components for the particular applications being used by the department personnel IE is installed for.

For example, in a business environment, it is appropriate to require a high level of security and to enforce security measures by locking down configuration options. It is also appropriate to limit users' access to trusted sources and appropriate materials. With that in mind, here's a rundown of the key security points to address in business installations:

- Enable Medium or High security for the Internet Zone.
- Enable Low security for the Local Intranet Zone.
- Provide configuration for the Trusted Sites Zone, including clients and vendors.
- Configure the Restricted Sites Zone to limit untrusted site access.

- Enable prompting for file, font, and component downloads.
- Accept only signed and marked safe ActiveX components.
- Prompt for user name and password for authentication.
- Prompt before submitting unencrypted data.
- Set Java security at a High level.
- Set software channel security to a High level.
- Pre-install site certificates.
- Restrict user certificate installation.

Of course, not all these settings are necessary in all applications. However, each of these issues should be addressed to help reduce the security risk to business users and your organization.

Active Channels

Objectives

With Internet Explorer 4.0, Microsoft has included a mechanism for providing push technology, in the form of Active Channels. The idea behind a *channel* is one you're already familiar with: Just like a radio station or a TV channel, an Active Channel for Internet Explorer is designed to deliver a specific kind of Web-based content directly to your workstation.

In fact, Active Channels are simply Web sites that have been extended to allow subscriptions through Internet Explorer. In fact, you can create a channel using the same HTML files, graphics, and other media files you have used to create a Web site. The only difference is that with a channel, you create a file called a Channel Definition Format (CDF) file that specifies the details about your channel, such as the channel name, subscription update schedule, and so on.

The CDF is a special file format from Microsoft; it is based on the eXtensible Markup Language (XML). With the CDF file, you can specify information about your channel that will be available to users in IE. Some of the information you can specify about your channel includes the following:

- Channel title
- Update schedule
- An abstract that describes channel content
- URLs for channel content

By specifying the URLs that point to channel content, Internet Explorer can download the associated HTML files. Channel content is kept up to date when Internet Explorer contacts your site to update the specified channel files according to the schedule specified in the CDF file.

Using the CDF mechanism, you can provide subscriptions to Web sites so that users always have the most current version of your site available on their machines. This can be useful for distributing content to users so that they can use the content from local resources rather than the network, and still ensure that all users have the same versions. Users also have the option of not downloading all the site content, but instead downloading just the CDF file with the update information. IE still contacts the channel site for updates, but does not download all of the site's content. Users can also choose to be notified of channel updates through email or through the channel bar.

The channel model also has another use; it can be used to provide a special type of channel called a software distribution channel. A *software distribution channel* is similar to a site channel except that the content delivered is in the form of application software for the user's workstation.

Managing software updates can be one of the most challenging problems facing many organizations. With software updates becoming more and more frequent, it can be difficult to make sure that all users in an organization have the most current version of the software they need. And if that weren't challenging enough, it is even more difficult to coordinate updates to make sure that all users have the same versions.

Software distribution channels are based on the Open Software Distribution (OSD) format, which is also based on XML. OSD provides a mechanism by which client machines can be queried for the versions of software installed on the machine; updates can be provided when the machine's versions are no longer current. OSD channels can be used to provide software in the form of Java applications, ActiveX controls, and even native code applications.

Additionally, the OSD model allows you to download only the components that have to be updated. The user does not have to reinstall the entire software package. OSD channels can download missing or corrupted software components so that users are always using current software versions with the correct components.

The Internet Explorer Administration Kit provides administrators the ability to customize the Active Channel bar to specify what channels are provided for the users automatically. Administrators can use this feature to subscribe end users to sites that provide internal resources and to subscribe users to software distribution channels so that their software packages are updated as well.

Administering Channels

Several issues face administrators who want to use channels for distribution of content and software updates. These include scheduling, installation methods, notification methods, and creating CDF and OSD files:

- **Scheduling Updates.** Administers control the update schedule for both content and software channels. Using the `<schedule>` tag in the CDF or OSD file, administrators can configure the `INTERVALTIME`, `EARLIESTTIME`, and `LATESTTIME` parameters for the `<schedule>` tag to specify when updates are performed. It is best to schedule updates for periods when the user is not likely to be using the machine (for example, late at night or extremely early mornings). Software updates consume network and machine resources.

- **Update Notification.** Although content can be updated automatically, the user must be notified that the content for the channel has been changed. The user configuration can be altered in Internet Explorer to provide email notification of channel updates. Additionally, the channel bar and the Favorites list graphically reflect updates.

- **Installation Methods.** When creating software distribution channels, you can choose from three methods to perform installation of new software components. You can have the software updates installed and configured automatically, so they don't have to interact with the application at all to receive the update. You can also choose to simply have the update files and installers downloaded to the end user's machine, and then provide instructions for the users to perform the installation. And finally, you can simply choose to notify users through email that upgrades are available, and point users to the resources needed to update the software on their own.

- **Creating CDF and OSD Files.** Creating CDF and OSD files is not too complicated, and there are many resources available to help you master the CDF format and the OSD format. Three of these resources are available on Microsoft's Web site.

  CDF 101 can be found at this site:

  `http://www.microsoft.com/workshop/prog/ie4/channels/cdf1.htm`

  CDF 201 can be found at this site:

  `http://www.microsoft.com/workshop/prog/ie4/channels/cdf2.htm`

  The OSD specification and information can be found at this site:

  `http://www.microsoft.com/standards/osd`

Both of these tutorials and the OSD specification can help you understand how to author a simple CDF file and then understand the more complex functionality that can be provided through channels with OSD.

Windows Desktop Update

Objectives

The Windows Desktop Update package includes many of the shell integration features that make Internet Explorer a new type of integrated browser. The Windows Desktop Update contains some very powerful features for customizing the user interface and features of Internet Explorer. Here is a list of some of the features provided in the Windows Desktop Update:

- The Active Desktop
- Shell integration
- Customized Web views
- Customized control panels
- Customized My Computer

By customizing each of these features, administrators can control the look and feel of users' desktops so that machines throughout an organization have similar user interfaces. In fact, administrators can even specify what parameters users can alter, so that the end user cannot alter the user interface. Administrators have the following options:

- **Locking Down All Settings.** If administrators so choose, they can lock down all the settings so that users cannot alter any of the security, shell, and desktop settings. In environments where security is a primary concern, this option can help ensure network security.
- **Locking Down Local Settings, but Allowing Roaming Profiles.** If users in your organization might use more than one workstation, it is possible to lock down the local machine settings so that they cannot be altered but still allow a user to download a user profile so that the user's current machine is configured for him or her.
- **Customizing Settings, but Not Locking Down.** Finally, administrators can simply choose to configure the machine initially with all recommended settings but still allow users to alter their settings.

Shell integration provides a way for users to browse the Web from the various areas of their computers, such as folders and the desktop. It also allows users to view their local file systems as Web pages (for example, single-clicking a file to view its contents). Users can access features of the Internet Explorer browser such as the Go button and the Favorites list from within file folders and other operating system features.

The *Active Desktop* allows administrators to incorporate Active Desktop components into the user's desktop. Active Desktop components can consist of HTML-based information sources, ActiveX controls, and so on. Some examples include dynamically updated stock tickers or weather status updates that can be added to the desktop, the Taskbar, or both. Active Desktop components can be used by administrators to make important information readily available to end users in a convenient fashion on the desktop, rather than buried in menus or folders.

The Windows Desktop Update also allows you to *customize Web views* to control how the user interacts with the My Computer interface, the Control Panel interface, and even folders and printers. This type of customization allows administrators to completely customize the user environment to provide the exact range of services necessary for your organization.

Customizing Web Views

You can customize Web views by modifying the files Windows uses to determine how environment variables should be set. The customization is controlled by four files, which are located in either `C:\Windows\Web` or `C:\Winnt\Web`:

File	Description
`MYCOMP.HTT`	The `MYCOMP.HTT` file controls the settings for interacting with My Computer on the user's desktop.

File	Description
CONTROLP.HTT	The CONTROLP.HTT file controls the settings for interaction with the Control Panel interface, as selected through the Start menu.
FOLDERS.HTT	The FOLDERS.HTT file controls the settings for Folders Web Views, allowing folders to be configured to behave like Web sites. *Note:* Although the FOLDERS.HTT file can be modified, it is not currently distributed with custom IE builds.
PRINTERS.HTT	The PRINTERS.HTT file controls settings that deal with available printers and their configurations. *Note:* Although the PRINTERS.HTT file can be modified, it is not currently distributed with custom IE builds.

By editing these files with a text editor, administrators can customize the user interface to tailor the interaction with the Windows GUI.

Caution

> Because the .HTT files do control the user interface settings for the Windows operating system, you should always make backup copies of any .HTT file before you attempt to edit it.

The .HTT files are hypertext templates that define all the parameters Windows uses to control how information is displayed in Web views. Most of the functionality in these files is provided through scripting, such as JavaScript or VBScript.

If you choose to edit the files, you will find that they have a format very similar to HTML, with some slight differences. For example, the variables %THISDIRNAME%, %THISDIRPATH%, and %TEMPLATEDIR% reflect environment variables processed through MIME filters to provide the template files and scripts with information about the current directory, and so on.

If you are familiar with scripting, you can alter the behavior of the scripts and the template files to provide a highly customized windows interface. However, always be sure to back up system files before editing.

Migration Issues

Objectives

Unless you are performing installations of Internet Explorer on new machines that have not yet been configured in any way, you will likely have to address some issues when moving users from the browsers and support applications they are currently using to Internet Explorer 4.0.

You should address these three primary areas of concern before testing a migration solution:

- **Hardware Compatibility Issues.** Administrators should verify the current hardware configurations of user machines scheduled for installations. The hardware on these machines should be checked for potential conflicts. Verifying compatibility with Microsoft—and with the hardware vendor—can help eliminate hardware problems with the new installation before they occur.
- **Software Compatibility Issues.** A software inventory of the user's machine should also be completed, and the applications installed should be checked for potential conflicts. Checking for software conflicts with the Internet Explorer 4.0 Release Notes, and with the IE Support Center (`http://www.microsoft.com/iesupport`) can help you determine whether there are known conflicts with your existing installed software.
- **Migration Issues.** If there are hardware or software conflicts, a solution for dealing with the conflict should be developed and tested extensively in a laboratory setting before attempting installation for end users. Additionally, software

upgrades or transitions from older applications should also be tested in a lab setting before attempting installation on end users' machines. And of course, any settings and data on user's machines should be backed up before an upgrade or migration is attempted.

Although hardware and software conflicts are uncommon, the potential still exists. If the task is approached with caution, it is possible to migrate a vast majority of users to IE 4.0 without incident.

Objectives

Replacing Other Browsers with Internet Explorer 4.0

The most common area in which compatibility and migration problems arise is with replacing the user's current browser with Internet Explorer. Of course, if the user is already using IE4, and you are simply updating the configuration, you should only have to check the Release Notes for the most recent version to check for incompatibilities.

However, the more likely scenario is a migration from Internet Explorer 3.*x* or from a Netscape browser product. For each of these types of migration, you must address a different set of issues.

Replacing Previous Versions of Internet Explorer

Migration from an installation of Internet Explorer 3.*x* is probably the simplest migration of all. Because both are Microsoft products, there is a high degree of portability. The Internet Explorer 4.0 installation process automatically retains the following IE 3.*x* settings:

- User cookies
- Proxy settings
- User favorites

The exception is that any installed plug-ins present under IE 3.*x* must be reinstalled after the installation of Internet Explorer 4.0 has been successfully completed.

You can include any existing plug-ins or add-ins with your new installation of IE4 by including them as custom components during the custom build. Of course, there may be updates of the plug-ins from IE3.*x* to IE4.0, so you should verify the correct version with the plug-in vendor.

Caution

> Many organizations retain multiple versions of browsers for an overlap period to ensure full migration compatibility. However, although IE and Netscape products may coexist on a machine, IE3.*x* and IE4.0 cannot. If you install IE 4.0 on a machine, you can no longer use IE3.*x* on that machine without creating a separate bootable partition with its own operating system.

Replacing Netscape Browser Products

Another very common migration scenario is migrating from a Netscape Navigator or Communicator product to the Internet Explorer browser. One significant advantage of migration from a Netscape browser to Internet Explorer is that both browsers can coexist on the same machine, so even after you install Internet Explorer on users' machines, they can retain their Netscape settings and still be able to launch the Netscape browser and run it alongside IE4.

Internet Explorer does import settings from Netscape browsers. It automatically detects and imports the following settings:

- User cookies
- Proxy settings
- User bookmarks

Netscape browsers also feature helper applications. If you want to retain those helper apps, you can specify them as the default applications for the appropriate file types in the Windows File Types option.

As is true in a migration from Internet Explorer 3.*x*, Internet Explorer does not import plug-ins from Netscape applications. To migrate plug-ins, you must find the equivalent IE4.0 version of the appropriate plug-in and configure it for installation as a custom package.

Objectives

Replacing Other Internet Mail and News Clients

In addition to the functionality provided by the Internet Explorer browser, you can configure the IE installation to use Outlook Express for email and news capabilities. Similar functionality was provided by Internet News and Mail in Internet Explorer 3.*x* and Netscape's Navigator and Communicator suites. Additionally, a number of other mail options have been available for some time, including Eudora, Exchange, and Outlook.

Two issues are involved in the migration of mail/news clients. First, the server settings from the previous application must be imported or altered. Second, the user's current mail messages and folders must be imported into Outlook Express so that users can still access old mail.

In fact, there are actually two options for migration:

- Users can continue to use their current applications in conjunction with IE4.
- Users can use the Outlook Express client.

If you choose to allow your users to continue using their current applications, you must configure your custom build of IE4.0 to use the end users' current external application as the mail and news programs. Similarly, if you choose to install an external mail program other than Outlook Express, you can specify that mail program as a custom package and then configure your IE build to use it for mail services.

If you are currently using another Microsoft mail client (such as Microsoft Exchange or the full version of Outlook), users can work with both mail clients. The Internet Explorer installation procedure imports Exchange and Outlook settings into Outlook Express so that the user can continue to use Exchange or Outlook, but also have the functionality of Outlook Express.

When migrating from a third party email/news application, Internet Explorer offers support for the following packages:

- Netscape Mail
- Eudora Light
- Eudora Pro

Users' mail folders from any of these mail clients are automatically imported for Outlook Express so that users can access old mail from within the Outlook Express client. Although these are the only third-party mail applications officially supported by the IE setup, other vendors may offer conversion utilities for switching your mail client. If you are using a third-party solution not mentioned here, contact the software vendor for additional information about conversion.

Choosing a Configuration Strategy for Microsoft Outlook Express

Objectives

The Microsoft Outlook Express component is a fully functional mail and news reader that can be configured in conjunction with the Internet Explorer Administration Kit to provide users with access to email and Internet newsgroups. The IEAK provides a number of configuration specifications you can alter with Outlook Express to provide a messaging component customized for your organization. The following sections describe the elements you can customize for Outlook Express, along with why you might want to customize each setting.

User Interface and InfoPane

As with other IE components, you can customize the look and feel of the Outlook Express client by altering the title bar text that appears when you launch the client. You can also alter the bitmap background for the toolbar, just as you can with IE.

The Outlook Express client also features a user interface element called the InfoPane. The InfoPane is displayed at the bottom of the Outlook Express client on startup and can be a great way to present users with important information that might aid them in using the Outlook Express client. For example, the InfoPane can contain information about how to reach your organization's help desk or where to find support documentation. It can include some Frequently Asked Questions, or it may simply contain information about your organization. Administrators can configure the contents of the InfoPane by providing a URL from which you want to load the InfoPane or by specifying a local file. Either way, the InfoPane is a valuable resource you can use to provide users with information.

Finally, you can specify that the Outlook Express client be considered the default mail or news client. If you specify the default option, your users can access Outlook Express from other Web view elements such as the Go menu. Any time an external application calls a news or mail client, Outlook Express will be used.

Welcome Message

The IEAK also allows administrators to populate the user's Inbox automatically after installation with a welcome message. The welcome message can be used to provide users with important mail service information at your organization, to point them to help resources, or simply to welcome users to your version of Outlook Express!

You can specify the location of the welcome message as a URL or as a local file path; after the initial launch of Outlook Express, your message will appear in the user's Inbox. You can also specify the sender of the message, so that you can customize the name of the party that originated your welcome message (for example, `"The IS/IT Team!"`).

Finally, you can specify a reply-to address for the welcome message. With this arrangement, you can have a message that originates from the president of your organization with replies going to the support center or help desk. This feature can help you route inquiries to the welcome message to the appropriate party.

Mail and News Servers

To provide functionality, Outlook Express relies on three servers, each of which provides a different type of functionality to the client. Each of the settings for the following servers can be customized for the client as well:

- **Incoming POP3 Server.** The *incoming POP3 server* is the server from which Outlook Express downloads mail messages directed to the user. This server is usually hosted at your organization and should be specified using a Fully Qualified Domain Name (FQDN) (for example, `pop3.mycompany.com`).
- **Outgoing SMTP Server.** When users compose outgoing email, the mail is delivered to a destination over the Internet (or intranet) using a different server based on the Simple Mail Transfer Protocol (SMTP). The SMTP server is used by Outlook Express only for outgoing mail and should also be specified using the FQDN (for example, `smpt.mycompany.com`).
- **NNTP News Server.** The NNTP server is what Outlook Express contacts to send and to receive Internet News groups and articles. Unlike the mail servers, one server is used for all news functionality. It is also specified using a FQDN (such as `news.mycompany.com`).

Signature for Messages

Many organizations prefer their users to have signatures attached to all outgoing messages. *Signatures* are simply blocks of text added to the bottom of all outgoing messages automatically, so that they are always present when a message is sent by the user. The uses for a signature vary. Many organizations use them as a disclaimer to denote that the sender of the message does not necessarily speak on behalf of the organization. Some organizations use signatures to provide additional contact information about the user and company, such as address and phone number.

The IEAK and Outlook Express allow you to specify a default custom signature to be used. Separate signatures can be specified for the mail messages and news articles.

Choosing a Configuration Strategy for Microsoft NetMeeting

Objective

Microsoft NetMeeting is a conferencing application that allows users to confer from remote locations using the Internet or intranet. NetMeeting allows users to use audio conferencing, video conferencing, and to share data such as files or applications. Because of its flexibility and power to share information over networks, NetMeeting can be a very valuable tool.

However, with such power comes the potential for abuse. Because audio and video conferencing are very network-intensive applications, some administrators may want to limit some of NetMeeting's functionality. Additionally, sharing applications and data over the network can create a situation in which potentially sensitive information is accidentally presented to the public. Therefore, you can limit application sharing and data sharing in NetMeeting as well.

The following sections outline the various restrictions you can place on the NetMeeting client when it is installed in conjunction with Internet Explorer 4.0.

Settings

By using the Internet Explorer Administration Kit or the IEAK Profile Manager, you can preconfigure the following aspects of the NetMeeting client for the end user. Keep in mind that altering these settings also affects the functionality of NetMeeting, so you should choose these settings in accordance with your organization's planned use of NetMeeting.

The options can be divided into four main categories:

- Restrict the use of file transfer
- Restrict the use of application sharing
- Restrict the use of the Options dialog box
- Restrict the use of video

Each of these areas contains a number of configuration parameters you can use to further customize the functionality of NetMeeting.

Restrict the Use of File Transfer

NetMeeting allows conference participants to share files. However, sharing files opens your client to the risk of accidentally distributing sensitive files. It also opens the risk of infecting your local file system with a virus if documents are shared from a nonsecure source. Administrators may therefore:

- Prevent user from sending files
- Prevent user from receiving files

Preventing the user from sending files eliminates the risk of exposure by preventing any outgoing file transfers. Blocking the receipt of files can prevent security breaches.

Restrict the Use of Application Sharing

Sharing applications allows users to work collaboratively on documents and to further share information by allowing conference participants to make changes to the documents under discussion. Administrators have the following options:

- Disable all application sharing features
- Prevent users from sharing the Clipboard
- Prevent users from sharing MS-DOS windows
- Prevent users from sharing Explorer windows
- Prevent users from collaborating

The level of restrictions you place on your users depends on your security needs and the performance requirements of your local machines and network. Sharing application data over the network can decrease network performance and can cause the local machine to respond sluggishly. However, it can be a valuable way to exchange information.

Restrict the Use of the Options Dialog Box

Users can alter their own NetMeeting settings from the NetMeeting Options dialog box. If an administrator wants to enforce a policy decision and prevent users from bypassing that decision through the Options dialog box, the following options can be disabled:

- Disable the General Options page
- Disable the My Information Options page
- Disable the Calling Options page
- Disable the Audio Options page
- Disable the Video Options page
- Disable the Protocols Options page

In addition to disabling the Options pages, administrators may also do the following:

- Prevent user from answering calls
- Prevent user from using audio features

These restrictions can help you enforce usage policies for NetMeeting by forcing calls to originate from your organization and by limiting the audio features to prevent workplace disturbances.

Restrict the Use of Video

NetMeeting provides video conferencing features that can be used when user machines have a video capture device. If no video capabilities exist, administrators can limit the users' capabilities with the following options:

- Prevent user from sending video
- Prevent user from receiving video
- Prevent user from using directory services

These settings can also be used to protect the user's privacy and to limit the amount of network traffic generated by NetMeeting. Because video is a very bandwidth-intensive application, limiting the use of video conferencing can prevent network congestion.

Other Settings

In addition to all the restrictions that can be placed on the NetMeeting client, administrators also have the option of specifying the following configuration information:

- **Default Directory Server.** This is the directory server that NetMeeting contacts to find available conference participants. This option can be set to any public server (either provided by Microsoft or by a third party), or it can be set to an internal directory server maintained by your organization.

- **Exchange Server Property.** The Exchange Server Property allows administrators to select the appropriate Exchange Server setting for NetMeeting.

- **Preset User Information Category.** The Preset User Information Category option allows administrators to select the user information category, such as Personal or Business.

> **Note** The Preset User Information Category option is significant only for the Corporate Administrator deployment role when a silent installation is selected.

- **NetMeeting Home Page.** This option allows administrators to set the URL for the NetMeeting home page. This option can refer to the Microsoft NetMeeting page or to an internally hosted page.

- **Audio/Video Throughput Limit.** Setting an audio/video throughput limit can allow your users to use NetMeeting's video and audio conferencing capabilities while limiting the possibility of network bottlenecks. Of course, limiting throughput may adversely affect conference performance. However, with some fine-tuning, you should be able to find a usable limit for your network that allows adequate performance without dominating network resources.

Protocols

The NetMeeting configuration options available also allow administrators to disable the protocols NetMeeting uses to communicate between clients. NetMeeting can communicate between machines connected directly through Null Modem cables or through the Internet/intranet using the TCP/IP protocol.

Administrators have the following options:

- Disable TCP/IP

- Disable Null Modem

These options allow you to restrict the protocol users can use with NetMeeting. Of course, if both protocols are disabled, NetMeeting cannot function properly. By default, the Disable Null Modem setting is selected.

Choosing a Configuration Strategy for Microsoft NetMeeting Client

Objectives

In addition to all the settings that can be controlled with the system policies and restrictions, you can configure a number of settings within the NetMeeting client itself. These settings control how conference participants connect to each other to use NetMeeting's conferencing features.

Many of these settings can also be configured using the IEAK (however, the settings should be double-checked from within the NetMeeting Client). These settings control the server NetMeeting connects to, how the connection is made, and whether any proxy servers are required to make the connection. If these settings are not correct, users cannot connect to other participants, making NetMeeting less than useful.

Internet Locator Service

NetMeeting uses a server to connect users for conferences. This server is known as the Internet Locator Service (ILS). When users launch NetMeeting, they must connect to an ILS to connect to other users. When the user logs in to an ILS server, he or she can see a list of other users who are available for NetMeeting calls. The user can then select a user and initiate a call. They can also incoming calls from users on the same server.

A number of different ILS services are available—your company may operate its own. Public ILS servers are provided by Microsoft, Four11, and a number of other companies. The ILS server you decide to use will likely depend on your geographic location and the network performance of the server. You may want to try connecting with several servers before you decide which server you will normally use as the default ILS server.

IP Connectivity and Peer-to-Peer Networking

NetMeeting supports two methods of connecting users for conferencing. The first is through IP-based networks. The second is through a peer-to-peer connection, based on a physical connection between machines.

In a restricted environment, it is possible to link two machines together physically with a null modem cable to create peer-to-peer networking. For machines that are not networked, or for special conferencing purposes, peer-to-peer networking can be an easy way to connect two machines.

However, the majority of the time, you will want to configure NetMeeting for IP connectivity, using networks such as your corporate intranet or the Internet. Of course, the machines must be connected to an IP-based network, and the network settings must be configured using the Windows Network Control Panel. When the correct network settings are in place, IP-based networking allows connections over a wide geographic area and uses the features of NetMeeting to their fullest extent.

Proxy Settings

As is true for other network applications that make use of Internet-based resources, if your organization uses a firewall or proxy server, NetMeeting also has to use the proxy server for some of its features.

There is no specific setting for proxy services within NetMeeting; however, proxy services must still be correctly configured within Internet Explorer.

Strategies for Managing Automatic Configuration Using the IEAK Profile Manager

Objectives

One of the strengths of the Internet Explorer Administration Kit is the IEAK Profile Manager. The IEAK creates the custom build for your installation based largely on the configuration of Internet Explorer installed on the machine you are using to run the IEAK. The process of creating a customized build is pretty extensive and time consuming; as a result, creating a customized build every time some configuration information changes can be a real hassle.

The IEAK Profile Manager provides you with the ability to reconfigure your custom build of Internet Explorer without rebuilding it. The capabilities of Profile Manager are limited, of course. For example, you cannot use the Profile Manager to add new packages to the installation. However, many of the user configurations that can be set inside the browser can be altered in the installation profile, which is stored in an `.INS` file that is with your custom package.

The IEAK Profile Manager is an executable separate from the IEAK and can be accessed from the Start menu under the IEAK folder. After the Profile Manager is launched, you can create a new profile file (`.INS`) from scratch, or you can load one from an existing custom build. You can also create customized profiles for Windows 95/NT, Windows 3.1/WFW/NT 3.5.1, or UNIX platforms. Keep in mind that some of the configurations available differ depending on the platform.

Here's a list of the types of configuration information you can alter using the IEAK Profile Manager:

- Browser title
- Support, Search, and Start page locations
- Preinstalled favorites

- Desktop wallpaper
- User agent string
- Proxy settings
- Imported channels
- Imported software update channels
- LDAP settings
- Outlook Express settings
- Signatures
- URLs for automatic browser configuration
- File locations for custom Web views (`.HTT` files)
- Security zone and content ratings
- Certificate settings

In addition to these interface and cosmetic configurations, you can also edit the system policies and restrictions of many IE settings and those of other packages, including the following:

- Microsoft Chat
- Microsoft NetMeeting
- Internet Restrictions
- Outlook Express
- Web Desktop
- Subscriptions

By altering these settings in the `.INS` files using the IEAK Profile Manager, you can create different installation profiles for different applications within your organization. In this way, you can distribute the same custom build with different `.INS` files. You can also take advantage of the Profile Manager to provide updates to your installer should any of the configuration information change (for example, the URL of any .JS or .PAC files for automatic browser configuration). If you have to alter this type of information, you can do so using the Profile Manager instead of the full IEAK.

Developing Configurations for Active Setup Components

Objectives

Internet Explorer features the Active Setup component for installing IE4.0. Active Setup is an executable that controls the user configuration, downloading, and installation of IE4.0 files; it simplifies the process for end users.

The major advantage of using Active Setup for installation is its modularity. The Active Setup component itself is only 407KB in size, so it can fit easily onto a floppy or be downloaded quickly over a 28.8Kbps modem to allow users to get started installing IE4 without a long wait.

Once the Active Setup component is downloaded, users run it as they would any other application; the component prompts the user for any configuration input required for the installation. After the user has entered the required information, Active Setup connects to the specified server and begins downloading the necessary files to perform the installation. After the files have been downloaded, the installation occurs according to the information already supplied by the user.

Before downloading the files however, Active Setup searches the user's machine for already installed components and determines whether or not there is enough disk space to perform the installation. This search can save the user valuable time by preventing the download of all the installation files only to conclude that there is not enough disk space. By downloading only the components that are not already installed, Active Setup also helps decrease download time. Finally, because Active Setup prompts the user for all necessary input before downloading the IE .CAB installation files, the user is free to do other work while the actual installation takes place. Because the download of a full IE installation can take quite a bit of time, users can even let the Active Setup run overnight. Here are some other advantages of Active Setup:

- **Distribution Site Cycling.** If the specified download site is not available, Active Setup automatically tries other listed download sites.
- **Progressive Downloading.** If the downloading process is interrupted for any reason, Active Setup keeps track of components already downloaded so that the download can pick up where it left off.

After Active Setup has successfully downloaded all the necessary components, it launches the standard Microsoft installer. Corporate administrators also have the option of customizing the IE4 setup with the IExpress tool.

The Internet Explorer Administration Kit allows administrators to customize the look and feel of many of the features of the Active Setup Wizard and to present choices to the user when he or she runs Active Setup. When you use the IEAK Wizard, the following features are customizable.

> **Note** Not all customizations are available to all administrative roles. Options may vary from one role to another; when an option is limited to a particular role, this fact is noted.

- Customize the CD-ROM Autorun screen
- Customize the Active Setup Wizard title bar and bitmap
- Import a custom Internet Connection Manager profile (ISP role)
- Choose the silent installation (Corporate Administrator role)
- Specify up to 10 install options

- Specify up to 10 download sites
- Specify unique version numbers and ID
- Specify installation directory (Corporate Administrator role)
- Customize Windows Desktop Update (Corporate Administrator role)

These options allow you to customize the images and titles in Active Setup to alert users to your customized version. These options also allow you to change the choices Active Setup presents to the user so that you can limit or suggest specific choices to the user performing the installation.

To aid administrators in troubleshooting and administrative functions, the Active Setup component also performs extensive logging. The log information is stored in two files that administrators can use to see what may have gone wrong with an installation. The two logs created are described here:

Log File	Description
`Active Setup Log.txt`	This log keeps track of every action performed by the Active Server component. It contains information about the servers contacted, files downloaded, files installed, and so on. If you are trying to determine why a component was not installed, or if you are diagnosing a component that is not functioning correctly, this log can provide valuable information.
`RunOnceEx Log.txt`	The IE components make extensive use of Dynamic Link Libraries, and this log reflects errors that occur in the `.DLL` registration phase. This log file can aid administrators in diagnosing errors related to `.DLL`s or random installation errors.

Both of these log files are located in the `C:\Windows` or `C:\Winnt` directories as plain-text files.

Developing Strategies for Using the Connection Manager Administration Kit

The Microsoft Connection Manager Administration Kit (CMAK) Wizard allows Internet Service Providers to create customized versions of the Microsoft Connection Manager.

The Connection Manager is a dialer that allows Windows users to easily keep track of dial-up network Points-of-Presence (POPs) and to easily connect to network resources. Configuring the inclusion and configuration of the Connection Manager allows ISPs and corporate administrators to provide access to network resources, configure TCP/IP settings on the user's machine, enable dial-up networking and dial-up scripting, and use a modem.

The CMAK Wizard allows administrators to create service profiles for network resources and to configure the look and feel of the Connection Manager. Installation of the Connection Manager in conjunction with Internet Explorer 4.0 can provide users with a simple solution to obtaining Internet connectivity to enjoy IE and its features.

Customizing the Connection Manager

The Connection Manager Administration Kit Wizard allows many of the features of the Connection Manager to be customized by administrators. These features include the following:

- **Graphics and Text.** Administrators can customize the title text and bitmaps displayed within the Connection Manager. They can also specify custom animations to be played during the connection process, and can specify some information such as support phone numbers or notifications. Administrators can also specify information such as help files.

- **Setting Up Phone Books.** Service providers can create phone books using Connection Point Services, which contain the information about the phone number to dial and the services offered (modem, ISDN, and so on). By using the CMAK, you can specify the phone book to be used with your Connection Manager; you can also specify the server location of the phone book so that you can automatically update it.
- **Automating System Configuration.** Using the automatic system configuration features, administrators can configure the TCP/IP settings of the user's machine. They can also customize the dial-up networking settings based on entries contained in the specified phone book. This arrangement eliminates much of the information that must be entered by users to create a dial-up connection.
- **Secure Connections.** For organizations that require or make use of PPTP to provide secure connections to network dial-up resources, the CMAK allows administrators to configure users' machines to connect to secure servers with the proper information to establish a secure connection.
- **Merging Service Profiles.** Administrators can merge service profiles that contain useful information for users into one service profile. This arrangement provides users with a simplified interface and choices of options while still retaining the functionality of multiple service profiles.
- **Connect Actions and Auto-Applications.** Administrators can use connect actions and auto-applications to configure user machines to automatically connect to network resources when certain applications are run. These features are handy when you want to automatically download phone book updates and to automatically disconnect from network resources when they are not in use.
- **Sign-In.** Administrators can customize any information that must be provided to servers during the sign-in process, such as user names, passwords, realm names, and so on. Additionally, this option allows administrators to configure dialing options such as the number of busy retries and the delay between retries.

By using the Connection Manager and the Connection Manager Administration Kit Wizard, organizations can create simple dial-in solutions for end users. Organizations can also tailor the dial-in parameters for users ahead of time to eliminate the risk of mistyped or misentered configuration information.

Exercises

Exercise 1.1: Licensing the Internet Explorer Administration Kit

In this exercise, you register for the Internet Explorer Administration Kit and sign up for your customization number.

1. Point your Web browser to `https://ieak.microsoft.com`.
2. Click the Get the IEAK link in the navigation bar.
3. Click the New Registration link.
4. Enter your email address, company name, first name, and last name; click the Register button.

   You will receive an email message containing confirmation of your registration.
5. Select the appropriate use for your installation of Internet Explorer.
6. Carefully read the licensing agreement; if you agree to it, select Accept.
7. After you agree to a license, you will be sent an email message that contains your customization code. Keep this code in a safe place because you will have to enter it when you run the IEAK.
8. You are now ready to download and install the IEAK software.

Exercise 1.2: Downloading the Internet Explorer Administration Kit

In this exercise, you download and install the Internet Explorer Administration Kit.

1. After you have completed the registration and obtained your customization code, point your browser to `https://ieak.microsoft.com`.
2. Click the Get the IEAK link in the navigation bar.

3. Click the Download link.
4. Select the appropriate version of the IEAK for your operating system and hardware.
5. Click Next.
6. Select the language you want for the IEAK. (This option you select here will not affect the language options available for custom builds.)
7. Click Next.
8. Select a download site based on geographic proximity to you.
9. Click Next.
10. Click Install Now. This action downloads the IEAK to your machine and installs the IEAK on your system.

Exercise 1.3: Planning Customization for Deployment

Following is an outline you can use to plan the customizations you will make to the Active Setup and Internet Explorer Installation, depending on your deployment. You can use this outline as a template for the considerations that should go into planning your deployment. The details for completing each stage are covered in subsequent chapters.

- Stage 1: Gathering Information
  1. Gather Custom Graphics and Custom Text
  2. Select Language for Installation
  3. Select the Distribution Media
- Stage 2: Specifying Active Setup Parameters
  1. Select the Microsoft Download Site
  2. Determine the Automatic Version Synchronization Policy

continues

Exercise 1.3: Continued

3. Determine Any Active Setup Components (up to 10)

4. Determine Trusted Publishers

- Stage 3: Customizing Active Setup

1. Select Bitmaps and Text for Customizing the Autorun Screen

2. Select Bitmaps and Text for Customizing the Active Setup Wizard

3. Select Title for Custom Components Install Section

4. For Corporate Administrators, Determine Whether Installation Will Be Silent

5. Determine Installation Options (up to 10)

6. Specify the URLs for Downloading IE Files

7. Determine the Version Number and Product ID for the Custom Build

8. Determine the Installation Directory

9. Determine the Policy for Integration of the Windows Desktop Update

- Stage 4: Customizing the Browser

1. Select Window Title Text and Toolbar Bitmap

2. Create Customized Animation Logos

3. Create the Customized Static Toolbar Logo

4. Determine URLs for Custom Start, Search, and Support Pages

5. Determine Favorites Configuration

6. Create a Custom Welcome Page

7. Create Desktop Wallpaper
8. Determine Channel Configurations
9. Determine Any Active Desktop Components to Be Installed
10. Determine Any Modifications to Desktop Toolbar
11. Determine Any Customizations to Be Made to My Computer
12. Determine Any Customizations to Be Made to Control Panels
13. Specify Automatic Browser Configuration Options
14. Specify Proxy Settings
15. Develop Security Policy
16. Determine Security Zone Settings

- Stage 5: Component Customization

1. Determine Mail Server Settings
2. Determine News Server Settings
3. Determine Mail and News Client Options
4. Specify LDAP Settings
5. Create Customized Signatures for Mail and News

- Stage 6: System Policies and Restrictions

1. Determine NetMeeting Settings and Policies
2. Determine Active Desktop Settings
3. Determine Desktop Wallpaper
4. Determine Desktop Toolbar Properties

continues

Exercise 1.3: Continued

5. Determine Internet Explorer Browser Properties
6. Determine Outlook Express Client Properties
7. Specify Shell Restrictions and Policies
8. Develop Channel and Subscription Settings
9. Determine Internet Explorer Advanced Settings

Of course, this exercise is left open ended and fairly ambiguous on purpose. The options you choose to use and choose to ignore should be based on the application you have in mind for your installation of Internet Explorer. By using this outline, however, you should be able to develop the materials you will need when configuring your custom build; this outline can make the process go much more smoothly.

Review Questions

The review questions in this section can help you assess your understanding of the terms, concepts, and objectives covered in this chapter. These questions are written in the style of the questions presented on the MCSE exam and are an excellent way to prepare yourself for the material you will see on the exam. After you complete the review questions, you will find the answer to each question—along with an explanation of the answer—in the following section.

1. You are selecting the Internet Explorer installation for your organization, which uses the browser for intranet capabilities so that departments can manage their own Web areas. Management wants to provide video conferencing as well. Select the best installation to provide the required services.

    A. Standard installation

    B. Full installation

    C. Enhanced installation

    D. Standard installation with FrontPage

2. For corporate administrators, an Internet connection and an installed version of Internet Explorer are required to (select all that apply):

    A. Use the IEAK Profile Manager.

    B. Build custom installations for Internet Explorer.

    C. Use the Internet Explorer Administration Kit.

    D. Use the Connection Manager Administration Kit.

3. What are the advantages of an Internet/intranet distributed custom installation? (Select all that apply.)

    A. Central build location is easier to administer.

    B. Access provided to entire organization.

C. Active Setup Wizard is small and quickly downloadable.

D. Security is increased.

4. Your organization wants to provide a simple installer that can be used by virtually anyone in your organization. What is the best solution?

    A. A CD-ROM and floppy disk combined distribution

    B. A complete set of installation floppy disks

    C. A network installer with Active Setup distribution

    D. A CD-ROM–only distribution

5. You operate a small network installation company and are beginning to allow clients dial-in access to your network for software upgrades. What role would provide you with the optimal set of IEAK features?

    A. Content Provider/Developer

    B. Corporate Administrator

    C. Internet Service Provider

    D. Internet Content Administrator

6. In planning your corporate deployment strategy, you've tested your custom IE build with various user software packages. You now have to rebuild the final distribution. How can you be sure that your components will still be compatible?

    A. By locking down your Desktop Update settings

    B. By copying the `.CAB` files from your previous build

    C. By disabling the Automatic Version Synchronization option

    D. By altering your build using the IEAK Profile Manager

7. Which of the following configuration options is granted only to the Corporate Administrator role?

    A. Multiple Download Sites

    B. Custom Version Number and ID

    C. Silent Installation

    D. Customized Logos and Animations

8. What security zone would the URL `http://deptserver` be automatically assigned to?

    A. Trusted Sites

    B. Internet Zone

    C. Restricted Sites

    D. Intranet/Local Zone

9. What must a Web site administrator do to allow users the ability to subscribe to a Web site and receive regular content updates?

    A. Create an OSD file for the site

    B. Configure the channels component for IE

    C. Create a CDF file for the site

    D. Nothing; sites are already enabled for updates

10. To configure Active Channel subscriptions for custom installations, administrators must:

    A. Have the necessary channel subscriptions in Internet Explorer on the IEAK machine

    B. Alter the channel settings from within the IEAK Profile Manager

    C. Prepare the necessary `.CDF` files for any channels to be subscribed to

    D. Configure the Connections Manager to connect to sites automatically for downloads

11. Which of the following scenarios is an appropriate use of the OSD Channel model?

    A. Allowing users to subscribe to sites in their Favorites folder

    B. Distributing the latest version of an in-house application

    C. Providing access to channels through the Active Desktop

    D. Providing users with subscriptions to the company news site

12. As a Corporate Administrator, you want to integrate browser features into clients' folder views in Windows Explorer. This requires:

    A. The Connection Manager Administration Kit

    B. The Windows Desktop Update

    C. Cannot be performed in the Corporate Administrator role

    D. The IEAK Profile Manager

13. As a Corporate Administrator, you want to customize the Control Panel appearances for users. This can be done by (select all that apply):

    A. Using the Windows Desktop Update

    B. Customizing the Intranet/Local Security Zone

    C. Editing the `CONTROLP.HTT` file

    D. Using the IEAK Profile Manager

14. Which of the following files can be used in the Corporate Administrator role to provide customization of the OS environment with a custom IE install? (Select all that apply.)

A. `PRINTERS.HTT`

B. `MYCOMP.HTT`

C. `FOLDERS.HTT`

D. `CONTROLP.HTT`

15. You are updating users' browsers from Netscape 3.0 with a VRML plug-in to Internet Explorer 4.0. You must be sure to configure the following (select all that apply):

    A. Nothing; IE will migrate all user settings

    B. Network server settings for mail and news

    C. A custom plug-in package for the VRML plug-in

    D. User favorites, so that bookmarks are imported

16. Which of the following clients is not supported for mail migration with Internet Explorer 4.0?

    A. Eudora Pro

    B. Lotus Notes

    C. Netscape Mail

    D. Microsoft Exchange

17. What options exist for administrators to provide customized help options for Outlook Express? (Select all that apply.)

    A. Customizable InfoPane

    B. Title bar customization

    C. Customizable server settings

    D. Initial user welcome message

18. Which of the following options allows administrators to provide audio/video conferencing on a congested network?

    A. Prevent user from using audio features

    B. Restrict the use of video

C. Audio/video throughput limit

D. Restrict the use of application sharing

19. Which file is altered by the IEAK Profile Manager to alter some customized installation options?

    A. The `.PAC` automatic browser config file

    B. The `.INS` installer file

    C. The `.HTT` template file

    D. The `.JS` scripting file

20. Once you have created a customized build of Internet Explorer, you can use the IEAK Profile Manager to (select all that apply):

    A. Customize user browser settings

    B. Alter the preconfigured user channel options

    C. Create a foreign language installer edition

    D. Alter system policies and restrictions

21. Active Setup offers the following benefits to users (select all that apply):

    A. Small download size

    B. Connection to a single distribution site

    C. Progressive component downloads

    D. Configuration prompting before downloads

22. One of your users is having trouble with his or her Active Setup Wizard not correctly installing the IE browser. Which tool can provide troubleshooting information?

    A. The installer `.INS` file

    B. The Active Setup `RunOnceEx` log

    C. The Active Setup log

    D. The Windows NT event viewer

23. Using a custom phone book file with the Connections Manager Administration Kit, ISP administrators can (select all that apply):

    A. Customize user's TCP/IP settings

    B. Configure the dial-in numbers available to users

    C. Alter the modem installation of users' machines

    D. Maintain a single phone book for automatic updates

Review Answers

Now that you have completed the review questions, check your answers against those provided here. Explanations are provided for each answer so that you can see whether you arrived at the correct solution for the right reason, or so that you can see how your answer varied from the correct one.

1. **B** The Full installation of Internet Explorer includes both the FrontPage Express package (which allows users to create and edit HTML documents) and Microsoft NetMeeting (which provides audio and video conferencing capabilities). The Enhanced version does include FrontPage Express but does not include NetMeeting.

2. **B and C** The Internet Explorer Administration Kit requires that administrators have a currently installed version of Internet Explorer and a connection to the Internet. The installed version of IE is used to copy some configuration settings such as channel subscriptions. The connection to the Internet is used to verify the most recent versions of the components through AVS. Without a current installation of IE and a connection to the Internet, the IEAK Wizard may run; however, a complete customized build cannot be produced.

3. **A and C** By making a custom installation available on the Internet/intranet, administrators can maintain a single copy of the installer while still providing a mechanism for reaching a large number of users. The Active Setup Wizard can

then be deployed to users remotely using a modem or floppy disk to manage installations from the network site for users who are not centrally located.

4. **C** A network installation, available through the Internet, can be accessed both internally and externally. By providing the Active Setup Wizard to users, the installation can proceed with minimal user input; downloading the necessary components and so on would be managed by the wizard.

5. **C** The Corporate Administrator role does not provide a license for public distribution of your customized installer. Because you want to provide dial-in services by taking advantage of the Connection Manager Administration Kit, the Content Provider/Developer role is not appropriate. To combine the features of a publicly distributable installer with dial-in features, you should select the ISP role.

6. **C** Disabling the Automatic Version Synchronization eliminates the IEAK Wizard's process of retrieving the most recent components from Microsoft. By eliminating this step, you can make sure that the components on your machine and in your installer are the same ones that were tested in a lab setting.

7. **C** Only the Corporate Administrator role can choose a silent installation where the user is not prompted for any configuration information during the IE installation.

8. **D** Any URL that is not a Fully Qualified Domain Name (containing periods) is considered local. Because `http://deptserver` contains no periods, it is automatically assigned to the Intranet/Local Zone. Had the URL been `http://deptserver.myorg.com`, it would be assigned to the Internet Zone.

9. **C** Web site content can be used as channel content without any changes. However, to engage the channel mechanism for the client, site administrators must create a CDF channel for their Web site that includes information that defines the channel content and its subscription schedule.

10. **A** Because the IEAK imports channel settings for custom builds from the current installed version of IE on the machine running the IEAK, that installation of IE must be correctly configured for channel subscriptions if they are to be included in the custom build.

11. **B** The Open Software Distribution (OSD) channel is another type of Active Channel that allows users to subscribe to applications rather than to Web-based content. The OSD channel allows users to receive automatic software updates using Internet Explorer and the channel mechanism.

12. **B** Shell integration features, such as the Active Desktop and Web views, are components included with the Windows Desktop Update. To take advantage of these features, Corporate Administrators must include the Windows Desktop Update in their custom installations.

13. **A and C** To alter the appearance of the Control Panels in the Windows interface, you must have installed the Windows Desktop Update. From there, you can alter Control Panel features by editing the hypertext template file for Control Panels (`CONTROLP.HTT`).

14. **B and D** The `MYCOMP.HTT` and `CONTROLP.HTT` files can be used by Corporate Administrators to alter the user interface features of Windows with IE 4.0. The `FOLDERS.HTT` and `PRINTERS.HTT` files can be altered as well; however, the latter two files are not included in a customized build, so the process of configuring these features cannot be automated through the IEAK and a custom build.

15. **C** When migrating to IE from Netscape, the IE installer automatically imports user bookmarks, server settings, and cookies. However, it does not transfer plug-ins. You should double-check plug-ins for compatibility with IE4 and then added them to the installation as a custom package.

16. **B** The Internet Explorer installer supports the automatic migration of mail from previous versions of IE, Netscape clients, and Eudora. It also supports settings imported from

Microsoft Exchange and Outlook. However, Lotus Notes, cc:Mail, and Pegasus are not supported clients for migration.

17. **A, B, and D** Administrators can configure the Outlook Express InfoPanel to point users to FAQs or help sites or to contain phone numbers for assistance. In addition, administrators can populate the user's Inbox with an initial welcome message that contains information about anything they choose, including pointers to help resources.

18. **C** Limiting the amount of network bandwidth that can be consumed by audio and video conferencing can help eliminate network congestion and bottlenecks when using the conferencing facilities of NetMeeting.

19. **B** The `.INS` file is used by the installer to determine customized profile information. The IEAK Profile Manager makes changes and additions to the `.INS` file for a customized build.

20. **A, B, and D** The IEAK Profile Manager can be used to alter many of the settings for an existing custom build, including customizing browser settings, importing new channel configuration features from the working IE version, and editing the systems policies and restrictions. However, the Profile Manager cannot create a new build from the ground up, and each language version of the installer must have a separate build.

21. **A, C, and D** The Active Setup Wizard offers several benefits to users: Its compact size (407K) allows it to be downloaded quickly or distributed on floppy disks; it manages the progressive download of components so that if the download is interrupted, it can pick up where it left off; and it prompts the user for configuration information before the download and install, so that the installation can be unattended. However, the Active Setup component does not connect to a single distribution site. It can contain up to 10 sites and will cycle through the available sites if the site the user selected is unavailable.

22. **C** The Active Setup Wizard keeps a text format log file of every task it performs. By reviewing this log, administrators can determine the point at which the installation was corrupted and try to take steps to resolve the problem.

23. **B and D** By using customized phone books, ISP Administrators can configure the phone numbers and server settings used by the Connections Manager to dial in to network resources. Because the phone book can be updated from the server, administrators have an easy way to maintain a single file and still provide updates for many users.

Answers to Test Yourself Questions at Beginning of Chapter

1. The Internet Explorer Administration Kit Wizard requires:

    - Internet Explorer 4.0 installed and functional on the machine to run the IEAK
    - A 486 66MHz or greater processor
    - Windows 95 or Windows NT 4.0
    - 8MB RAM for Windows 95, 16MB RAM for Windows NT
    - 40MB to 60MB of disk space for the IEAK installation
    - 40MB to 100MB of additional disk space per each customized build
    - A working connection to the Internet

    Sections Referencing This Material:

    - "Choosing the Appropriate Internet Explorer Installation"
    - "Internet Explorer Requirements"
    - "Requirements for the Internet Explorer Administration Kit Configuration Wizard"

2. The Standard installation includes the Internet Explorer 4.0 browser, Outlook Express for email and news, and the ActiveMovie component for multimedia functionality.

The Enhanced and Full versions build on the same components found in the Standard installation. The Enhanced installation adds FrontPage Express, which allows users to create and edit Web content.

The Full installation includes all the features of the Standard and Enhanced versions and adds Microsoft Wallet for Web-based commercial transactions, NetShow for Internet-based multicasting, and NetMeeting for network-based audio/video conferencing and data sharing.

Sections Referencing This Material:

- "Choosing the Appropriate Internet Explorer Installation"
- "Which Installation: Standard, Enhanced, or Full?"

3. There are three deployment roles for the Internet Explorer Administration Kit:

   - Internet Content Provider/Developer
   - Internet Service Provider (ISP)
   - Corporate Administrator

   The Content Provider role is designed for IEAK administrators who develop content for the Internet and want to distribute a customized version of Internet Explorer to provide turnkey solutions for clients.

   The ISP role is designed for Internet Service Providers who want to provide customers with a customized browser for the Internet. The amount of customization the ISP role allows is limited. However, the ISP role has additional functionality available, such as the Connection Manager Administration Kit, which allows configuration of dial-up accounts for network access.

   The most complete customization options are provided by the Corporate Administrator role. In the Corporate Administrator role, completely customized packages can be created, including the use of the Windows Desktop Update to customize the complete Windows environment for the user.

Each deployment role requires a different license agreement from Microsoft.

Sections Referencing This Material:

- "Custom Installation Strategies"
- "Administrative Roles"

4. A network-based IE installation allows administrators to manage the customized IE package in one location, so that, by updating the centrally located files, all users have access to the revised IE installer.

   By using the Active Setup component, administrators can distribute a small, portable installer that will contact a central network resource to obtain the complete installation package.

   Sections Referencing This Material:

   - "Custom Installation Strategies"
   - "Distribution Mechanisms"

5. The four security zones used by Internet Explorer are:

   - Local/Intranet Zone
   - Internet Zone
   - Trusted Sites
   - Restricted Sites

   The Local/Intranet Zone is for network resources located on a Local Area Network or on a corporate intranet. These hosts are assumed to be trustworthy, so security measures against them are more relaxed. Machines with URLs that do not contain periods (.) are considered part of the Local/Intranet Zone.

   The Internet Zone contains all machines on the Internet as well as network resources accessed using a Fully Qualified Domain Name, such as `www.mycompany.com`.

   The Trusted and Restricted Sites Zones allow administrators to specify sites that are considered Trusted or Restricted based on individual URLs. Trusted sites are treated with relaxed security precautions; Restricted sites are given the maximum security precautions.

Sections Referencing This Material:

- "Developing Secure Internet Explorer Usage Strategies"
- "Internet Explorer Security Zones"

6. The Windows Desktop Update provides several innovative features to Internet Explorer. It adds shell integration (such as the ability to incorporate components into the Taskbar) and the ability to manipulate Web views with folders. It also adds the functionality of the Active Desktop, all of which allows users to access network information from nearly any Windows interface.

   Additionally, the Windows Desktop Update allows Corporate Administrators the ability to manage nearly all aspects of the user's environment, including the functionality of My Computer and Control Panels. Administrators can alter the user's desktop, screen saver, and Web views. Administrators can also lock down these components to prevent users from altering them on their own.

   Sections Referencing This Material:

   - "Windows Desktop Update"
   - "Customizing Web Views"

7. Because the Internet Explorer installer can successfully migrate many of the settings from Netscape products, the transition should be fairly easy. IE automatically reads any server settings and user information and can import bookmarks into favorites.

   The only major concern is with any installed browser plug-ins. These plug-ins must be added to the IE installation as custom packages; compatibility with IE 4.0 should be checked.

Sections Referencing This Material:

- "Migration Issues"
- "Replacing Other Browsers with Internet Explorer 4.0"
- "Replacing Netscape Browser Products"

8. Internet Explorer supports email migration from the following clients:

   - Netscape
   - Internet News and Internet Mail
   - Eudora and Eudora Pro

   Internet Explorer retains server settings (unless they are overridden during the installation) and will import users' mail folders.

   Sections Referencing This Material:

   - "Migration Issues"
   - "Replacing Other Internet Mail and News Clients"

9. The Active Setup Wizard provides an easy-to-use, lightweight installation mechanism for installing Internet Explorer 4.0. Because of its small size (407K), it can be easily downloaded or distributed on floppy disks. When it is run, it prompts the user for any information that must be input before beginning the component download. This approach saves the user from having to be present during the entire installation process. Additionally, the Active Setup Wizard manages the download of components so that, if the download is interrupted, Active Setup can pick up where it left off.

   Section Referencing This Material:

   - "Developing Configurations for Active Setup Components"

10. The Connection Manager Administration Kit provides ISPs and Corporate Administrators the capability to configure a customized Connection Manager for clients, which allows

the clients to connect to the Internet or to corporate-based dial-up resources.

Section Referencing This Material:

- "Developing Strategies for Using the Connection Manager Administration Kit"

11. The Internet Explorer Administration Kit Profile Manager gives administrators the ability to edit the installation configuration file (.INS) for a customized installation of Internet Explorer. In this way, administrators can change the configuration of the customized installation without rerunning the IEAK Wizard.

    Section Referencing This Material:

    - "Strategies for Managing Automatic Configuration Using the IEAK Profile Manager"

12. Many of Outlook Express's options can be configured using the IEAK. These options include the following:

    - The title bar text
    - The InfoPane
    - The initial welcome message in the user's Inbox
    - The POP3 server for incoming mail
    - The SMTP server for outgoing mail
    - The NNTP server for news functionality
    - Email signature
    - Newsgroup signature

    Section Referencing This Material:

    - "Choosing a Configuration Strategy for Microsoft Outlook Express"

13. The Active Channel features of Internet Explorer allow administrators to create Web sites that add subscription functionality using a Channel Definition Format (.CDF) file. Users can then subscribe to the Web site and receive email

notices when the site is updated—or have the site's updated content automatically downloaded to their machines.

Open Software Distribution (OSD) channels are similar to CDF channels, but instead allow administrators to automatically update actual applications to users' desktops. OSD channels can be configured to provide users with an email notice of upgrades, to automatically download the upgrade installers, or to automatically install the updated software.

Sections Referencing This Material:

- "Active Channels"
- "Administering Channels"

14. Although NetMeeting provides robust conferencing facilities, it has some potential for abuse. Allowing file sharing and application sharing can leave a user's machine vulnerable to viruses and security leaks. Video conferencing can also represent a potential user privacy issue.

    However, the biggest concerns with audio and video conferencing stem from network bandwidth concerns. Both applications are network intensive; if left to run unchecked, they can seriously hamper network performance. However, administrators can use features such as the ability to limit audio/video bandwidth to balance NetMeeting functionality with Network performance.

    Section Referencing This Material:

    - "Choosing a Configuration Strategy for Microsoft NetMeeting"

Chapter 2

Installation and Configuration

Before you can begin using Internet Explorer and the Internet Explorer Administration Kit, you have to install and configure the software. This chapter covers all aspects of obtaining Internet Explorer and the IEAK from Microsoft and the process of installation and configuration.

Because Internet Explorer is a complex piece of software, its configuration and installation are involved processes. However, Microsoft has gone out of its way to provide a robust installation process that is easy to follow and complete.

This chapter also tackles one of the most important aspects of using the Internet Explorer Administration Kit: customizing the browser. This chapter takes you step by step through a browser configuration in the Corporate Administrator role and explains how to customize the component of Internet Explorer to build an install that is right for you and your organization.

This chapter helps you prepare for the exam by covering the following objectives:

Objectives

- Install and configure Internet Explorer 4.0, with or without the Windows Desktop Update, on computers that run various operating systems. Operating systems include
  - Microsoft Windows NT Server 4.0
  - Microsoft Windows NT Workstation 4.0
  - Microsoft Windows 95

continues

- Microsoft Windows 3.*x*
- Macintosh

- Specify and customize Active Setup components
- Customize the browser
- Configure built-in and custom components of Internet Explorer 4.0 by using the IEAK wizard. Components include
  - Microsoft Outlook Express
  - Microsoft NetMeeting
- Configure channels, software distribution channels, and site subscriptions
- Configure Outlook Express for custom installations of Internet Explorer 4.0

Test Yourself! Before reading this chapter, test yourself to determine how much study time you will need to devote to this section.

The following prechapter quiz is designed to help you get a feel for how well you currently understand the material covered in this chapter. If you feel that you have a strong understanding of the objectives outlined in the previous list, try the quiz. Based on your score on this quiz, you may feel well enough prepared to skip ahead to the Review Questions at the end of the chapter, or you may determine that you would like to study the chapter material more closely.

1. Identify the minimum installation requirements for installing Internet Explorer 4.0 on a Windows 95/NT machine.
2. What restrictions does performing a silent installation place on the customization options for the Active Setup Wizard?
3. What are some of the concerns with allowing file transfers with NetMeeting?
4. How would you add a disclaimer for all outgoing messages with Outlook Express?
5. How many download sites and custom components can be added to the Active Setup Wizard in the Corporate Administrator role?
6. What is the mechanism for specifying custom channels for installation?
7. What is the function of `.INS`, `.JS`, and `.PAC` files?

The answers to this prechapter quiz are located at the end of this chapter. Score your answers against those provided to determine your course of study for this chapter.

Test Objectives Overview

Chapter 1 reviewed the process for planning the creation of a customized version of Internet Explorer using the IEAK and the IEAK Profile Manager. Although Chapter 1 dealt with the Internet Explorer platform at a fairly high level of abstraction, this chapter dives right into the practical aspects.

Now that you have planned all the configuration options and customizations you intend to make using the IEAK, it is time to put your choices into real situations and begin the process of creating your customized build.

This chapter addresses the installation and configuration of Internet Explorer, including all the components you can customize, tweak, and make your own in order to create the installation that best suits the needs of your organization.

The chapter starts out by reviewing the installation procedures for Internet Explorer on various platforms. Because the installation and configuration of Internet Explorer on the machine on which you are running the IEAK Administration Kit is critical to the success of your system-wide implementation, this seemingly trivial task takes on a great deal of importance. If you recall from the last chapter, the IEAK obtains many of the configuration details for your custom build from the version of IE running on your machine. This means that the installation and configuration of the version on your machine plays a major role in determining the nature of what appears on other machines.

The chapter moves on to the configuration of various components using the IEAK. We will take a look at how you can customize various aspects of the Active Setup Wizard so that the installation for your clients proceeds exactly as you have planned. We will also look at the configuration of various browser components within the IEAK Wizard so that you understand how each of the settings impacts your users' features and functionality.

Finally, we will look at the customization of various IE components that can be a part of your custom installation to provide supplementary services to Internet Explorer. Features such as Outlook Express, NetMeeting, channels, and subscriptions all play roles in how your users interact with Internet Explorer 4.0 every day.

With all this information under your belt, you'll be well on your way to completely managing your organization's Internet Explorer configuration. Here's a rundown of the specific topics covered in this chapter:

- Installing Internet Explorer 4.0
- Customizing Active Setup components
- Customizing the browser
- Configuring Microsoft Outlook Express
- Configuring Microsoft NetMeeting
- Configuring channels and subscriptions

Installing Internet Explorer 4.0

Objective

The first order of business in getting started with Internet Explorer and the Internet Explorer Administration Kit is the actual installation of the Internet Explorer suite itself. Although this may seem like an obvious step, there are some important aspects to installation that anyone using the IEAK should be familiar with.

First, because you are using the IEAK to create a customized installer and version of Internet Explorer, it's important that you are familiar with the installation process. Knowing how the process works and how the user interacts with the installation process can be an important part of customizing your installer.

Second, the Internet Explorer Administration Kit relies heavily on the installation of Internet Explorer that resides on the same machine as the IEAK. For example, channel configuration information is not actually configured within Internet Explorer but is imported from the resident IE 4.0 installation.

Finally, you must create your customized build with the system requirements for running it and the configuration of your users' machines in mind. The next several sections cover the installation procedures for Internet Explorer on various platforms, including the installation requirements, using Active Setup, and the step-by-step procedure for getting Internet Explorer 4.0 onto the machine.

Installing Internet Explorer 4.0 for Windows NT and Windows 95

Although Windows 95 and Windows NT differ significantly as operating systems, the installation procedures for Internet Explorer 4.0 are identical on both systems.

The requirements for installing IE 4.0 on the system vary from operating system to operating system, however, because some of the basic requirements for Windows 95 are different from those of Windows NT. Table 2.1 shows the requirements for the various installations of Internet Explorer combined with the requirements for each operating system. Reviewing these requirements before you begin the installation procedure can save you time and headaches by ensuring adequate resources for the installation.

Table 2.1

Installation Requirements for Internet Explorer 4.0 for Windows 95/NT

Installation	OS	Requirement
All	Windows 95/NT or higher	486/66 processor
Browser Only and Outlook Express	Windows 95	12MB RAM
Standard Installation w/o Windows Desktop Update	Windows 95	8MB RAM
Standard or Full w/ Windows Desktop Update	Windows 95	16MB RAM

Installation	OS	Requirement
All	Windows NT	24MB RAM
Browser Only	Windows 95/NT	40MB disk space
Standard Installation	Windows 95/NT	47MB disk space
Full Installation	Windows 95/NT	73MB disk space
Browser Only	Windows 95/NT	12.3MB download
Standard Installation	Windows 95/NT	16MB download
Full Installation	Windows 95/NT	24.2MB download

The installation procedure for Internet Explorer 4.0 for Windows 95/NT starts on the 95/NT download page:

```
http://www.microsoft.com/ie/ie40/download/win95.htm
```

From here, you can download the Active Setup Wizard to begin the installation procedure for Windows 95. Here's the installation procedure:

1. Click the Download link on the download page. You will be prompted to select the version of IE 4.0 you want to install. Because you're installing for Windows 95/NT, select that option and click Next to continue.

2. You are prompted to select the language you want to use with Internet Explorer. Select the appropriate language for your installation and click Next to continue.

3. You are prompted to select a download site to get the Active Setup Wizard. Select the site that is nearest to your geographic location to ensure the quickest download.

4. You are prompted to save the Active Setup Wizard to your hard drive. After you have saved it, you are ready to begin the installation procedure. Double-click the `IE4SETUP.EXE` file you have saved to begin the installation.

5. The Active Setup Wizard, shown in Figure 2.1, guides your installation of IE from this point on. After it launches, click Next to continue.

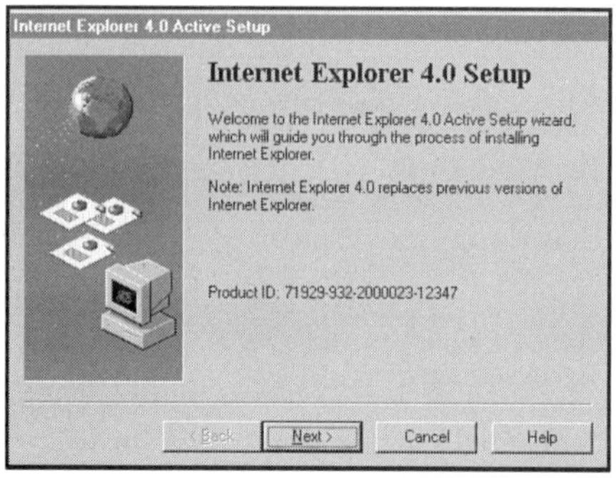

Figure 2.1

The Active Setup Wizard provides users with step-by-step guidance through the IE 4.0 installation.

6. You see the license agreement for Internet Explorer 4.0. Before you can continue to install IE 4.0, you must agree to the license agreement. If you choose not to agree, you cannot continue.

7. After agreeing to the license, you are offered the option to either download the components to your hard drive for installation later or to Install IE 4.0. Because we're installing, select the Install option and click Next to continue.

8. You are asked to choose the type of installation you want to perform, as shown in Figure 2.2. You can select from Browser Only, Standard Installation, and Full Installation. Choose the installation option you want and click Next to continue.

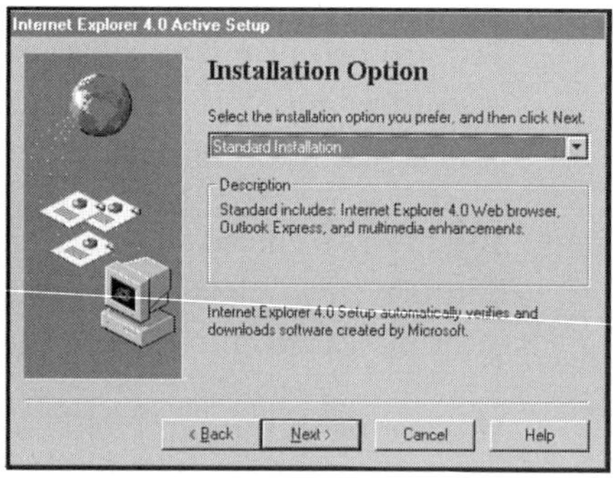

Figure 2.2

Using the Active Setup Wizard to select the browser installation.

9. The Active Channel Selection screen, shown in Figure 2.3, is the next configuration option. Microsoft preinstalls various Active Channel subscriptions based on your location. Select your location and click Next to continue.

Figure 2.3

Selecting preinstalled Active Channels based on your geographic location.

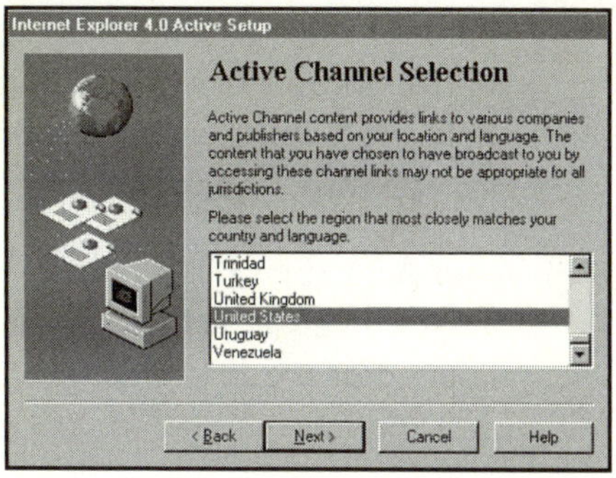

10. You are prompted to enter the location of the installation directory in which you want the installer to place IE and its support files. The default location is `C:\Program Files\Internet Explorer`. If you want to install IE in another location, enter that path on this screen. When you've entered the information for the installation directory, click Next to continue.

11. The Active Setup Wizard contacts the Microsoft server to determine the possible download sites from which you can obtain the components for the actual installation. After Active Setup has determined the download sites as shown in Figure 2.4, you are given the opportunity to select a site. Pick the download site that is closest to your physical location to maximize download efficiency; then click Next to continue.

Figure 2.4

Selecting a download site with Active Setup.

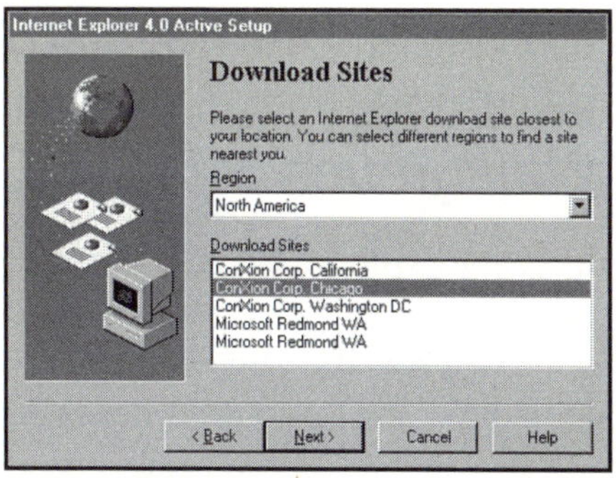

12. Internet Explorer connects to the selected download site to obtain the latest components. Depending on the configuration you have selected and the speed of your connection to

the Internet, this portion of the installation can take up to several hours. Fortunately, Active Setup manages the connection; if the download fails in the middle, when you rerun Active Setup, it picks up where it left off.

13. After Active Setup has downloaded all the necessary components, it begins the installation process, as shown in Figure 2.5. Again, the length of time needed to finish the installation process depends on the installation options you have chosen.

After completing the installation for the version of IE 4.0 and the components you have selected, the Active Setup Wizard configures your system. If required for your installation, you are prompted to restart your machine. When you reboot, you will be ready to run Internet Explorer 4.0.

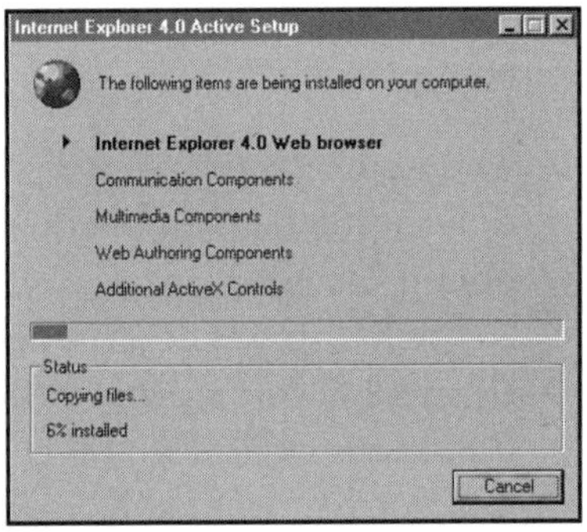

Figure 2.5

The Active Setup Wizard installs all the necessary Internet Explorer components.

Installing Internet Explorer 4.0 for Windows 3.1, 3.11, Windows for Workgroups 3.11, and Windows NT 3.51

Internet Explorer 4.0 is supported for Windows 3.x systems; however, you must have a connection to the network and a TCP/IP stack (such as the Microsoft Stack or Trumpet WinSOCK) installed to connect to the Internet correctly.

The requirements for installing IE 4.0 vary from operating system to operating system because some of the basic requirements for Windows 3.x are different from those of Windows 95/NT. Table 2.2 shows the requirements for the various installations of Internet

Explorer combined with the requirements for each operating system. Reviewing these requirements before you begin the installation procedure can save you time and headaches by ensuring adequate resources for the installation.

Table 2.2

Installation Requirements for Internet Explorer 4.0 for Windows 3.x

Installation	OS	Requirement
All	Windows 3.x	486 processor or higher
All	Windows 3.x	12MB RAM
To Run Java	Windows 3.x	16MB RAM
All	Windows 3.x	25MB to 62MB disk space
All	Windows 3.x	7.5MB to 12.5MB download

The installation procedure for Internet Explorer 4.0 for Windows 3.1 versions starts on the Windows 3.1 download page:

`http://www.microsoft.com/ie/ie40/download/win31.htm`

From this site, you can download the Active Setup Wizard to begin the installation procedure for older versions of Windows.

The following installation procedure uses the Active Setup installation process:

1. From the Microsoft IE 4.0 for Windows 3.1 page, click the Download Active Setup Installer link to download the Active Setup installer to your local machine.
2. You are prompted to select the language you want to use. Select the appropriate language and click Next.
3. You are prompted to select the site from which you want to download the Active Setup installer and components. Select a site that is near your location to provide optimal download rates.

4. You are prompted to either open the file or download/save to disk. Save the Active Setup installer to your hard drive.

   After the Active Setup installer is downloaded, you are ready to begin running the application. Simply double-click the Active Setup installer to begin installing IE 4.0!

5. The Active Setup Wizard guides your installation of IE from this point on. After it launches, click Next to continue.

6. You see the license agreement for Internet Explorer 4.0. Before you can continue to install IE 4.0, you must agree to the license agreement. If you choose not to agree, you cannot continue.

7. After you agree to the license, you are offered the option to either download the components to your hard drive for installation later or to install IE 4.0. Because we're installing, select the Install option and click Next to continue.

8. You are asked to choose the type of installation you want to perform. You can select from Browser Only, Standard Installation, and Full Installation. Choose the installation option you want to install and click Next to continue.

9. The Active Channel Selection screen is the next configuration option. Microsoft preinstalls various Active Channel subscriptions based on your location. Select your location and click Next to continue.

10. You are prompted to enter the location of the installation directory in which you want the installer to place IE and its support files. When you've entered the information for the installation directory, click Next to continue.

11. The Active Setup Wizard contacts the Microsoft server to determine the possible download sites from which you can obtain the components for the actual installation. After Active Setup has determined the download sites, you are asked to select one. Pick the download site closest to your physical location to maximize download efficiency. After you have selected the download site, click Next to continue.

12. Internet Explorer connects to the site to obtain the latest components. Depending on the configuration you have selected and the speed of your connection to the Internet, this portion of the installation could take up to several hours. Fortunately, Active Setup manages the connection; if the download fails in the middle, when you rerun Active Setup, it picks up where it left off.

13. After Active Setup downloads all the necessary components, it begins the installation process. Again, the length of time required to finish the installation process depends on the installation options you have chosen.

After completing the installation of the version of IE 4.0 and the components you have selected, the Active Setup Wizard configures your system. If required for your installation, you are prompted to restart your machine. When you reboot, you will be ready to run Internet Explorer 4.0.

Installing Internet Explorer 4.0 for Macintosh

Microsoft provides two versions of Internet Explorer for the Macintosh: one for older 68x0x-based machines and another native Power PC version for newer Macintoshes. The procedure for installation of IE 4.0 on both is the same.

The installation procedure begins at the Microsoft home page for Internet Explorer for the Macintosh:

```
http://www.microsoft.com/ie/ie40/download/mac.htm
```

This page contains the links to download the Internet Explorer Active Setup Wizard for installation, or the option to download all the installation files without Active Setup. Before making your choices, you should familiarize yourself with the requirements for installing Internet Explorer on your system:

- Power PC or 68030 processor, or higher
- MacOS System 7.1 or higher
- 8MB RAM minimum

The disk space requirements for Internet Explorer on the Macintosh vary considerably depending on the components you are installing. Table 2.3 shows the various components for IE 4.0 on the Macintosh and the required disk space for each.

Table 2.3

Disk Space Requirements for IE 4.0 Installation on the Macintosh

Installation	Processor	Disk Space
Minimum	PowerPC	9.1MB
Minimum	68K	8.8MB
Recommended	PowerPC	20.8MB
Recommended	68K	19.7MB
Recommended	PowerPC and 68K	27.6MB
Full	PowerPC	28.5MB
Full	68K	23.6MB
Full	PowerPC and 68K	36.6MB
Java VM	PowerPC	7.7MB
Java VM	68K	7.5MB
Outlook Express	PowerPC	7.3MB
Outlook Express	68K	7.1MB

In addition to these requirements for the installation, you should also consider the requirements for the download, because the necessary components must also be downloaded to your Macintosh before they can be installed. Table 2.4 shows the various disk space requirements for the component downloads for the Macintosh.

Table 2.4

Disk Space Requirements for Component Downloads for IE 4.0 on the Macintosh

Installation	Processor	Download Disk Space
Minimum	PowerPC	4.3MB
Minimum	68K	4.1MB
Recommended	PowerPC	10.9MB
Recommended	68K	10.5MB
Recommended	PowerPC and 68K	14.3MB
Full	PowerPC	14.3MB
Full	68K	12.4MB
Full	PowerPC and 68K	24.5MB
Java VM	PowerPC	5.2MB
Java VM	68K	5.1MB
Outlook Express	PowerPC	3.3MB
Outlook Express	68K	3.2MB

After you have determined the correct requirements for installing Internet Explorer on your Mac, you are ready to begin the installation process.

For the following installation, we're going to use the Active Setup installation process:

1. From the Microsoft IE 4.0 for Macintosh page, click the Download Active Setup Installer link to download the Active Setup installer to your local machine. Because the Active Setup installer is only 350KB, this shouldn't take too long, even over a modem.

2. You are prompted to select the language you want to use. Select the appropriate language and click Next.

3. You are prompted to select the site from which you want to download the Active Setup installer and components. Select a site that is geographically near your location to provide optimal download rates.

4. You are prompted to either open the file or download/save to disk. Save the Active Setup installer to your hard drive.

5. If your machine already has StuffIt Expander installed, or if you are currently using IE 3.0 or later, the installer downloads and is automatically expanded. If it is not automatically expanded, you must get a copy of StuffIt Expander and manually expand the archive.

After the Active Setup installer is expanded, you are ready to begin running the application. Follow these steps to begin installing IE 4.0 on your machine:

1. Double-click the Active Setup installer to launch the installation program. The Active Setup installer manages the entire IE 4.0 installation process (see Figure 2.6).

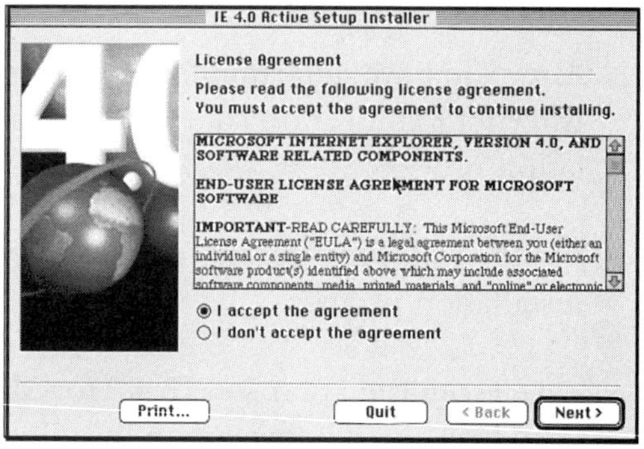

Figure 2.6

The Macintosh version of the Internet Explorer Active Setup Wizard.

2. The Active Setup installer first prompts you with the license agreement. Before you can proceed with the installation, you must select I Accept the Agreement and then click Next to continue.

3. The installer presents you with a text overview of the process. After reading through the overview, click Next to continue.

4. The screen shown in Figure 2.7 appears; you can decide to download and install Internet Explorer, or to only download the components to your hard drive and perform the installation later. Because we are going to install it now, select Install and click Next to continue.

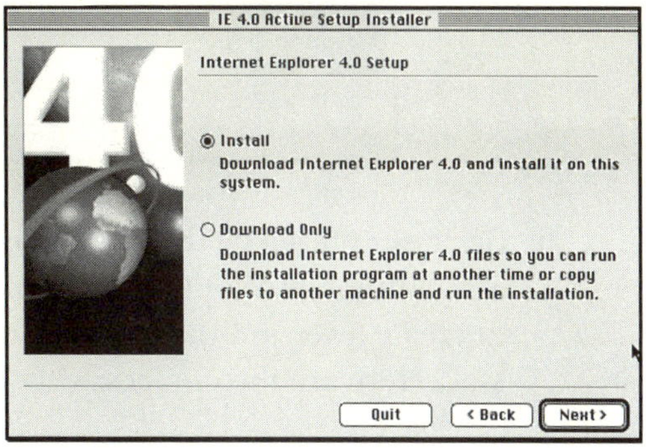

Figure 2.7

The Active Setup Wizard allows you to perform an IE installation or to grab files for installation at a later time.

5. The next screen, shown in Figure 2.8, allows you to select the type of installation you want to complete:

    - Recommended Install
    - Custom Install
    - Full Install
    - Minimal Internet Explorer
    - Minimal Outlook Express
    - Remove

    Because this chapter is about customization, choose the Custom Install option.

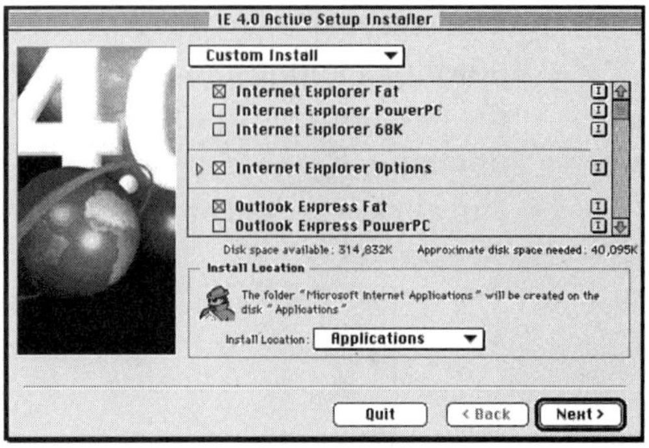

Figure 2.8

Selecting the type of IE installation to perform.

6. Because you selected Custom Install, you are now presented with a number of options. For this installation, we're going to create a version that will run on either a 68K or Power Mac. Here are the choices:

   - Internet Explorer Fat
   - All Internet Explorer Options
   - Outlook Express Fat
   - System Extensions
   - Internet Config

   If you want to vary the installation for your machine at this point, that's fine. Simply make sure that you select the options you want to install before proceeding to step 7.

7. Specify the location of the hard drive on which you want to install IE 4.0, based on the disk requirements. Click Next to continue.

8. You see the prompt to download files (see Figure 2.9). If your organization is behind a firewall or uses a proxy server, you must enter that information here. Also, if you have to start a dial-up connection to the Internet, you should do that before proceeding. Once you're ready for the next step, click Next to continue.

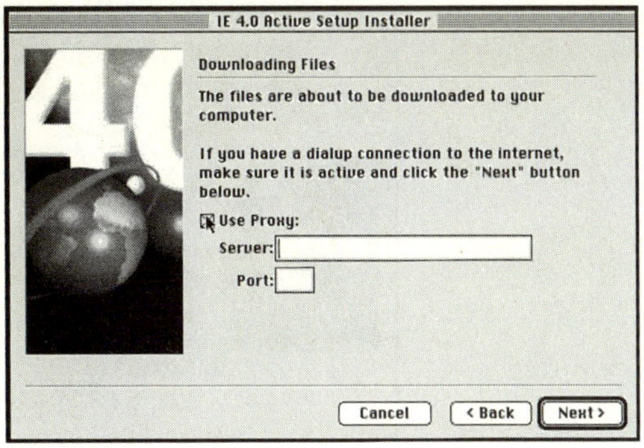

Figure 2.9

Configuring the Active Setup Wizard to download files and specifying proxy settings.

9. The Active Setup installer downloads a list of sites available to you to perform the component installation. When the list is ready, it is displayed as shown in Figure 2.10. Select the download site closest to you to provide the fastest download time and click Next to continue.

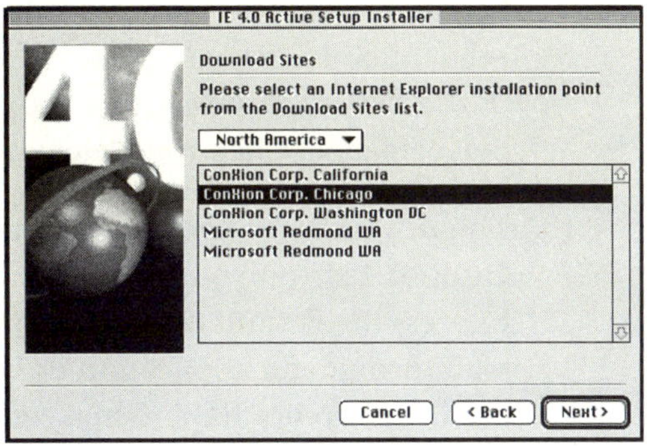

Figure 2.10

The Active Setup Wizard allows you to specify download sites based on your geographic location.

10. The Active Setup installer connects to the download site you selected and begins downloading components, as shown in Figure 2.11. You can cancel the installation at any time by clicking Cancel.

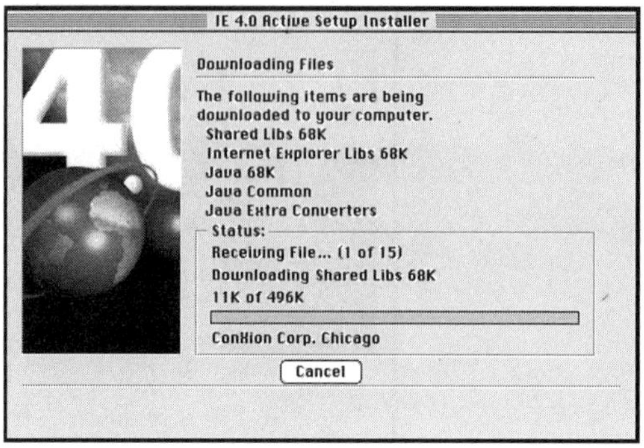

Figure 2.11

The Active Setup Wizard downloads all the selected IE components before beginning the IE installation.

11. After your files have been downloaded, you can disconnect your machine from the Internet as necessary. Click Next to continue.

12. You are prompted to see whether you want to make Internet Explorer your default browser. If you choose to make it your default browser, any time you click an Internet resource, you will launch Internet Explorer. If you do not choose to make IE the default browser, it will not affect Internet Explorer's performance. Click your selection to continue.

13. The next prompt concerns whether or not you want to make Outlook Express your default mail client. Making Outlook Express the default mail client means that any time you send mail through an application or browser, Outlook Express is used. You do not have to make Outlook Express your default client. Click your selection to continue.

14. The Microsoft Installer installs the necessary software components for Internet Explorer 4.0 on your machine, as shown in Figure 2.12. This might take some time, depending on any custom choices for installation that you have made. When the installation program has finished, you are prompted to restart your computer.

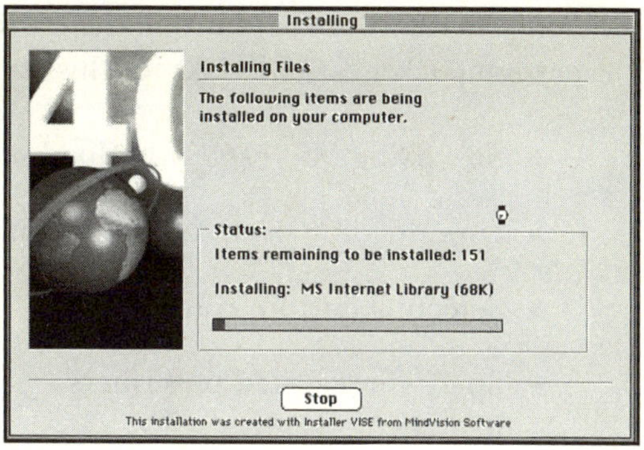

Figure 2.12

After completing the download process, the Active Setup Wizard installs all the necessary IE components.

After your machine restarts, your installation of Internet Explorer 4.0 is complete. Now you are ready to use Internet Explorer on the Macintosh.

Using the IEAK Wizard to Customize Active Setup Components

Objective

Customizing the Active Setup components with the IEAK allows you to specify how users will interact with your custom installation for Internet Explorer 4.0. There are five stages involved in creating customized packages and customizing the components of the Active Setup Wizard as described by the IEAK Wizard. The stages include

- Gathering Information
- Specifying Active Setup Parameters
- Customizing Active Setup
- Customizing the Browser
- Component Customization (if necessary)

The first stage involves checking the information that the Wizard has gathered about your current setup and supplying information that the Wizard needs to begin the customization process. The second stage involves providing the information used by Active

Setup to download and install the correct IE 4.0 components and custom packages. The tasks for this stage include the following:

- Specifying Microsoft download sites
- Downloading or updating IE components
- Selecting custom components
- Specifying trusted publishers

After this information is provided, you move on to stage three of the IEAK Active Setup customization, which involves customizing Active Setup. From this stage, you can alter the appearance and functionality of Active Setup for your custom build. The third stage includes the following tasks:

- Customizing the CD-ROM Autorun screen
- Customizing the Active Setup title bar text and bitmap
- Importing a custom profile from the CMAK (for the ISP role)
- Specifying a silent installation (for the Corporate Administrator role)
- Specifying installation options (up to 10)
- Specifying download sites (up to 10)
- Specifying version numbers
- Specifying the installation location for IE (for the Corporate Administrator role)
- Specifying Windows Desktop Update integration (for the Corporate Administrator role)

Because much of the customization and specialization regarding the Active Setup Wizard can be performed only in the Corporate Administrator role, that is the role we will be using for this section. Keep in mind that you must apply for and be granted a

Corporate Administrator customization number from Microsoft (you have to sign a license agreement for creating an internally distributed version of IE). You can apply for the license at this URL:

```
https://ieak.microsoft.com/release2/licenseProducts.asp
```

Stage 1: Initial Steps in the Customization Process

After you have your customization code from Microsoft, you can launch the IEAK and go through the initial steps to begin customizing the Active Setup Wizard:

1. Launch the IEAK Wizard from your installed folder or the Start menu. The wizard should launch and provide you with an overview of the five stages in the process, as shown in Figure 2.13. Click Next to continue.

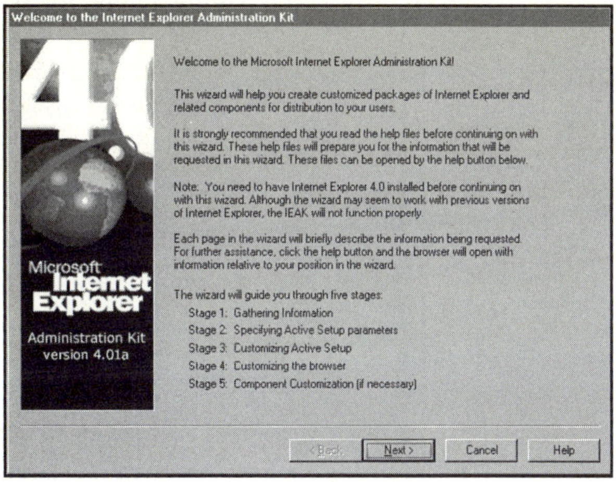

Figure 2.13

The Internet Explorer Administration Kit Wizard guides administrators through the creation of custom builds.

2. After reviewing the information on the next screen, click Next to continue. You are then prompted to enter your company name and customization code, as shown in Figure 2.14.

   After you enter this information, you can select the appropriate role for creating your custom build. Because we are going to proceed as a Corporate Administrator, select that role and click Next to continue.

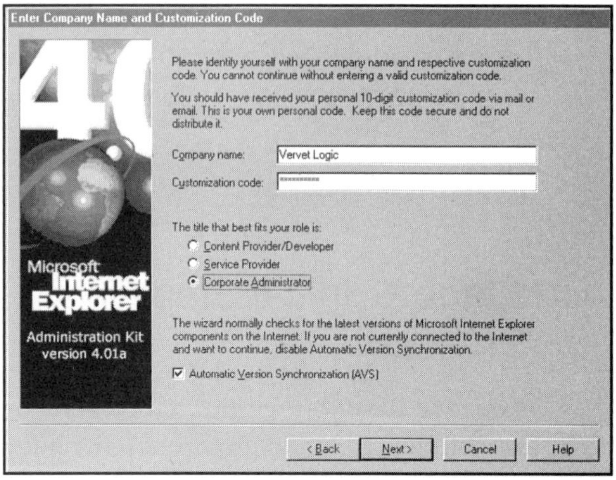

Figure 2.14

The administrative roles available are specified by the customization code based on your license agreement.

3. You are prompted to select the platform for which you are creating a build, as shown in Figure 2.15. Select the appropriate platform and click Next to continue. Keep in mind that some of the options in the following steps may differ depending on the version you choose in this step. For the sake of this exercise, we are creating a build for Windows 95/NT.

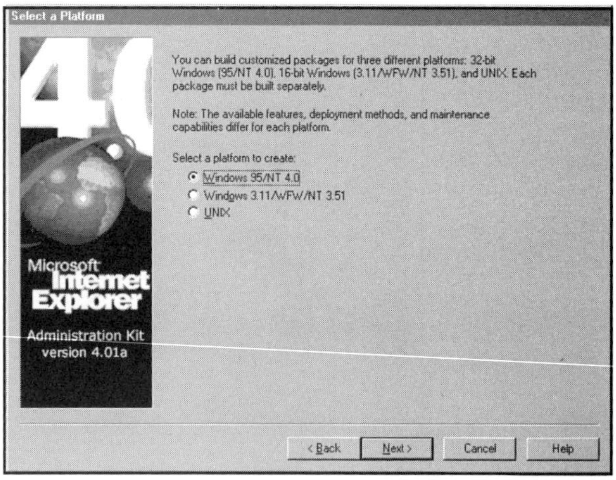

Figure 2.15

Using the IEAK Wizard to build custom versions for different platforms.

4. You are asked to identify the target language for this build. You can select any language you want. However, you must create a separate custom build for each language you choose.

5. You are prompted to specify the directory in which you want to create your custom build for Internet Explorer 4.0, as shown in Figure 2.16. You can use any directory you want; just make sure that there is adequate disk space in the chosen directory. You can also select the deployment method you are going to use.

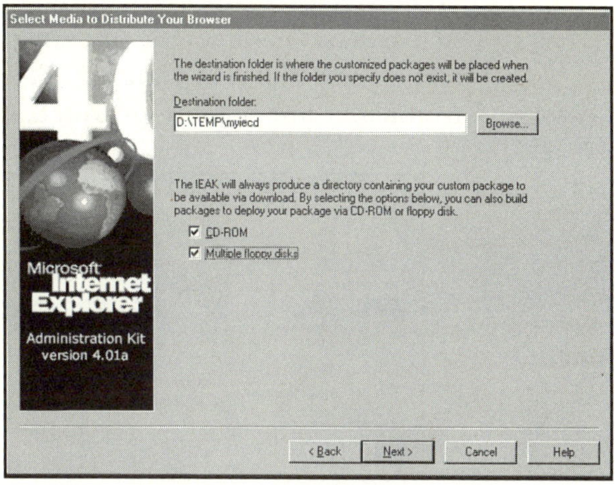

Figure 2.16

Specifying the directory in which the IEAK will create the customized build.

For this exercise, we are going to build a custom build for deployment on CD-ROM. When you have entered your directory and selected your deployment method, you are ready to continue by specifying the information for Active Setup and customizing the Active Setup Wizard.

Stage 2: Specifying Active Setup Information

In this stage of the Internet Explorer Administration Kit, you will be customizing the information used by the Active Setup Wizard to download the necessary components from various installation sites on the Internet. Here is a list of some of the information you will provide for the customized Active Setup Wizard:

- Specifying the Microsoft download site
- Downloading or updating IE components

- Selecting custom components
- Specifying trusted publishers

Follow these steps to customize the information used by the Active Setup Wizard:

1. When you are ready to begin the process of specifying the Active Setup parameters, you are greeted by the introductory screen shown in Figure 2.17. After reviewing the introductory information provided, click Next to continue.

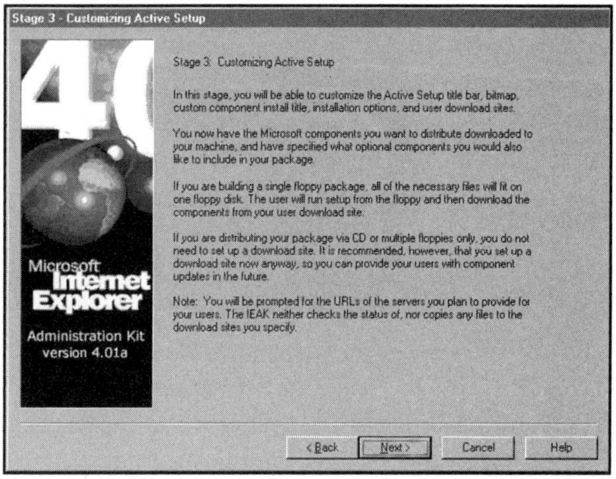

Figure 2.17

Beginning the specification of Active Setup parameters with the IEAK Wizard.

2. Select the site from which you want to download the components that will be used in your custom build. This is not the same as the site to which your users will connect, and it is not a configuration option. This information just lets the IEAK Wizard know where to look for the packages to download for including in your installer. Select the site closest to you and click Next to continue.

3. The Automatic Version Synchronization (AVS) checks to see that you have all the latest components for IE. If you do not, you can choose to synchronize so that all your packages are the most recent versions available. Once AVS has completed its check, click Next to continue.

4. Provide Active Setup with the information for any custom components you will install along with Internet Explorer. *Custom components* can be any number of applications created by your organization, an outside vendor, or Microsoft. For example, if you want to include a special plug-in for Internet Explorer, you can include it here as a custom component. If you want to add a custom component, simply click Add, as shown in Figure 2.18.

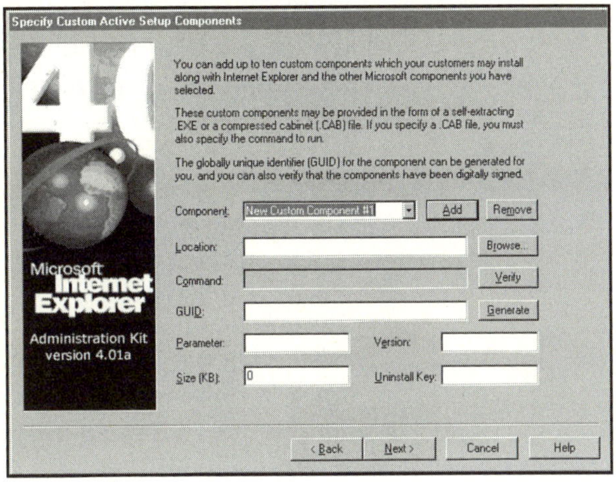

Figure 2.18

The IEAK allows you to configure Active Setup for custom components to be installed with IE 4.0.

5. You must enter some information about the component in order to include it:

   - **Component.** This is the name of your component. You can use any name you want, but it should probably describe the component you are adding in some way so that users know what it is.

   - **Location.** This is the location of the component that you want to install. Components can be in the form of `.CAB` files, created with Microsoft's cab utility, `makecab.exe`, or they can be self-extracting `.EXE` archives. The location is simply the location of the installation files.

   - **Command.** This is the command that runs the component. It is usually filled in for you automatically when you have selected the location of the component if the component is an `.EXE`. If you specify a .CAB file, you must specify the command. Next to this parameter is a Verify button. Because IE requires that some custom components be digitally signed, you can use the Verify button to check the digital signature of the component. If the component does not verify correctly, you may want to obtain the component from another source.

- **GUID.** The GUID is a unique identifying string used by the operating system and other components to uniquely identify your custom component. You can use the Generate button located next to this parameter to automatically generate the GUID.
- **Parameter.** With the parameter setting, you can specify any command switches or parameters required for your custom components if they are executable files.
- **Version.** The Version parameter allows you to specify a special version number for keeping track of your customized components. You can use any versioning system you like (it is not necessary for IE; the field is provided as a convenience for tracking your own components).
- **Size.** This parameter is simply the size of your custom component in KB.
- **Uninstall Key.** This parameter allows you to specify the uninstall key for your custom component so that users can correctly uninstall the component using the Add/Remove Program utility. Without this information, you cannot assure users that an uninstallation of your components will actually remove the custom component. To enter this information, you must enter the correct uninstall subkey for your component:

```
HKEY_LOCAL_MACHINE\Software\Microsoft\Windows\CurrentVersion\Uninstall\
ApplicationName\UninstallString
```

In this syntax, *`ApplicationName`* is the display name of your custom component, and *`UninstallString`* is the command (with any switches) for running your Uninstall application.

After you have entered all the information for your custom package, you can add another package by clicking Add, or you can remove a custom package by clicking Remove. When you are finished with the custom components, click Next to continue.

6. You are prompted to select the name of the trusted publisher you want to assign to customized components and to your customized build of Internet Explorer. To assign a trusted publisher value to your customized build or component, you must first install a valid digital certificate and sign any custom components.

When you have entered the necessary information for Active Setup to retrieve its components and have added your custom packages, you are ready to enter the next stage of customization: customizing the Active Setup Wizard, in which you can specify various look-and-feel elements regarding the Active Setup Wizard.

Stage 3: Customizing the Active Setup Wizard

The Internet Explorer Administration Kit allows for many customization options regarding the look, feel, and functionality of the Active Setup Wizard. In the preceding section, you provided the IEAK with the information needed to begin customizing the Active Setup Wizard. In this section, you will customize the actual components themselves so that the Active Setup Wizard will function within the parameters you have established for your users.

The following list identifies some of the functionality of the Active Setup Wizard you can customize:

- The CD-ROM Autorun screen
- The Active Setup title bar text and bitmap
- Importing a custom profile from the CMAK (for the ISP role)
- Specifying a silent installation (for the Corporate Administrator role)

- Specifying installation options (up to 10)
- Specifying download sites (up to 10)
- Specifying version numbers
- Specifying the installation location for IE (for the Corporate Administrator role)
- Specifying Windows Desktop Update integration (for the Corporate Administrator role)

With all these customizations, you can control not only how the Active Setup Wizard looks when users launch it, you can also control much of the installation functionality. This includes components and sites for downloading and even the power to restrict the installation choices of users, such as the silent installation feature. Remember that some of these features are not available in all custom builds (for example, ISP Administrators cannot choose the silent installation).

The following steps go through the customization process for the Active Setup Wizard when running the IEAK in the Corporate Administrator role:

1. In the first step of stage 3, you are presented with another welcome screen announcing the next stage of the IEAK Wizard and the Active Setup customization. Once you have reviewed the information presented, click Next to continue.
2. The first customization you can make to the Active Setup wizard involves altering the Autorun screen for CD-ROM based installations. This screen is automatically presented to users when they place a CD in their CD-ROM drives. The customization options for the Autorun screen are shown in Figure 2.19.

You can make the following customizations to the Autorun screen using the IEAK:

- **Title Bar Text.** The title bar text is the text that appears in the window's title bar; it can be customized by entering your text in this field.
- **Custom Bitmap Location.** If you want to specify a custom bitmap for the background of the Autorun screen (that is, if you want to replace the standard Microsoft bitmap with something like a company logo), you can specify the location of the custom bitmap here.

  The custom bitmap for the Autorun splash screen must be a 256-color bitmap that is 540×347 pixels in size. The bitmap should also contain one button to run the installation program and another to show more information.
- **Standard Text Color.** You can select the standard color of the text to be displayed in the Autorun screen, if you want something other than black text.
- **Highlight Text Color.** You can also alter the highlight color to specify one to match your text color.
- **Button Style.** You can alter the style of buttons that are displayed. For example, you can choose a special 3D button if that fits better with the look you are trying to achieve.

When you are finished customizing the Active Setup Autorun screen, click Next to move on to customize the Active Setup Wizard itself.

3. The first options you have for customizing the Active Setup Wizard include specifying the title bar text for the Active Setup Wizard and specifying a replacement, custom bitmap for the wizard, as shown in Figure 2.19.

   The custom bitmap should be 120×239 pixels and must be 256-color (16-color for Windows 3.*x*). Only the Windows Active Setup bitmap can be customized. When you have entered the information for customization, click Next to continue.

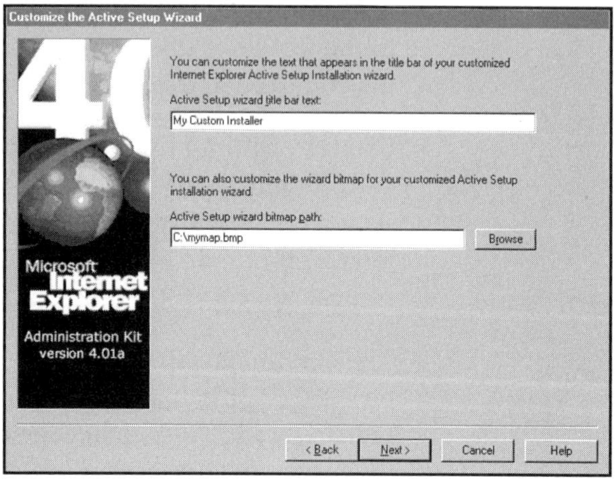

Figure 2.19

The IEAK allows you to customize the Autorun screen for the Active Setup Wizard.

4. Because we are creating a custom IE installation using a Corporate Administrator deployment role, the next option is whether you want to perform the installation as a silent installation. This option is available only if you have agreed to the Corporate Administrator license and have obtained the proper customization code for the IEAK Wizard.

   Choosing a silent installation places some additional restrictions on other configuration choices you have to make. Because a silent installation does not prompt the user for any information, you must specify several configuration options for the user:

   - **Specify a Single Download Site for the Download of Components.** Because the user will not be presented with 10 choices for download, you must specify one, and you should make sure that it is a reliable site. If the user can't reach the site and is not allowed to choose alternates, this could lead to frustration.

   - **Specify a Single Installation Option.** The silent installation does not allow users to select an installation option with various components. Therefore, you must choose an installation option for the user.

- **Specify the Installation of the Active Desktop/Windows Desktop Update.** Because users will not be presented with the options necessary to install the component for themselves, you must specify that option for them.

If you are creating a very specific installation, one for which most configuration choices are already mandated, a silent installation can produce an Active Setup Wizard that is extremely easy for the user. Once the user launches it, there is nothing more for him or her to do. However, if you want to provide users with any sort of flexibility, a silent installation might not be the best option. When you have made your selections, click Next to continue.

5. The next section contains the parameters you can use to create up to 10 configuration options. For example, you may want to offer the Standard, Enhanced, or Full options normally provided with IE. However, you may also want to include a custom option (for example, "Corporation X") that includes custom packages or special installation options for your company.

   Specifying customized installation options can allow you to provide a special option for your organization that supplies the precise components your users need. You can leave the other installation options to provide maximum flexibility, or you can limit the choices to any options you want. The IEAK Wizard for customizing the installation options is shown in Figure 2.20.

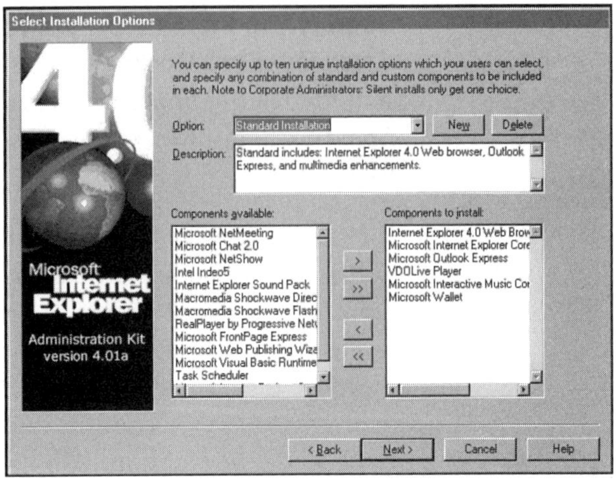

Figure 2.20

Creating customized installation options can make it easier for users to install the correct components.

By default, the IEAK Wizard offers Minimal, Standard, and Full installation options. You can create new installation options by clicking the New button.

> **Note** If you have chosen the silent installation feature, you cannot add new installation options. You are forced to configure only one option.

This dialog box offers the following insallation options:

- **Option.** This field is the name for your particular set of installation options.
- **Description.** This field can be used to present users with a description of the components contained in the installation or to indicate which applications are available. The Description field can be very useful for presenting users with information they need to make an educated decision about what version of IE to install.
- **Components Available.** This field represents the list of components available to include in your customized installation package. You can select any number of these components to include in your custom option.

- **Components to Install.** This list box represents the components that will be installed by Active Setup when the user has selected the current installation option.

After you have added any customized installation options to present to users, click Next to continue.

6. The IEAK Wizard allows you to specify what download sites your Active Setup can contact to download the necessary components. These sites can be any site accessible by HTTP or FTP. Note, however, that you have to put all the files for your custom build on the site to make them available. The specification as it would be entered in the wizard is shown in Figure 2.21.

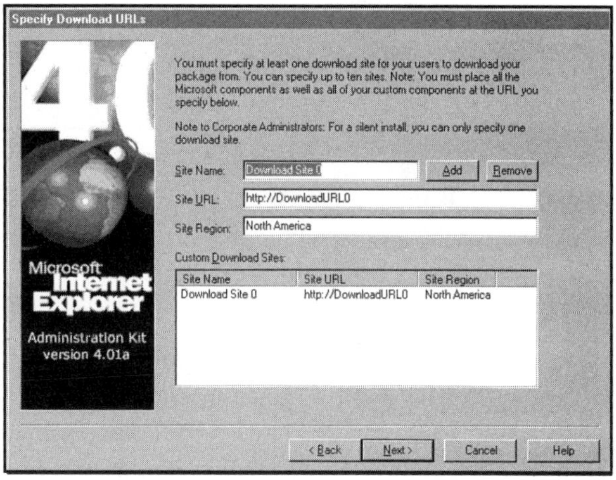

Figure 2.21

Specifying the download URLs that Active Setup is to contact to retrieve IE components.

On this wizard page, you can enter a name for the site so that users know where the download site is. You must then enter the full URL for the download site. You can also add a download region so that users have a better idea of the download site's geography. When you have entered all the information, you can add it to the available list by clicking Add.

If you have selected to run a silent installation, you are allowed to configure only one download site. If you are not using the silent installation option, you can enter up to 10 download sites. When you have entered all your specified download sites, click Next to continue.

7. With the Select Version Information option shown in Figure 2.22, you can add a customized version number for your version of IE. Active Setup increments this number for each installation so that only the newest components are installed.

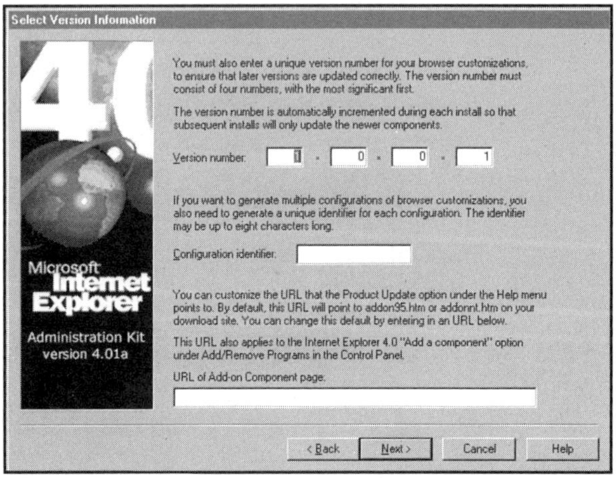

Figure 2.22

The IEAK Wizard allows customized version numbers to keep track of custom builds.

You can also create a configuration identifier that can be used to uniquely identify your custom build. This identifier is also passed along to browsers so that they are aware of the custom build. The identifier can be up to 8 characters long.

Finally, you can enter a URL for the location of the add-on component page. The links for this page are found in the Help menu in IE 4.0, or in the Add/Remove Programs Control Panel. This information allows users to click and get information about additional packages they can download and install for IE 4.0. The default value for this URL is to the `ADDON95.HTM` or `ADDONNT.HTM` on the download site the user has specified.

When you have customized your version numbers and other identifying information, click Next to continue.

8. The Active Setup Wizard allows users to select where they want to install Internet Explorer. You can also direct Active Setup to install IE in specific locations, as shown in Figure 2.23.

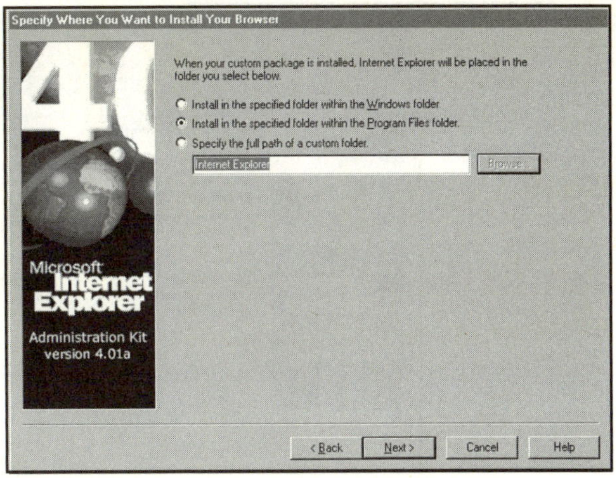

Figure 2.23

Administrators can configure the location of the IE files to be installed.

You can select from the following locations in which to install IE:

- Install in the specified folder within the `Windows` folder
- Install in the specified folder within the `Program Files` folder
- Specify the full path of a custom folder

When you have selected where you want to place the IE installation files, click Next to continue.

9. The final step in customizing the Active Setup Wizard is to specify the inclusion of the Windows Desktop Update, as shown in Figure 2.24.

   If you are performing a silent installation, you must make the choice for the user. However, if you are not, you can select User Choice to specify that the user is to be presented with an option asking whether they want to install the Desktop Update. If you choose not to offer the Desktop Update as a custom package, users can always select it later as an add-on. When you have selected the Windows Desktop Update option, click Next to continue.

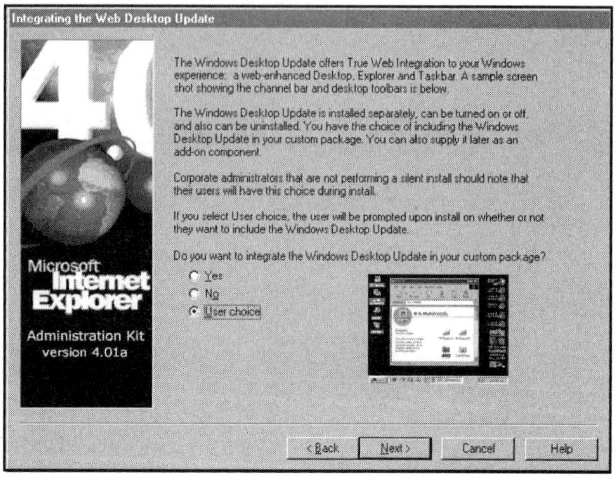

Figure 2.24

The Windows Desktop Update can be installed by Active Setup or added later by the user.

Stage 4: Customizing the Browser

Objective

In this section, we examine Stage 4 of the IEAK Wizard: customizing the browser. In this section, you can alter the look and feel of many of the Internet Explorer browser settings and change the behavior of the browser for users.

Because the nature of the browser is different for different applications, the options available to you in this section vary depending on your deployment role. For example, those administrators in the ISP role can customize server settings and login scripts. Administrators in the Corporate Administrator role can alter the security configuration of the IE browser.

Regardless of your role, and some of the slight modifications presented to you, here is the procedure for altering the browser settings. Following these steps, you can create a fully customized version of Internet Explorer for your organization:

1. In Stage 4, the first screen for the IEAK Wizard is a customary welcome screen. It explains the changes you will be making to the browser in the next section of the wizard. When you have reviewed this information, click Next to continue.

2. The first set of options presented allows you to customize some aspects of the appearance of the browser, such as the title bar (see Figure 2.25).

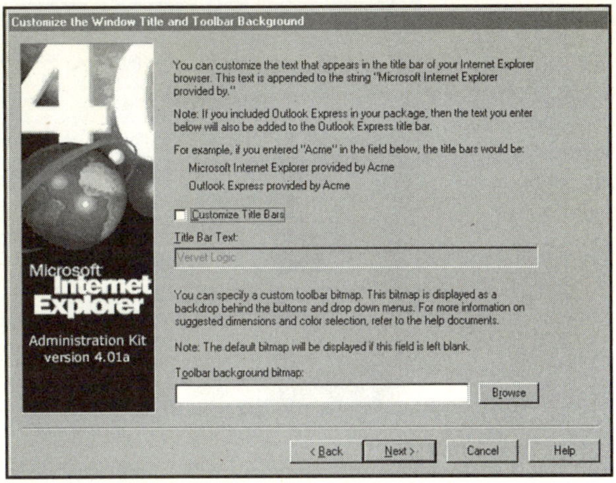

Figure 2.25

The IEAK Wizard allows administrators to customize browser appearance.

With this screen, you can add a text string that will appear in the Internet Explorer title bar to indicate that the user is running a customized version of IE, provided by your organization. If you choose to customize title bars, the text you enter in the Title Bar Text field will appear in the IE title bar, preceded by the text `Microsoft Internet Explorer provided by`. The same is true for Outlook Express; if you enter `My Company`, the title bar would read `Outlook Express provided by My Company`.

Administrators can also specify a bitmap that will appear as the background in the IE toolbar. This bitmap can further customize the look and feel by being displayed as the custom graphic in the IE toolbar. There are no specific dimensions for the bitmap—it is treated as a repeating background. However, it should be 256 colors, and it should be light enough so that you can read the black text in the toolbar (the text appears on top of the bitmap).

If you are specifying a custom toolbar bitmap, enter the location of the bitmap file here. When you are finished, click Next to continue.

3. Internet Explorer features customizable Start and Search pages as shown in Figure 2.26.

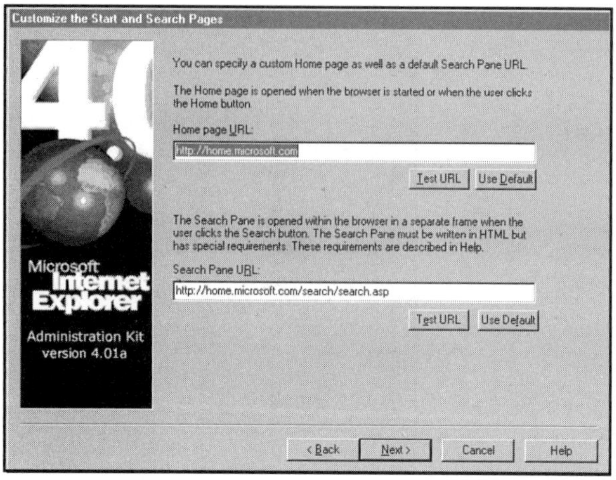

Figure 2.26

By customizing the Start page and Search page, you can point users to the right resources for your organization.

The *Start page* is the page loaded when the browser is first launched; it is also displayed whenever the user clicks the Home button within the browser. Customizing the Start page simply involves specifying the URL for the page you want to designate as the default user Start page.

The *Search page* is a special frame that opens in Internet Explorer when users select the Search option. However, because it is a special frame that is opened, the Search page has some important restrictions:

- Search pages open initially in a 200-pixel-wide frame. Because the goal is to let users access searches like they would a navigation bar, customized search pages should fit within the initial 200-pixel width.
- Search pages extend the length of the browser, so there is no height limit. However, you may want to keep it short so that users do not have to scroll.
- Results from customized searches should be displayed in the main browser window. This can be done using the `TARGET=_MAIN` syntax to direct output from the search frame to the main browser window.

If you decide to build a customized search page, you can specify the URL here. However, it's a good idea to test it before you assign a possibly malfunctioning search page to your new browser.

After you enter the URLs for your customized pages, click Next to continue.

4. On this screen, you can enter a URL for a customized support page, as shown in Figure 2.27.

   There are no restrictions on the size or content of the help page. However, it is a good idea to specify the URL for a custom support page, launched from the Help menu's Online Support option, especially if you have made extensive browser modifications. After you enter the URL for your support page, click Next to continue.

Figure 2.27

Adding a customized support page can aid users in getting help quickly.

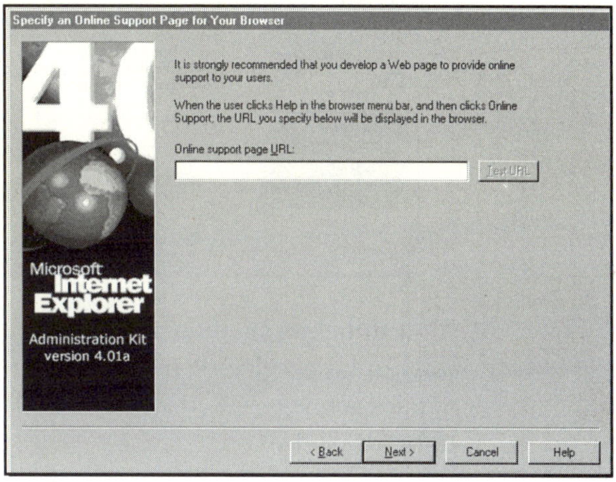

5. The next step for customizing the browser functionality is to provide the links for the Internet Explorer link bar and to add preset favorites to the users' Favorites folders.

   Specifying new links and favorites is as simple as adding a new URL along with a text label, as shown in Figure 2.28.

   By simply clicking the Links or Favorites heading in the list box, you can then add a folder, add a URL, or remove them. There is no limit to the number of links or favorites you can provide; however, keep the list short and simple to make users more likely to investigate your preinstalled choices.

You can also use the Import button to import the current links and favorite settings from the browser currently installed on your machine; you can also use the Import button to specify the path to a network location containing favorites. This allows you to easily import large favorite files without having to enter them by hand.

When you have finished customizing the links and favorites, click Next to continue.

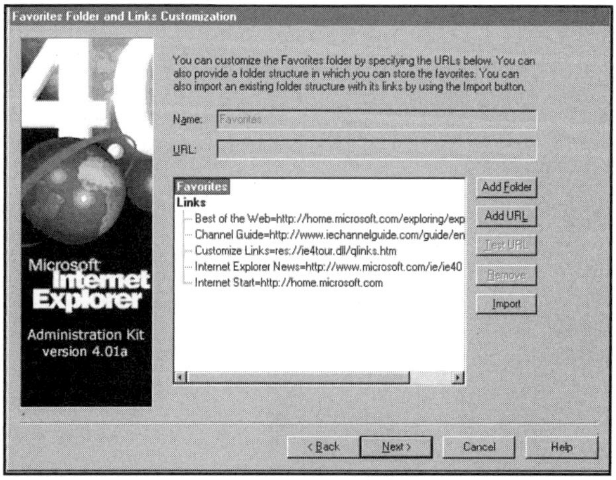

Figure 2.28

Customizing the users' links and favorites in Internet Explorer.

6. After initial installation and first launch, Internet Explorer will display a welcome message to users to indicate that the application is installed and to give them a chance to run tutorials, and so on.

   Administrators have the option of customizing the welcome message—or, indeed, choosing to display it at all—using the options shown in Figure 2.29.

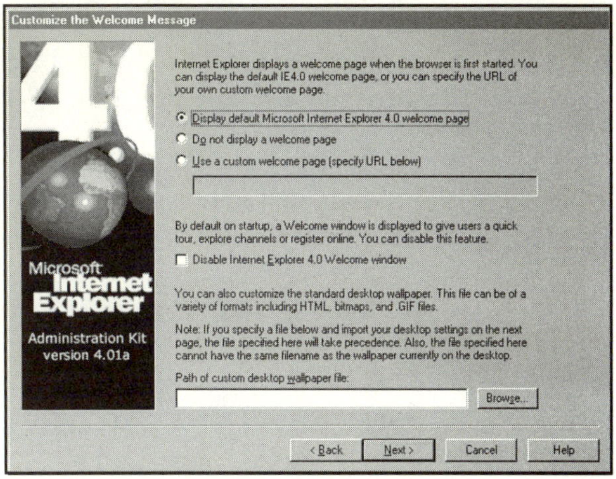

Figure 2.29

Customizing the Internet Explorer welcome message.

The first option displays a welcome page for Internet Explorer. This welcome page is shown only once; administrators have the option of specifying the use of the standard Microsoft welcome page, a custom welcome page, or none at all.

In addition to the welcome page, IE launches a welcome window, which is essentially a separate browser window that gives users the options for tutorials, tours, and so on. If you do not want this window to display, you can disable it here.

Finally, you can specify a custom desktop wallpaper to be used. Keep in mind that not all users may want a custom wallpaper. However, you can specify bitmaps, HTML, or a `.GIF` file to be used as the default wallpaper.

When you have selected your options for the welcome messages, click Next to continue.

7. The IEAK allows you to customize the channels that appear in the user's channel bar. These settings are based on the settings for the version of Internet Explorer currently installed on your machine.

   The process for customizing the channels for your installation of IE is pretty straightforward: Using the channel bar from your desktop, add and remove any channels that you want until you have the settings you want your users to have when they install IE.

When you have customized the channels, you can choose whether or not to include your customized channels in the distribution, as shown in Figure 2.30.

If you choose to customize the channels, the IEAK imports all your channel settings into the custom IE package it builds. When you are ready to continue, click Next.

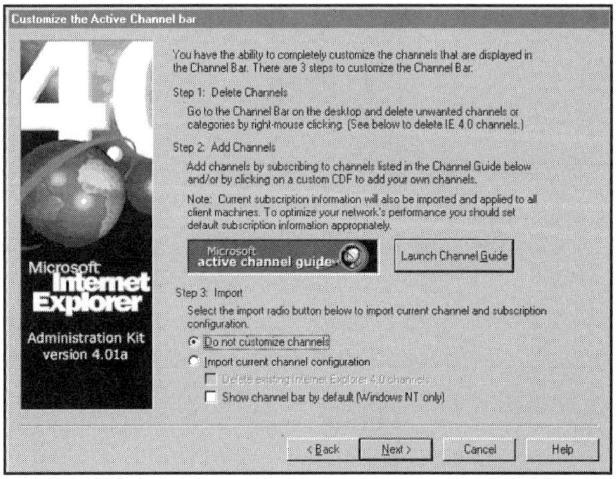

Figure 2.30

Importing customized channels from Internet Explorer with the IEAK.

8. Just as you can import Active Channel settings, you can also customize software distribution channels, as shown in Figure 2.31.

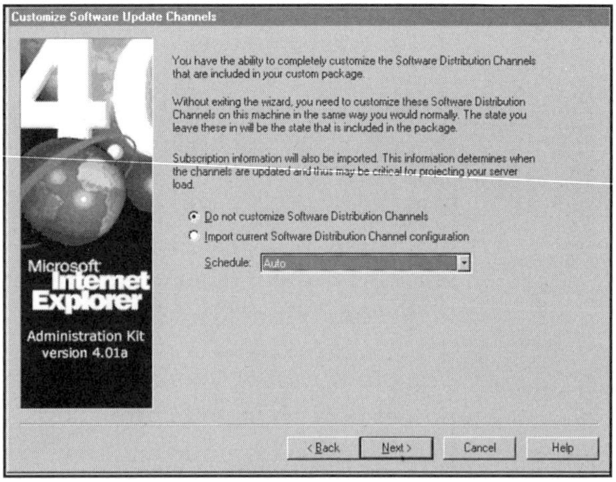

Figure 2.31

You can customize software distribution channels by importing Internet Explorer settings.

When you have established the software distribution channels you want to install for users within Internet Explorer on the administrator's machine, you can import the settings with the IEAK. When you are ready to continue, click Next.

9. If you have chosen to install the Windows Desktop Update, you can also choose to customize the settings for the Active Desktop, as shown in Figure 2.32.

   In the same way you configure channel settings, you configure the Active Desktop: by importing the settings from your installed version of Internet Explorer. After you have selected the settings you want, you can import the settings. When you are finished, click Next to continue.

Figure 2.32

Customizing the Active Desktop involves importing settings from Internet Explorer.

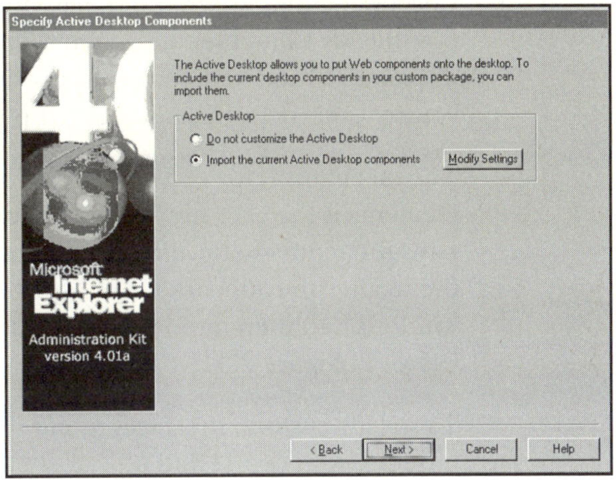

10. You can also import the settings for any desktop toolbars, as shown in Figure 2.33.

    As with other components based on the administrator's machine, toolbar settings are imported from the current version of Internet Explorer on the machine running the IEAK.

    Further on in the customization process, Corporate Administrators also have the option of restricting the changes a user may or may not make to configurations such as desktop toolbars.

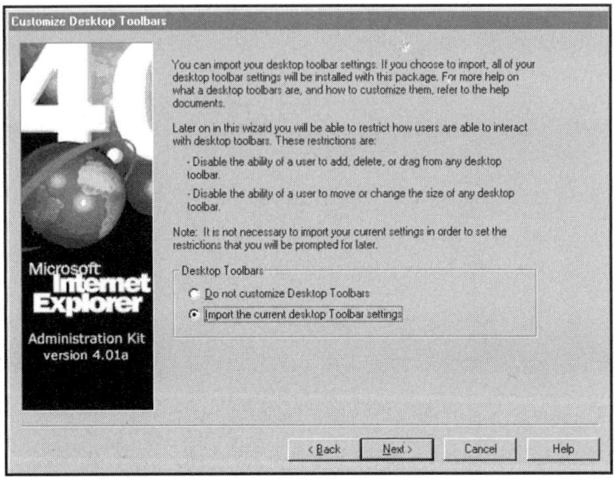

Figure 2.33

Importing desktop toolbar settings with the IEAK.

11. Corporate Administrators also have the option of configuring how the My Computer and Control Panel window elements are displayed. These configuration options can provide greater control over users' machines for corporate environments.

    The mechanism for controlling the customization of these elements is the `.HTT` file, a HyperText Template file that contains the template for displaying data. You can edit the `.HTT` file to alter the appearance of My Computer and the other windows and then import the file into the IE install, as shown in Figure 2.34.

    To specify custom interfaces, point the IEAK Wizard to the modified `MYCOMP.HTT` and `CONTROL.HTT` files. If you do not want to customize these settings, simply leave the fields blank. When you are ready to continue, click Next.

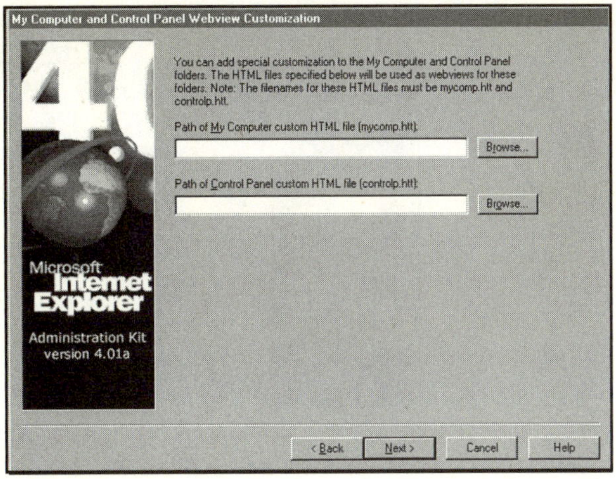

Figure 2.34

Customizing Windows functionality with `.HTT` files.

12. When the Internet Explorer browser contacts a Web site, one of the pieces of information it makes available to the server is the *user agent string*. This string identifies the browser type and version so that any special features of the site for one specific type of browser (for example, IE 3.0 features or IE 4.0 features) can be correctly displayed.

    Many sites use the information in the user agent string to determine the kinds of browsers being used to view the sites. Adding a custom string to the user agent should not affect performance, but it does add an enhancement that allows site administrators to see that your version of IE has been customized.

    Simply add the text to the screen shown in Figure 2.35 to append it to the user agent string. For example, if you enter **`IE Custom Build`**, the full string given by the browser would be as follows:

```
Mozilla/4.0 (compatible; MSIE 4.01; Windows NT); IE Custom Build
```

    This string includes both the standard IE 4.0 user agent string and your customized information. When you are ready to continue, click Next.

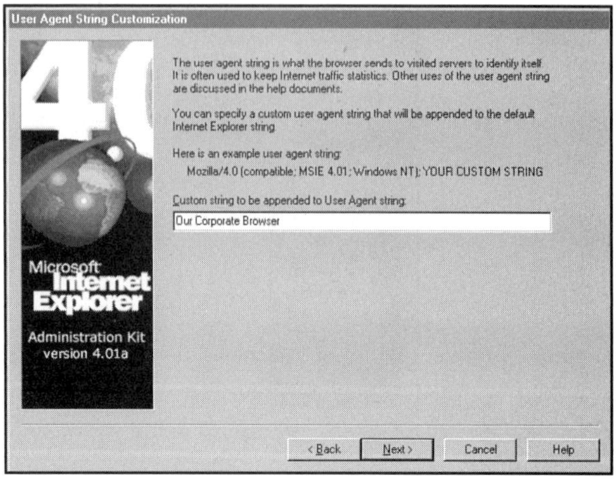

Figure 2.35

Entering a custom user agent string provides Web servers with more information.

13. Internet Explorer provides a mechanism for updating the browser and components without reinstalling. This process is called *automatic browser configuration*, and it can be accomplished by one of the following file types:

    - **.INS files.** These are the installation files created by the IEAK and maintained using the IEAK Profile Manager. If you specify an .INS file, you can make modifications to the file using the IEAK Profile Manager and then have the browser check this file for new configuration information.

    - **.JS or .PAC files.** These files allow you to perform autoproxy configuration so that the proxy server settings of your browser can be maintained remotely and automatically.

    Depending on your requirements, you can use either type of file for automatic browser configuration. Finally, as shown in Figure 2.36, you can customize the interval at which the browser will autoconfigure. If you leave this last field blank (or set it to 0), the browser will reconfigure when the system is rebooted.

    The specifics of creating autoconfiguration files are covered in Chapter 3, "Configuring and Managing Resource Access."

    When you are ready to continue, click Next.

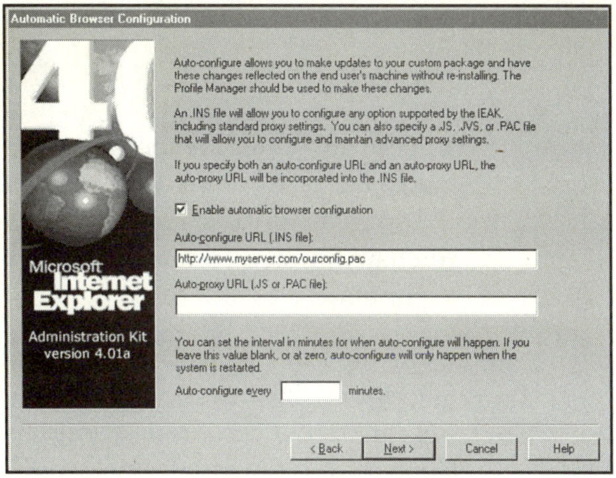

Figure 2.36

Specifying files for automatic browser configuration.

14. Even if you do not choose to use automatic browser configuration to manage the proxy settings for your IE installation, you can still specify the initial proxy information provided to IE, as shown in Figure 2.37.

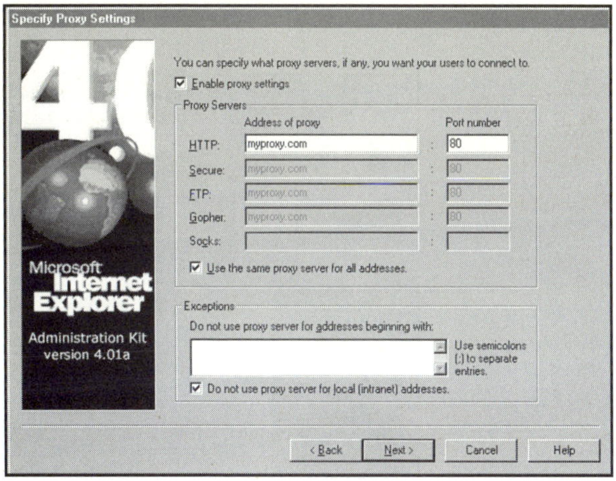

Figure 2.37

Specifying the proxy server settings for Internet Explorer.

From this screen, you can enter specific proxy information for each type service used by IE, including the following:

- HTTP
- Secure HTTP
- FTP

- Gopher
- SOCKS

You can also enter the specific addresses of sites that IE will bypass the proxy server to reach; you can also choose to have IE bypass the proxy server for local intranet addresses. When you have finished customizing your proxy settings, click Next to continue.

15. Using the IEAK Wizard, you can configure the security settings for certificates. As you can for other IE components, you can import certificate settings from the current IE installation, or you can install a new root certificate, as shown in Figure 2.38.

    The security settings also allow administrators to import Authenticode settings. Authenticode allows IE to download and automatically install ActiveX and other types of components when they are supplied by trusted sources. After choosing the settings to import, if any, click Next to continue.

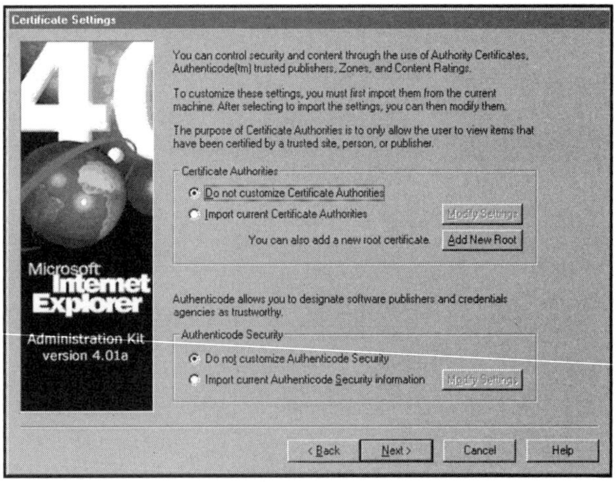

Figure 2.38

Modifying the certificate settings for IE 4.0.

16. Additional security settings, such as the configuration of security zones and the settings for content ratings, can be specified with the IEAK Wizard, as shown in Figure 2.39.

Security zone settings can be customized from within the IEAK; content ratings are imported from the currently installed version of Internet Explorer. Creating customized security policies is covered extensively in Chapter 3.

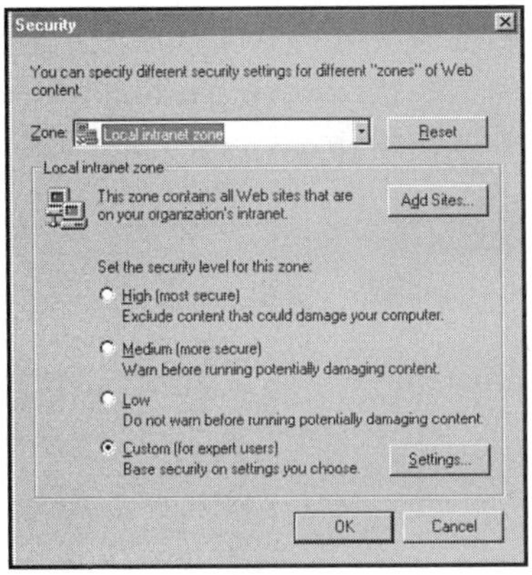

Figure 2.39

Altering security zone settings and content ratings with the IEAK.

The following section looks at the customization of specific components: Outlook Express and NetMeeting.

Stage 5: Configuring and Customizing Components

Objective

The following sections take a look at how some of the IE components can be configured using the IEAK, specifically Outlook Express, NetMeeting, and channel subscriptions. Each of these options has a number of parameters that can be altered with the IEAK Wizard—either as a part of the wizard itself or by modifying System Policies and Restrictions.

The next stage of the IEAK Wizard is stage 5, Component Customization. When you have looked over the introductory screen for this section, click Next to continue. The next options presented are primarily for the configuration of Outlook Express, so let's take a look at how that is configured.

Microsoft Outlook Express

The Outlook Express mail and news client has a number of settings administrators can alter to provide maximum functionality. Here are the steps for configuring Outlook Express:

1. The first step for configuring Outlook Express is to provide information regarding the servers Outlook will use to send and receive messages. The wizard screen is shown in Figure 2.40.

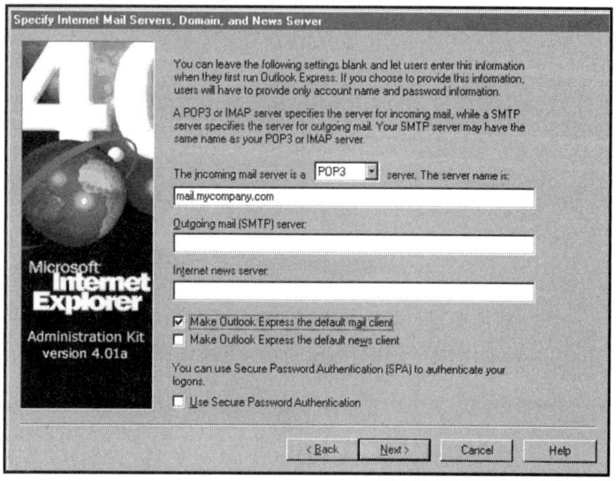

Figure 2.40

Customizing the server settings for Outlook Express.

Select the type of server that will be used for incoming mail. Outlook supports the POP3 and IMAP protocols. Select the appropriate protocol and enter a name for the server in the text field.

Enter the fully qualified domain name for the incoming mail server (for example, `mail.mycompany.com`). This information allows Outlook to connect to that server for incoming mail.

In the Outgoing Mail (SMTP) Server field, provide the fully qualified domain name for your organization's SMTP server. You must also specify the fully qualified domain name for the Internet news server so that the client can access newsgroups.

When you have configured this information, you can choose to make Outlook Express the default mail or news client, and also elect to use secure password authentication for security purposes. When you are finished entering server information, click Next to continue.

2. The next option allows you to configure the information for a Lightweight Directory Access Protocol (LDAP) server (see Figure 2.41), if you want to provide directory services to Outlook Express users.

   In the same way you entered server information, enter the information for your LDAP server in the text fields and then select an authentication type. When you are finished configuring LDAP server settings, click Next to continue.

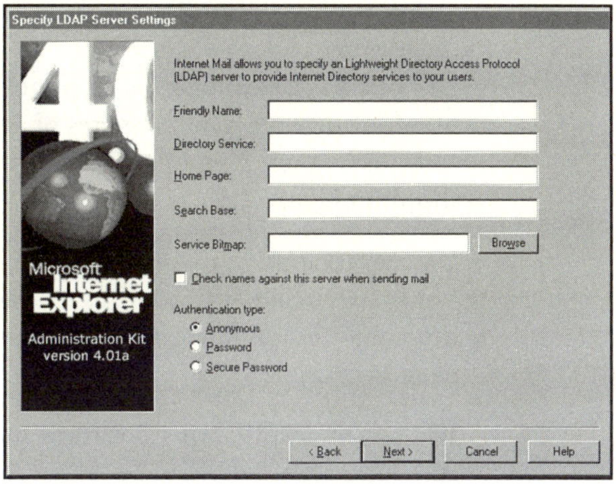

Figure 2.41

Specifying LDAP server information to provide directory information.

3. The customization of Outlook Express provides a way to customize the InfoPane that appears at the bottom of the Outlook Express client and the welcome message that first appears in a user's Inbox. Specify the location of these files using the wizard screen shown in Figure 2.42.

   The InfoPane can be a customized HTML file located on a server, or it can be included as a local file. The welcome message is also an HTML file that must be specified as a local file. You can also customize the sender of the welcome message and indicate a reply-to address in case a user responds to the welcome message with questions.

   When you have specified the location of your InfoPane and welcome message HTML files, click Next to continue.

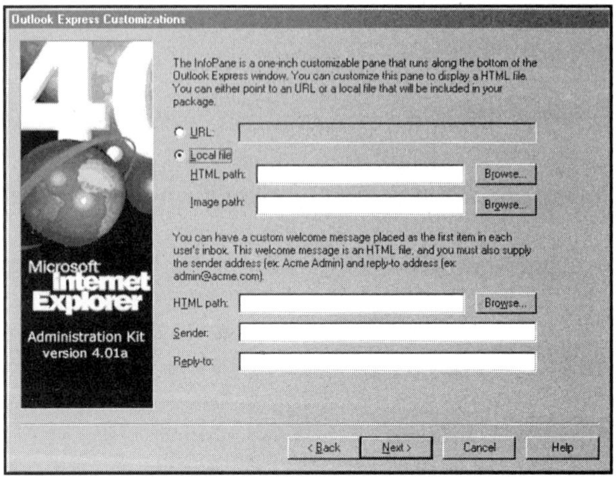

Figure 2.42

Customizing the Outlook InfoPane and establishing a welcome message for new users.

4. Outlook Express allows you to create customized signature files for outgoing mail messages or for news postings. You can specify these signature files in the IEAK Wizard, as shown in Figure 2.43.

   You can use one signature for both mail and news, or you can specify separate signatures for each purpose. The size of the signature is limited to 1K and should be entered on this page as plain text.

   When you've written the signatures and are ready to continue, click Next.

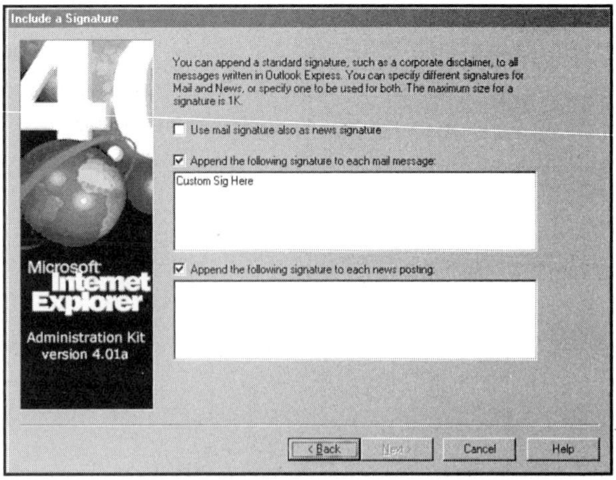

Figure 2.43

Specifying automatic signatures for email and news messages.

5. The remaining customization options for Outlook Express can be found under the System Policies and Restrictions. In this view, you can click the Outlook Express folder to see the remaining configuration options for Outlook Express, which fall into two categories: General Settings and View Customization.

   From the General Settings screen shown in Figure 2.44, you can alter three specific features:

   - Put Mail and News in the Restricted Sites Zone
   - Mail: Make Plain-Text Message Composition the Default for Mail Messages.
   - News: Make HTML Message Composition the Default for News Posts.

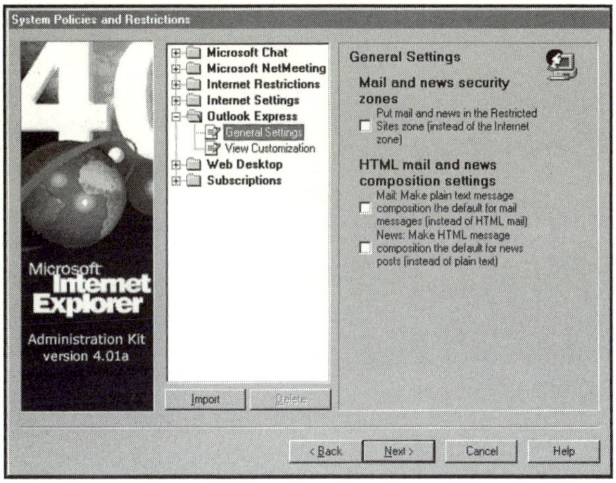

Figure 2.44

Customizing the General Settings for the Outlook Express client.

Changing the security zone of mail and news affects the news sites that can be accessed by the Outlook Express client. Changing the default message formats can help with compatibility. For example, because many mail clients do not support HTML formatted mail, you may want to make the default plain text by selecting that option so that your users have maximum compatibility.

From the View Customization screen shown in Figure 2.45, you can select four settings:

- Turn on Outlook Bar
- Turn off Folder List
- Turn on Folder Bar
- Turn off Tip of the Day

Each of these options changes the look and feel of the Outlook client. The settings can be altered by the user later.

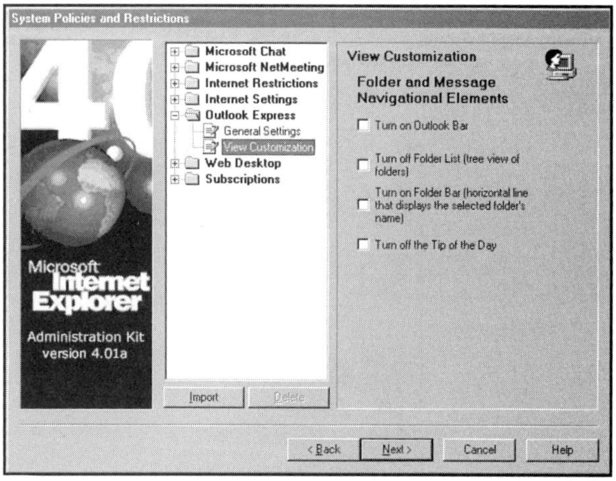

Figure 2.45

Specifying the View Customization options for Outlook Express.

That's it for configuring Outlook Express! The following section looks at configuring the settings for NetMeeting.

Microsoft NetMeeting

Microsoft NetMeeting is a powerful tool that lets you share data and collaborate and conference over the Internet or intranet. However, the power of NetMeeting can be abused or can sometimes place a strain on network resources.

Administrators can therefore specify several different parameters for the use of NetMeeting under the System Policies and Restrictions, as shown in Figure 2.46.

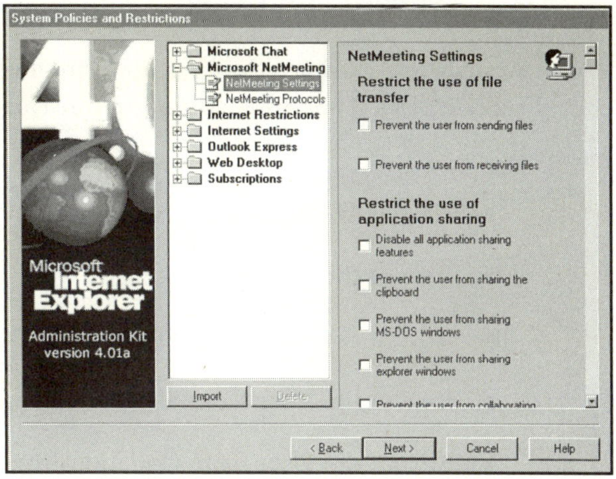

Figure 2.46

Specifying NetMeeting settings within the System Policies and Restrictions.

By placing restrictions on what the user can do with NetMeeting, the administrator can help provide the best mix of tools for the environment without compromising privacy, security, or performance. The following sections examine the NetMeeting settings you can control from the System Policies and Restrictions area of the IEAK Wizard.

Restrict the Use of File Transfer

Transferring files with NetMeeting can be a valuable tool for collaboration, allowing users to exchange data in real time. However, this freedom to exchange information can be a potential security risk: Users can inadvertently exchange viruses; worse, users can accidentally release sensitive documents over the net. Therefore, administrators can select the following options:

- Prevent the User from Sending Files
- Prevent the User from Receiving Files

By limiting the data users can exchange, administrators can minimize the security risks.

Restrict the Use of Application Sharing

Application sharing is another powerful tool that represents possible security risks. Therefore, administrators can select the following options:

- Disable All Application Sharing Features
- Prevent the User from Sharing the Clipboard
- Prevent the User from Sharing MS-DOS Windows
- Prevent the User from Sharing Explorer Windows
- Prevent the User from Collaborating

Limiting the ability to share applications can increase security; it can also help preserve user resources by not placing additional processing and memory strains on conferencing machines.

Restrict the Use of the Options Dialog Box

As a Corporate Administrator, you can use the IEAK to control the user's ability to configure many options for NetMeeting. Because some of the settings that allow administrators to control resource access or to limit the functionality of NetMeeting are found in Options dialog boxes, the potential for the user to override preset values exists.

To help "lock down" the settings, administrators can restrict users' access to certain Options dialog boxes. Because the users cannot alter the Option dialog boxes, they cannot alter the settings. Administrators can select the following options from the System Policies and Restrictions area of the IEAK Wizard:

- Disable the General Options Page
- Disable the My Information Options Page
- Disable the Calling Options Page
- Disable the Audio Options Page

- Disable the Video Options Page
- Disable the Protocols Options Page
- Prevent the User from Answering Calls
- Prevent the User from Using Audio Features

Restrict the Use of Video

One of the biggest consumers of network resources is the video conferencing features of NetMeeting. Video consumes large amounts of network bandwidth and can also represent a privacy concern to users. To help keep network resources under control and to protect users' privacy, administrators can select the following options from the System Policies and Restrictions area of the IEAK Wizard:

- Prevent the User from Sending Video
- Prevent the User from Receiving Video
- Prevent the User from Using Directory Services

Here are some of the additional parameters administrators can customize for NetMeeting:

- **Set the Default Directory Server.** This parameter specifies the directory server that NetMeeting will connect to for conference hosting. Although the defaults are Microsoft NetMeeting servers, you can also specify a third-party server or a private site.
- **Set Exchange Server Property for NetMeeting Address.** When using Exchange in conjunction with NetMeeting, you can specify an address listing.
- **Preset User Information Category.** The User Information Category lets other NetMeeting users know how you are using NetMeeting (for example, for business or personal use). This option can be used only if you are in the Corporate Administrator role and have selected the silent install option.

- **Set NetMeeting Home Page.** You can enter a URL for the NetMeeting home page to provide users with information about NetMeeting.

- **Set Limit for Audio/Video Throughput.** This parameter allows administrators to limit the amount of network bandwidth consumed for audio/video conferencing. By limiting the amount of throughput that can be used for conferencing, administrators can make sure that conferences do not adversely affect network performance. Of course, limiting bandwidth decreases the quality of audio and video. However, you can still achieve a balance between quality and performance.

In addition to the feature configurations, the IEAK Wizard allows you to specify settings for the NetMeeting protocols, as shown in Figure 2.47.

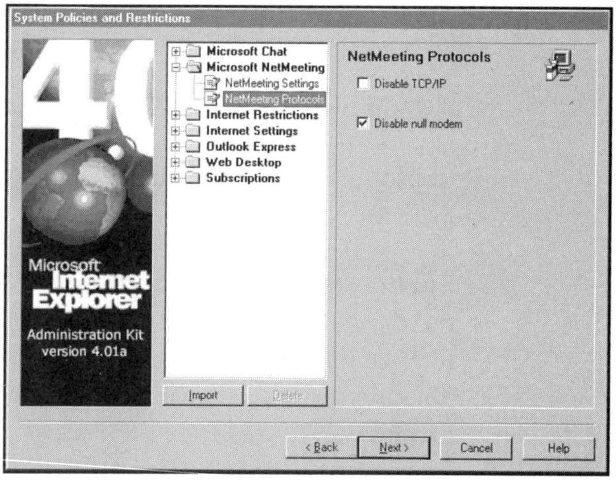

Figure 2.47

Specifying the NetMeeting protocols.

NetMeeting can operate over a TCP/IP connection to the Internet/intranet or between two machines connected by a null modem cable. From the NetMeeting Protocol section of the System Policies and Restrictions area of the IEAK Wizard, administrators can select the following options:

- Disable TCP/IP

- Disable Null Modem

These options allow administrators to limit the protocols and types of conferencing that can be performed by NetMeeting by imposing physical limits on the networking protocol. Disable Null Modem is selected by default (in most situations, disabling TCP/IP renders NetMeeting useless).

Configuring Channels and Subscriptions

Objective

Site subscriptions can be a mixed blessing for users. On one hand, having sites downloaded automatically is a great convenience because it allows users to always have access to the most current information. However, if the site has a lot of information or is updated too frequently, it can become a resource burden. To help administrators control the behavior of site subscriptions, Internet Explorer allows for various restrictions in the System Policies and Restrictions area of the IEAK Wizard, as shown in Figure 2.48.

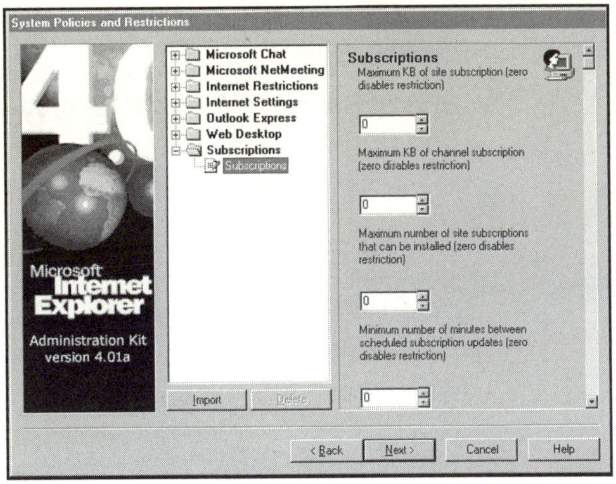

Figure 2.48

Configuring subscription restrictions within the System Policies and Restrictions area of the IEAK Wizard.

These restrictions allow administrators to control exactly how subscriptions are updated and when they are updated. Here are the parameters the administrators can specify with the IEAK Wizard:

- **Maximum KB of Site Subscription.** This parameter puts a physical limit on the amount of disk space that can be used for Web site subscriptions.

- **Maximum KB of Channel Subscription.** This parameter puts a physical limit on the amount of disk space that can be used for channel subscriptions.
- **Maximum Number of Site Subscriptions That Can Be Installed.** This parameter sets a limit on the number of sites to which the user can subscribe.
- **Minimum Number of Minutes Between Scheduled Subscription Updates.** This interval sets a time period between the downloading of subscription updates. This parameter can be used to force an update to occur less frequently than may have been specified by the publisher.
- **Beginning of Range in Which to Exclude Scheduled Subscription Updates.** This parameter allows administrators to block out a time during which no subscription updates can occur. This specification can help ensure that valuable network resources are not used for subscription updates during productivity periods.
- **End of Range in Which to Exclude Scheduled Subscription Updates.** This is the end of the block of time during which subscription data may not be downloaded.

Note

The range for excluding scheduled updates is specified using minutes after midnight. For example, if you want to block updates from 9 a.m. to 5 p.m., you use the values 540 and 1020 because 9 a.m. is 540 minutes after midnight and 5 p.m. is 1020 minutes after midnight.

- **Maximum Site Subscription Crawl Depth.** This setting limits the number of pages into a site that the subscription mechanism will crawl. Limiting the number of crawl levels can significantly reduce the size of the download.

With these options customized within Internet Explorer, the benefits of subscriptions can far outweigh any disadvantages, allowing users the most current information without creating undo stress on system or network resources.

Exercises

The following exercises are designed to give you step-by-step, hands-on guidance through some of the setup tasks outlined in this chapter. Some of these exercises require you to be at a particular section of the IEAK Wizard. You can use these exercises as a guide while reviewing the rest of the chapter to perform specific tasks.

Exercise 2.1: Creating a New Installation Option

This exercise takes you step by step through the creation of a customized installation option for Internet Explorer 4.0.

1. Launch the IEAK Wizard with a Corporate Administrator customization code.
2. Bypass the silent mode installation option. When you reach the Select Install Options screen, click the New button to create a new installation option.
3. Click the Option text field and type the name of your custom install. For example, type **`My Company's Official Install`**.
4. Click the Description text box and type a description for your custom install option. For example, type **`Our Company's Officially Endorsed Installation`**.
5. Select the components you want to add to your install from the Components Available list box. You can select multiple components by clicking them.
6. Add the components you selected to the Components to Install list box by clicking the > button.

You have just created a customized installation option. You can add other options by repeating steps 1 through 6, or you can click Next to continue with the wizard.

Exercise 2.2: Customizing Outlook Express

This exercise covers the steps involved in customizing the installation of Outlook Express from the IEAK Wizard. Because this exercise begins part way through the IEAK Wizard, you must step through the wizard to the Outlook Express customization screens.

1. Launch the IEAK Wizard with a Corporate Administrator customization code.
2. Step through the IEAK Wizard until you reach the Stage 5—Customizing Components section. Click Next to begin customizing Outlook Express.
3. From the Specify Internet Mail Servers, Domain, and News Server screen, select the type of server for the incoming mail server (POP3 or IMAP).
4. Enter the Fully Qualified Domain Name (FQDN) for the incoming mail server.
5. Enter a FQDN for the outgoing mail (SMTP) server.
6. Enter the FQDN for the Internet news server.
7. You can make Outlook Express the default mail client and the default news client. You can also select the option to use Secure Password Authentication if your server supports it.
8. When you finish entering server information and selecting options, click Next.
9. Enter information for your LDAP server. If you are not using LDAP for directory services, click Next to continue.

   If you are using an LDAP server for directory services, you must supply the following settings for your LDAP server:

   - Friendly name
   - Directory service
   - Home page

- Search base
- Service bitmap

You can configure Outlook Express to check the LDAP directory when sending mail by selecting the Check Names Against This Server When Sending Mail option. Finally, select the authentication type for your LDAP server. When you are finished, click Next to continue.

10. You can customize the InfoPane displayed by Outlook Express. Enter the URL for the InfoPane content or enter the path for the local file.

11. You can also specify information for the welcome message sent to users when they install Outlook Express. Specify the path to the HTML file for the message; also specify a sender for the message and a reply-to address so that users can respond to the welcome message.

12. When you are finished configuring the InfoPane and welcome message, click Next to continue.

13. You can enter the text for signatures that are automatically appended to mail and news messages in Outlook. You can specify different messages for mail and for news, or you can use the same signature for both purposes.

14. When you are finished entering signature text, click Next.

You are now finished configuring Outlook Express with the IEAK Wizard.

Exercise 2.3: Customizing NetMeeting

This exercise covers the steps involved in customizing the restriction settings for NetMeeting from within the IEAK Wizard. Because this exercise begins part way through the IEAK Wizard, you must step through the wizard to the System Policies and Restrictions screen.

continues

Exercise 2.3: Continued

1. Launch the IEAK Wizard with a Corporate Administrator customization code.
2. Step through the IEAK Wizard until you reach the System Policies and Restrictions section and click Next to begin customizing NetMeeting.
3. Click the + next to the `Microsoft NetMeeting` folder in the list box to expand the options for NetMeeting.
4. Click `NetMeeting Settings` to display the system settings for NetMeeting on the right side of the dialog box. Now you are ready to begin setting the options for NetMeeting.
5. Set the Restrict the Use of File Transfer option.
6. Using the scroll bar on the right side of the dialog box, scroll to the Restrict the Use of Application Sharing settings.
7. Scroll to the next set of restrictions in the Restrict the Use of the Options Dialog category. These restrictions prevent users from changing the settings within NetMeeting. Select the Options dialog boxes you want to disable.
8. Scroll down to the Restrict the Use of Video category. These options prevent users from using the video conferencing capabilities of NetMeeting. Select your options and scroll down to continue.
9. You must enter some configuration information. In the Set the Default Directory Server field, enter the FQDN for the ILS server you want to use with NetMeeting.
10. In the Set Exchange Server Property for NetMeeting Address section, select the appropriate extension attribute if you are using Exchange in conjunction with NetMeeting.
11. If you selected the silent installation option, you must set the Preset User Information Category. Otherwise, leave this field blank and continue.

12. In the Set the NetMeeting Home Page field, you can specify a home page for the NetMeeting client that offers help and instructions for users.

13. You can restrict the amount of bandwidth used for audio/video using the Set Limit for Audio/Video Throughput field. Enter the value for the average bandwidth in bits per second (bps).

14. From the list box on the left of the dialog box, click NetMeeting Protocols.

15. Select the protocols you want to disable. Most likely, you will want to disable only the null modem protocol.

You are finished configuring NetMeeting. You can continue configuring other options or click Next to proceed with the IEAK Wizard.

Exercise 2.4: Configuring Subscription Configurations

This exercise covers the steps involved in customizing the restriction settings for subscriptions from within the IEAK Wizard. Because this exercise begins part way through the IEAK Wizard, you must step through the wizard to the System Policies and Restrictions screen.

1. Launch the IEAK Wizard with a Corporate Administrator customization code.

2. Step through the IEAK Wizard until you reach the System Policies and Restrictions section and then click Next to begin customizing subscriptions.

3. Click the + next to the `Subscriptions` folder in the list box to expand the options for subscriptions.

4. Click the `Subscriptions` item under the main `Subscriptions` folder to display the system settings for subscriptions on the right side of the dialog box.

continues

Exercise 2.4: Continued

5. Fill in the value for the Maximum KB of Site Subscription option. This value sets a limit for the amount of disk space used by subscriptions.

6. Fill in the Maximum Number of Site Subscriptions That Can Be Installed option. This value limits the total number of subscriptions the user can configure.

7. To increase the efficiency of subscription updates, you can enter a value for the Minimum Number of Minutes Between Scheduled Subscription Updates option.

8. The next two options allow you to restrict when updates can occur. Enter a value for the Beginning of Range in Which to Exclude Scheduled Subscription Updates option. The trick is that the time is specified in the number of minutes after midnight. For example, if you want to restrict updates starting at 9 a.m., enter `540` for this value.

9. Enter a value for the End of Range in Which to Exclude Scheduled Subscription Updates option. This is the ending time for update restrictions, also specified in minutes after midnight. For example, if you want to end the update restriction at 6 p.m., enter `1080`.

10. Specify the Maximum Site Subscription Crawl Depth, which is the number of links down the site tree that the subscription mechanism will download page content during updates.

You are finished configuring subscription options. You can configure other options or click Next to proceed with the IEAK Wizard.

Review Questions

The review questions in this section can help you assess your understanding of the terms, concepts, and objectives covered in this chapter. These questions are written in the style of the questions presented on the MCSE exam and are an excellent way to prepare yourself for the material you will see on the exam. After you complete the review questions, you will find the answer to each question—along with an explanation of the answer—in the following section.

1. Select the appropriate requirements for performing a full installation of IE 4.0 for Windows 95.

   A. 486/66 MHz or higher, 8MB RAM, 64MB disk space

   B. Pentium, 24MB RAM, 64MB disk space

   C. 486/66 MHz or higher, 16MB RAM, 73MB disk space

   D. Pentium, 24MB RAM, 50M disk space

2. To limit the number of user choices during installation, you want to use the silent installation feature. What role(s) have access to the silent install? (Select all that apply.)

   A. Internet Service Provider

   B. Corporate Administrator

   C. Content Provider/Developer

3. When creating a custom component for installation with your custom build, what is crucial to include to allow users the option of removing the component correctly?

   A. Version number

   B. Uninstall key

   C. GUID

   D. Parameter

4. Which of the following are restrictions placed on the administrator who chooses the silent install option? (Select all that apply.)

   A. Limited to specifying one download site

   B. Limited to specifying one installation option

   C. Limited to specifying one custom component

   D. Must select option for Windows Desktop Update

5. Custom channel configurations are created

   A. By the IEAK Wizard

   B. In the IEAK Profile Manager

   C. In IE and imported into the IEAK Profile Manager

   D. In IE and imported to the IEAK Wizard

6. HyperText Template files (`.HTT`) are used to

   A. Customize software distribution channels

   B. Perform automatic browser updates

   C. Customize My Computer and Control Panel interfaces

   D. Customize the Active Desktop

7. To receive mail with Outlook Express, you must specify values for

   A. The server protocol and the FQDN for the mail server

   B. LDAP server settings

   C. The SMTP server FQDN

   D. A custom InfoPane URL

8. To "lock down" settings for NetMeeting so that users cannot override the settings specified by administrators, you must

   A. Limit audio/video bandwidth

   B. Disable file transfer features

   C. Restrict the use of Options dialog boxes

   D. Restrict the use of application sharing

9. To manage users' proxy settings remotely without forcing the reinstallation of IE, you use which of the following mechanisms?

   A. Automatic browser updates with a `.HTT` file

   B. Automatic version synchronization with a `.HTT` file

   C. Automatic browser updates with a `.PAC` file

   D. Automatic version synchronization with a `.JS` file

10. What range value would you specify in the option to restrict scheduled subscription updates to prevent updates from occurring between the hours of 9 a.m. and 6 p.m.?

    A. 9:00 and 6:00

    B. 0900 and 1800

    C. 540 and 1080

    D. 900 and 600

Review Answers

Now that you have completed the review questions, check your answers against those provided here. Explanations are provided for each answer so that you can see whether you arrived at the correct solution for the right reason, or so that you can see how your answer varied from the correct one.

1. **C** 486 or higher, 16M RAM, and 73M disk space.

2. **B** Because the silent installation option creates so many restrictions for the user, you can perform a silent install only if you are a Corporate Administrator.

3. **B** To successfully uninstall a component, the uninstall key must be in the Windows Registry. The uninstall key allows the user to select the component from the Add/Remove Programs Control Panel to launch the component's uninstaller.

4. **A, B, and D** Administrators who choose the silent install option can specify only one download site, can specify only one installation option, and must select the Windows Desktop Update option.

5. **D** The IEAK does not allow the direct manipulation of channel configurations. Instead, administrators must configure the custom channel settings in the version of IE installed on the machine on which the IEAK is running, and then import the channel settings into the IEAK Wizard.

6. **C** HyperText Template files (`.HTT`) are used to customize My Computer and Control Panel interfaces.

7. **A** The SMTP server must be specified to send mail, but only the incoming mail server and protocol must be specified to receive mail.

8. **C** If you deny users access to the Options dialog boxes, users cannot alter the settings created by the IEAK for NetMeeting.

9. **C** Proxy settings are manipulated with automatic browser updates and can use either a `.JS` or a `.PAC` file.

10. **C** The range of time to restrict scheduled updates is specified in the number of minutes past midnight (with midnight being zero). Therefore, 9 a.m. is 540 and 6 p.m. is 1080.

Answers to Test Yourself Questions at Beginning of Chapter

The following answers are provided for the prechapter quiz at the beginning of this chapter. You can use these questions and answers to determine how familiar you may already be with this chapter's material. Each of the questions relates to a specific goal for the Installation and Configuration section of the "Implementing and Supporting the Microsoft Internet Explorer Administration Kit for Microsoft Internet Explorer 4.0" MCSE exam. Each of the following answers references the section in this chapter that deals with the covered objective so that you can easily locate the material you may want to review or clarify.

1. The minimal requirements for installation of IE4.0 vary depending on what specific components you have selected to install. The following chart shows the minimal requirements for different installation options:

Installation	OS	Requirement
All	Windows 95/NT	486 processor or higher
Browser Only and Outlook Express	Windows 95	12MB RAM
Standard Installation w/o Windows Desktop Update	Windows 95	8MB RAM
Standard or Full w/Windows Desktop Update	Windows 95	16MB RAM
All	Windows NT	24MB RAM
Browser Only	Windows 95/NT	40MB disk space
Standard Installation	Windows 95/NT	47MB disk space
Full Installation	Windows 95/NT	73MB disk space

continues

Installation	OS	Requirement
Browser Only	Windows 95/NT	12.3MB download
Standard Installation	Windows 95/NT	16MB download
Full Installation	Windows 95/NT	24.2MB download

Sections Referencing This Material:

- "Installing Internet Explorer 4.0"
- "Installing Internet Explorer 4.0 for Windows NT and Windows 95"

2. Selecting a silent installation option means that your users are not prompted for any information regarding the installation of Internet Explorer on their system. A silent installation places the following requirements on administrators:

    - Administrators can specify only one installation option
    - Administrators can specify only one download site
    - Administrators can configure the user information for NetMeeting

    Because the user does not have any input in a silent installation, the administrator must specify all relevant configuration information.

    Section Referencing This Material:

    - "Customizing Active Setup Components"

3. Although NetMeeting allows the transfer of files to and from a user's machine while he or she is participating in a conference, doing so poses some security risk. Users may obtain a virus through a transmitted document, or they may inadvertently release a confidential document to conference participants. Because of the potential hazards, administrators can restrict the functionality of file transfers within NetMeeting.

Sections Referencing This Material:

- "Configuring Components Using the IEAK Wizard"
- "Microsoft NetMeeting"

4. From the browser configuration stage of the Internet Explorer Administration Kit Wizard, you can add a custom signature for Outlook Express. You have the option of using the same signature or disclaimer for both mail messages and news posts; alternatively, you can use separate disclaimers for each type of message.

   Sections Referencing This Material:

   - "Configuring Components Using the IEAK Wizard"
   - "Microsoft Outlook Express"

5. Administrators can specify up to 10 download sites and up to 10 custom components, provided they did not choose the silent installation option. For a silent installation, administrators can specify only one download site.

   Section Referencing This Material:

   - "Customizing Active Setup Components"

6. Custom channel settings for both Active Channels and software distribution channels are imported from the running installation of Internet Explorer 4.0 that resides on the same machine as the IEAK. To configure custom channel settings, administrators must first configure the channels they want to install within IE. Then they can import the channel settings using the IEAK Wizard.

   Section Referencing This Material:

   - "Customizing the Browser"

7. The `.INS`, `.JS`, and `.PAC` files are all used for automatic browser configuration. By specifying the automatic browser configuration option and pointing IE to the appropriate file, administrators can alter settings within IE without requiring users to reinstall Internet Explorer. You can use `.INS` files to configure the same settings specified using the IEAK Wizard; you can use `.JS` and `.PAC` files to alter the information for proxy server settings.

   Section Referencing This Material:

   - "Customizing the Browser"

Chapter 3

Configuring and Managing Resource Access

The power of the Internet Explorer Administration Kit does not come exclusively from its capability to alter the physical appearance of Internet Explorer and its components. Certainly, cosmetics are very nice, but the real power of the IEAK can be found in its capability to control other aspects of the browser, such as security and proxy settings.

This chapter looks at how administrators can create customized security and proxy settings and can manage browser configuration when building an installation of IE 4.0 in the Corporate Administrator deployment role.

This chapter helps you prepare for the exam by covering the following objectives:

Objectives

- In Corporate Administrator mode, create and assign various levels of security for security zones.
- In Corporate Administrator mode, manage proxy server support for custom installations of Internet Explorer 4.0.
- Manage automatic configuration by using the IEAK Profile Manager. Methods include:
  - JScript autoproxy
  - `.INS` files
  - `.ADM` files

STOP

Test Yourself! Before reading this chapter, test yourself to determine how much study time you will need to devote to this section.

The following prechapter quiz is designed to help you get a feel for how well you currently understand the material covered in this chapter. If you think you have a strong understanding of the objectives outlined in the previous list, try the quiz. Based on your score on this quiz, you may feel well enough prepared to skip ahead to the Review Questions at the end of the chapter, or you may determine that you would like to study the chapter material more closely.

1. What advantages do Authenticode and certificates offer for Internet security?
2. What are the four Internet Explorer security zones, and how is each one used to classify sites?
3. In what ways can administrators alter the Java security settings to isolate Java applets from the user's operating environment?
4. What system of content ratings are used by default in IE 4.0, and what are the limitations of rating systems in general?
5. What is the purpose of a proxy server, and what proxy server settings can be altered by administrators using the IEAK?
6. What components of Internet Explorer and the IEAK are used for automatic browser configuration?
7. What is the purpose of the IEAK Profile Manager? How does it function?
8. What are `.INS`, `.INF`, `.ADM`, and `.CAB` files, and how are they used?

The answers to this prechapter quiz are located at the end of this chapter. Score your answers against those provided to determine your course of study for this chapter.

Test Objectives Overview

This chapter deals with the Microsoft test objectives geared towards configuring and managing resource access. To manage these resources with the IEAK Wizard or Profile Manager, you must be running the IEAK as a Corporate Administrator. Remember that the license for the Corporate Administrator role is for the private deployment of IE; the ISP or Content Developer role is for a public deployment of IE.

The first area covered in this chapter involves assigning levels of security to browser features. Recall from Chapter 1, "Planning," that the various sites to which Internet Explorer can connect fall into four security zones, each with its own customizable levels of security features. This chapter looks at those features in depth and examines how they are configured. These features include the configuration of security measures for additional browser add-ons, such as ActiveX components, scripting, and Java.

After we cover the direct configuration of security within the browser, we will look at configuring another type of security with Internet Explorer: the proxy server. Proxy servers are used to add a layer of network protection for organizations and to help increase network performance. Regardless of the reason a proxy server is in place, Internet Explorer must be configured to work with the proxy server if users are to run Internet Explorer. This chapter takes a look at configuring proxy information with the IEAK.

Finally, you can change or manage proxy settings and many other features of Internet Explorer through automatic browser configuration, which makes use of some scripting files to alter the settings of Internet Explorer without forcing the user to reinstall components. We will take a look at the types of automatic configuration available and when it is appropriate to use each method. Here's a list of the topics covered in this chapter:

- Creating and assigning security levels
- Managing proxy server support for Internet Explorer 4.0

- Managing automatic configuration using the IEAK Profile Manager
- JScript autoproxy
- .INS Files

Creating and Assigning Security Levels

The ability to configure the security settings of Internet Explorer gives the administrator a tremendous amount of power and responsibility over how users make use of Internet Explorer. The administrator can restrict access to sites, specify what types of services can be used on sites, and alter the type of secure connections that can be used when connecting to secure sites.

By altering these settings, the administrator effectively controls what can and cannot be done with Internet Explorer. This control makes it possible to configure the browser to protect the end user by limiting access to types of data that might be harmful, preventing the user from inadvertently damaging his or her local system. You can also increase the security of data on your corporate networks by making sure that users do not accidentally open doors to files or services that should be inaccessible. The following sections look at the configuration of various security features for Internet Explorer 4.0, including certificate authority settings, Authenticode, security zones, and content ratings.

Certificate Authorities

The foundation of security for browsers is the *certificate*. Because the browser and the server for Web sites and information must have some way of verifying that you are who you say you are (and vice versa), the security certificate is used to make sure that everyone is dealing with a trusted source of information.

Let's review some basics about certificates. A certificate is simply an electronic file that contains information regarding you and your organization. This information is provided in a certificate file format that has been digitally signed by a *certificate authority*, a third party responsible for verifying your information. The digital signature process involves using *public key encryption*, a process by which the certificate authority signs your certificate with its public key. In this way, the certificate authority lets your browser and servers know that your certificate is valid and has not been tampered with. Because of the signatory process, if your certificate is compromised (for example, if the certificate file is edited), it becomes invalid.

The certificate process also allows certificate authorities to let certificates expire after a specific length of time. The expiration date helps make sure that the information provided to the certificate authority is accurate.

Administrators can configure certificate authority settings for Internet Explorer using the IEAK Wizard, as shown in Figure 3.1.

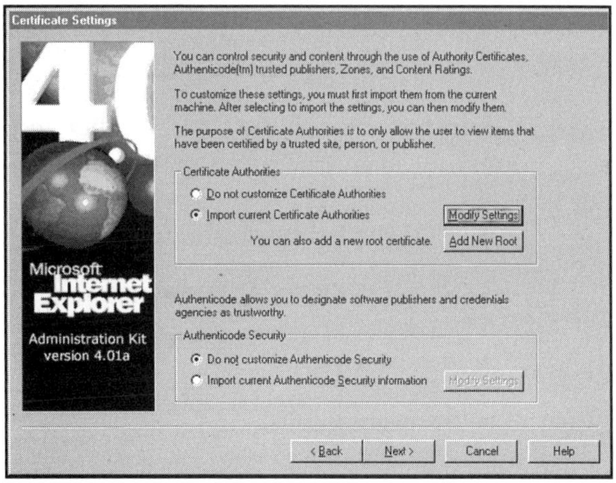

Figure 3.1

The IEAK Wizard allows you to configure the installation of new security certificate authorities.

The mechanism for incorporating certificate authority configurations is based on the installation of Internet Explorer 4.0 on the IEAK machine. Certificate authorities installed for that installation of IE can be imported into the customized build, in much the same manner as channel settings or desktop settings.

The mechanism for incorporating certificate authority configurations also provides a way to add a new root certificate, if you want to create a version for deployment that uses a different root certificate as the main security mechanism. Click the Add New Root button and select the location of the new root certificate file; that certificate is then added to the custom build.

Once your certificate authority settings have actually been imported, you can customize the settings for the certificate authorities that will actually be accessible to users, as shown in Figure 3.2.

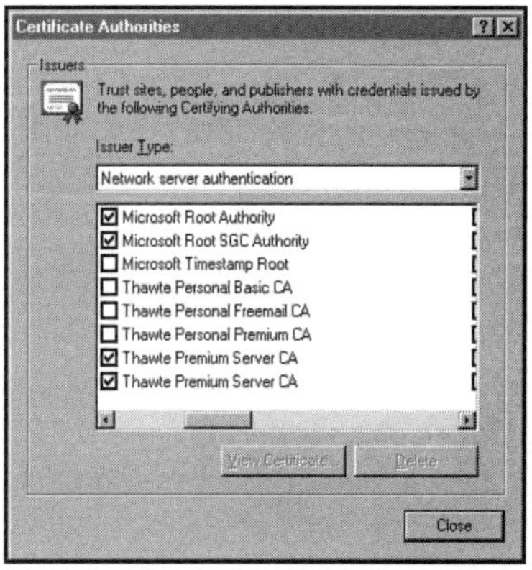

Figure 3.2

Administrators can configure which certificates authorities are available and which are not.

Certificate authorities (CAs) installed in Internet Explorer fall into four main categories (also called *issuer types*):

- Network Server Authentication
- Network Client Authentication
- Secure Email
- Software Publishing

You can select which of the available CAs in each of these categories is considered a valid issuing CA by clicking the Modify Settings button in the Certificate Authorities section of the Certificate Settings dialog box. Internet Explorer will then examine the presented certificates when connecting to a service; if the certificate is issued by a trusted source—one defined here—the content will be accepted.

Selecting the certificate authorities to accept gives you a lot of control over the content that can be downloaded. Trusted certificate authorities can relate directly to information content (such as Web pages) or software content (such as ActiveX controls). For example, if you choose not to allow the Microsoft Corporation as a trusted certificate authority for Software Publishing, your users may be unable to download ActiveX controls from Microsoft.

If you aren't sure whether or not you want to add or remove a CA from your trusted build, you can view the certificate from a CA by clicking the View Certificate button. Figure 3.3 shows a certificate's Properties dialog box.

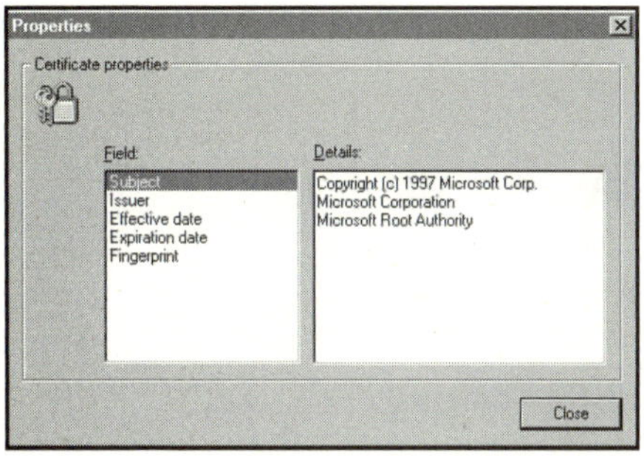

Figure 3.3

The IEAK allows administrators to view certificate details.

Viewing the certificate issued by a CA gives you details about the name of the certificate authority, the certificate's expiration date, and other information you can use to decide whether or not you want to include that vendor's information.

Certificates from the various CAs configured by default with Internet Explorer, and from those added later to your machine, are stored in the *Root Store*, which is simply a repository for all the installed certificates. If you choose to delete a certificate or certificate authority from your customized installation, it is deleted from the Root Store and is no longer available to users.

Note

The information in this section concerning certificates and Authenticode apply only to the Windows 95 version of the IEAK and Internet Explorer. UNIX and Windows 3.x platforms do not support the certificate and Authenticode technologies in Internet Explorer 4.0.

Caution

Be careful when deleting certificate authorities that are initially bundled with IE. These CAs are generally trusted sources licensed to Microsoft; they are installed because they are the more common certificate authorities users will encounter. However, if security is a very high concern for your organization, being able to delete CAs gives you much tighter control over the trusted network resources your users can access. As discussed later in this chapter, you can modify the System Policies and Restrictions to restrict users from downloading content or software from any sites that do not have a certificate from a valid, trusted, certificate authority.

Authenticode

One of the key components to the security mechanism provided with certificates is Microsoft's Authenticode technology, which is used by software developers to identify them as the authors of the code and to verify that the code has not been tampered with.

Authenticode is based on several protocols and standards that are already widely used with certificate technology:

- PKCS #7, a cryptographic message syntax standard
- PKCS #10 for certificate request formats
- X.509 for certificate specification
- SHA and MD5 hash algorithms for encryption

The technology allows developers to obtain a digital certificate and then to "sign" their components so that users can be assured that the software they are downloading has the following characteristics:

- Has actually come from the company/entity represented
- Has not been altered from the original code

Authenticode provides users with some security that they are getting the right software from the right source—and minimizing their risks of getting a virus. As the popularity of components such as Java applets and ActiveX controls increases, this kind of security can be important, not only for users, but also for corporate network security.

The IEAK Wizard allows you to specify Trusted Publishers and Issuers of Credentials for your customized build of Internet Explorer, as shown in Figure 3.4.

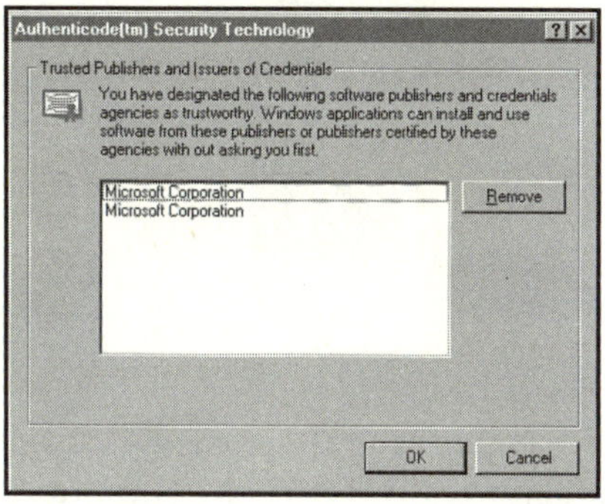

Figure 3.4

Administrators can control the Authenticode settings for trusted publishers.

Whenever Internet Explorer encounters a new component that it is asked to download, it checks the component against entities on this "trusted" list. If the source of the component is trusted, the component is downloaded automatically by the browser. If the source of the component is not on this list, users are prompted about whether or not they want to download the component, or they are forbidden from installing the component, depending on the security configuration.

Security Zones

Recall that Internet Explorer features security zones that allow users and administrators to divide the sites visited by IE into four categories: Internet, Intranet (Local), Trusted Sites, and Restricted Sites.

Using these four divisions, administrators can control the individual security features, or levels of security, applied to each type of site. For example, administrators may want to have low security for sites on the local intranet while maintaining high security for sites on the Internet. With security zones, this kind of flexibility is possible.

The IEAK Wizard allows administrators to accept or modify the default settings for the security zones, as shown in Figure 3.5.

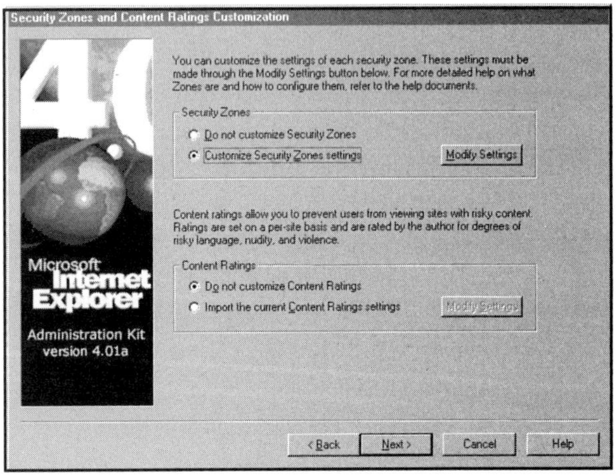

Figure 3.5

The IEAK Wizard allows the modification of security zone settings and content ratings.

By customizing the security settings, administrators can exert greater control over the content users can access and can even restrict content from sites.

Each of the four security zones can be assigned a default level of security from one of the following four choices:

- **High (Most Secure).** Exclude content that could damage your computer.
- **Medium (More Secure).** Warn before running potentially damaging content.
- **Low.** Do not warn before running potentially damaging content.
- **Custom (for expert users).** Bases security on settings you choose.

Each of these security choices has a specific set of security features associated with it, as shown in Table 3.1.

Table 3.1

Default Security Zone Settings in Internet Explorer and the IEAK Wizard

Setting	Low	Medium	High
Download Unsigned ActiveX Controls	Prompt	Disable	Disable
Script ActiveX Controls Marked Safe for Scripting	Enable	Enable	Enable
Initialize and Script ActiveX Controls not Marked as Safe	Prompt	Prompt	Disable
Download Signed ActiveX Controls	Enable	Prompt	Disable
Run ActiveX Controls and Plug-Ins	Enable	Enable	Disable
Logon	Automatic logon with current user name and password	Automatic logon only in Intranet Zone	Prompt for user name and password
Font Download	Enable	Enable	Prompt
File Download	Enable	Enable	Disable
Java Permissions	Low Safety	High Safety	High Safety

continues

Table 3.1 Continued

Setting	Low	Medium	High
Software Channel Permissions	Low Safety	Medium Safety	High Safety
Launching Applications and Files in an `IFRAME`	Enable	Prompt	Disable
Installation of Desktop Items	Enable	Prompt	Disable
Submit Non-encrypted Form Data	Enable	Prompt	Prompt
Drag and Drop or Copy and Paste Files	Enable	Enable	Prompt
Scripting of Java Applets	Enable	Enable	Disable
Active Scripting	Enable	Enable	Enable

In addition to choosing a preconfigured security choice such as Low, Medium, or High security, administrators comfortable with the security options available can create a customized security setting to apply, as shown in Figure 3.6.

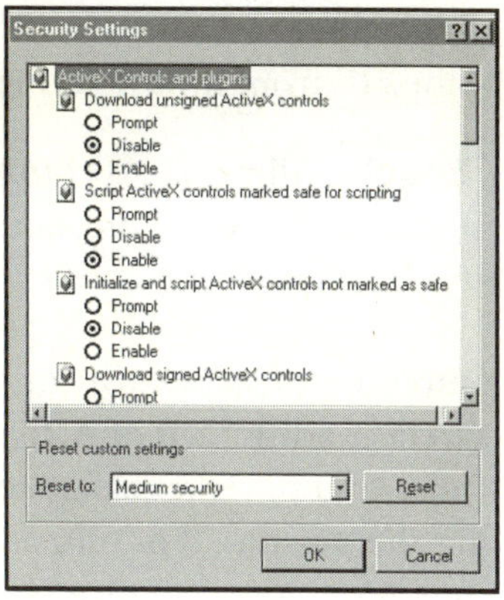

Figure 3.6

Applying a customized security setting to a zone offers administrators complete flexibility over the safety features of IE.

How each of these settings is applied to the security zone determines the overall security for how sites within that zone are treated. As listed in Table 3.1, administrators can make a number of choices regarding the configuration of security options. The options in Table 3.1 represent the individual options, which break down into six categories of security.

ActiveX Controls

The ActiveX Control section of the Security Settings dialog box allows administrators to configure how the customized security zones will react to ActiveX components to be run or downloaded by Internet Explorer. There are five configuration options:

- Download Unsigned ActiveX Controls
- Script ActiveX Controls Marked as Safe for Scripting
- Initialize and Script ActiveX Controls not Marked as Safe
- Download Signed ActiveX Controls
- Run ActiveX Controls and Plug-ins

The administrator can customize each of these options using the following settings:

- **Prompt.** Causes Internet Explorer to notify the user before proceeding with the action (for example, prompts the user before downloading a component).

- **Disable.** Prevents the action from occurring (for example, stops IE from downloading any ActiveX controls).
- **Enable.** Allows IE to continue the action without notifying the user (for example, runs an ActiveX control without notifying the user).

By combining these security options, administrators can allow users to take advantage of ActiveX controls from trusted sources and those that have been signed using Authenticode, while preventing the download of untrusted components. Alternatively, the administrator can configure IE to warn users and let them make their own security choices. This flexibility provides maximum options and allows for different policies based on the type of site being connected to. For example, an administrator may want to disable the downloading of unsigned ActiveX controls from sites in the Internet Zone while enabling them for sites in the Intranet (Local) Zone.

User Authentication

The User Authentication section of the Security Settings dialog box controls how Internet Explorer handles the default logon for sites that require authentication. Administrators can choose from four methods for logon:

- **Automatic Logon with Current User Name and Password.** The Automatic Logon option automatically uses the current user name and password pair for the IE user when it encounters a site that requires authentication. This allows users to enter a protected site without interrupting their workflow to enter a user name and password. However, if the user name and password pair aren't the same for various sites, this option may not work.
- **Automatic Logon Only in Intranet (Local) Zone.** The Automatic Intranet Logon option allows a seamless logon to sites located on the local intranet.

- **Prompt for User Name and Password.** This option causes IE to prompt the user to enter his or her user name and password when accessing a site that requires authentication. This is the most common option because many users have a different user name/password combination for Windows and for various Web sites.
- **Anonymous Logon.** The Anonymous Logon option allows IE to submit an anonymous user name along with the user's email address as the password. This logon scheme is commonly used on the Internet to provide access to download sites.

By specifying the method for logon used in each security zone, administrators can control how users interact with sites by making users aware that they are logging into a site, by prohibiting users from automatically logging onto a site on the Internet, or by making the logon to local intranet sites seamless.

Downloads

The Downloads section of the Security Settings dialog box controls how Internet Explorer reacts to the downloading of fonts and files. The fonts downloaded are fonts specifically designed to work with Internet Explorer and features such as Dynamic HTML. Files can include any type of download link on a page that results in a file being transferred from the site's server to the local machine, where it is to be saved and then launched by another application.

Controlling the fonts and files downloaded to the user's machine can help minimize the risk of corrupting the local file system with bad files, viruses, and so on. Because this is an issue of balancing user convenience with security, many administrators choose simply to prompt the user before proceeding with downloads. In this way, the user is made aware of the possible security problems and takes the risk on his or her own initiative.

Java

The Java section of the Security Settings dialog box controls how Internet Explorer interacts with Java applications and applets it encounters on a site. Java represents the same potential security risk that ActiveX controls do. Because there are a number of settings you can use to control how Java runs, configuring the Java settings can be quite complex.

Administrators have the option of choosing from the following settings for Java security:

- Medium safety
- Low safety
- High safety
- Disable Java
- Custom

The Low, Medium, and High settings are based on the same settings administrators can set individually using the Custom option. Administrators can also disable Java altogether, which prohibits users from accessing Java applets or applications. Because of the widespread use of Java on the Web, however, disabling Java completely can render many pages useless. For most organizations, Java can be used safely with some precautions that limit its access to the local system. Table 3.2 shows the Java security settings available for customization and their defaults for Low, Medium, and High safety.

Table 3.2

Java Safety Custom Settings and the Default Values of Settings for Low, Medium, and High Safety

Java Security Feature	Low Security	Medium Security	High Security
Run Unsigned Content	Run in Sandbox	Run in Sandbox	Run in Sandbox
Run Signed Content	Enable	Prompt	Prompt
Access to All Files	Disable	Disable (Unsigned)	Disable (Unsigned)
		Prompt (Signed)	Prompt (Signed)
Access to All Network Addresses	Disable	Disable (Unsigned)	Disable (Unsigned)
		Prompt (Signed)	Prompt (Signed)
Execute	Disable	Enable (Unsigned)	Enable (Unsigned)
		Prompt (Signed)	Prompt (Signed)
Dialogs	Disable	Disable (Unsigned)	Disable (Unsigned)
		Prompt (Signed)	Prompt (Signed)
System Information	Disable	Disable (Unsigned)	Disable (Unsigned)
		Prompt (Signed)	Prompt (Signed)
Printing	Disable	Disable (Unsigned)	Disable (Unsigned)
		Prompt (Signed)	Prompt (Signed)

continues

Table 3.2 Continued

Java Security Feature	Low Security	Medium Security	High Security
Protected Scratch Space	Disable	Disable (Unsigned)	Disable (Unsigned)
User Selected File Access	Disable	Disable (Unsigned)	Disable (Unsigned)
		Enable (Signed)	Prompt (Signed)

All the settings for Java applications are divided into two sections: unsigned content and signed content. The settings are the same, but administrators may want to apply a greater degree of security to unsigned Java content. What do these settings control? Let's take a look:

- **Run Unsigned Content.** As this option's name indicates, it controls how IE treats unsigned Java content. Very few Java developers or individuals placing Java-based content on the Web sign their applets. This means that a majority of Java content is questionable from a security standpoint. However, Java applets run inside a protected area of memory that prohibits them from interacting with other applications or the operating system. This protected area is called a *sandbox*. The idea behind the sandbox is simple: Isolation equals security. Because the Java content is isolated from the other software components on your machine, allowing it to run inside the sandbox doesn't give it enough power to damage your system. Most unsigned Java applets are required to run inside the sandbox.

- **Run Signed Content.** Java developers have the option of signing their content (just as developers of ActiveX controls can), which permits a greater degree of trust and security regarding the source of the applet. Administrators can therefore extend the same security options to signed Java code that they can to ActiveX controls: Enable, Disable, or Prompt.

- **Access to All Files.** Because Java has restricted access to the file system, many Java applets cannot interact with user files and cannot save data. However, administrators can give Java code access to the file system so that it can read and write files to the user's hard drive. Keep in mind that unless you are using signed Java code, this can be a serious security flaw: You are providing any Java applet with the opportunity to corrupt files on the user's machine.

- **Access to All Network Addresses.** By design, Java applets can use the network to connect only to the machine the code originated from. This limitation prevents someone from writing an applet on a machine you trust, and then having that applet contact a mysterious third machine to which the applet uploads information about your computer. For most Java applications, accessing the network is not really an issue; a majority of the time, you will want to connect to the server anyway. Occasionally, however (for example, with a chat application), direct peer-to-peer connections have advantages. This option allows administrators to bypass the traditional Java networking restrictions.

- **Execute.** By design, Java programs cannot interact with programs or applications on the local file system; they cannot even launch "helper" applications. This option allows administrators to grant permission to Java applets to launch external executables. If you are using unsigned Java applets, you should enable this option with caution, especially if the applet is also granted access to the file system. Imagine this: A Java applet is allowed to write files and launch executables. The application writes a small executable to the hard drive, which installs a virus, executes it, and then removes it. Although this isn't a likely scenario, with the right security loopholes, it's a possible one.

- **Dialogs.** Java applications have limited user interface capabilities, and this includes prompting for user input. This option allows administrators to grant permission to applets to communicate with users through dialog boxes.

- **System Information.** Java applets are limited in the amount of information they can gather about your system, including configuration, installed software, Registry entries, and so on. Keeping applets from this information isolates them in their sandboxes and prevents them from doing harm to the local user's machine or from serving as reconnaissance applications for nefarious coders. Administrators can bypass this security feature to allow applets to access system information, but they should do so with caution.

- **Printing.** In accordance with Java's limited access to the local file system, printing is generally disabled for Java applets. This option allows administrators to bypass this limitation and allow Java to print.

- **Protected Scratch Space.** Some Java applets are designed to make use of disk "scratch space" for performing some functions. Using scratch space is a common programming technique and does not necessarily indicate a problem. However, unlimited access to scratch space can represent a security hole. Administrators can use the IEAK to limit Java to interaction with a protected scratch space, or a hard drive sandbox, that allows Java the use of scratch space while limiting overall exposure.

- **User Selected File Access.** Allowing Java access to files selected by the user can be a way for administrators to provide some level of file access to Java applets so that they can save and read user data, while maintaining user control. Users can select the files applets can access, and therefore can limit the exposure of their local file system. Of course, this freedom represents a slight security risk; but limited file access can be a reasonable alternate to granting Java access to the entire collection of files on the user's machine.

All these options can be configured with the IEAK Wizard, as shown in Figure 3.7.

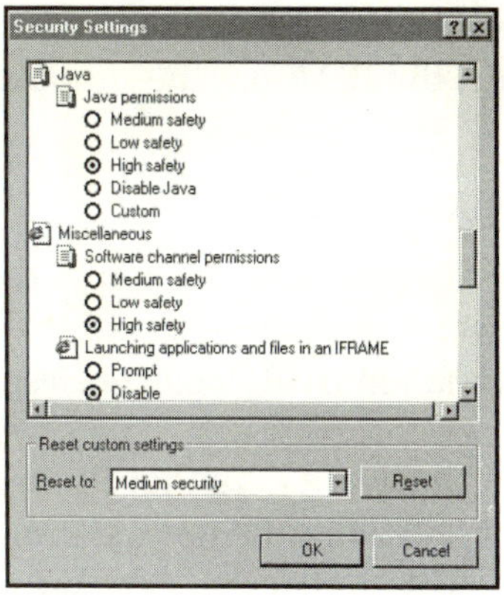

Figure 3.7

The IEAK Wizard allows the customization of many settings for running Java applets within Internet Explorer.

You can also edit many more advanced settings using the advanced editing section, shown in Figure 3.8. By editing the advanced settings for signed and unsigned content, administrators can literally control every aspect of the applet, including threads and Registry entries! This power allows a very flexible security environment, but only someone intimately familiar with Java in the browser context should edit these settings.

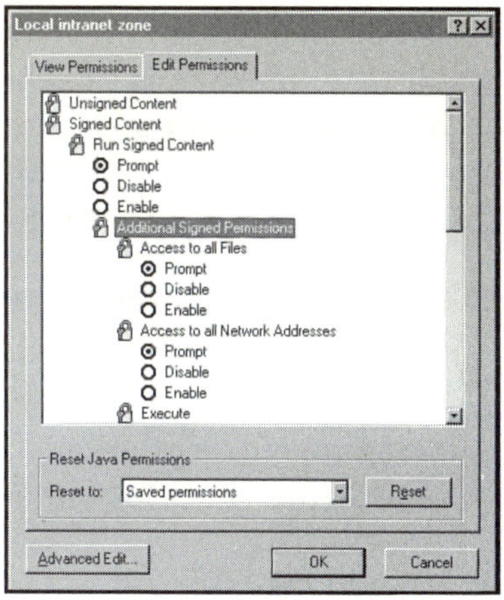

Figure 3.8

Editing advanced Java security permissions can alter settings from thread control to the Registry.

Failing to properly edit some of the more advanced settings can lead to serious security holes that can be exploited to allow access to your users' data and your network. The general settings and control offered by the IEAK will meet about 98 percent of your security needs. If you have a unique situation that requires a minute level of control over Java, you'll have to make yourself a

Java expert; take comfort in the fact that should that day ever come, the IEAK has the support you'll need.

Miscellaneous

The Miscellaneous section of the Security Settings dialog box allows administrators to control a number of settings that don't really fall into other categories:

- **Software Channel Permissions.** Because software channels allow the downloading of executable content that controls updates for user software, administrators will generally want to make sure that the information provided is secure. This option allows administrators to apply various levels of security to software channels to make sure that the update information is from trusted, reliable sources.
- **Launching Applications and Files in an `IFRAME`.** Internet Explorer features support for `IFRAME` tags, which allow the launching and display of some content from other applications within a frame in the current browser window. This is similar to a plug-in type extensibility of the browser's capabilities. Administrators can choose to disable this feature, or they can prompt the user before launching external applications so that the user is aware that he or she is not interacting directly with Internet Explorer.
- **Installation of Desktop Items.** Administrators can control user capabilities to install desktop items to be used in conjunction with the Windows Desktop Update. Installation of desktop items is prohibited; users are unable to configure their Active Desktops with new components.
- **Submit Nonencrypted Form Data.** Many sites use forms as a way of gathering input from users visiting their sites. Many of these forms are not hosted on secure servers and are therefore vulnerable to having the information stolen on the network while it is in transit. For example, if a user purchases something with a credit card from a secure form, the credit-card number is encrypted, preventing theft in transit. However, on a nonencrypted form, the credit-card number is

plain text and can easily be grabbed and used illegally. Disabling nonencrypted forms can limit users' interaction with many sites and generally isn't necessary. However, prompting users to make sure that they are aware that a form is not secure can help prevent users from unknowingly submitting data insecurely without limiting their options.

- **Drag and Drop or Copy and Paste Files.** Drag-and-drop capabilities and copying and pasting files allows users to browse the local file system with Internet Explorer. However, these functions can also give the impression that the user is viewing local data, when in fact, that data might reside on another machine on the network. Disabling or enabling this option can allow administrators to help users keep track of where they are in the network by limiting file system interaction for remote resources.

Scripting

The Scripting security settings control how Internet Explorer interacts with pages that contain scripts—in VBScript, JScript, or any other scripting language that can be added on to Internet Explorer. Using these scripting options, administrators can limit the capability of scripts to control Java applets or of Internet Explorer to run active scripts from a contacted site.

By creating security policies that consider all the options outlined above, administrators can create a security environment that works for their organization while balancing the organization's needs with users' convenience. The goal of a security policy is not to stifle the productivity of the user, but to protect the organization and user from threats they may not be aware of. Using the flexibility of Internet Explorer and the IEAK Wizard, it should be possible for any administrator to achieve that goal.

Content Ratings

The Internet frequently comes under fire as the playground of the sick and twisted—and to an extent, that is true. The nature of the Internet makes it difficult to censor content and to keep things decent for people of all ages. That said, the Internet can still be an incredible resource for productivity. Communicating with clients and vendors and gathering news and information has never been easier or faster. So how do individuals and administrators balance the good with the bad?

Many Internet vendors and sites now support self-rating systems that allow sites to rate their content based on criteria such as nudity and language. The ratings allow sites to volunteer information about their content—and allow administrators to restrict information based on these ratings. The self-rating system is becoming increasingly popular; surprisingly, many controversial sites are willing to rate their content voluntarily to help keep government restrictions to a minimum. So how do these rating systems fit into the IEAK and Internet Explorer? IE 4.0 supports content ratings based on one of the more popular self-rating systems: the Recreational Software Advisory Council (RSACi) Internet rating system.

The RSACi system is not the only system Internet Explorer can support. IE can read in `.RAT` files for other rating system configurations. However, the standard support is for RSACi ratings, and that is what is discussed primarily in this section.

To configure content ratings using the IEAK Wizard, administrators must select the Import the Current Content Ratings Settings option from the Security and Content Ratings Customization dialog box. This action imports the current ratings settings from the installation of IE on the administrative machine. Administrators can then customize the settings by clicking the Modify button.

Before configuring the content settings, administrators must enter a supervisor password as shown in Figure 3.9. This password is required to alter the ratings settings or to override content ratings. The password prevents users from modifying the content ratings on their own, bypassing the rating system established by the administrator.

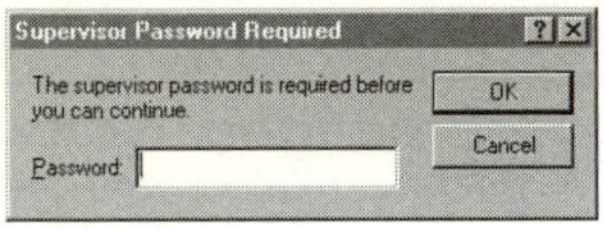

Figure 3.9

Configuring content ratings settings requires a supervisor password to prevent user modification.

As shown in Figure 3.10, the RSACi rating system is divided into four different categories:

- Language
- Nudity
- Sex
- Violence

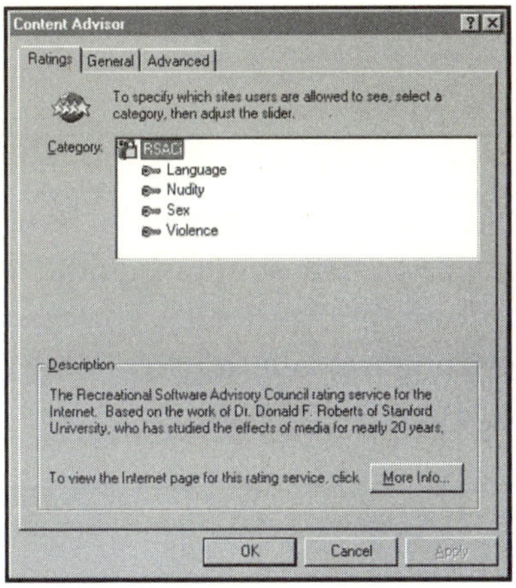

Figure 3.10

Editing the Content Rating setting with the IEAK Wizard.

Each of these categories allows for a numeric rating from 0 to 4; Level 0 is the least offensive and Level 4 is the most offensive.

Of course, no rating system can be perfect; what someone considers “frontal nudity” may be what someone else considers “provocative frontal nudity.” Opinions vary considerably. However, the RSACi ratings make an attempt to categorize most of the content users may find offensive—or certainly what is inappropriate for the workplace. A breakdown of the RSACi categories and levels is provided in Table 3.3.

Table 3.3

The Recreational Software Advisory Council Internet Rating System and Values

RSACi Category	Level 0	Level 1	Level 2	Level 3	Level 4
Language	Inoffensive Slang	Mild Expletives	Moderate Expletives	Obscene Gestures	Explicit or crude language
Nudity	None	Revealing Attire	Partial Nudity	Frontal Nudity	Provocative Frontal Nudity
Sex	None	Passionate Kissing	Clothed Sexual Touching	Non-explicit Sexual Touching	Explicit Sexual Activity
Violence	No Violence	Fighting	Killing	Killing with Blood and Gore	Wanton and Gratuitous Violence

When you have selected the level of the site you want your users to be able to view, simply slide the scale to the top level they can view, as shown in Figure 3.11. For example, placing the scale on Level 2 for Language allows users to see sites up to, and including, Level 2 Language-rated sites.

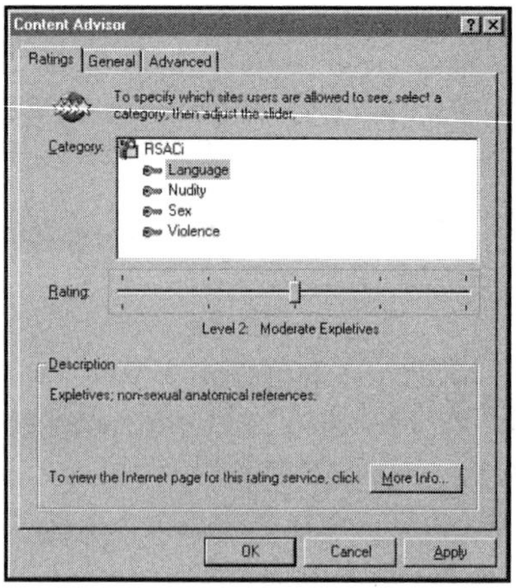

Figure 3.11

The severity of each rating setting can be manipulated on a sliding scale from 0 to 4.

On the General page of the Content Advisor dialog box, administrators can make a few adjustments to the content ratings, as shown in Figure 3.12.

Figure 3.12

Administrators can also configure password requirements and bypass content ratings.

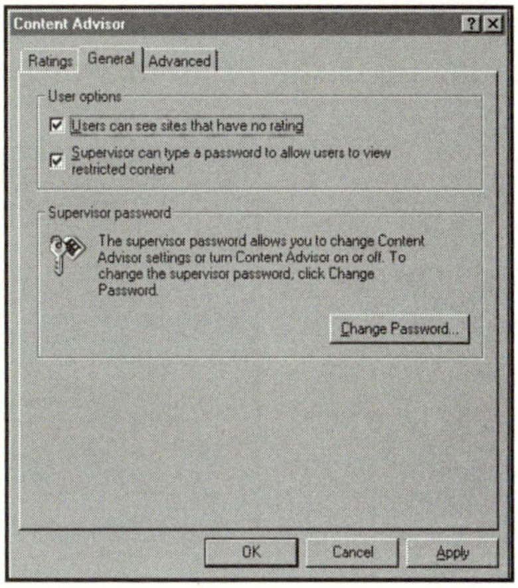

The first option is that administrators can provide access to sites that have not been rated. Because participation in RSACi ratings is voluntary, many sites are not rated. These sites may not be offensive at all; they may be business sites that haven't considered the option of (or see no need for) rating their sites. If you restrict access to sites that are not rated, you limit your users to only the sites that have voluntarily rated themselves. And because it is the controversial sites that are most likely to have voluntarily rated themselves, you might be creating a paradox regarding site ratings. Fortunately, even if you do allow users access to sites that are not rated, remember that many controversial sites do rate themselves, which greatly cuts down on the potential for abuse.

Administrators can also specify that a supervisor can override a site restriction using the supervisor password. This mechanism provides a way for administrators to allow users to access sites that might contain questionable material when they have supervisory approval.

Finally, on the General page of the Content Advisor dialog box, administrators can change the supervisor's password for altering content rating settings and overriding restrictions.

Of course, the RSACi rating system is not the only Internet rating system—and there may be even more systems in the future. There are also services that provide updates to ratings and sites over the Internet. On the Advanced page of the Content Advisor dialog box, shown in Figure 3.13, administrators can import .RAT files to configure IE for different rating systems.

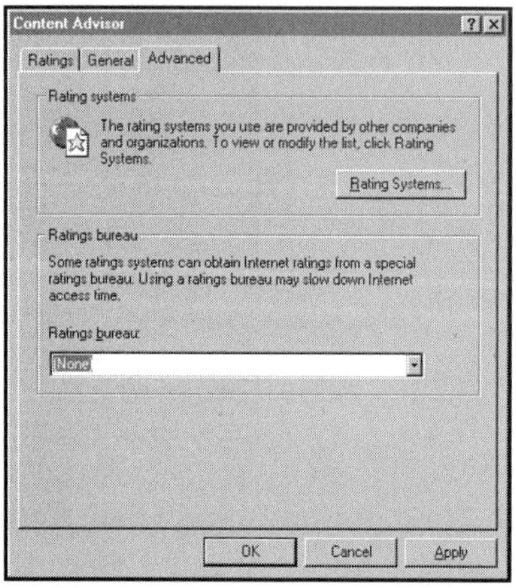

Figure 3.13

The IEAK Wizard also allows additional rating systems to be configured and imported.

Administrators can also point IE to a ratings bureau that will supply IE with content ratings updates over the Internet, if your organization chooses to subscribe to such a service.

With some advanced planning and careful consideration of what your users should and should not access, you can use content ratings to increase productivity and keep users from questionable material. It's important to realize, however, that rating systems are not foolproof nor are they a guarantee that the users will not be able to access such material. If you consider content ratings as a first step and an important safeguard, you will probably get satisfactory results with content ratings. If you are looking for a panacea to cure the ills of the Internet, you will likely be disappointed.

Managing Proxy Server Support for Internet Explorer 4.0

Many organizations want to protect their internal networks and machines from direct exposure to the Internet. At the same time, many organizations want to increase the speed and efficiency of their network resources. Fortunately, there is a mechanism that can help organizations with both of these goals: the proxy server.

Whenever a machine on your network contacts a site on the Internet, it provides the site's server with information about your network. The machine in your organization lets the site it is contacting know the machine's IP number—and that can lead to a vulnerability in your network. Another pitfall of the Internet is a user who checks the same page repeatedly within a short period of time. Each time he or she reloads the page, it causes traffic on your network. And if a co-worker is looking at the same page, your network traffic is further increased by two users who could increase their efficiency and reduce your traffic by sharing the page resource.

A *proxy server* is a mechanism that both masks your internal network from the outside and increases your network's efficiency. How does it work? It works by acting as the agent your users contact to reach the Internet, and it stores the resources the users have downloaded, as shown in Figure 3.14.

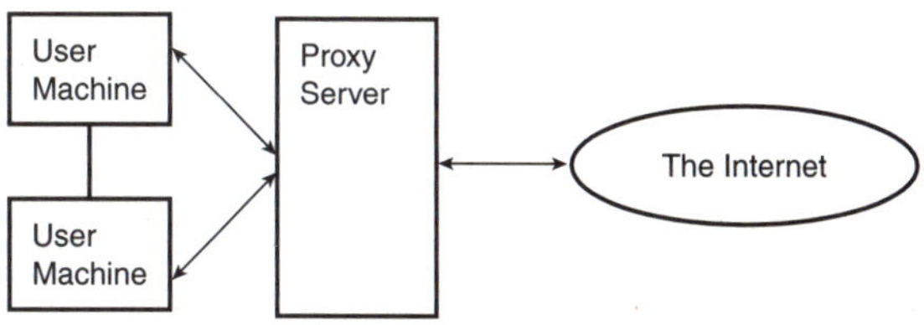

Figure 3.14

The proxy server acts as your organization's gateway to the Internet.

When a user wants to get information from a Web site or some other Internet resource, the user's browser contacts the organization's proxy server. The proxy server records the information and contacts the site on the Internet to retrieve the information. When the proxy server has the information it requested, it stores it in a local cache and then passes the information back to the user's computer. All this activity takes place at very high speeds, so the extra steps are not generally noticeable to the end user. However, there are some distinct benefits to using a proxy server:

- The user's machine is never directly exposed to the Internet.
- The proxy server is the only machine outside organizations see on your local network.
- The information is stored locally, should the user need to revisit it soon. And because the information is stored locally, other users can access the information without the proxy reconnecting to the network.

Of course, the individual configurations of how many documents the proxy caches and how long documents stay in the cache can vary, but the preceding explanation provides a good overview of what a proxy server is and how it functions.

If your organization uses a proxy server, your users will have to configure Internet Explorer to use the proxy server when they connect to the Internet. Without the proper proxy server settings, users cannot view any online content that doesn't exist on the local intranet.

The IEAK Wizard allows administrators to specify proxy server settings, as shown in Figure 3.15.

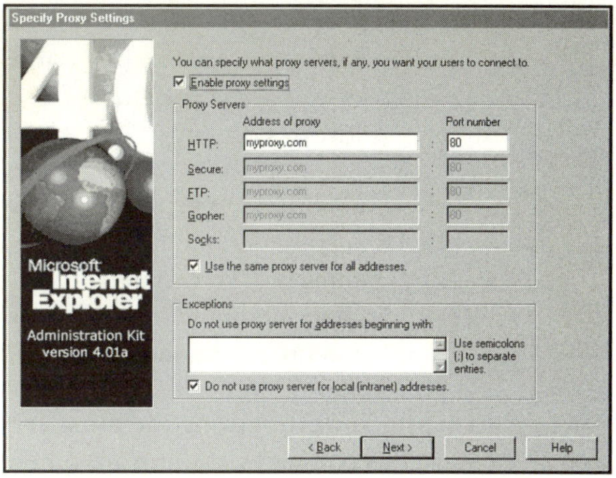

Figure 3.15

Using the IEAK Wizard to specify the proxy settings for Internet Explorer.

Using the IEAK Wizard, administrators can enable the use of proxy settings for Internet Explorer 4.0. Because proxy servers function in a way similar to other types of Internet servers, you must specify a Fully Qualified Domain Name (FQDN) and a port number for your organization's proxy server. Internet Explorer supports the following types of proxy servers:

- **HTTP.** This option is used for Web proxy servers that use the HyperText Transfer Protocol.
- **Secure.** This option is used for secure Web servers (those that use HTTPS or SSL for encrypted transactions).
- **FTP.** This option is for servers that use the File Transfer Protocol to exchange files.
- **Gopher.** This option is for Gopher servers that provide information similar to the Web.
- **SOCKS.** This option is for proxy servers that support the SOCKS protocol, which is a limited type of firewall protocol that can be used with some servers.

Administrators can also choose to use the same proxy settings for all proxy services (some proxy servers support multiple protocols on a single server).

Finally, the IEAK Wizard offers a way for users to bypass the proxy settings: The administrator can enter addresses that bypass the proxy server or can select the Do Not Use Proxy Server for Local (Intranet) Addresses option.

By entering an address to bypass the proxy server, you are instructing IE to contact directly any server containing your entered text string. Similarly, if you enable proxy bypass for local addresses, any address entered into the browser that is not an FQDN or does not contain any periods is contacted directly.

This method of configuring the proxy server is the simplest and the most direct. However, there are times when it is necessary to change the configuration of the proxy server. Doing this after your browser has been deployed can be a hassle and can lead to user problems if users do not alter their proxy settings correctly.

Because many organizations must alter the configuration of older browsers (or even new browsers) after the browsers have been installed, the IEAK and Internet Explorer support a mechanism called *automatic browser configuration.* Automatic browser configuration allows administrators to alter the configuration of a user's browser without forcing the user to reinstall the browser. The next section takes a look at how IE and the IEAK support auto configuration, and how you can use autoconfiguration to manage IE and proxy settings.

Managing Automatic Configuration Using the IEAK Profile Manager

From an administrative standpoint, one of the most frustrating problems with today's browsers and the rapid pace of changes with the Internet is managing browser deployment. New versions of the browser, new custom features, bug fixes, updates—all these things can create a nightmare for IS organizations struggling to keep users current while keeping services running smoothly. Installing and updating a browser as complex as Internet Explorer can take valuable time—time that could be used by the IS organization on other projects, and time that could be used by the employee on something productive.

Beginning with IE 3 and continuing with IE 4.0, Microsoft has supported a process that allows administrators to alter the configuration files for the IE browser and then to have that information downloaded by the browser and updated automatically. This process is called automatic browser configuration.

There are two main components to automatic browser configuration:

- Automatic proxy management
- Component and browser configuration

Automatic proxy management allows administrators to configure an autoproxy file that contains rules and functions about how the browser is to use proxy services. Then instead of hard-coding proxy information into the browser configuration, administrators maintain an autoproxy file that the browser uses to configure itself for proxy services.

Component and browser configuration uses a similar mechanism to update browser settings and custom component installations. By using the IEAK Profile Manager, administrators can build a special `.INS` file that contains configuration information for the browser installation. The browser is then configured to check this file on the network periodically and updates its configuration based on the contents of the file.

The next few sections look at the autoproxy configuration mechanism, `.INS` files, and the IEAK Profile Manager. In combination, these tools allow an almost completely remote management scheme for IE 4, freeing up administrative and end-user time and energy.

JScript Autoproxy

Organizations may often have a need to change proxy settings (for example, when a new proxy server is introduced or proxy settings change to better meet user demands). However, asking users to alter their own proxy settings can lead to misconfigurations and more headaches for users and IS. To compensate for the need to change proxy settings without troubling the user—and without the need to reinstall IE—IE 4.0 supports autoproxy configuration.

The autoproxy mechanism is simple:

1. Administrators use the IEAK Wizard to configure IE to look for an autoproxy file (a `.JS` or `.PAC` file).
2. IE locates the file on the network and uses its contents in place of the traditional proxy settings.
3. The administrator then updates the network copy of the `.JS` or `.PAC` configuration file, and browsers are automatically updated at the predetermined interval.

Figure 3.16 shows the IEAK Wizard and the configuration for autoproxy.

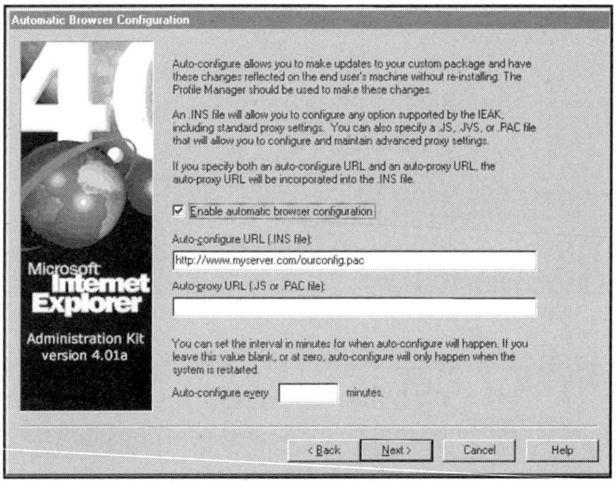

Figure 3.16

Specifying the location (URL) for autoproxy configuration files using the IEAK Wizard.

On the IEAK Wizard's Automatic Browser Configuration screen, you enter the URL that points to your local `.JS` or `.PAC` file, including the filename. Here's a sample URL:

```
http://myserver/proxy/myproxy.pac
```

This URL tells Internet Explorer where the autoproxy file is located on the network.

Note

> Make sure that the autoproxy file is correctly written and installed in the location you've specified on your Web server before you begin browser deployment.

You can also specify the interval at which IE should check the file for updates. You can specify this interval in minutes, or you can leave the field blank, which forces IE to check the autoproxy file each time IE is restarted. Keep in mind that having the browser check the autoproxy file too frequently can unnecessarily increase network traffic, especially if your configuration changes only every few weeks.

.JS and .PAC Files

After you have configured IE to use an autoproxy file, you must create the file and place it on your Web server. IE can use both .JS and .PAC files; both have the same format and use JScript to construct the rules for when to use certain proxy settings.

Note

> The contents of autoproxy files are written in JScript; therefore, the .JS extension is accepted by Internet Explorer as the file type. However, Netscape also supports autoproxy configuration and uses JScript as well. Netscape, however, supports .PAC as the file extension for its autoproxy files. Therefore, IE accepts both .JS and .PAC files to increase compatibility.

The format of the autoproxy file is simple: it is a text file that contains the JScript code that determines how the browser should connect when given a specific URL. Here's a sample autoproxy file:

```
function FindProxyForURL(url, host) {
     if (isResolvable(host))
   return "DIRECT";
     else
        return "PROXY myproxy:80";
}
```

In this example, the JScript function is passed a URL and a host name. The script checks to see whether the host name can be resolved into an IP address. If it can, the host is contacted directly with the `return "DIRECT";` statement; if the host name cannot be resolved, the script points the browser to the proxy server with the statement `return "PROXY myproxy:80";` (where *myproxy* is the host name of your server).

You can customize your autoproxy file to contain any number of combinations or functions for determining the proxy to be used or to be bypassed. Here are some examples:

- Connect to a proxy if the host contains any periods:

```
function FindProxyForURL(url, host) {
     if (dnsDomainLevels(host) > 0) {
        return "PROXY myproxy:80";
     }
        return "DIRECT";
}
```

- Connect to a different proxy for different protocols:

```
function FindProxyForURL(url, host) {
     if (url.substring(0, 5) == "http:") {
        return "PROXY myproxy:80";
     }
     else if (url.substring(0, 4) == "ftp:") {
        return "PROXY myFTPproxy:80";
     }
     else if (url.substring(0, 7) == "gopher:") {
        return "PROXY myGOPHERproxy";
     }
     else if (url.substring(0, 6) == "https:") {
        return "PROXY mySECUREproxy:8080";
     }
     else { return "DIRECT";
     }
}
```

If you are unfamiliar with JScript, there are many texts available, such as *Sams Teach Yourself JavaScript 1.3 in 21 Days, Third Edition*

(Sams Publishing) that you can use to learn more about the scripting language.

Here's one final example, in the form of a commented, fully functional .PAC or .JS file:

```
/* A JScript Auto-Proxy Configuration File.
   This file simply checks to see if a host is local,
   and if it is, it connects directly. If it is not,
   the connection is made via the proxy. */
function FindProxyForURL(url, host) {
   if (isPlainHostName(host))   //Check the host name
      return "DIRECT";          //If it has no periods, connect
directly
   else
      return "PROXY myproxy:80";  //Otherwise, use the proxy
}
 //Make sure to substitute myproxy for your proxy name
```

This is a very simple file, but it gets the job done. It gets the host name from the browser and then examines it to determine whether the host is local or not. If it is local, the browser is instructed to connect directly. If the host is not local, the browser is passed the proxy information and is instructed to connect through the proxy. Configuring an autoproxy file can be this simple. This file, placed on your server at the previously specified autoproxy file URL, allows proxy connections without any configuration input from the user. You can modify this file using any of the other sample scripts in this chapter, and the user's configurations would reflect the changes automatically.

Preparing for Autoconfiguration

Now that you have an idea of how autoproxy configuration works, you are ready to move on to the configuration of the browser and components using automatic browser configuration.

You must go through a few steps to prepare your build to use automatic browser configuration: You must set up the build, sign and create updated .CAB files, and place the files on your server.

Preparing the Build

Preparing your custom build of IE to use automatic browser configuration is a very straightforward process. From the IEAK Wizard's Automatic Browser Configuration screen (refer to Figure 3.16), simply click the Enable Automatic Browser Configuration check box.

You must also enter the URL for the location of the `.INS` file you will be creating in the Auto-Configure URL (`.INS` File) text field.

Finally, you must enter the interval at which you want IE to check the `.INS` file for updates. This interval is specified in minutes; however, if you leave this field blank, IE will check for updates each time it is restarted.

Server Preparations

For your automatic browser configuration to function properly, you must also prepare the automatic configuration files on your Web server. You must create the directory for the URL where the `.INS` and the associated `.CAB` files for the automatic update will be hosted. For example, if you have entered `http://myserver/autoconfig/` as the URL for the location of the `.INS` and `.CAB` files, you must make sure that you have an `autoconfig` directory on your Web server. You must also ensure that when you have finished creating the `.INS` and `.CAB` files (as outlined in the next section), that they are placed in this location on the server. The files must also be readable by the users who will be accessing them, just as would any files on your server that are available over the Web.

To avoid potential conflict, it is a good idea *not* to edit the `.INS` and `.CAB` files directly on your server. That is, when you are going to create new autoconfiguration files, you should do so in another location, and then transfer them to the Web site when they are completed. This approach helps eliminate potential problems with users trying to connect and update their versions of IE while you are in the process of creating a new update.

The IEAK Profile Manager

The Internet Explorer Administration Kit is not simply the IEAK Wizard. The IEAK also installs the IEAK Profile Manager, which is a tool that can easily be used to create customized configuration changes, after you have used the IEAK Wizard to create your custom build.

The idea behind the IEAK Profile Manager is that after you have created your custom build, there may be times when you want to update your configuration. To update the configuration, you can use the IEAK Wizard to create a completely new installation, which you might do for future use, anyway. However, what about updating users who have already installed Internet Explorer? Requiring them to completely reinstall IE for configuration changes is cumbersome and annoying—especially because IE has a mechanism in place for updating itself: automatic browser configuration.

You know that the automatic browser configuration mechanism uses `.INS` files to control the information that is updated. How do you create those `.INS` files? That's where the IEAK Profile Manager comes in.

You can use the IEAK Profile Manager, shown in Figure 3.17, to alter the `.INS` file created with your customized installation of Internet Explorer.

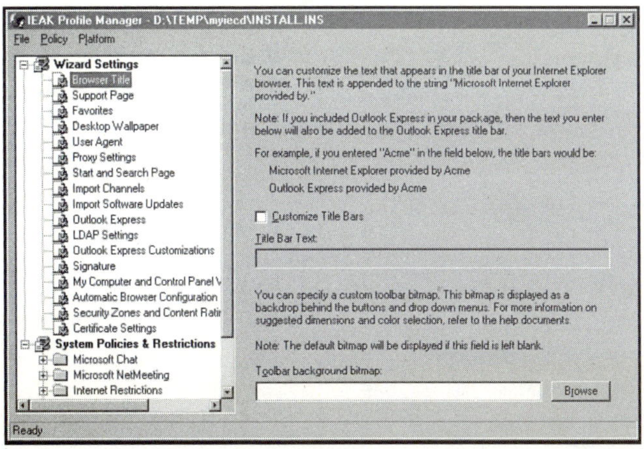

Figure 3.17

The IEAK Profile Manager allows administrators to create customized `.INS` *update files.*

How does the IEAK Profile Manager work? It's a pretty simple process:

- **Creating the original `.INS` files.** When you create your customized build of Internet Explorer using the IEAK Wizard, the build creates a number of files used to control the configuration of your customized installation. These files include the `.INF` files used to configure customized components and the master `.INS` file used to customize your entire installation.

  The original `.INS` file for your customized installation is in the directory you have specified as the location in which the IEAK Wizard is to place your custom build. You can then launch the IEAK Profile Manager and use it to make changes to the `.INS` file and your build's configuration.

- **Editing the `.INS` file with the IEAK Profile Manager.** After you have loaded your build's `.INS` file, you can edit all the attributes you specified earlier in the IEAK Wizard. The available attributes are displayed in a tree on the left side of the IEAK Profile Manager (see Figure 3.18).

  When you click a configurable attribute, the right side of the screen presents you with screens similar to those in the IEAK Wizard, allowing you to change the configuration information you have already entered.

  You can also edit the System Policies and Restrictions section to alter the security and usage settings for Internet Explorer and other components.

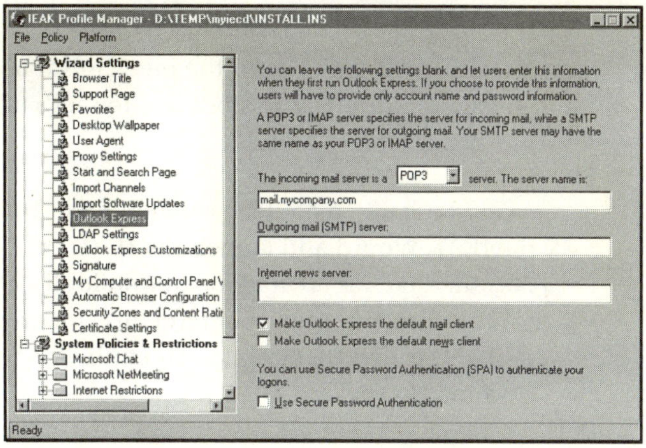

Figure 3.18

Using the IEAK Profile Manager to edit settings for your custom build.

- **Creating an update `.INS` file and `.CAB` files.** After you finish using the IEAK Profile Manager to make changes to your browser's configuration, you can save the new `.INS` file to a separate location. The IEAK Profile Manager then creates the new `.INS` file and the necessary `.CAB` files that contain any new `.INF` files required to customize components. For example, if you alter the channel settings, a new `.INF` file for channels is created. This information must be stored in a `.CAB` file that is used by automatic browser configuration to get the new information. The IEAK Profile Manager creates these files as well.

- **Updating the browser.** After you have created the `.INS` file and the `.CAB` files for your update, you must place the files on the server in the directory you specified in the Automatic Browser Update URL filed in the IEAK Wizard. After you correctly place the files, users' browsers can download the updated `.INS` file (which tells the browser which settings to change) and the `.CAB` files (which contain the `.INF` files that allow the browser to change the configuration of installed components).

This may sound a bit confusing at first, but the next few sections look more closely at using the IEAK Profile Manager. We'll also include a discussion of the file formats floating out there to give you a better idea of what they do.

Using the IEAK Profile Manager

Now that you understand the mechanism behind the IEAK Profile Manager and what it can be used for, let's take a look at the actual use of the tool.

After you have created a custom build of Internet Explorer, quit the IEAK Wizard and launch the IEAK Profile Manager. Open the `.INS` file that was created in your build directory. This file most likely is located in the root level directory for your build and is probably called `INSTALL.INS`. Open the file to begin creating your custom `.INS` file.

The IEAK Profile Manager's interface is very straightforward. Attributes you can edit are divided into two broad categories:

- **Wizard Settings.** These are the same customization settings you altered to create your custom build using the IEAK Wizard. You can click the + to expand the listing of options and then click a setting (such as Browser Title) to edit the value of that setting.
- **System Policies and Restrictions.** The System Policies and Restrictions settings are configuration options for the various custom components you have chosen to install, such as Outlook Express or the Web desktop. Again, you can click a folder and expand it to see the options you can edit.

The Wizard Settings you can alter are shown in Table 3.4; the System Policies and Restrictions settings are listed in Table 3.5. You can also import new policies from the Policy menu, which allows you to read in policies from existing `.ADM` files. Finally, you can alter the platform of your new `.INS` file from the Platform menu.

Table 3.4

Internet Explorer IEAK Wizard Settings That Can Be Modified Using the IEAK Profile Manager

Wizard Setting	Description
Browser Title	Alters the settings for customized IE and installer titles
Support Page	Alters settings for the default IE support page
Favorites	Specifies a preinstalled favorites list for users
Desktop Wallpaper	Selects the bitmap used as the default desktop wallpaper
User Agent	Specifies the user agent string passed from the IE client to servers
Proxy Settings	Alters the proxy server configuration for IE
Start and Search Pages	Specifies the default start and search pages for IE
Import Channels	Imports new channel subscriptions and settings from the IE version installed on the administrative machine
Import Software Updates	Imports new software channel subscriptions and settings from the IE version installed on the administrative machine
Outlook Express	Alters customization settings for the appearance of Outlook Express mail and news servers
LDAP Settings	Alters settings for a Lightweight Directory Access Protocol server
Outlook Express Customizations	Alters customizations for Outlook Express client, such as a welcome message and the InfoPane

continues

Table 3.4 Continued

Wizard Setting	Description
Signatures	Adds custom signatures to the Outlook Express mail and news client
My Computer and Control Panel Webview Customization	Provides custom .HTT files to control user access to My Computer and the Control Panel
Automatic Browser Configuration	Specifies URLs for ABC and autoproxy updates
Security Zones and Content Ratings	Configures customized settings for security zones and applies content ratings to sites
Certificate Settings	Alters the installed certificate authorities and trusted publishers for IE

Table 3.5 ***Internet Explorer System Policies and Restriction Settings That Can Be Modified Using the IEAK Profile Manager***

System Policies and Restrictions	Description
Microsoft Chat	Settings for Microsoft Chat, including Chat Servers and so on
Microsoft NetMeeting	Settings for Microsoft NetMeeting, including protocols, default configurations, and usage restrictions
Internet Restrictions	Lock-down settings for Internet configurations, preventing the user from altering many IE configuration options
Internet Settings	Preconfigure Internet settings, such as default fonts and colors

System Policies and Restrictions	Description
Outlook Express	Customizes user options for the Outlook Express client
Web Desktop	Restricts changes for the Web desktop configuration, including shell features and components
Subscriptions	Establishes policies for channel subscriptions, such as maximum download size and update times

After you have changed any of the settings you want to alter for your update, save the files by selecting Save As from the File menu, as shown in Figure 3.19. You are prompted to specify the full path (including the filename) of the `.INS` file you are creating. Where you save it doesn't matter because you will be transferring it to your server.

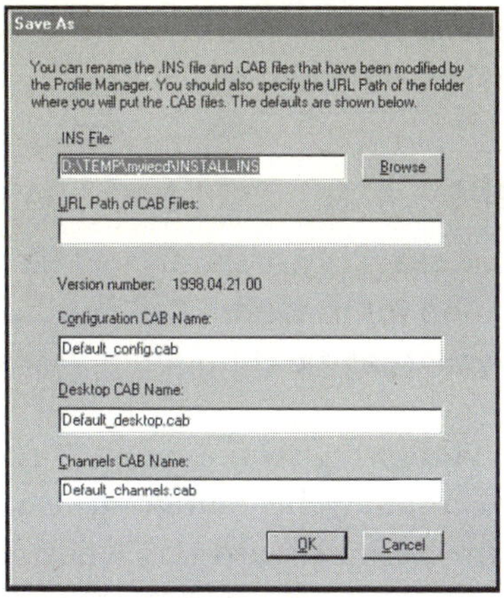

Figure 3.19

Saving your customized `.INS` files and creating the necessary `.CAB` files.

Next, you must enter the URL path of the `.CAB` files the IEAK Profile Manager is going to create. The actual `.CAB` files themselves are created in the same directory as the `.INS` file. However, in the URL Path of CAB Files text box, you should specify the location *where the `.CAB` files will be placed on your server.* The IEAK Profile Manager saves the location of your `.CAB` files in the `.INS` file, so you must enter the correct server URL here.

You can change the names of the configuration, desktop, and channels .CAB files if you want. The contents of these files are unaffected, and the new names are written to the .INS file. If you are worried about confusion later, simply use the default names; if you want to develop your own naming system to keep track of revisions, enter the new names here.

When you are finished, click OK and the IEAK Profile Manager goes to work. It creates the .INS file and the .CAB files in the directory you specified, and it places all the new data needed to complete the update into those files. Once IEAK Profile Manager is done, exit from it and transfer the files to your Web server.

After the .INS and .CAB files are in place on your server, the automatic update process is complete. Following the schedule you specified, users' versions of IE will contact the Web server at your specified URL. They will check the .INS file to see whether it has changed; if it has, IE will automatically download the new .INS and .CAB files and then install the changes. If there has been no update, IE goes about business as usual, using the most current version available.

.INS, .ADM, .INF, and .CAB Files

The .INS files are simply text files divided into sections for configuration information. Each of these sections contains the parameters that can be configured in that section and their values.

The following section of an .INS file section is called ActiveSetup and contains the configuration information for customizing the Active Setup Wizard with a custom title and a bitmap. As you can see, the section contains a WizardTitle and a WizardBitmap variable, each with a value. That's all there is to it.

```
[ActiveSetup]
WizardTitle=Vervet Logic IE Install
WizardBitmap="ourlogo.bmp"
```

If you are familiar with Windows .INI files, you will notice the similarity of the format of .INS files. Because the file is a text file, you can even edit the file by hand. However, it's best to leave the editing of the file to the IEAK Profile Manger. The format of the file isn't specific, but the phrasing of values is important to the configuration.

Listing 3.1 shows a sample `.INS` file for a customized build. Each of the sections corresponds to settings that administrators can configure using the IEAK Wizard and the IEAK Profile Manager.

Listing 3.1

Sample `.INS` File for a Customized Internet Explorer 4.0 Build

```
[Branding]
Type=2
WizardVersion=4.73.2226.0
CompanyName=Vervet Logic
Wizard_Version=4.73.2226.0
Custom_Key=C349993
Language Locale=EN
Language ID=1033
CMBitmapPath=
CMBitmapName=
CMProfilePath=
CMProfileName=
CMUseCustom=0
Version=1,0,0,5
Configuration ID=
Add on Url=
Window_Title_CN=Vervet Logic
Window_Title=Microsoft Internet Explorer provided by Vervet Logic
Toolbar Bitmap=D:\TEMP\vervet.bmp
IE4 Welcome Msg=1
User Agent=Vervet Logic Example Browser
Serverless=0
NoDial=0
SignupCustomDir=D:\Program Files\IEAK\reskit\isp\server\client
```

continues

Listing 3.1 Continued

```
Silent Install=0
InstallDir=%w\Internet Explorer
WebIntegrated=1
WebChoice=0
Platform=2
CabsURLPath=D:\TEMP\
InsVersion=1998.04.02.00
[Batch]
Build_CD=1
Build_Floppy=0
Build_MultiFloppy=0
Build_Win31=0
[ActiveSetup]
WizardTitle=Vervet Logic IE Install
WizardBitmap=""
[ActiveSetupSites]
SiteUrl0=http://DownloadURL0/WIN95_NT/ie4site
SiteName0=Download Site 0
SiteRegion0=North America
SiteUrl1=http://DownloadURL1/WIN95_NT/ie4site
SiteName1=Download Site 1
SiteRegion1=North America
SiteUrl2=/WIN95_NT/ie4site
SiteName2=
SiteRegion2=
SiteUrl3=/WIN95_NT/ie4site
SiteName3=
SiteRegion3=
SiteUrl4=/WIN95_NT/ie4site
SiteName4=
SiteRegion4=
SiteUrl5=/WIN95_NT/ie4site
SiteName5=
SiteRegion5=
```

```
SiteUrl6=/WIN95_NT/ie4site
SiteName6=
SiteRegion6=
SiteUrl7=/WIN95_NT/ie4site
SiteName7=
SiteRegion7=
SiteUrl8=/WIN95_NT/ie4site
SiteName8=
SiteRegion8=
SiteUrl9=/WIN95_NT/ie4site
SiteName9=
SiteRegion9=
[Internet_Mail]
Window_Title=Outlook Express provided by Vervet Logic
Use_IMAP=No
SMTP_Server=mail.mcp.com
POP_Server=mail.mcp.com
Default_Client=Yes
Logon_Using_SPA=No
Infopane=
Welcome_Message=
Welcome_Name=admin@mcp.com
Welcome_Address=info@mcp.com
Infopane_Bitmap=
Install_Mail_16=0
[URL]
Home_Page=http://www.mcp.com
Search_Page=http://home.microsoft.com/search/search.asp
Help_Page=http://www.vervet.com
Quick_Link_1_Name=Channel Guide
Quick_Link_1=http://www.iechannelguide.com/guide/en/en_us.asp
Quick_Link_2_Name=Customize Links
Quick_Link_2=res://ie4tour.dll/qlinks.htm
Quick_Link_3_Name=Internet Explorer News
Quick_Link_3=http://www.microsoft.com/ie/ie40
```

continues

Listing 3.1 Continued

```
Quick_Link_4_Name=Internet Start
Quick_Link_4=http://home.microsoft.com
Quick_Link_5_Name=New Quick Link 6
Quick_Link_5=http://www.new6
NoWelcome=0
FirstHomePage=
Signup=Specify Location of HTML or CGI Script
AutoConfig=1
AutoConfigURL=
AutoConfigJSURL=
AutoConfigTime=
Quick_Link_6_Name=New Quick Link 7.url
Quick_Link_6=http://www.new7
Quick_Link_7_Name=
Quick_Link_7=
[Favorites]
[DesktopObjects]
Desktop Wallpaper Path=vervet.bmp
Channel Bar=0
Desktop Component URL=
Desktop Component Local Flag=0
Delete Old Channels=0
NumChannels=44
ImportChannels=1
ImportObjects=0
ImportToolbars=0
My Computer Path=
Control Panel Path=
Option=1
[Proxy]
HTTP_Proxy_Server=proxy.vervet.com:80
FTP_Proxy_Server=proxy.vervet.com:80
Gopher_Proxy_Server=proxy.vervet.com:80
Secure_Proxy_Server=proxy.vervet.com:80
```

```
Socks_Proxy_Server=proxy.vervet.com:80
Use_Same_Proxy=1
Proxy_Override=<local>
Proxy_Enable=1
[Entry]
Entry_Name=Internet Signup
[Phone]
Phone_Number=7037957
Area_Code=206
Country_Code=1
Country_ID=1
Dial_As_Is=No
[User]
Requires_Logon=Yes
[Server]
SW_Compress=Yes
PW_Encrypt=No
Type=PPP
Negotiate_TCP/IP=Yes
[TCP/IP]
Specify_Server_Address=No
IP_Header_Compress=Yes
Gateway_On_Remote=Yes
DNS_Address=0.0.0.0
DNS_Alt_Address=0.0.0.0
[Scripting]
Path32=
Name32=
[Internet_News]
NNTP_Server=news.mcp.com
Default_Client=Yes
Logon_Using_SPA=No
Logon_Required=0
[LDAP]
FriendlyName=
```

continues

Listing 3.1 Continued

```
Server=
HomePage=
SearchBase=
Bitmap=
CheckNames=0
AuthType=0
[ExtRegInf]
chat=*,chat.inf,DefaultInstall
conf=*,conf.inf,DefaultInstall
inetset=*,inetset.inf,DefaultInstall
oe=*,oe.inf,DefaultInstall
Desktop=
Toolbars=*,toolbar.inf,DefaultInstall
SITECERT=
AUTHCODE=*,AUTHCODE.inf,DefaultInstall
RATINGS=*,RATINGS.inf,DefaultInstall
SECZONES=*,SECZONES.inf,DefaultInstall
inetres=*,inetres.inf,DefaultInstall
shell=*,shell.inf,DefaultInstall
subs=*,subs.inf,DefaultInstall
[Wallpaper]
NumFiles=0
file0=bkgd.bmp
ComponentsPositioned=10
[Quick Launch Files]
NumFiles=0
[Security Imports]
ImportSITECERT=0
ImportAUTHCODE=1
ImportRATINGS=1
ImportSECZONES=1
Win16SiteCerts=0
[Signature]
Use_Signature=1
```

```
Signature_Text=Custom Sig.
[Mail_Signature]
Use_Signature=1
Use_Mail_For_News=0
Signature_Text=Custom Sig
[Subscriptions]
{5C832350-CF51-01bC-7600-00000A000000}=http://www.microsoft.com/ie/
➥ie40/download/cdf/ie4updates-en.cdf
[SWUpdates]
SoftwareUpdates=0
[Custom Wallpaper]
NumFiles=1
file0=vervet.bmp
[Custom Branding]
Branding=D:\TEMP\/Default_config.cab,1998.04.02.00,-1,
[Custom Desktop]
Desktop=D:\TEMP\/Default_desktop.cab,1998.04.02.00,-1,
[Custom Channels]
Channels=D:\TEMP\/Default_channels.cab,1998.04.02.00,-1,
```

In addition to the `.INS` file that controls the configuration of Internet Explorer options, System Polices and Restrictions are controlled through Windows administration file templates (`.ADM` files). When you alter the settings for policies using the IEAK Profile Manager, the changes from the `.ADM` template files are incorporated into `.INF` files built into the `.CAB` files for each component. If you are familiar with the `.ADM` format, you can modify the files directly to create custom templates for system policies. The different `.ADM` files and the components they control are listed in Table 3.6.

Table 3.6

Internet Explorer .ADM Files and Components

Components	Template File	Description
NetMeeting	CONF.ADM and CONF.INF	NetMeeting access configuration information
Internet Properties	INETRES.ADM and INETRES.INF	User Internet settings
Outlook Express	OE.ADM and OE.INF	Specifies policies regarding Internet news and mail usage
Web Desktop	SHELL.ADM and SHELL.INF	Specifies access policies to shell features
Channels and Subscriptions	INETRES.ADM, SUBS.ADM and INETRES.INF, SUBS.INF	Specifies system policies for channel and site subscriptions
Microsoft Chat	CHAT.ADM and CHAT.INF	System policies for access to Chat features and functions
IE Advanced Settings	INETRES.ADM and INETRES.INF	Specifies IE advanced settings and system policy lock downs
Internet Code Download	INETRES.ADM and INETRES.INF	Specifies system settings for Internet code download
Active Desktop	SHELL.ADM and SHELL.INF	Specifies System Polices and Restrictions for desktop components

When you launch the IEAK Profile Manager, the application reads the template files (.ADM) created during your customized build. When you use the IEAK Profile Manager to make changes to System Policies and Settings, you are altering these profiles. To incorporate those changes into the user's browser, the IEAK Profile Manager creates new .INF files that are used to configure the custom components.

The trick is that these new `.INF` files must be delivered to the browser in an easy-to-access and easy-to-download file format. The Microsoft Cabinet (`.CAB`) file format is how the automatic browser configuration mechanism achieves this goal. By building all the possible `.INF` files into `.CAB` files, the IEAK can create three `.CAB` files that can be quickly downloaded with the new `.INS` file. In this way, the browser can access all the files and information it needs to complete an update, without having to download more than a handful of files.

By default, when you create an update with the IEAK Profile Manager, you produce four files:

- The new `.INS` file
- `Default_config.CAB`
- `Default_desktop.CAB`
- `Default_channels.CAB`

Depending on the options you selected, some of these `.CAB` files may not be created (for example, `Default_desktop` and `Default_channels` may not be created). Otherwise, these are the files you place on your server; these are the files IE downloads to update itself.

Exercises

The following exercises are designed to give you step-by-step, hands-on guidance through some of the setup tasks outlined in this chapter. Some of these exercises require you to be at a particular section of the IEAK Wizard or the IEAK Profile Manager. If that is the case, simply follow the guidelines through the wizard until you reach the section described by the exercise.

Of course, the specifics of how you approach each exercise may vary depending on the type of deployment you are developing. However, these exercises present the guidelines you need to step your way through the task at hand.

Exercise 3.1: Modifying a Security Zone

The first exercise covers modifying a security zone. Because the most commonly used zone is also the zone with the most potential for problems, this exercise modifies that zone: the Internet Zone. You are going to edit the security zone for the Internet using the IEAK Profile Manager. The steps for modifying the zone with the IEAK Profile Manager are the same as those for the IEAK Wizard.

1. Launch the IEAK Profile Manager and expand the Wizard Settings category.

2. Select Open from the File menu and then select the `.INS` file from the folder in which you created your custom build.

3. From the list of settings, select Security Zones and Content Ratings Customization.

4. Under the Security Zones options, select Customize Security Zones Settings and click the Modify Settings button.

5. You should see the Security dialog box. From the Zone list, select Internet Zone.

6. Under the Zone combo box, you should see the settings for the Internet Zone; the level of security selected by default will most likely be Medium (More Secure). Assume that you

want to create a more secure environment for the Internet Zone. Click High (Most Secure) to select this level of security for the Internet Zone.

7. Click OK to exit the Security dialog box. You have altered the security zone settings for the Internet Zone to create a more secure environment.

Exercise 3.2: Setting a Content Rating for Business Use

In this exercise, you are going to create a content rating configuration for business use. You won't allow access to severe language, sex, nudity, or violence. But because many business sites are not rated at all, you want to configure the content ratings to allow access to sites that are not rated. You are going to edit the content ratings for the Internet using the IEAK Profile Manager. The steps for modifying the content rating with the IEAK Profile Manager are the same as those for the IEAK Wizard.

1. Launch the IEAK Profile Manager and expand the Wizard Settings category.
2. Select Open from the File menu and then select the `.INS` file from the folder in which you created your custom build.
3. From the list of settings, select Security Zones and Content Ratings Customization.
4. From the Content Ratings section, select the Import the Current Content Ratings Settings option and click the Modify button.
5. You are prompted to create a password as the supervisor so that the content ratings cannot be altered by the user without a supervisor override. Enter a password and click OK.
6. You see the Content Advisor dialog box. Use this dialog box to set the levels for ratings that users will be allowed to view. Because you are configuring this rating specification for business use, you are going to be fairly restrictive.

continues

Exercise 3.2: Continued

7. In the Category list, click Language. Slide the rating scale to Level 2: Moderate Expletives.
8. In the Category list, click Nudity. Slide the rating scale to Level 0: None.
9. In the Category list, click Sex. Slide the rating scale to Level 0: None.
10. In the Category list, click Violence. Slide the rating scale to Level 1: Fighting.
11. Click the General tab to display the general settings.
12. Under User Options, click both options:
    - Users Can See Sites That Have No Rating
    - Supervisor Can Type a Password to Allow Users to View Restricted Content

    These options ensure that users can still reach business sites that don't self-rate using RSACi, and that a supervisor can override any restricted sites.
13. Click OK in the Content Advisor dialog box. Your new ratings policy is now complete.

Exercise 3.3: Editing Proxy Settings with the IEAK Profile Manager

Proxy servers allow you to mask users' machines and your network behind one machine that acts as a liaison to the Internet. However, for IE to work properly with a proxy server, you must configure Internet Explorer to work with your proxy settings. You are going to edit the proxy settings for Internet Explorer using the IEAK Profile Manager. The steps for modifying the proxy settings with the IEAK Profile Manager are the same as those for the IEAK Wizard.

1. Launch the IEAK Profile Manager and expand the Wizard Settings category.

2. Select Open from the File menu and then select the `.INS` file from the folder in which you created your custom build.
3. From the list of settings, select Proxy Settings.
4. Select Enable Proxy Settings.
5. Enter the address information for your proxy server (for example `myproxy.mycompany.com` on port `80`).
6. Repeat this process for each proxy server at your organization. If you use the same address for all proxy services, click the Use the Same Proxy Server for All Addresses check box.
7. Enter the exception for sites you do not want IE to use the proxy server to connect to (for example, `mycompany.com`). If you want to exclude sites that exist on the intranet, select the Do Not Use Proxy Server for Local (Intranet) Addresses check box.
8. That's it. Your proxy settings are configured, and you can edit other settings or exit from the IEAK Profile Manager.

Review Questions

The review questions in this section can help you assess your understanding of the terms, concepts, and objectives covered in this chapter. These questions are written in the style of the questions presented on the MCSE exam and are an excellent way to prepare yourself for the material you will see on the exam. After you complete the review questions, you will find the answer to each question—along with an explanation of the answer—in the following section.

1. To establish a trusted connection with a site, IE must have been configured with:

   A. A root certificate from a valid certificate authority

   B. Public key encryption technology

   C. Security zone settings

   D. Proxy server settings

2. To assure users that the applications they download are from a trusted source and have not been altered, administrators can leverage

   A. Proxy server settings

   B. Certificate authorities

   C. Public key encryption

   D. Authenticode

3. Sites accessed using a Fully Qualified Domain Name are automatically assigned to what security zone?

   A. Intranet (Local) Zone

   B. Trusted Sites Zone

   C. Internet Zone

   D. Restricted Sites Zone

4. Using security zone settings, administrators can prevent users from downloading which of the following? (Select all that apply.)

   A. Fonts

   B. Unsigned ActiveX controls

   C. Security certificates

   D. Unsigned Java code

5. Which of the following isolates Java code from the user's environment?

   A. Certificate authorities

   B. Authenticode

   C. Proxy servers

   D. The sandbox

6. Which of the following are content rating categories in the Recreational Software Advisory Council Internet rating system?

   A. Language, Nudity, Sex, and Violence

   B. Language, Nudity, Pornography, and Violence

   C. Obscenity, Nudity, Sex, and Violence

   D. Obscenity, Nudity, Pornography, and Violence

7. A proxy server

   A. Establishes encrypted connections with sites

   B. Serves as a gateway to the Internet for user clients

   C. Controls Authenticode and certificate settings

   D. Provides user directory information

8. Administrators can configure Internet Explorer to automatically configure proxy settings by using

   A. JScript with `.PS` and `.PRX` files

   B. VBScript with `.VB` and `.PAC` files

   C. JScript with `.JS` and `.PAC` files

   D. VBScript with `.PS` and `.PRX` files

9. Which of the following sets of protocols can be used with proxy servers in IE 4.0?

   A. HTTP, FTP, IMAP, and SMTP

   B. HTTP, NNTP, SMTP, and SOCKS

   C. HTTP, FTP, Gopher, and SOCKS

   D. HTTP, IMAP, POP3, and SOCKS

10. To construct the necessary files for automatic browser configuration, administrators can use

    A. The IE Express Wizard

    B. The CMAK

    C. The IEAK Profile Manger

    D. The IEAK Wizard

11. The IEAK Profile Manager edits which of the following file types?

    A. `.ADM` files

    B. `.INS` files

    C. `.CAB` files

    D. `.INF` files

Review Answers

Now that you have completed the review questions, check your answers against those provided here. Explanations are provided for each answer so that you can see whether you arrived at the correct solution for the right reason, or so that you can see how your answer varied from the correct one.

1. **A** (A root certificate from a valid Certificate Authority) Without an installed certificate, the server has no way of verifying the identity of the user and therefore cannot establish a secure connection.

2. **D** Authenticode technology allows developers to digitally sign their applications so that users can be sure that they are receiving code from a trusted source, and that the code has not been altered.

3. **C** Sites that use an FQDN or that contain periods in the domain name are automatically considered part of the Internet Zone. Sites that do not make use of periods are assigned to the Intranet (Local) Zone.

4. **A, B, and D** Fonts, unsigned ActiveX controls, and unsigned Java code can all be prohibited from downloads using the security zone settings.

5. **D** The sandbox is a mechanism employed by Internet Explorer and other applications that support Java to isolate Java code from the system memory and file system. The sandbox creates a closed sphere of influence for the application and prevents it from altering the user's environment.

6. **A** Language, Nudity, Sex, and Violence are the four content categories for ratings based on the RSACi system. Each of these four categories also includes five levels (from Level 0 to Level 4), with Level 4 being the most potentially offensive material.

7. **B** By connecting to a proxy server, which in turn connects to Internet clients, users' machines are never allowed direct contact with Internet resources. This configuration helps shield users' machines from interaction with the server, protecting the privacy of the user and increasing network security.

8. **C** Using JScript, administrators can write functions the browser can use to determine whether or not it should connect to a site with a proxy server. When autoproxy is configured for IE, and a `.JS` or `.PAC` file is made available to the browser, IE uses the file's instructions in place of proxy server settings.

9. **C** IE 4.0 supports the following proxy server types:

   - HyperText Transfer Protocol
   - File Transfer Protocol
   - Secure Web services
   - Gopher
   - SOCKS

10. **C** The IEAK Profile Manager is used by administrators to edit the `.INS` files necessary for automatic browser configuration. In addition, the IEAK Profile Manager creates the necessary `.INF` files for updates and incorporates them into the `.CAB` files that IE downloads to perform auto updates.

11. **B** The IEAK Profile Manager *edits* `.INS` files for automatic browser configuration. However, it also *creates* the `.INF` files for upgrades and packages them into Cabinet (`.CAB`) files for updates.

Answers to Test Yourself Questions at Beginning of Chapter

The following answers are provided for the prechapter quiz at the beginning of this chapter. You can use these questions and answers to determine how familiar you may already be with this chapter's material. Each of the questions relates to a specific goal for the Configuring and Managing Resource Access section of the "Implementing and Supporting the Microsoft Internet Explorer Administration Kit for Microsoft Internet Explorer 4.0" MCSE exam. Each of the following answers references the section in this chapter that deals with the covered objective so that you can easily locate the material you may want to review or clarify.

1. The Authenticode and certificate technologies allow developers to sign the applications they have created by using a digital certificate that is authenticated from a trusted third-party organization.

   Digital signing of applications (such as custom packages and ActiveX components) prevents them from being altered and provides the user with assurance that the code is the same as that from the source, so there is less risk in downloading and running the application. In fact, administrators can set the security settings for IE 4.0 to require that users install only code that has come from and been signed by a trusted organization to minimize the security exposure of the organization.

   Sections Referencing This Material:

   - Creating and assigning security
   - Certificate authorities
   - Authenticode

2. There are four security zones for Internet Explorer:

   - Internet Zone
   - Intranet (Local) Zone
   - Trusted Sites Zone
   - Restricted Site Zone

   Each zone can have specific security policies regarding how the browser treats sites that fall into one of the zones. For Trusted and Restricted Zones, administrators must enter the

URL of the site to include that site in either zone. Sites with addresses that are Fully Qualified Domain Names or that contain periods are automatically treated as members of the Internet Zone. Sites on the local network or that do not contain periods are treated as members of the Intranet (Local) Zone.

The flexibility to provide different levels of security to different zones allows administrators to balance user features with network security to maximize the usability of IE 4.0.

Sections Referencing This Material:

- "Creating and Assigning Security Levels"
- "Security Zones"

3. By using the custom Java security settings when specifying zone-level security, administrators can apply the following restrictions to Java applets and applications:

    - Restrict Java network connectivity
    - Restrict signed or unsigned Java to running in a sandbox
    - Restrict signed or unsigned Java's access to the file system
    - Restrict signed or unsigned Java's access to scratch space
    - Restrict signed or unsigned Java's access to printing

   By placing these restrictions on either signed or unsigned Java code, administrators can effectively isolate Java from interaction with the user's environment, making the download and execution of Java code more secure.

   Sections Referencing This Material:

    - "Creating and Assigning Security Levels"
    - "Java"

4. Internet Explorer supports the Recreational Software Advisory Council Internet (RSACi) rating system for site content ratings. The RSACi rating system is a voluntary rating system; sites that choose to participate can rate themselves on the categories of Language, Nudity, Sex, and Violence.

   The pitfall of the RSACi rating system is that, because the system is voluntary, all offensive sites may not participate in the rating system. The ratings apply only to participating sites, although administrators can also choose to block access to sites not participating in the rating system.

   As with nearly any rating system, RSACi ratings are subjective. Because what one individual considers "frontal nudity" may be what someone else considers "provocative frontal nudity," there is still no guarantee that offensive content will be blocked for all sites.

   Sections Referencing This Material:

   - "Creating and Assigning Security Levels"
   - "Content Ratings"

5. A proxy server acts as a gateway agent between a user's machine and resources on the Internet. By connecting to the Internet through a proxy server, users' machines are protected from direct interaction with Internet servers. This separation provides a greater level of security and privacy for users and organizational networks.

   Administrators can use the IEAK to force IE users to connect to the Internet through a proxy server and to automatically configure the addresses for available proxy servers. Administrators can also configure IE for autoproxy, a method in which proxy settings are specified in a JScript (`.JS` or `.PAC`) file that contains rules for when to use the proxy server. Autoproxy allows administrators to maintain a single configuration file for all proxy use for all users.

   Section Referencing This Material:

   - "Managing Proxy Server Support for Internet Explorer 4.0"

6. Automatic browser configuration is established by enabling the feature and entering the URLs for the autoconfiguration files using the IEAK Wizard. After the browser has been set to use automatic browser configuration, administrators can use the IEAK Profile Manager to create update files that will be automatically downloaded by the browser and used to configure changes and updates without reinstalling the browser.

   Sections Referencing This Material:

   - "Managing Proxy Server Support for Internet Explorer 4.0"
   - "Managing Automatic Configuration Using the IEAK Profile Manager"
   - "JScript Autoproxy"

7. The Internet Explorer Administration Kit Profile Manager allows administrators to modify the configuration settings for a custom IE build without rerunning the IEAK Wizard. The Profile Manager also allows administrators to alter the settings in System Policies and Restrictions and exports the new settings into the files used for automatic browser configuration updates.

   The IEAK Profile Manager works by allowing administrators to edit the `.INS` files IE uses to determine its configuration. When administrators create a new update, the `.INS` file is saved, and any `.INF` files or other configuration files required by the browser to perform the update are written into Cabinet (`.CAB`) files that are located at the URL specified for automatic browser configuration. When the IE browser checks for an update, it downloads any new update files and reconfigures itself without requiring a full reinstallation.

   Sections Referencing This Material:

   - "Managing Automatic Configuration Using the IEAK Profile Manager"
   - "The IEAK Profile Manager"
   - "Using the IEAK Profile Manager"

8. .INS, .INF, .ADM, and .CAB files are created by the IEAK Profile Manager to perform automatic browser configuration. Here's what each file does:

    - The .INS file is the overall configuration file created by the Profile Manager. The file is used to direct the new configuration parameters and to specify the location of additional files to be installed.
    - .ADM files are the policy templates used by the Profile Manager to import System Policies and Restrictions settings for Internet Explorer and components.
    - .INF files provide special configuration information to components that require it. These files are similar to configuration files for components of IE, such as Outlook Express.
    - To facilitate the download of update information, the Profile Manager incorporates .INF files and any additional support files into the Windows Cabinet (.CAB) file format. The .CAB file format is a compressed format, similar to that of ZIP files; it allows the browser to update itself by downloading a few small files that it can then use to extract the other files for the final update.

    Sections Referencing This Material:

    - "Managing Automatic Configuration Using the IEAK Profile Manager"
    - "The IEAK Profile Manager"
    - "Using the IEAK Profile Manager"
    - ".INS, .ADM, .INF, and .CAB Files"

Chapter 4

Integration and Interoperability

Internet Explorer is a core productivity application in many organizations. It can be used to distribute information and to gather information. Like any other good co-worker, Internet Explorer is a team player. IE interacts with other software applications regularly, including the components of IE that allow users to access a variety of Internet information resources.

This chapter takes a look at the integration and interoperability of Internet Explorer 4.0. The chapter addresses the issues that face administrators when they are migrating users from other vendors' applications to Internet Explorer 4.0. The chapter also looks at migrating from other versions of Internet Explorer.

Finally, it's important to see how Internet Explorer interacts with supplementary applications like NetMeeting and other browsers, and how administrators can configure other components of Internet Explorer in addition to the browser. This chapter looks at IE interoperability with mail clients and components such as NetMeeting that give IE the full feature set that makes it so powerful.

Objectives

- In Corporate Administrator mode or Internet Service Provider mode, deploy a preconfigured version of Internet Explorer 4.0 by using the IEAK. Distribution methods include
  - Download
  - CD-ROM
  - Floppy disk

continues

- Replace other Internet browsers. Other browsers include
  - Microsoft Internet Explorer 3.*x*
  - Netscape Navigator
- Replace other Internet mail clients. Other mail clients include
  - Internet Mail and News
  - Netscape Mail
  - Eudora
- Configure NetMeeting for various tasks. Tasks include
  - Multipoint application sharing
  - Transferring files
  - Video conferencing

Test Yourself! Before reading this chapter, test yourself to determine how much study time you will need to devote to this section.

The following prechapter quiz is designed to help you get a feel for how well you currently understand the material covered in this chapter. If you think you have a strong understanding of the objectives outlined in the previous list, try the quiz. Based on your score on this quiz, you may feel well enough prepared to skip ahead to the Review Questions at the end of the chapter, or you may determine that you would like to study the chapter material more closely.

1. What are the specific files and folders created for network-based installations of Internet Explorer? What about CD-ROM–based installations? Multiple floppies?
2. What issues are faced when migrating from a previous version of IE to IE 4.0?
3. What issues are faced when migrating from Netscape Navigator to IE 4.0?
4. What email clients does the Internet Explorer installation process support for automatic migration?
5. What types of conferencing and collaboration are supported by NetMeeting?
6. What are some of the security risks associated with application sharing and file transfer?
7. What are some of the issues with audio and video conferencing?

The answers to this prechapter quiz are located at the end of this chapter. Score your answers against those provided to determine your course of study for this chapter.

Test Objectives Overview

The issues of integration and interoperability really apply to two areas of Internet Explorer:

- The migration from other browsers and components to IE 4.0.
- The interaction of IE with other components, such as NetMeeting.

Many administrators deploying Internet Explorer will most certainly face these issues. This chapter starts off by discussing the deployment methods available for Internet Explorer so that administrators are aware of how those options can affect the migration path with other applications.

The chapter continues with specific issues that spring from migrating from other browsers (such as Netscape Navigator) to Internet Explorer 4.0, and the issues that might stem from migrating from a previous installation of Internet Explorer.

Because Internet Explorer is more than just a browser, the chapter also looks at the integration of mail clients and explains how to migrate from previous versions of Netscape, Eudora, and Internet Mail to the Outlook Express client. Some of the issues covered include preserving server settings and migrating user mail.

Finally, the chapter looks at how Internet Explorer and the IEAK let administrators configure the NetMeeting client to meet the needs of users. All this leads to building the most functionally complete build of Internet Explorer possible, and successfully getting it on users' machines with the minimum inconvenience to users and IS staff.

Here's a rundown of the specific topics addressed in this chapter:

- Deploying a preconfigured version of IE 4.0
- Replacing Internet browsers

- Replacing Internet mail clients
- Configuring NetMeeting

Deploying a Preconfigured Version of IE 4.0

In previous chapters, we have discussed the mechanism for creating your customized build of Internet Explorer. Using the IEAK Wizard, you enter the configuration information as prompted to alter the settings for your version of Internet Explorer. When you are finished, the IEAK Wizard creates the necessary files and places them in the location you specified during the initial configuration process.

Once the IEAK Wizard has done its job and finished creating your custom package, you are ready to begin the process of assembling the package for distribution through one of the following methods:

- Download
- CD-ROM
- Floppy disk

Your preconfigured version of Internet Explorer 4.0 can be distributed through download sites, either on the Internet or your intranet. In this approach, users download the Active Setup Wizard to begin the installation. When they run the Active Setup Wizard, the rest of the installation files are downloaded from the network site.

If you are concerned about network traffic or connections, you can distribute IE through other media as well. You can burn the installation files onto a single CD-ROM that can be used to perform the installation without a network connection. And if you are building an installation for older machines, for example, you can also create a set of installation floppy disks.

When you tell the IEAK Wizard the method you are going to use for distribution, the IEAK Wizard automatically creates the necessary files to properly deploy your version of IE. For example, if you have chosen to create both a CD-ROM installation and a floppy disk installation, the IEAK Wizard creates three folders:

- `DOWNLOAD`
- `CD`
- `Mfloppy`
- `INS`

Each of these directories contains the necessary files for its media distribution. The following sections take a look at the specifics.

Distribution by Download

The IEAK Wizard automatically assumes that you are creating a version of IE that you will want to deploy over the network. If you choose additional methods of installation, you can find the download version in a `DOWNLOAD` folder. Otherwise, you can find the files for your version of IE in the folder you specified for the build.

When you have run the IEAK Wizard, and it has finished creating your customized build, you are ready to proceed with the preparation of your Web site.

Recall from the IEAK Wizard process that you were asked to specify a download site on your server, as shown in Figure 4.1.

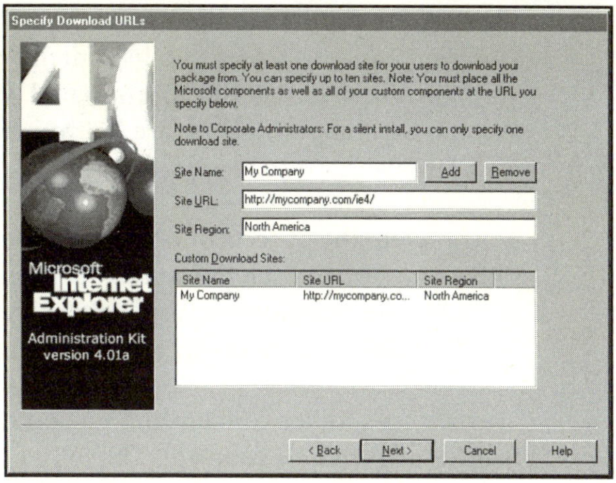

Figure 4.1

Specifying a download site for IE installation with the IEAK Wizard.

For example, you may have specified the URL `http://www.mycompany.com/ie4/` as the location from which your clients will download IE. Now you must prepare your Web server.

On the Web server, you must make sure that the path you specified exists and that it is publicly readable. For the preceding example, that means you would have to create an `ie40` directory in the root document directory on your Web server.

When that directory is created and ready to go, you can transfer the files for downloading. Within the directory you told the IEAK Wizard to create for the custom installation, there should be a folder named for the platform version you created (for example, `WIN95_NT`). Within that folder is a second folder called `IE4SITE`.

The IE4SITE folder contains the files to be placed on your system. The IE4SITE folder contains two items:

- **`IE4SITES.DAT`.** This text file contains the URL information for download sites you specified during the IEAK Wizard process.
- **`En`.** This folder contains the installation files. The folder is actually named after the language version you have chosen to create. For example, the folder name is `En` if you have chosen to build an English language version of IE.

The contents of the installation folder are what is really important. The entire En folder and its contents must be moved to your Web site and placed at the appropriate URL. When they are there and the correct permissions are set, you are ready for network installations.

To complete the process of deploying a network installation version, you must go back into your root level directory where the IEAK Wizard created your installation. There you will find another folder within the WIN95_NT folder called DOWNLOAD.

The DOWNLOAD folder contains the version of Active Setup that has been configured for your site. The folder is nested within several folders, one for the platform WIN95_NT followed by a folder for the language version En. In the ~/DOWNLOAD/WIN95_NT/EN folder, you should find the IE4SETUP.EXE file. This is the Active Setup Wizard.

You can copy this version of the Active Setup Wizard onto a single floppy to distribute to users, or you can add it to a page on your Web site. After users copy it from a floppy or download it to their machines, the Active Setup Wizard will connect to your download site to run the installation.

Distribution by CD-ROM

Sometimes, a network-based installation is not the best method for installing Internet Explorer 4.0. For example, administrators may want to minimize network traffic. Or they might want to provide a faster installation method to users with modem connections. If this is the case, administrators can opt to create a CD-ROM–based installation from within the IEAK Wizard, as shown in Figure 4.2.

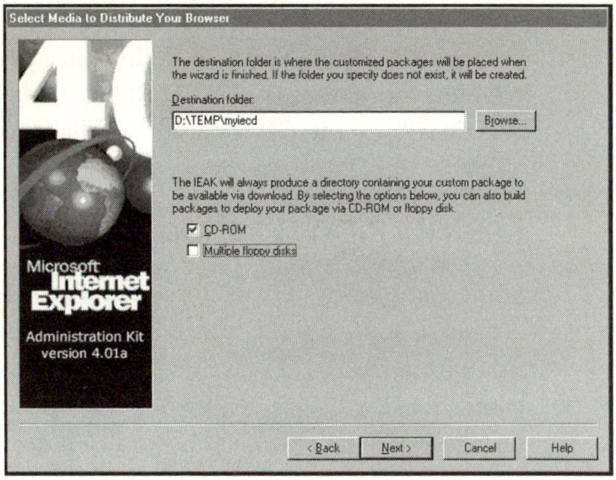

Figure 4.2

Specifying a CD-ROM–based installation for Internet Explorer with the IEAK Wizard.

If you selected the CD-ROM–based installation option from the IEAK Wizard, the wizard will create an IE 4.0 installer and installation files designed to run from a CD-ROM. This option adds some features to your deployment, such as an autorun file to automatically launch the CD when the user places the CD in his or her CD-ROM drive. This option also includes any customized splash screen specified for CD-ROM–based installation.

Just as for the network-based installation, the CD-ROM–based installation places its files in a folder located in the root directory you specified to the IEAK Wizard. Within that root directory is a folder for the platform, such as `WIN95_NT`.

Within the platform folder is a folder called `CD`, which contains all the files needed for a CD-ROM-based installation. There should be three items in the `CD` folder:

- **`AUTORUN.INF`.** This is the autorun file for automatically launching the IE Setup Wizard when the disc is inserted into the drive.
- **`IESETUP.EXE`.** This is the Internet Explorer installation program used to guide the user through the installation.
- **`Win95`.** This folder contains the helper applications, Cabinet files, and other items used to complete the actual installation.

To create the CD-ROM, you use your burning software, or you create a CD image that places the contents of the CD folder in the root level directory of the CD-ROM. Then you can mass produce and distribute the CD for user installations.

Distribution by Floppy Disk

Sometimes, both network-based and CD-ROM–based installations are just not possible. Perhaps a user with an older machine does not have a CD-ROM drive or a network connection. For such cases, the IEAK Wizard allows you to specify a multiple floppy disk-based installation, as shown in Figure 4.3.

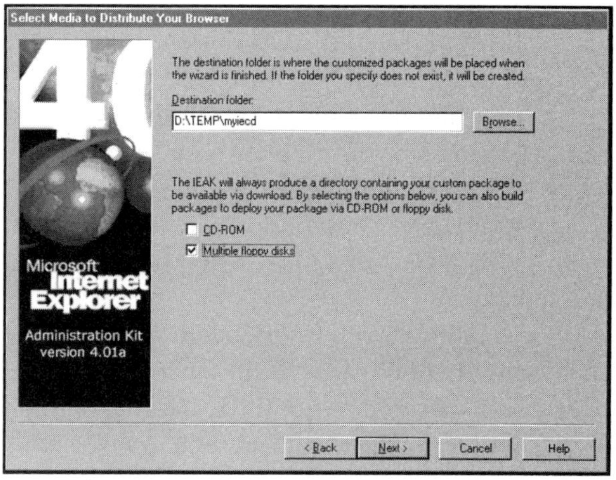

Figure 4.3

Specifying a multiple floppy disk-based installation for Internet Explorer with the IEAK Wizard.

Just as with the methods for network-based and CD-ROM–based installations, the IEAK Wizard creates the files for a floppy disk installation in the root directory you specified for the build. Within that folder is a folder for the platform, such as `WIN95_NT`.

Within the platform folder is a folder called `Mfloppy`. This folder contains the files necessary to create the floppies for this installation. Within the `Mfloppy` folder are specific folders for each platform (for example, `Win95`, `WinNT`, and, if appropriate, a multiplatform folder such as `Win95_NT`).

Within each of these folders you should find the familiar folder for the language version (for example, the `En` folder for the English language). The language folder contains a number of subfolders, each labeled with a title such as `Disk1` or `Disk9`. These folders correspond to the floppies that must be created for the installation. `Disk1` contains the Active Setup Wizard; the subsequent disks contain the necessary installation files.

You must copy the contents of each folder to a floppy disk, so that the files are in the root level directory of the floppy—not in the numbered folder! This set of disks can be used for the installation or as a master set for duplicating additional sets of disks.

The final directory contains the `.INS` file used for your custom version of Internet Explorer to establish the correct user settings. As you see in Chapter 5, "Monitoring and Optimization," this `.INS` file can be edited manually or by using the IEAK Profile Manager to customize the build after it has been created using the IEAK Wizard.

As you can see, the IEAK provides a number of mechanisms for deploying your preconfigured version of IE 4.0. Working with these methods, you should be able to find deployment options that work for all the users in your organization.

Replacing Internet Browsers

Unless your organization is just getting started on the Internet, or unless you are deploying Internet Explorer onto new machines within your organization, chances are that your user base already has a browser installed.

You may have several concerns when migrating from an older browser to a newer version or replacing another vendor's browser altogether. A number of different browsers are on the market today; however, Internet Explorer 4.0 supports migration only from previous installations of Internet Explorer 3.*x* and from Netscape Navigator.

If you are migrating from another browser (such as Mosaic), none of the user settings can be preserved. If that is the case, you should treat the installation of Internet Explorer as a fresh installation and specify any user components using the IEAK Wizard.

However, if you are upgrading your user's browser from a previous version of Internet Explorer 3.*x* or Netscape Navigator, there are some migration issues you might want to consider.

Microsoft Internet Explorer 3.*x*

The easiest migration path of all possible browsers is from Internet Explorer 3.*x* to Internet Explorer 4.0. Because both are Microsoft products and because there is such similarity between browsers, many settings are preserved during the transition.

There is one very important caveat, however. Although the migration from IE 3.*x* to IE 4.0 is easy, the two browsers cannot coexist on the same machine. With other browsers such as Netscape Navigator and Communicator, you can have multiple versions of the browser installed, for whatever reason. Then you can simply allow the user to run whichever version they need for a task. Internet Explorer 4.0, however, completely removes Internet Explore 3.*x* from the user's system. Further, IE 3.0 cannot reside on the same machine as IE 4.0.

There is one solution if you have to have coexisting IE versions for a user. But the solution is quite complicated: create a dual boot system. You can partition the user's hard drive so that there are two bootable partitions, one with Windows 95 for example, and another with Windows NT. The Windows 95 installation can contain IE 3.01 and the Windows NT partition can have Internet Explorer 4.0. When the machine restarts, the user can choose which OS to boot into, making the different browser versions available.

If this sounds like a real hassle to go through to maintain different IE versions, it is. Unless there is a very important reason to do so, coexisting IE versions is not recommended.

Assuming that you have decided to leave your IE 3.*x* days behind you and go with IE 4.0, what issues do you have to consider?

The answer is really not much. The Active Setup Wizard and the installation process take care of the details for you, importing a variety of user settings, including these:

- Proxy settings
- Favorites
- Cookies

If you do not specify new values for these settings in the IEAK Wizard for your installation, they are preserved from the user's previous IE installation. In the case of elements such as cookies (which can't be specified in the IEAK Wizard), the settings are imported automatically.

What considerations are there for a migration from IE 3.x to IE 4.0? One area of concern is plug-ins and add-on components. If your user base is using a plug-in (such as a VRML viewer or some other type of browser extension), you will have to specify that as a custom package with your IE 4.0 deployment. The reason for this is simply that the plug-in architecture differs between IE 3.0 and IE 4.0. Although a plug-in from IE 3.0 might work in IE 4.0, there is no guarantee. Therefore, you should evaluate all your user's plug-ins carefully.

Keep in mind that some plug-ins might provide functionality that is now built into IE 4.0, making them obsolete. After you determine that you still want users to have access to a plug-in, you should obtain the Internet Explorer 4.0 version of the plug-in and then use the IEAK Wizard to include it as a custom package for your installer.

Netscape Navigator

Of course, the major competitor to Internet Explorer in the browser market is Netscape—both the Navigator and Communicator versions of the browser software. Because Netscape is a major competitor, and because Microsoft wants to make the transition easier for users making the switch, the migration from Netscape products to Internet Explorer 4.0 is very easy.

As it does for the migration from earlier versions of Internet Explorer, the Active Setup Wizard and the IE installation process automatically detect versions of Netscape previously installed on the user's machine. And as it does for the migration from IE 3.*x*, the installation process also migrates and preserves a number of Netscape Navigator settings, including these:

- Proxy settings
- Bookmarks (favorites)
- Cookies

Of course, when you are creating a custom version of Internet Explorer, you can specify that these settings override the imported settings. However, if you leave the proxy settings blank, for example, the installation process imports the proxy settings from Netscape.

To make the process complete, the biggest issue to be addressed is the migration of browser plug-ins. Here, the plug-in architecture for the two browsers is different; that means you must find the IE versions of any plug-ins you want users to retain and add them as custom packages to your IE installation.

So what is the difference between migration from IE 3.*x* and migration from a Netscape product? There is one critical difference: Internet Explorer 4.0 and Netscape products can safely coexist on the same machine.

Keep in mind that your users must select one of the browsers as their default browser, but the two browsers can both be used on the same machine without any complicated dual-boot system.

Replacing Internet Mail Clients

Now that you have addressed the issues facing the migration of an older browser to Internet Explorer 4.0, there is the issue of migrating important components. No other component is more closely associated with the browser than Internet news and email clients.

A host of clients for email and news are available on the Internet; some are shareware, some are commercial. Unfortunately, their architectures and features vary wildly, and users become very attached to their mail clients.

Mail clients range from applications such as Elm and Pine (text-based clients that run on shared UNIX systems) to Pegasus and Eudora (graphical mail clients for Windows and other platforms). So how does Internet Explorer deal with the complexities of migrating from such a wide variety of clients? By limiting the participants.

It would be almost impossible (and certainly likely to lead to mistakes) if Internet Explorer supported migration from every available email client. Therefore, migration support for Internet Explorer 4.0 has been limited to some of the more popular clients:

- Internet Mail and News
- Netscape Mail
- Eudora (and Eudora Pro)
- Outlook
- Microsoft Exchange (includes Windows Messaging)

If you are planning to migrate to Internet Explorer 4.0 for email using the Outlook Express client, and you don't see your mail client in the preceding list, there is little you can do. If the address information is separated by commas, Outlook Express will read addresses from a text file. You might also check to see whether messages can be imported/exported from your mailer to one of the supported clients, and then imported a second time into Outlook Express. If none of these options work, you can really only start over with your new mail once you have installed Internet Explorer. You may want to contact the manufacturer of the old client and see whether it has a mechanism for exporting its mailbox formats to IE.

Keep in mind that if you are using another mail client—and are happy with it—you don't have to change. Outlook Express can coexist with other email applications (with the exception of Internet Mail) without any problems.

A couple of options exist for using email clients other than Outlook Express and Internet Explorer 4.0. The first is simply to keep using the email client you were using before IE came to your system.

You can configure Internet Explorer to use another email client from the Internet Preferences dialog box, on the Programs page, as shown in Figure 4.4.

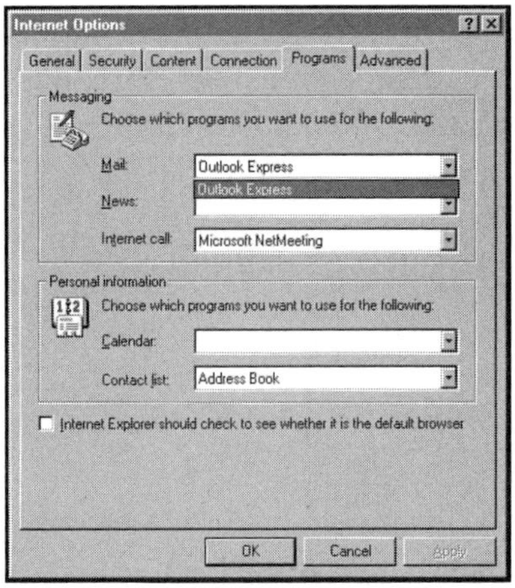

Figure 4.4

Configuring Internet Explorer 4.0 to work with other email clients.

To configure IE to work with an existing client, make sure that the client is installed and present on the user's desktop. After IE has been configured to use the new client, that client will be launched automatically, instead of Outlook Express, when the mail service is needed.

You can configure your installation of Internet Explorer to use another email client even in a custom installation. To do this, you include the new email client as a custom package in your installation. The IE installer will launch the installer for the new email client, installing it on the machine so that it can be used with IE.

Internet Mail and News

The easiest path for migrating email services is from Microsoft's Internet Mail and News to Outlook Express. Because Internet Mail and News are components of Internet Explorer 3.*x*, their settings are imported into Outlook Express automatically.

After the installation of IE 4.0 is complete, messages and settings from Internet Mail and News will be present in the Outlook Express client, and Outlook Express will be the default mail application for IE 4.0.

Netscape Mail

The Internet Explorer installation process can automatically detect installed email packages and import the settings from those applications along with any existing messages.

This process can be used to convert from a previous version of Netscape Mail to Outlook Express. The first step in the conversion process is to specify the Outlook Express client as the default mail and news client for your custom installation of IE 4.0, as shown in Figure 4.5.

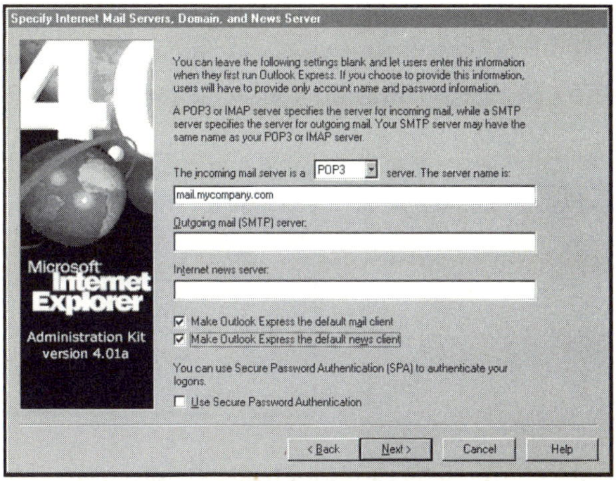

Figure 4.5

Specifying Outlook Express as the default mail and news client in the IEAK Wizard.

When you have specified that Internet Explorer is to use the Outlook Express client, the rest is automatic.

During the installation process, the Active Setup Wizard and the IE installation process automatically detect installed mail clients and import existing mail messages and folders. Of course, the installation process uses the server settings you specified in the IEAK Wizard.

Eudora

If you are currently using a Eudora mail client and are migrating to Outlook Express, you can configure Outlook Express as the default client in the IEAK Wizard. This causes the same process to occur with Eudora as occurred for Netscape: the installation process imports existing messages and folders into Outlook Express.

However, there is another method for importing messages and settings into Internet Explorer. If you install the Outlook Express client but do not set it to be the default mail client, your users can continue to use Eudora (or Netscape) for mail. Should they later choose to use Outlook Express, here's the process for importing settings with Outlook Express:

1. Launch the Outlook Express client and select Import from the File menu.

2. Select Address Book from the menu. You see a dialog box indicating the mail clients that Outlook supports when importing address books (see Figure 4.6).

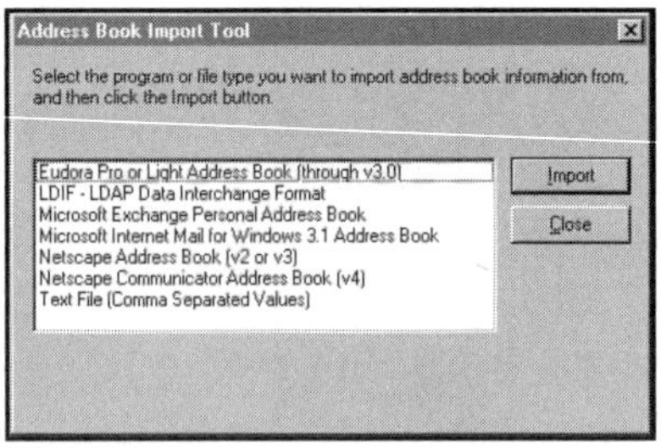

Figure 4.6

Importing address book settings with Outlook Express.

3. Select Eudora from the presented choices.

4. Click Import. When you are notified of the successful import, click OK.

5. From the File menu, select Import and then select Messages. This action launches the Import Messages Wizard, as shown in Figure 4.7.

   Select the client you want to import (for example, Eudora) and click Next to continue.

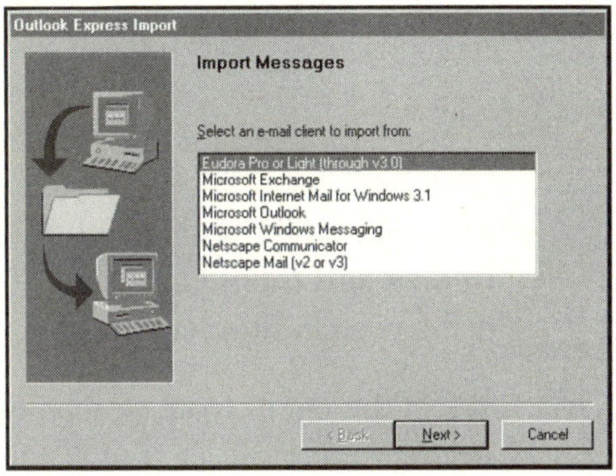

Figure 4.7

The Import Messages Wizard in Outlook Express can transfer messages from many mail clients.

6. You are prompted to enter the location of the mail messages (the default value is usually correct), as shown in Figure 4.8.

   Confirm that the message location is correct and click Next to continue.

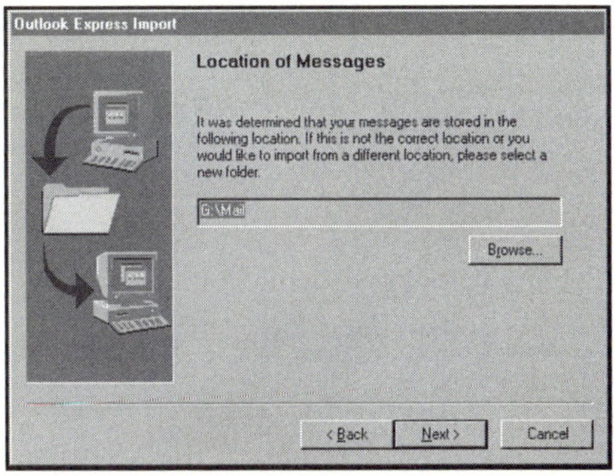

Figure 4.8

Selecting the location of mail messages.

7. You are prompted to select the folders you want to import. You can either import individual folders or import the whole bunch as a group, as shown in Figure 4.9.

When you have selected the folders you want to import, click Finish. The messages will be imported into Outlook Express.

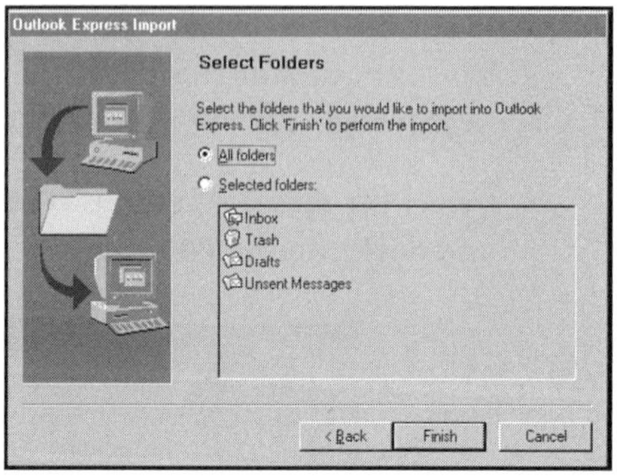

Figure 4.9

Selecting the message folders to import into Outlook Express.

8. Now import the server settings. From the File menu, select Import and then select Mail Account Settings. This action displays a client selection box, as shown in Figure 4.10.

   Select the client from which you want to import the server settings and click Next to continue.

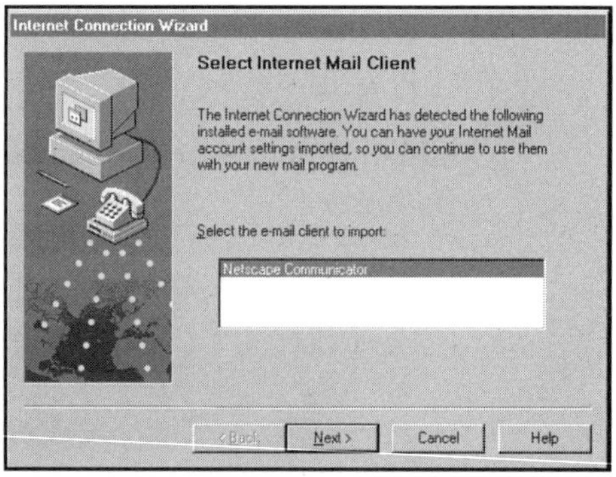

Figure 4.10

Selecting the client from which you want to import mail server settings.

9. You are shown a preview of the settings to confirm their accuracy (see Figure 4.11).

   If you have changes to make, you can step through the wizard to alter any of the settings. If the settings are acceptable, click Next to continue.

Figure 4.11

Confirming the mail server settings to be imported.

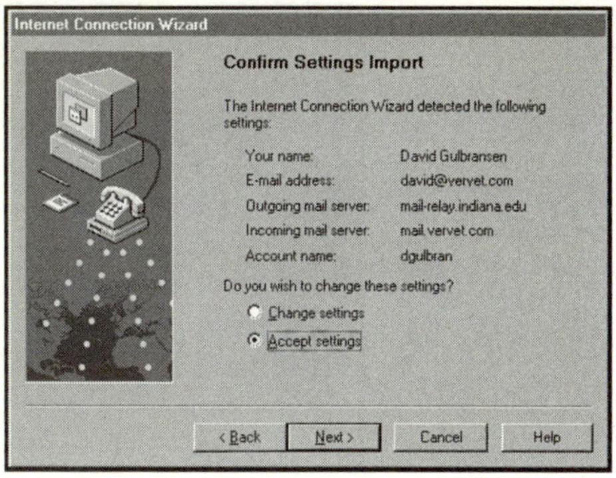

10. Because Outlook Express can handle multiple mail boxes, you are asked to enter a "friendly" name for the mail account, as shown in Figure 4.12.

    For example, your user name might be `JK343I`, but you could enter `Jackie` for your friendly name. When you've entered your friendly name, click Next to continue.

Figure 4.12

Entering a friendly name for the default email account.

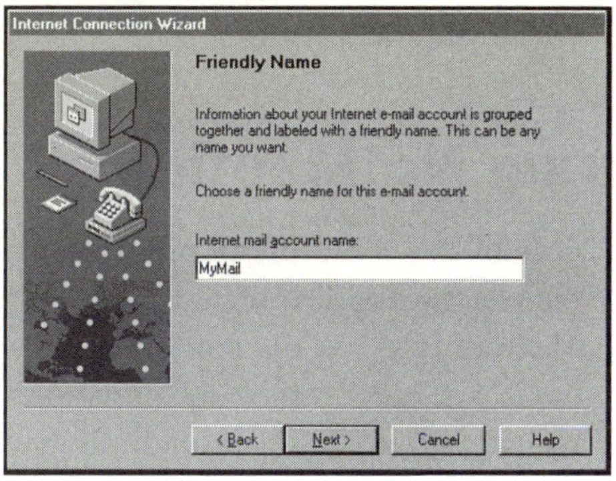

11. You are prompted to enter the method you use to connect to your mail server (see Figure 4.13).

    Select the method that applies (for example, a modem or a local network) and click Next to continue.

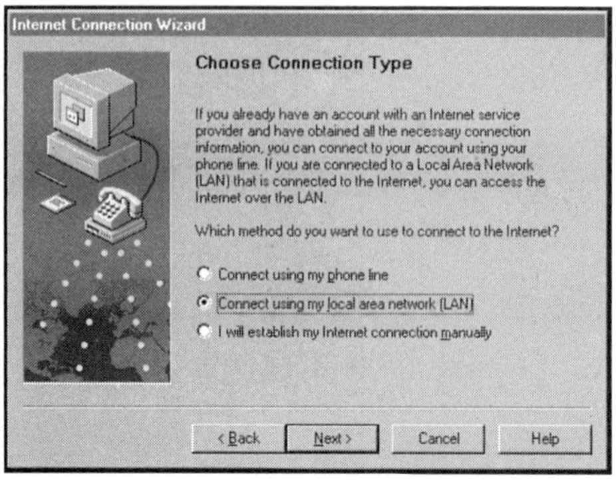

Figure 4.13

Selecting the connection method for retrieving email.

12. Finally, you are presented with some information regarding the transfer of settings. Review the information and click Finish. Outlook Express imports the settings, and your configuration is complete.

That's all there is to importing settings from an existing mail client after IE has already been installed. This process can be used for Eudora or Netscape—and hopefully for many other mail clients in the near future.

Configuring NetMeeting

One of the components administrators can choose to install in conjunction with Internet Explorer is Microsoft NetMeeting. NetMeeting is a versatile conferencing application that allows users to exchange data in files, to share applications, to share a whiteboard, and to make use of audio/video conferencing.

With the power of information and collaboration that comes with NetMeeting, there are several issues that face administrators when configuring clients for use with NetMeeting. First is the issue of security. When configuring elements such as application and file sharing, there is a risk of exposing network resources and information on the user's machine. And features such as audio and video conferencing bring up issues concerning privacy and the efficient use of network resources.

Fortunately, both the IEAK Wizard and Profile Manager allow administrators to set policies regarding NetMeeting use and features. This section takes a look at how administrators can use both IEAK tools and configure the NetMeeting client itself to achieve the best results for their organization.

Let's begin by taking a look at the initial configuration of the NetMeeting client:

1. When you first run NetMeeting, the client takes you through a series of dialog boxes designed to allow you to configure NetMeeting for your machine (see Figure 4.14).

   When you have read the introductory screen, click Next to continue.

Figure 4.14

Getting started with the NetMeeting client.

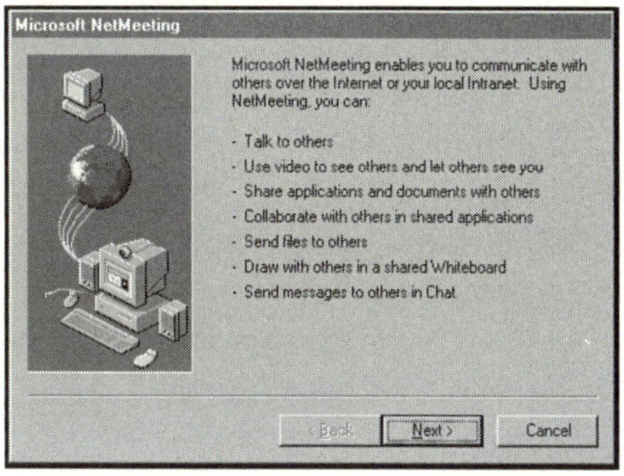

2. After you pass the notice dialog boxes, you are asked to select a server for NetMeeting and to decide whether you want NetMeeting to log into that server automatically, as shown in Figure 4.15.

   The NetMeeting server is the machine you use to connect to other users by placing and answering calls. You can choose a public server from the pull-down list, or you can enter your company's private ILS server. Your company can obtain the NetMeeting ILS software from the NetMeeting home page at `http://www.microsoft.com/netmeeting`.

   If you select the Log on to a Directory Server When NetMeeting Starts check box, you are automatically connected to the server you selected when you launched NetMeeting. Otherwise, you must connect to the server manually.

When you have selected your server options, click Next to continue.

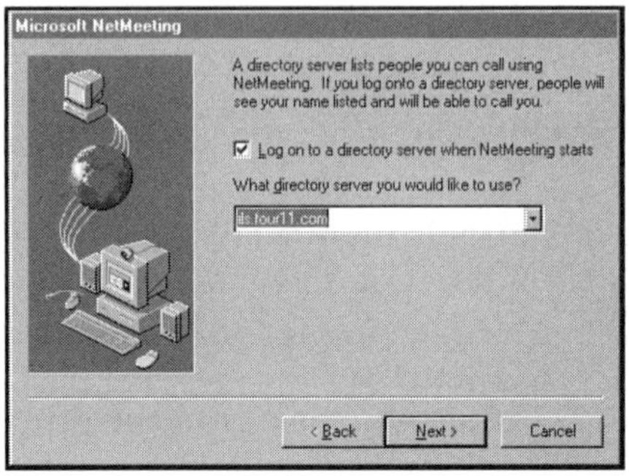

Figure 4.15

Selecting a NetMeeting server site during the initial NetMeeting client launch.

3. Enter your personal contact information, as shown in Figure 4.16.

   The NetMeeting directory server uses this information to let other NetMeeting users know who you are. When you have completed the information, click Next to continue.

Figure 4.16

Entering contact information for the NetMeeting client.

4. Select how you are going to use the NetMeeting client, as shown in Figure 4.17. You can select from the following options:

   - For personal use (suitable for all ages)
   - For business use (suitable for all ages)
   - For adults-only use

The category you select here lets other users know how you are using NetMeeting and what type of calls you might be willing to accept. Select the category that applies to you and click Next to continue.

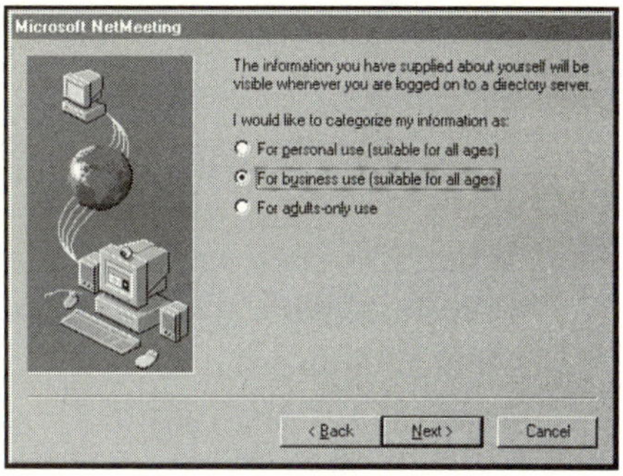

Figure 4.17

Users can specify how they are going to use the NetMeeting client to connect to other similar users.

5. You are prompted to select the type of connection to the network you are using, as shown in Figure 4.18. You can select from the following options:

    - 14400 bps modem
    - 28800 bps or faster modem
    - ISDN
    - Local Area Network

    When you have selected the type of connection you will be using with NetMeeting, click Next to continue.

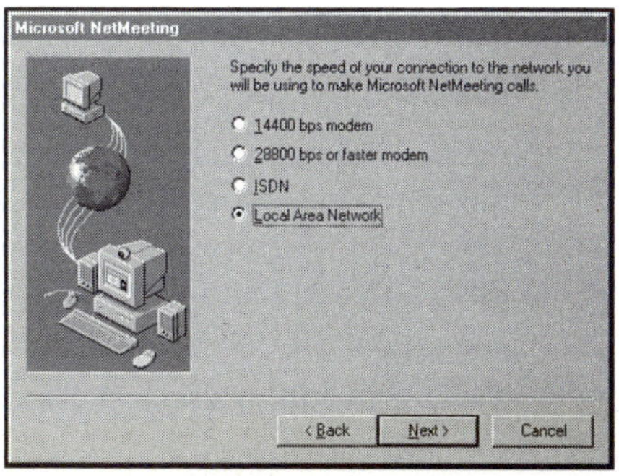

Figure 4.18

NetMeeting can be configured to work with a variety of network connection types.

6. The next section of the NetMeeting initial setup wizard involves specifying the audio settings for the client. This process ensures that NetMeeting uses the proper audio levels to record your voice and uses the proper volume levels to allow you to participate in the conference without disturbing other users in your area.

   The first step in setting audio levels is to set the volume for the NetMeeting client, as shown in Figure 4.19.

   When you click the Test button, the wizard plays a test sound that should allow you to gauge the volume of your speakers. You can adjust the volume by moving the sliding volume control until the volume is right for you.

   When you have set the volume accordingly, click Next to continue.

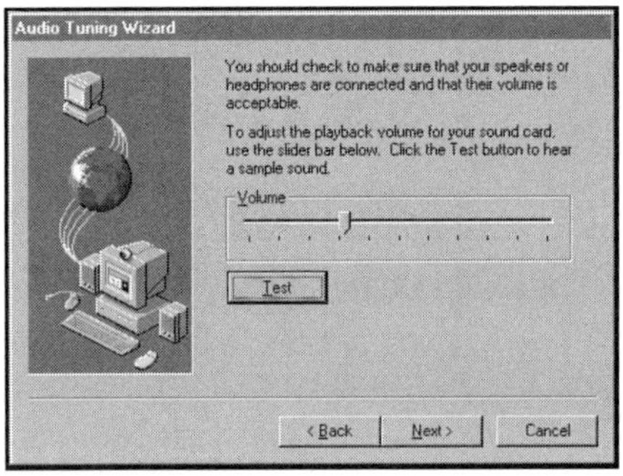

Figure 4.19

Testing the volume of NetMeeting can help prevent you from disturbing other users.

7. Set the input level for your microphone, as shown in Figure 4.20.

   Because peoples' voices vary, and because other environmental factors such as background noise affect audio transmissions, you must calibrate your microphone.

   Read the text from the dialog box into your microphone while you adjust the recording levels. When you have properly adjusted your input levels, click Next to continue.

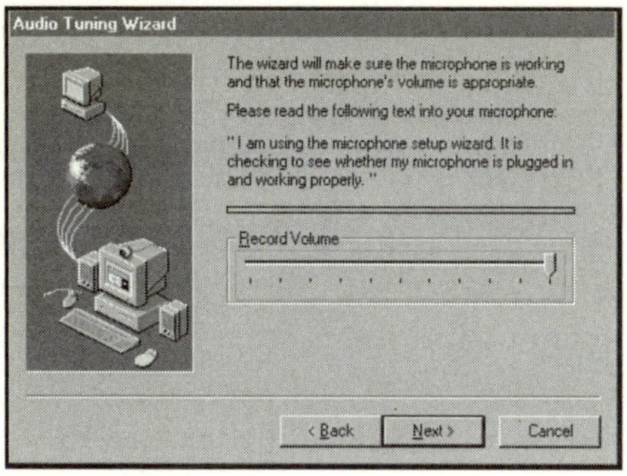

Figure 4.20

The microphone level in NetMeeting affects the quality of audio conferencing.

8. Now that you have specified the initial settings for NetMeeting, you are ready to move on to configuring the client. Click Finish to apply the new settings to NetMeeting.

   After a few minutes, the NetMeeting client launches as shown in Figure 4.21. You are ready to continue setting up your client for application and file sharing and for audio/video conferencing.

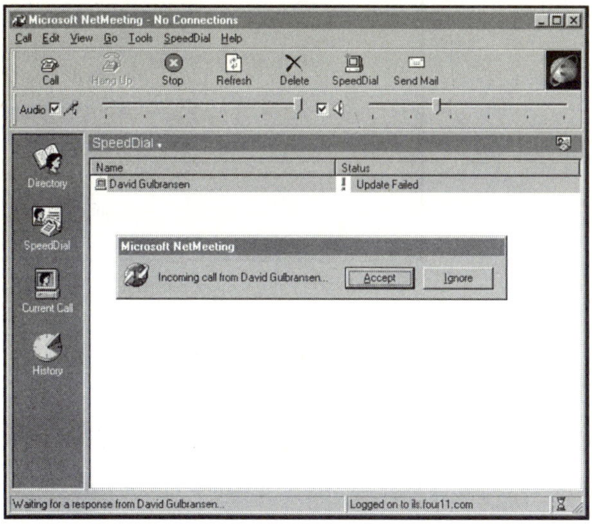

Figure 4.21

The Microsoft NetMeeting client allows users to establish a conference and to share data.

Multipoint Application Sharing

When you have completed your initial configuration for NetMeeting, you are ready to begin configuring the specifics for different NetMeeting applications. Each of these applications requires two types of configuration: configuration from within the IEAK Wizard and configuration from within the NetMeeting client.

The first application for NetMeeting we are going to configure is multipoint application sharing. You can alter settings for application sharing with the IEAK Wizard or the IEAK Profile Manager from within the System Policies and Restrictions settings.

From the System Policies and Restrictions dialog boxes of either the IEAK Wizard or the IEAK Profile Manager, administrators can disable certain applications for NetMeeting. One of the options in the NetMeeting Settings section is Restrict the Use of Application Sharing, as shown in Figure 4.22.

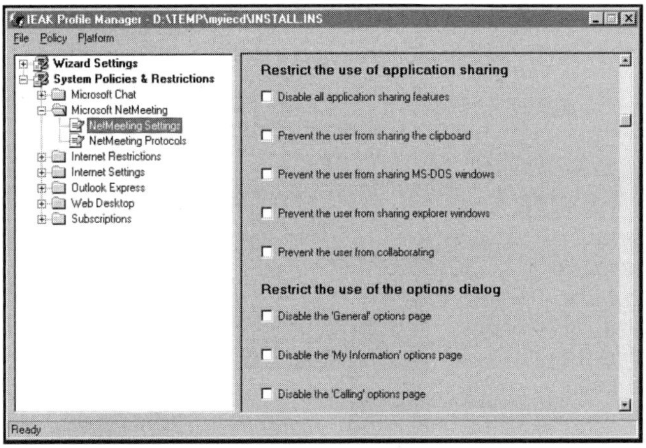

Figure 4.22

Configuring NetMeeting application sharing from the IEAK Profile Manager.

Within this section, administrators can select from the following options:

- Disable All Application Sharing Features
- Prevent the User from Sharing the Clipboard
- Prevent the User from Sharing MS-DOS Windows
- Prevent the User from Sharing Explorer Windows
- Prevent the User from Collaborating

Each of these settings can be used to restrict an aspect of application sharing to help protect the user's machine and resources.

However, if you want to allow full application sharing, do not select any of these options. Failing to place restrictions can leave some holes in security; however, if you want to perform full application sharing, these security risks may be necessary.

If you decide to allow application sharing, the client must still be configured as well. From the NetMeeting Tools menu, you may notice that Start Collaborating is disabled by default, as shown in Figure 4.23.

Figure 4.23

The NetMeeting client must be configured to allow application sharing.

To activate application sharing, you must first choose Enable Sharing from the Tools menu, which causes the installation of the NetMeeting components necessary for sharing.

Caution

> Installing and enabling sharing may require that your system be rebooted. You should quit all other applications and save any necessary data before proceeding.

After you have enabled sharing, you are ready to begin sharing applications. To start the process, you must have a call in place, and the application to be shared must be open. When the call is established, the person running the application can choose Share Application and then select the application to share from the menu, as shown in Figure 4.24.

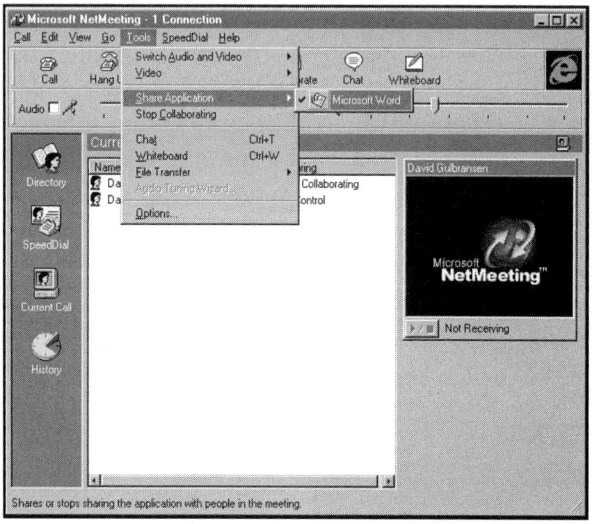

Figure 4.24

With sharing enabled, callers can launch and share applications between machines.

Now the application appears on the screens of the other members of the call. To allow users to contribute to the application, the hosting participant must select Start Collaborating, which allows the other participants to actually interact with the application (see Figure 4.25).

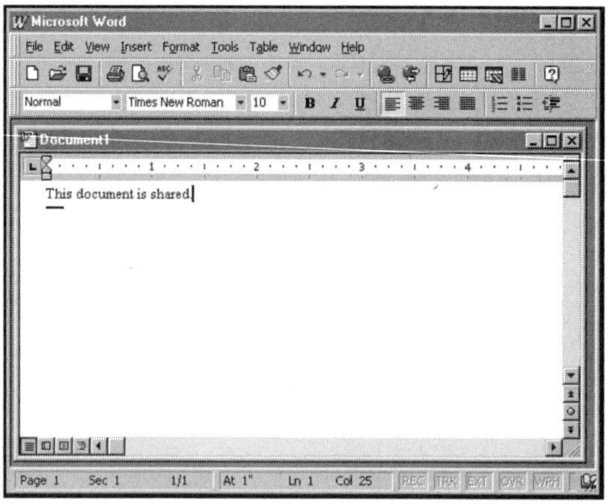

Figure 4.25

Application sharing allows connected users to work in the same application over the network.

That's all there is to application sharing! Although it is a straightforward process, it also provides an amazing amount of power and interaction among conference participants. When the application host shares and collaborates, he or she also relinquishes control of the application. Although this can be a great security risk, it can also be an excellent way to share data and workloads.

Transferring Files

Now that you know how to share applications and collaborate using NetMeeting, let's take a look at how you can use NetMeeting to exchange files. Although application sharing actually allows you to host and share applications, file transfer offers an alternative way to share data and collaborate with NetMeeting.

File transfer simply allows you to exchange files with other NetMeeting participants and then open or alter the files on your own machine. In this way, users can work collaboratively without the network bandwidth or security loopholes of application sharing. Let's take a look at how it's done.

First, as with other NetMeeting settings, administrators can use the IEAK Wizard or the Profile Manager to alter the System Policies and Restrictions concerning file transfer for NetMeeting, as shown in Figure 4.26.

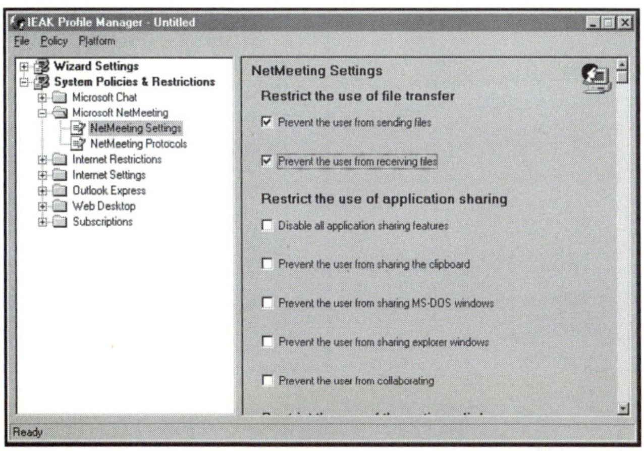

Figure 4.26

Altering file transfer settings for NetMeeting using the IEAK Profile Manager.

From the System Policies and Restrictions dialog boxes, administrators can choose the following options:

- Prevent the User from Sending Files
- Prevent the User from Receiving Files

Both of these options allow administrators to control security. Preventing the sending of files can help protect your company's data from falling into the wrong hands or exposing information inadvertently. Preventing the user from receiving data can help prevent the spread of viruses and protect the system from corrupt files. However, if you choose to allow file transfer with NetMeeting, you cannot select either of these options.

From within NetMeeting, configuring file transfer is simple:

1. Select a folder in which NetMeeting will store incoming file transfers. You can do this from the General page of the Options dialog box, in the File Transfer section (see Figure 4.27).

   After you have selected the folder in which files will be stored, you're ready to send and receive files.

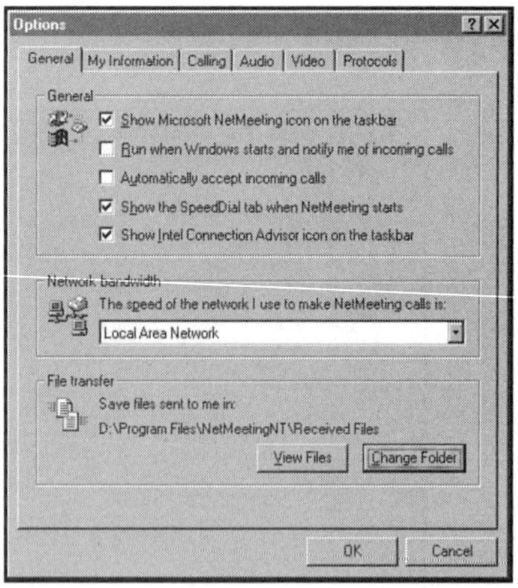

Figure 4.27

Selecting the storage folder for incoming NetMeeting file transfers.

2. To send a file, select Tools | File Transfer | Send File, and you will see the dialog box shown in Figure 4.28.

You can then browse the file system and select the file you want to send. When you click OK, the file is sent on its way. If the recipient refuses the file, you are alerted to this failure. When the file has been transferred, you are notified of the successful transfer.

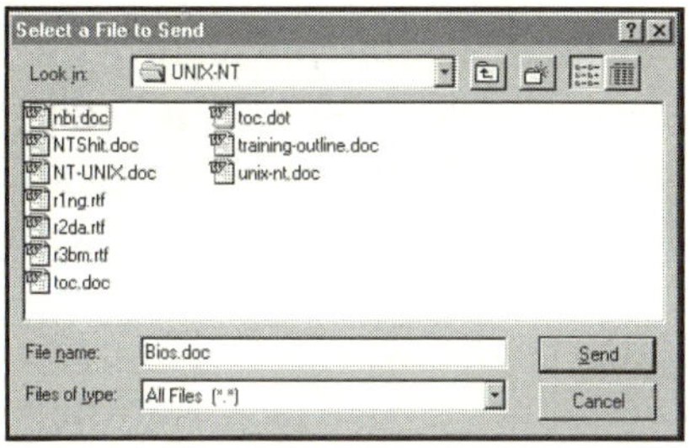

Figure 4.28

Preparing to send a file using the NetMeeting file transfer mechanism.

3. If a conference participant sends you a file, you are notified of the incoming file and asked whether you want to open or reject the file, as shown in Figure 4.29.

   If you choose to accept the file, the file is saved in the folder you specified, and the associated application launches so that you can view the file. If you reject the file, it is not saved on your hard drive, and the other participant is notified that you did not accept the file.

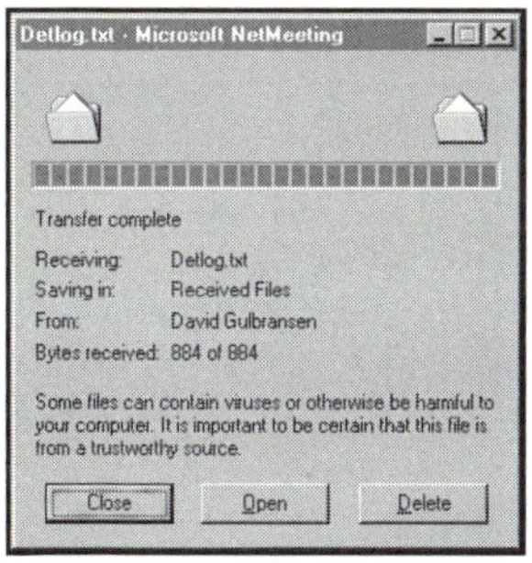

Figure 4.29

Receiving an incoming file using NetMeeting.

Caution

There is no way that NetMeeting can screen all incoming files. Opening a file from an unknown source may expose your system to hazards such as viruses. You should accept incoming file transfers only from trusted sources.

Now that you have seen how participants can share applications and file data, let's take a look at the more conference-like feature of NetMeeting: video conferencing.

Video Conferencing

The final NetMeeting feature discussed in this chapter is the video conferencing feature. When this feature is used on a machine that features a video capture card and a video camera, NetMeeting allows real-time video conferencing with audio.

Video conferencing is a powerful meeting tool, allowing users to conference face to face over the network. However, video is a very demanding application. Because video conferencing is a very network-intensive bandwidth application, results vary widely depending on the network connectivity being used.

Many administrators may want to restrict the use of video conferencing to preserve network bandwidth for other user applications. A handful of video conference participants on a network can quickly consume all the available network bandwidth, bringing other services to a halt. Because of this possibility, the IEAK Wizard and the IEAK Profile Manager allow administrators to configure NetMeeting video settings, as shown in Figure 4.30.

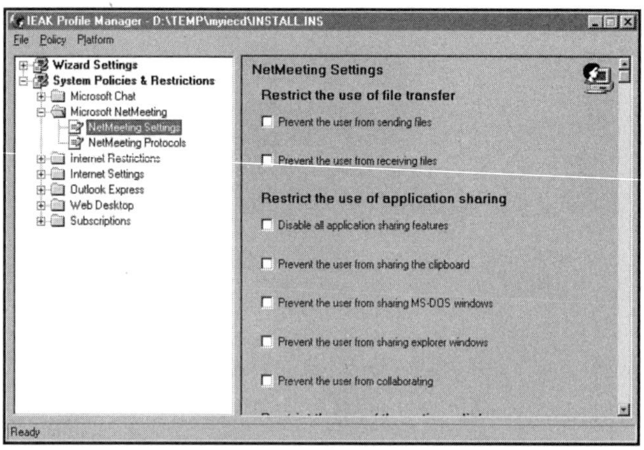

Figure 4.30

NetMeeting restrictions can be established through the IEAK Profile Manager.

Using the System Policies and Restrictions mechanism, administrators can select the following options:

- Prevent the User from Sending Video
- Prevent the User from Receiving Video
- Prevent the User from Using Directory Services

These options allow the administrator to stop conference participants from consuming bandwidth with resource-intensive video conferencing.

In addition, administrators can set a limit for audio/video throughput by specifying the average audio/video throughput limit (in bps) for the video and audio features of NetMeeting. By limiting these features, administrators can leave the video conferencing features intact and still make sure that video usage does not dominate the network. Being able to set limits can be a very handy feature for systems with limited network resources or systems hosting large conferences. Although limiting the throughput affects video performance, it is still possible to reduce the bandwidth (to preserve network resources) while still maintaining adequate video.

Now that you've seen how administrators can alter the video settings with the IEAK, let's take a look at how video works from within NetMeeting.

The NetMeeting client has a number of video settings that users may change to maximize their video performance. These settings are found in the Options dialog boxes, accessed from the Tools menu (see Figure 4.31).

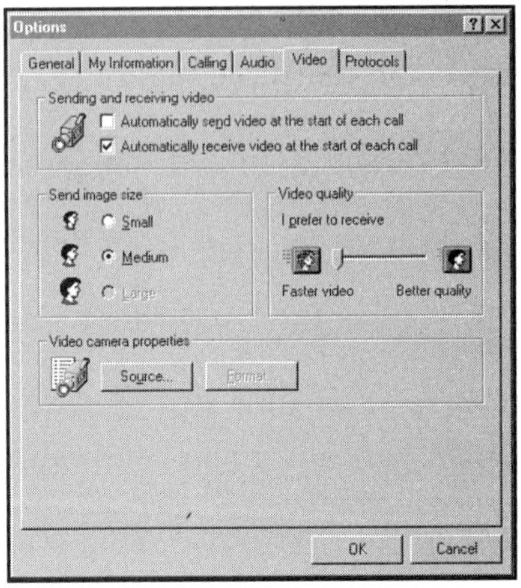

Figure 4.31

Adjusting video settings from the Options dialog box within the NetMeeting client.

The Video tab in the Options dialog box has four sections users can access to alter video settings:

- **Sending and Receiving Video.** In this section, users can choose to have video enabled automatically when they initiate a call. For example, users can select the Automatically Send Video at the Start of Each Call option, which causes video to be enabled by default. Users can also select the Automatically Receive Video at the Start of Each Call option, which allows them to see immediately the conference participants who are sending video.
- **Send Image Size.** In this section, users can select the size of the video they want to send. The larger the image, the slower the transmission. The default size is Medium.
- **Video Quality.** The video quality affects the resolution and frame rate of the video being sent or received. The user can adjust a sliding scale to indicate whether he or she would rather have faster video rates or better image quality.
- **Video Camera Properties.** This section allows the user to select the input source of the video and to alter any settings that might be associated with the user's capture equipment.

After these options are optimized for the user, the user is ready to begin conferencing with video, as shown in Figure 4.32.

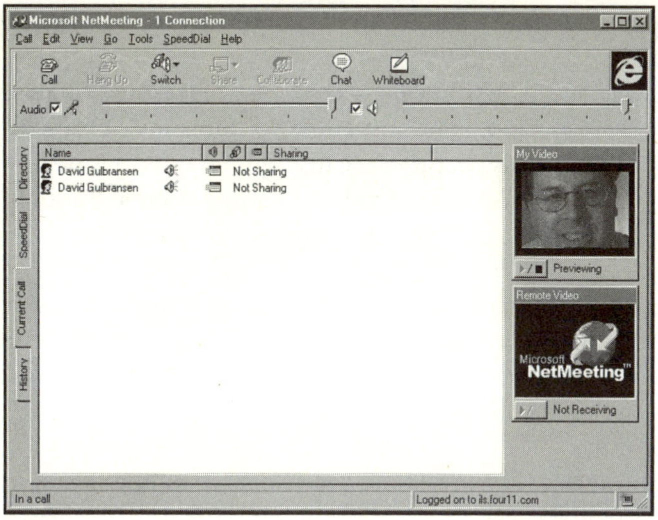

Figure 4.32

Video conferencing allows conference participants to share images as well as sound.

To begin conferencing with video, the user simply initiates a call; from the Tools menu, the user selects the Video option. From the Video submenu, the user can select to send or receive video and can detach the video windows from the application so that the windows are free floating on the desktop.

With the right equipment, video conferencing can be a valuable tool. And with some time and planning, you can optimize NetMeeting to take advantage of video conferencing without completely exhausting network resources.

Exercises

The following exercises are designed to give you some step-by-step, hands-on guidance for some of the setup tasks outlined in this chapter. Because this chapter has dealt with configuring many of Internet Explorer's components, most of these exercises take place within the component itself.

Remember that, as with any customization activity, you may notice slight variances in your settings from those in these exercises. Nonetheless, these exercises should serve as a basic framework for completing the outlined tasks.

Exercise 4.1: Importing Mail Messages from Netscape Communicator to Outlook Express

1. Launch the Outlook Express mail client.
2. From the File menu, select the Import submenu and then choose Messages. This action launches the Outlook Express Import Wizard.
3. Select the email client from which you want to import. For this exercise, select Netscape Communicator and click Next.

> **Note** If you want to follow this exercise with another mail client, select that client in step 3. If you select a client other than Netscape Communicator, keep in mind that some of the dialog boxes may differ slightly from those described in the following steps.

4. You are prompted to enter the location of your mail messages. The Import Wizard attempts to automatically determine the location; if it succeeds, click Next to continue. Otherwise, enter the message location and then click Next.
5. You are prompted to specify what folders you want to import. You can select individual folders to import, or you can select All Folders.

6. After you have selected the folder or folders to import, click Finish. You're done! Outlook Express reads the mail messages from the old mail application and makes them available to you within Outlook Express.

Exercise 4.2: Establishing a Video Connection with NetMeeting

1. Launch the NetMeeting client.
2. If your client does not automatically add you to a server, join the server that will be hosting your meeting by selecting it from the Server pull-down box located below the toolbars.
3. Select the person you wish to call from the directory listing and double-click to initiate the call.
4. Once the person has answered the call, you should begin sending and receiving video automatically. However, you may need to follow steps 5 and 6.
5. To begin sending your video signal, go to the Tools menu and make sure that under Video, the Send option is selected. This will send out your video signal.
6. To receive video from the other caller, go to the Tools menu and under Video, make sure that Receive is selected.
7. Now you should be able to use the video features of NetMeeting to their fullest.

Review Questions

The review questions in this section can help you assess your understanding of the terms, concepts, and objectives covered in this chapter. These questions are written in the style of the questions presented on the MCSE exam and are an excellent way to prepare yourself for the material you will see on the exam. After you complete the review questions, you will find the answer to each question—along with an explanation of the answer—in the following section.

1. Which of the following folders contains the files for network installation that must be placed on the Web server?

   A. `DOWNLOAD`

   B. `IE4SITE`

   C. `WIN95_NT`

   D. `Mfloppy`

2. Which of the following is a problem with migration from IE 3.x to IE4.0? (Select all that apply.)

   A. Plug-in compatibility between versions

   B. Importing user proxy server settings

   C. Coexistence of IE 3.0 and IE 4.0 on same machine

   D. Importing user cookie settings

3. Which of the following mail clients is not supported for importing with IE/Outlook Express?

   A. Internet Mail

   B. Pegasus Mail

   C. Netscape Mail

   D. Eudora Pro

4. To establish connections with three or more NetMeeting participants, users must specify a connection to a/an

   A. LDAP server

   B. NetMeeting home page

   C. User profile database

   D. NetMeeting directory server

5. To use NetMeeting's application sharing feature, users must first configure the NetMeeting client to

   A. Connect automatically to a directory server

   B. Enable sharing

   C. Limit audio/video throughput

   D. Specify a file download directory

6. Which of the following NetMeeting features poses a security risk to the local file system?

   A. Whiteboarding

   B. File transfer

   C. Video conferencing

   D. Audio conferencing

7. How can administrators preserve network resources while still retaining NetMeeting functionality?

   A. Disable application sharing

   B. Disable call answering

   C. Limit collaboration

   D. Limit audio/video throughput

8. What are the four folders created by the IEAK Wizard that contain the custom installation information?

   A. `DOWNLOAD, CD, Mfloppy, INS`

   B. `WIN95_NT, DOWNLOAD, Floppy, ADM`

   C. `DOWNLOAD, WIN95_NT, WIN311, INS`

   D. `INET, DOWNLOAD, CD, INS`

9. How can administrators prevent users from altering NetMeeting settings?

   A. Disable application sharing

   B. Disable the Options dialog boxes

   C. Limit collaboration

   D. Limit audio/video throughput

10. How might an administrator go about importing addresses and messages from a mail client that Outlook Express does not support for migration? (Select all that apply.)

    A. Import addresses as comma-separated values (CSVs)

    B. Import messages as text files

    C. Convert mail to a supported client and then convert to Outlook Express

    D. Import addresses as a `.DBM` file

Review Answers

Now that you have completed the review questions, check your answers against those provided here. Explanations are provided for each answer so that you can see whether you arrived at the correct solution for the right reason, or so that you can see how your answer varied from the correct one.

1. **B** The `IE4SITE` folder contains the files that must be placed on the Web server in the specified download URL. The `DOWNLOAD` folder contains the Active Setup files for the installation; although this folder *can* be placed on the Web site, it can also be distributed by disk.

2. **A and C** For any upgrade or conversion to Internet Explorer 4.0, plug-in compatibility should be checked and new plug-ins should be installed as custom packages. In addition, IE 3.0 and IE 4.0 cannot reside on the same machine.

3. **B** IE supports importing mail settings and messages from Internet Mail, Netscape, and Eudora. It can also import settings from Microsoft Exchange and Outlook (the full client version). IE/Outlook Express does not support Pegasus Mail.

4. **D** The NetMeeting directory server acts as a host mechanism for connecting users for conferences. When the user launches the NetMeeting client, he or she can either log in to a directory server automatically or can log on manually.

5. **B** Until sharing is enabled, clients cannot share applications and collaborate.

6. **B** The ability to exchange files with NetMeeting is a useful collaboration feature, however using the file transfer feature is a security risk. Because users are saving a file from the network, the content cannot be ensured; the threat that the file contains a virus that may corrupt the user's system is legitimate.

7. **D** Because audio/video conferencing is the most network-intensive application, limiting the audio/video throughput bandwidth can help relieve network congestion while still allowing users access to the feature.

8. **A** The four default folders that contain the information and files for each type of installation option created with the IEAK Wizard are `DOWNLOAD`, `CD`, `Mfloppy`, and `INS`.

9. **B** Disabling the Options dialog boxes from the System Policies and Restrictions section will prevent users from altering the settings of the NetMeeting client.

10. **A and C** Outlook Express addresses can be imported as a text file that uses comma-separated values. Mail messages from unsupported clients can be converted to a supported client, and then converted a second time into Outlook Express.

Answers to Test Yourself Questions at Beginning of Chapter

The following answers are provided for the prechapter quiz at the beginning of this chapter. You can use these questions and answers to determine how familiar you may already be with this chapter's material. Each of the questions relates to a specific goal for the Integration and Interoperability section of the "Implementing and Supporting the Microsoft Internet Explorer Administration Kit for Microsoft Internet Explorer 4.0" MCSE exam. Each of the following answers references the section in this chapter that deals with the covered objective so that you can easily locate the material you may want to review or clarify.

1. All the files created for a custom installation of Internet Explorer are located in the root level directory of the folder specified by the administrator during the IEAK Wizard process. There are however, several special folders and files that are created for each specific type of installation:

   - **Network.** This installation contains a folder named after the platform version being created, such as `Win95_NT`. Within that folder is an `En` folder (if the language is English) that contains the files to be placed on the Web site. You will also have a `DOWNLOAD` folder that contains the Active Setup Wizard that users must download to run the installation.

- **CD-ROM.** In the root level directory is a `CD` folder that contains the files for the CD-ROM. This folder includes the executable to launch the installation process, and the autorun file to configure the CD-ROM autorun feature. The contents of this folder should be placed on the CD-ROM as the root level directory.

- **Floppy Disk.** In the root level IE directory is a folder called `Mfloppy` that contains one subfolder for each floppy disk (these folders have the names `Disk1`, `Disk2`, `Disk3`, and so on). The contents of each disk folder should be copied to a floppy disk—without the folder—so that the folder contents are in the root level directory of the floppy.

What are the specific files and folders created for network based installations of Internet Explorer? What about CD-ROM based installations? Multiple Floppies?

Sections Referencing This Material:

- "Deploying a Preconfigured Version of IE 4.0"
- "Distribution by CD-ROM"
- "Distribution by Floppy Disk"

2. Migration from Internet Explorer 3.*x* to IE 4.0 is a very straightforward process. The IE installation process automatically preserves some of the user settings, including these:

   - Favorites
   - Cookies
   - Proxy settings

   Administrators should reconfigure any previously installed plug-ins as add-on packages for IE 4.0 to ensure compatibility. Administrators should also be aware that IE 3.*x* and IE 4.0 cannot coexist on the same machine because of software incompatibilities.

Sections Referencing This Material:

- "Replacing Internet Browsers"
- "Microsoft Internet Explorer 3.*x*"

3. Migration from versions of Netscape Navigator or Communicator to IE 4.0 is a straightforward process. The IE installer preserves the following settings:

    - Favorites (Bookmarks)
    - Cookies
    - Proxy settings

    Administrators should reconfigure any previously installed plug-ins as add-on packages for IE 4.0 to ensure compatibility. Unlike IE 3.*x*, versions of Netscape products can coexist on the same machine as Internet Explorer 4.0.

    Sections Referencing This Material:

    - "Replacing Internet Browsers"
    - "Microsoft Internet Explorer 3.*x*"

4. The large number of Internet Mail clients available makes it impossible for Outlook Express and IE to support the automatic migration from all email clients. However, the IE installation process does support migration from the following clients:

    - Internet News and Mail
    - Netscape Navigator and Communicator
    - Eudora (including Eudora Light and Eudora Pro)

    The installation process also imports settings from the following clients:

    - Microsoft Exchange
    - Outlook (the full client version)

Sections Referencing This Material:

- "Replacing Internet Mail Clients"

5. NetMeeting supports a wide variety of conferencing and collaboration tools, including the ability of users to share applications and to take turns controlling the application from remote machines. NetMeeting also supports white-boarding and file transfers, two additional ways to exchange data and work collaboratively on remote systems.

   NetMeeting also supports more traditional types of conferencing, include audio conferencing and video conferencing.

   Sections Referencing This Material:

   - "Configuring NetMeeting"
   - "Multipoint Application Sharing"
   - "Transferring Files"
   - "Video Conferencing"

6. Although application sharing and file transfer are powerful tools, both have associated risks.

   Application sharing allows remote users to control the functionality of an application running on your machine. As a result, the remote user has limited access to your file system—not to mention full control over documents you are currently editing.

   File transfer opens the user's local machine to exposure from corrupted files or to files that contain viruses. Because of the security risks associated with both conferencing features, application sharing and file transfer should be enabled only when conferencing with trusted individuals in a secure network environment.

   Sections Referencing this Material:

   - "Configuring NetMeeting"

- "Multipoint Application Sharing"
- "Transferring Files"

7. Although audio and video conferencing are both powerful conferencing tools, there are some limitations that administrators should be aware of.

   Both audio and video conferencing can represent disturbances in the workplace. If levels are not set correctly, conferencing can be louder than a speaker phone. Although this wouldn't be a problem in a conference room, it can be a problem in a small office environment or from an employee's cubicle.

   The biggest issue with audio and video conferencing is the consumption of bandwidth. Because both audio and video (especially video) are bandwidth-intensive applications, running NetMeeting with video can quickly erode network performance. Limiting audio/video throughput can help administrators limit this problem.

   Sections Referencing This Material:

   - "Configuring NetMeeting"
   - "Video Conferencing"

Chapter 5

Monitoring and Optimization

With the high degree of customization you can achieve with Internet Explorer administrators must address a number of considerations both during and after the deployment of a customized version of Internet Explorer.

Specifically, administrators should be aware of how to optimize the performance of Internet Explorer using the customization tools available in the IEAK. A number of settings are related to performance and network connectivity, and administrators can manipulate them to make the installed version of IE more tailored to the needs of the end user.

This section of the MCSE exam and this chapter address the issues of monitoring and optimization. That is, the chapter covers the steps administrators can take to make sure that the IE is configured for the best performance for their users.

This chapter helps you prepare for the exam by covering the following objectives:

Objectives

- Customize Active Desktop items and Active Channels
- Use the IEAK Profile Manager to optimize network resources and components
- Set up schedules for automatic updates. Locations include
  - Site subscriptions
  - Channels
  - The Active Desktop
- Optimize caching and performance

Test Yourself! Before reading this chapter, test yourself to determine how much study time you will need to devote to this section.

The following prechapter quiz is designed to help you get a feel for how well you currently understand the material covered in this chapter. If you think you have a strong understanding of the objectives outlined in the previous list, try the quiz. Based on your score on this quiz, you may feel well enough prepared to skip ahead to the Review Questions at the end of the chapter, or you may determine that you would like to study the chapter material more closely.

1. What feature must be installed to make use of the Active Desktop? How are Active Desktop components customized within the IEAK?
2. What type of folder customization is allowed with the Windows Desktop Update?
3. What functionality is added to Internet Explorer with Active Channels? How are Active Channels accessed? How are Active Channels configured using the IEAK?
4. What are the different types of scheduling mechanisms for active components and site subscriptions?
5. What policy settings and restrictions have the greatest impact on performance?
6. How does caching function in Internet Explorer 4.0? How does manipulating cache settings affect performance?

The answers to this prechapter quiz are located at the end of this chapter. Score your answers against those provided to determine your course of study for this chapter.

Test Objectives Overview

Internet Explorer is a large and complicated application. Its close integration with the shell and operating system leave it in a position to seriously affect many aspects of the user's machine without intention. When you add customized components to the mix, a situation develops in which the complex interactions of components and settings can cause performance problems that seriously impact the usability of the application.

This chapter examines the components and settings of Internet Explorer that have the greatest impact on usage and performance. The chapter looks at how these mechanisms work and what steps you can take to make sure that they work at the most optimal level.

The chapter begins by looking at the Active Desktop, how administrators go about customizing Active Desktop settings and items, and how those settings impact performance. We will also look at channel customization and configuration. Aspects of channels, such as subscription schedules and downloading content, can seriously affect the performance of a system with IE installed.

The chapter also looks at one of the most powerful and flexible tools available to administrators through the IEAK: the IEAK Profile Manager. Because administrators can alter System Policies and Restrictions through the IEAK Profile Manager, this chapter covers how those settings can impact performance and how administrators can maximize performance using policy settings.

Finally, the chapter looks at the Internet Explorer caching mechanism and how it affects performance. Administrators and users should both be aware of what the cache is, how it works in IE, and how altering the cache can seriously impact performance.

Here's a rundown of the topics covered in this chapter:

- Customizing Active Desktop items
- Customizing Active Channels

- Optimizing components with the IEAK Profile Manager
- Scheduling automatic updates
- Optimizing caching and performance

Customizing Active Desktop Items

Objective

The Active Desktop is a component of the Windows Desktop Update that allows users to customize their desktop environment to provide a number of enhancements that blur the lines between local and network resources.

For example, using the Active Desktop, users can alter the way they interact with the taskbar: They can add icons for applications so that the applications can be run with the click of a button.

Users can also customize their folder views: When users are browsing the local file system, items can be displayed like traditional windows or they can be altered to function as Web pages. If folders are viewed as Web pages, files become links, and you only have to single-click them.

Finally, users can add custom components to the Active Desktop, making the desktop function much like a Web page. Users can specify resources to list on the page, such as interactive stock tickers or weather maps. Components can be downloaded from a variety of sources, and the user can control what elements are added to the Active Desktop.

Customizing options for the Active Desktop starts with the IEAK Wizard when you are first creating your custom installation. You must configure your installation to install the Windows Desktop Update if you want to take advantage of the features found in the Active Desktop.

Then you can use the IEAK Wizard to import the settings of the Active Desktop components configured on the IE installation on the administrative machine, as shown in Figure 5.1.

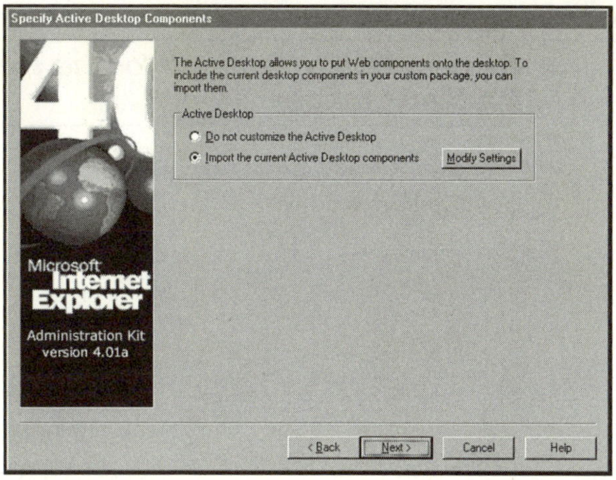

Figure 5.1

Importing the Active Desktop components from IE using the IEAK Wizard.

If you have chosen to install the desktop, the only remaining task at this stage is to configure the System Policies and Restrictions that will apply to the desktop settings. The policies can be configured for the installation using the IEAK Wizard, as shown in Figure 5.2, or they can be altered later using the IEAK Profile Manager.

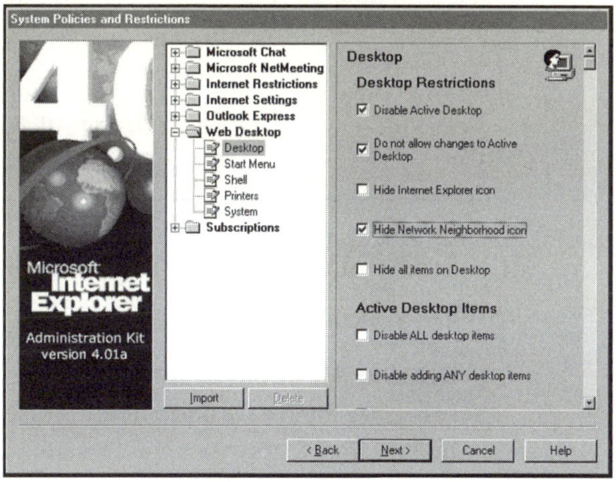

Figure 5.2

Specifying policy restrictions for the Active Desktop using the IEAK Wizard.

A number of restrictions can be applied to the usage and configuration of the desktop; the full list of policy choices is shown in Table 5.1.

Table 5.1

System Policy Settings for the Desktop in the IEAK Profile Manager

Policy	Settings
Desktop Restrictions	Disable Active Desktop
	Do Not Allow Changes to Active Desktop
	Hide Internet Explorer Icon
	Hide Network Neighborhood Icon
	Hide All Items on Desktop
Active Desktop Items	Disable All Desktop Items
	Disable Adding Any Desktop Items
	Disable Deleting Any Desktop Items
	Disable Editing Any Desktop Items
	Disable Closing Any Desktop Items
Desktop Wallpaper Settings	No HTML Wallpaper
	Disable Changing Wallpaper
Desktop Toolbars Settings	Disable Dragging, Dropping, and Closing All Toolbars
	Disable Resizing All Toolbars

Here is a list of the settings that deal specifically with the Active Desktop:

- **Disable All Desktop Items.** This setting restricts users from using the Active Desktop at all. This setting could be used to make other features of the Desktop Update available to users, while disabling Active Desktop components.
- **Disable Adding Any Desktop Items.** With this option selected, the preconfigured options from your custom build are available to the user; however, users are prohibited from adding any additional desktop items.

- **Disable Deleting Any Desktop Items.** Similar to the preceding option, this option leaves preconfigured items intact but prevents the user from removing items from the desktop.
- **Disable Editing Any Desktop Items.** If you want to install desktop items with specific settings, this option can prevent users from altering the configuration of any installed desktop items.
- **Disable Closing Any Desktop Items.** This option prevents users from closing preinstalled desktop items, keeping items always present on the desktop.

Although some configuration of the Active Desktop can be performed in the IEAK Wizard (and the Profile Manager), the majority of the Active Desktop configuration for the user takes place on the actual desktop. Let's look at how.

To access the Active Desktop configuration, users can simply right-click an empty area of the Desktop to display a pop-up menu that contains choices for the Active Desktop, as shown in Figure 5.3.

Figure 5.3

Use the Active Desktop pop-up menu to access desktop configuration choices.

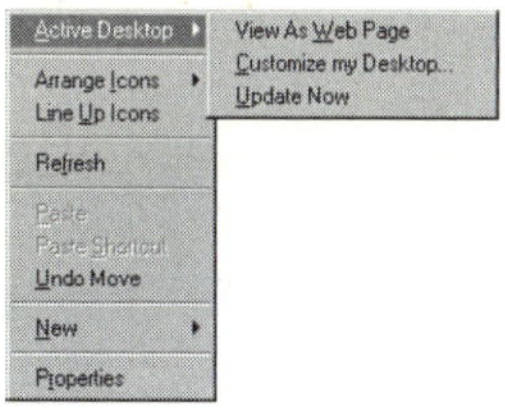

In the pop-up menu, under the Active Desktop submenu, users are presented with three choices:

- View as Web Page
- Customize My Desktop
- Update Now

The View as Web Page option is what actually activates and deactivates the Active Desktop. When this option is selected, any installed and selected desktop items appear on the desktop, where users can interact with them freely. If this option is not selected, the items are hidden.

The Customize My Desktop option is how users can alter the appearance of the desktop, add and remove components, and customize their folder views. The following sections cover customizing the desktop using this option.

Finally, the Update Now option forces any installed Active Desktop items that are active to connect to their sources and update their content. This option can be used if the user wants to force a content update outside the parameters of the subscription for the item.

Display Properties

When you select Customize My Desktop from the Active Desktop submenu, the Display Properties Control Panel launches, as shown in Figure 5.4. This action also automatically selects the Web tab, which is what controls the Active Desktop. Of course, you can also access these settings using the standard Control Panel methods as well.

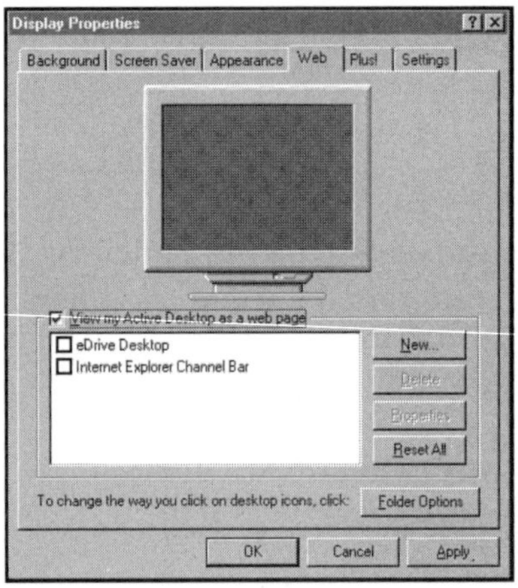

Figure 5.4

The Display Properties Control Panel Web tab controls Active Desktop properties.

From the Display Properties Control Panel, you can control all the Active Desktop settings. You can do any of the following tasks:

- Activate and deactivate the Active Desktop
- Add new Active Desktop items
- Delete Active Desktop items
- Edit the properties of installed items
- Reset to the default settings
- Edit folder view options

Users can activate (or deactivate) the Active Desktop by selecting the View My Active Desktop as a Web Page option, which simply turns the Active Desktop on or off.

The components displayed on the Active Desktop are found in the list box; you can add new items by clicking the New button. Items with a check mark are currently selected to appear on the Active Desktop.

You can delete items by selecting them in the list box and then clicking the Delete button. Similarly, you can edit the settings for the items by clicking the Properties button; you can return all the components and settings to their default settings by clicking Reset All.

Finally, users can alter the way their folders appear and display the contents of the local file system by clicking the Folder Options button.

The following sections present the specific details for each of these outlined customizations.

Adding Desktop Items

You can add items to the Active Desktop in two ways: by specifying a URL (or file) for the item, or by connecting to a gallery, such as the Microsoft Desktop Gallery, located at `http://www.microsoft.com/ie/ie40/gallery/`.

If you choose to add an item by specifying the URL, simply click New. When you are prompted to be taken to the Microsoft Desktop Gallery, click No; you are then asked to enter the URL, as shown in Figure 5.5.

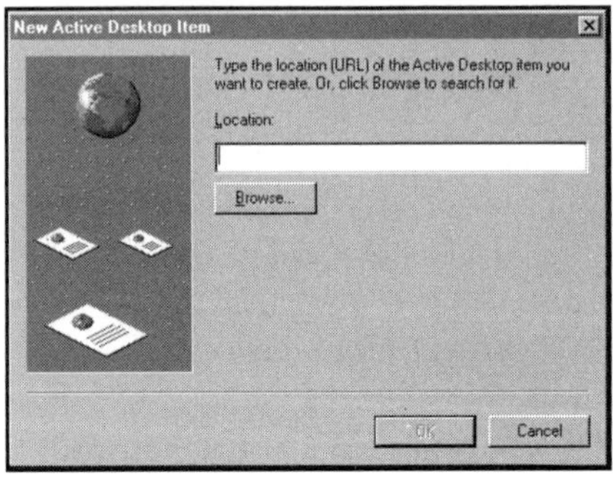

Figure 5.5

Adding a desktop item by specifying the URL for the item content.

You can add any Web site as an Active Desktop component by specifying the URL; however, items that have been developed specifically for the Active Desktop generally provide more dynamic content.

If you are just browsing items or are looking to add a specific type of item, the Microsoft Desktop Gallery can provide a good resource for items. To install items through the gallery, click New to add a new item. When prompted about whether you want to connect to the gallery, click Yes. This action launches Internet Explorer and loads the Microsoft Desktop Gallery page, as shown in Figure 5.6.

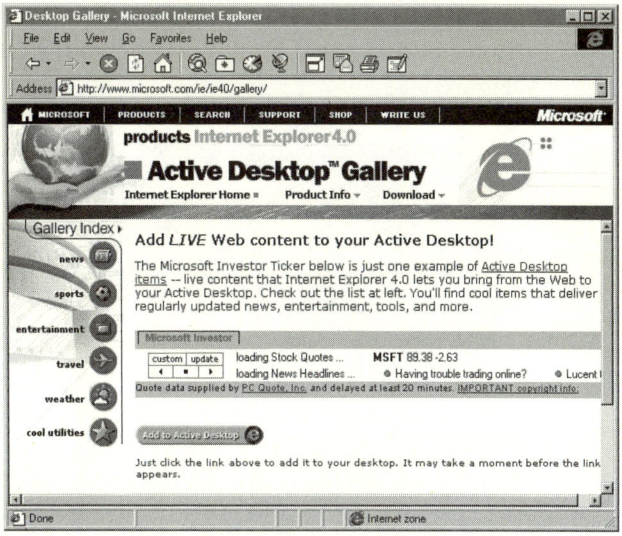

Figure 5.6

The Microsoft Desktop Gallery contains items available for the Active Desktop.

The Desktop Gallery contains a number of items, in categories, that you can add to your Active Desktop. Click the item to see a description page for the item; if you want to install that item, simply click the Add to Active Desktop button.

You are then prompted to confirm that you want to install the component and are asked to review subscription information. Item developers can specify subscription schedules for updating their items; however, you can override those schedules at this stage, as shown in Figure 5.7.

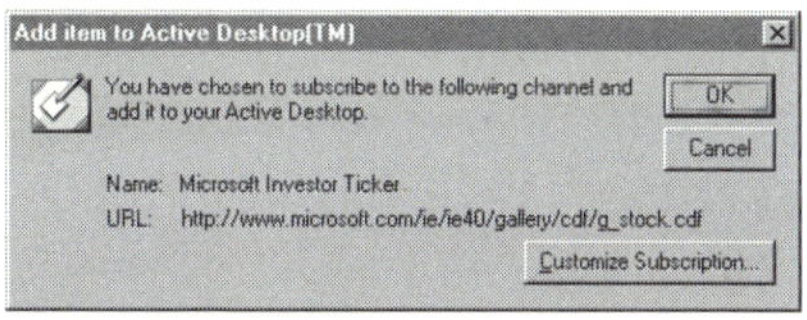

Figure 5.7

Adding a desktop item automatically configures subscription information and adds the component to the desktop.

Similarly, if you are subscribing to a Web site rather than a designed item, you can take this opportunity to specify the update schedule. After you agree to the schedule, the item is downloaded and installed on your Active Desktop. When the initial content is downloaded, the item appears on your desktop, as shown in Figure 5.8.

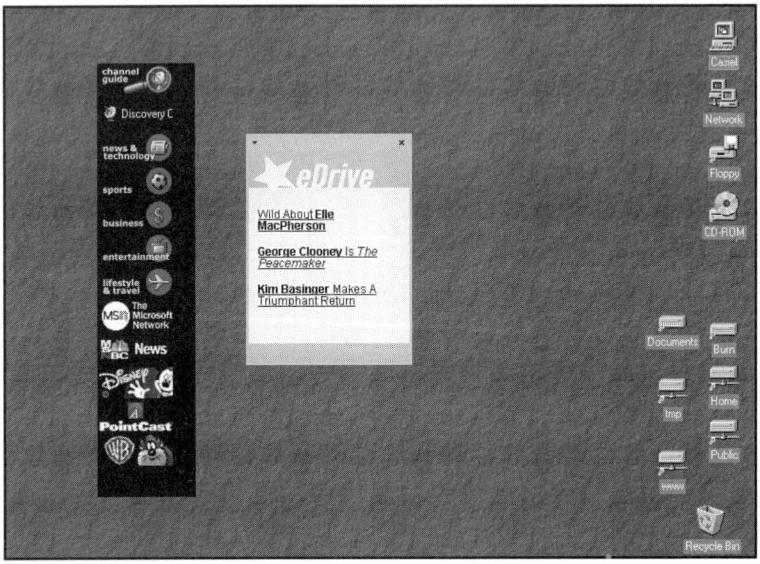

Figure 5.8

Items added appear on the Active Desktop as floating windows.

Deleting Desktop Items

Some desktop items are better than others; the only way to really evaluate one is to use it. So what if you decide that the desktop item you wanted so badly turns out to be a dud? Delete it.

Deleting a desktop item is easy. From the list box, simply select the item you want to remove and click the Delete button. You are prompted to confirm that you want to delete the item, as shown in Figure 5.9.

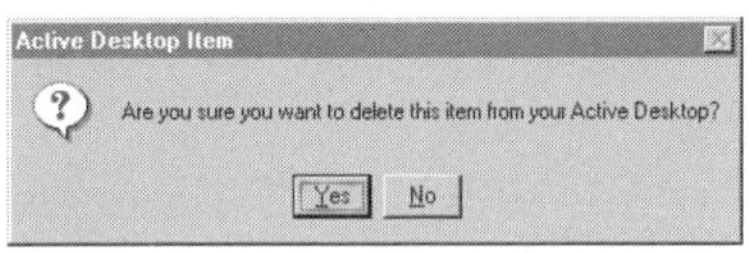

Figure 5.9

Deleting an item from the Active Desktop is easy and quick.

Assuming that you do want to delete the item, agree to the prompt; the item is removed from your desktop. Keep in mind that deleting the item from the desktop completely removes it from your system; if you want to add it to the desktop again, you must do so as if it were a new item. If you want to leave the item installed on your system but just don't want it to appear on your desktop, simply deselect the item in the list box. Only items with a check mark appear on the desktop.

Editing Desktop Items

Recall that when you installed a new desktop item, as described in "Adding Desktop Items," earlier in this chapter, you were prompted to confirm subscription information. At that time, we were in a hurry to install the component, so we simply accepted the assigned subscription and went about our business.

But now you've decided that you want to edit that subscription information to change the way your item downloads are updated. You can do so by editing the item's properties.

The first option you have is to subscribe or unsubscribe to an item's content. Because items are simply HTML or CDF channels, you can subscribe to them just as you can to Web sites and channels. Subscribing is how you keep desktop items current and updated. However, there may be occasions in which you want to keep the item on your desktop without receiving any automatic updates (for example, if you are taking your laptop on the road for an extended period of time).

If you select the item you want to update from the list box, you can then click Properties to edit the settings for that item, as shown in Figure 5.10.

The Subscription tab of the Desktop Properties dialog box provides information about the name of the item and the URL. You can use the Unsubscribe button to stop the automatic content update. Under the Unsubscribe button is a list of the following summary information:

- The type of subscriptions
- The update schedule

- The time of the last update
- The result of the last update
- The next scheduled update

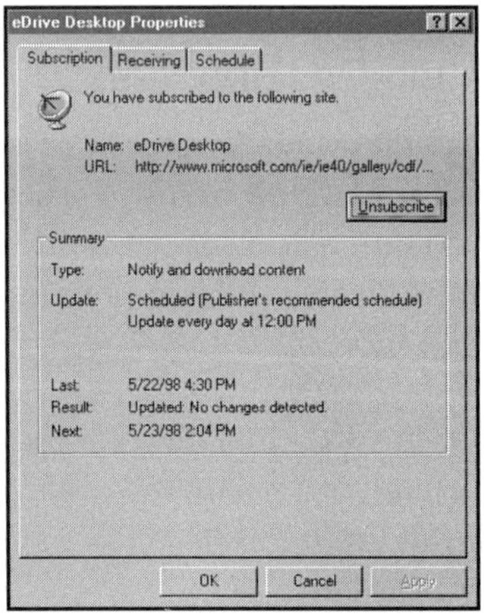

Figure 5.10

Editing the subscription properties for an Active Desktop item.

The Receiving tab of the item's Desktop Properties dialog box allows you to specify how the subscription mechanism functions, as shown in Figure 5.11.

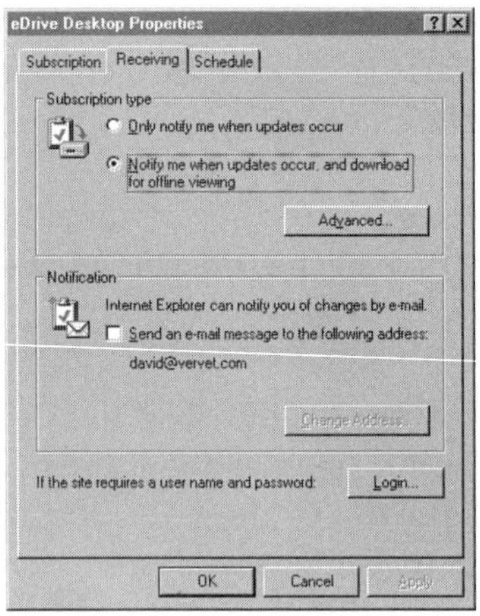

Figure 5.11

Users can be notified automatically about updates to the Active Desktop items.

The Subscription Type section of the Receiving tab allows users to alter the subscription type. Users can choose from two subscription types:

- **Only Notify Me When Updates Occur.** This option provides notification to the user of an item update, but the user must update the item content manually.
- **Notify Me When Updates Occur, and Download for Offline Viewing.** This option automatically updates the new item content and then notifies the user.

The user can also click the Advanced button to customize exactly what is updated. On the Advanced Download Options dialog box, users can specify the following:

- **Content for Offline Use.** This option provides two selections for the user:
  - **Download Linked Pages Within a Depth of *X*.** This option allows the user to specify how many levels down the new content will be downloaded. It is generally not wise to set this option higher than 1 or 2 levels.
  - **Follow Links Outside of This Page's Web Site.** This is a very dangerous option to select; it can result in the download of additional content not provided by the item author.
- **Items to Download.** This option allows users to select whether or not to download certain types of content. With this option, users can specify that large files (such as video files) should not be automatically downloaded.
  - Images
  - Sound and video
  - ActiveX controls and Java applets

- **Never Download More than X KB per Update.** This option allows users to restrict the amount of information downloaded during an update based on the size in kilobytes. This option allows users to specify that an update for this item cannot be, for example, over 500KB in size.

The final tab in the Properties dialog box, the Schedule tab, is also available for specifying properties, as shown in Figure 5.12.

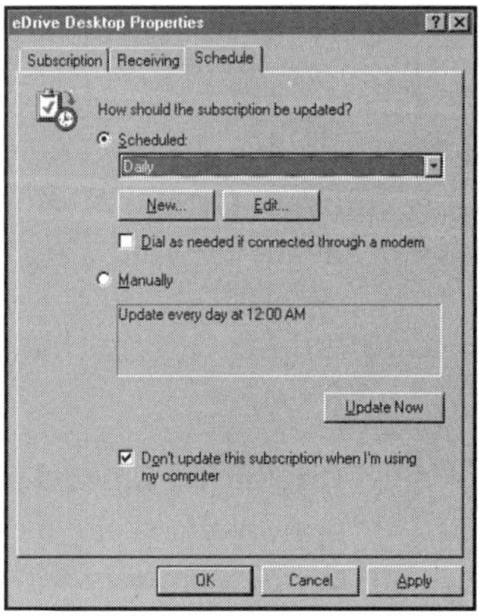

Figure 5.12

Altering subscription schedules can balance the timeliness of information with network resources.

The Schedule tab allows users to select the methods to be used for scheduling the item. The options allow user to specify that an update should occur at the following times:

- **Scheduled.** This option allows users to update the item according to the schedule determined by the item's creators or according to a custom specified schedule, such as the following:
  - Daily
  - Monthly
  - Weekly

  The Dial As Needed If Connected Through a Modem option causes the computer to automatically connect to the Internet for an update if it is connected with a modem.
- **Manually.** This option reminds users to update the item but requires that they manually run the update.

Users can also select the Don't Update This Subscription When I'm Using My Computer option, which prevents an item from consuming network and system resources while it is in use.

If users choose to edit the schedule or create a new custom schedule, they can do so using the custom schedule mechanism shown in Figure 5.13.

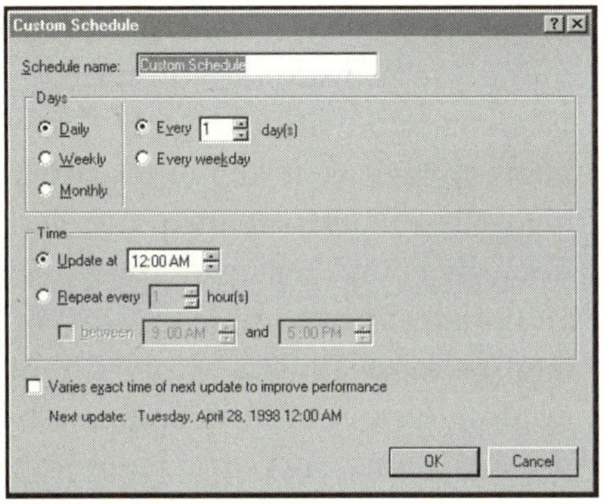

Figure 5.13

Users can create custom update schedules based on their working habits.

In the Custom Schedule dialog box, users can change the specifics of the Daily, Weekly, or Monthly updates, or they can create a new update from scratch.

First, the user must specify the days on which the update is to occur. The options for the day are as follows:

- **Daily.** For this option, the user can either select the Every Weekday option or specify the interval of days between updates.
- **Weekly.** For this option, the user must specify the interval of weeks and the days of the week on which the update is to occur.
- **Monthly.** For this option, users can specify a specific date in the month and the number of months between updates. For example, the user can specify day 15 of every 2 months. The user can also specify a weekday and a month interval, such as the first Saturday of every month.

Users must also specify the time for the update. They can choose a specific time, such as 2:00 a.m., or they can specify an interval, such as Repeat Every 4 Hours. If they choose an interval, they may also specify an update period, such as Repeat Every 2 Hours Between 9:00 a.m. and 5:00 p.m.

The final option for custom scheduling is the Varies Exact Time of Next Update to Improve Performance option. This option is really a human safeguard. Generally, individuals tend to schedule updates for even time periods, for example 12:00 or 12:30. Even if they try to provide variation, they generally select times such as 12:45 or 1:15. Unfortunately, this type of scheduling means that many clients are trying to update items at the same time, decreasing network performance. By selecting the Varies Exact Time option, the computer varies the time slightly each time it performs an update. For example, instead of updating at 12:00 a.m., it might choose 12:07 a.m. or 11:59 p.m. By adding this somewhat random element to the update schedule, the load should be dispersed, increasing performance and making the update go more quickly.

Folder Options

Another component of the Active Desktop is the capability to manipulate the appearance of folders within the file system. The user can select the functionality of icons within the folder, the file types associated with applications, and the folder elements that are seen and that are hidden.

On the General tab of the Folder Options Control Panel, shown in Figure 5.14, you can select from three styles of folder views:

- Web Style
- Classic Style
- Custom

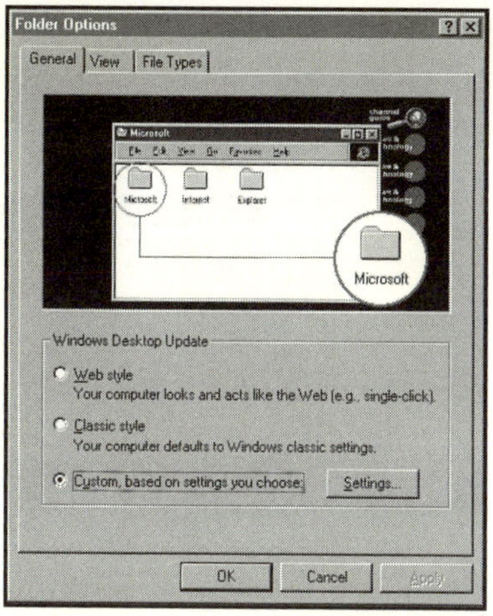

Figure 5.14

The Folder Options Control Panel allows you to select the type of folder view you want for the local file system.

The first option is the Web Style, represented in Figure 5.15. The Web Style option causes folder contents to appear as though they were the contents of a Web page. That is, folders, documents, and so on are treated like links and are underlined. They are also activated with a single click instead of a double click. This interface blurs the distinction between content located on the Internet, content on the intranet, and content on the local file system.

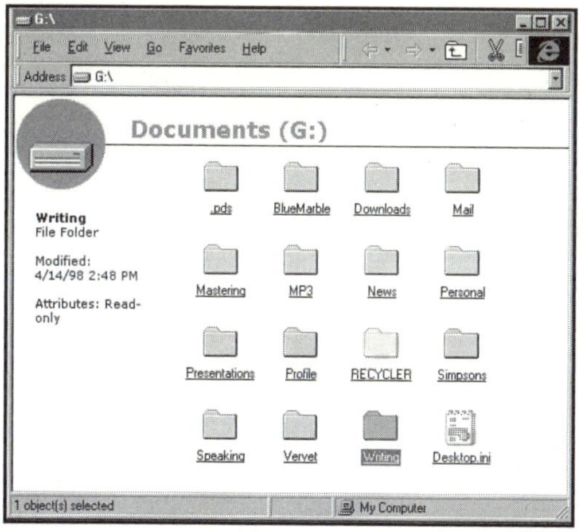

Figure 5.15

The Web Style option for folder views features an interface like the Web, including single-clicking files.

The second option is the Classic Style, represented in Figure 5.16. The Classic filter causes folders to behave as they have in previous versions of Windows. Files are shown normally and require a double-click to be activated. System files are hidden, and the overall appearance is that of a standard Windows 95 folder.

Figure 5.16

The Classic Style features the conventional Windows folder interaction.

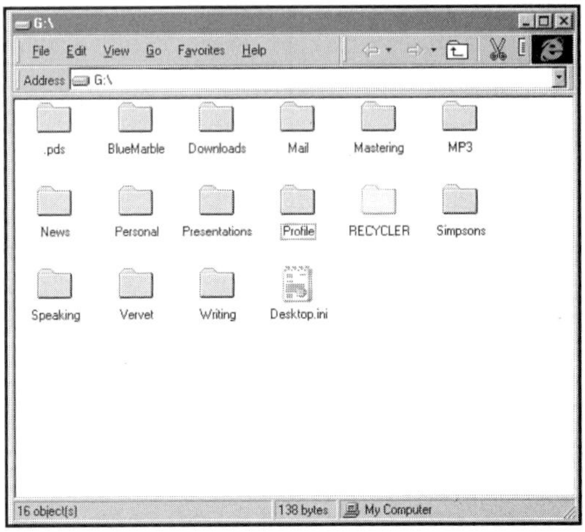

Finally, users can select a Custom style, based on settings you choose using the Custom Settings dialog box, shown in Figure 5.17.

Figure 5.17

Users can configure customized settings for folder views to use combinations of their favorite features.

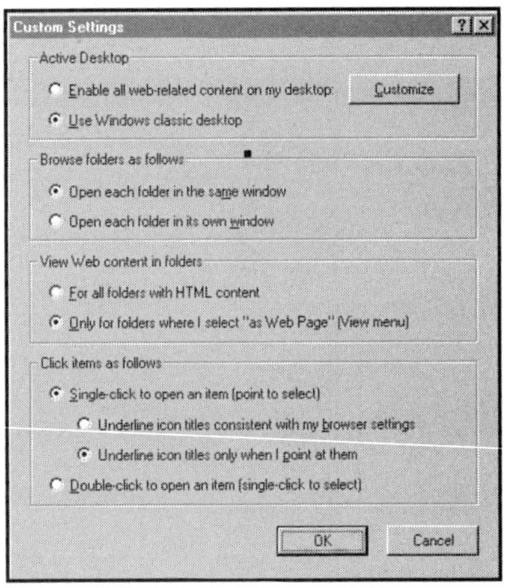

By selecting a Custom view, users can pick the features of the Web view and the Classic view that they like. The features are divided into four categories:

- **Active Desktop.** With the Active Desktop options, users can choose the Enable All Web-Related Content on My Desktop option or choose the Use Windows Classic Desktop option. Any customizations made to the Active Desktop from the Display Control Panel apply if Web content is enabled.

- **Browse Folders as Follows.** This option controls how folders are spawned as users traverse through folder levels. You can choose the Open Each Folder in the Same Window option, which does not spawn a new folder but displays the new content in the currently open window. The Open Each Folder in Its Own Window option causes a new window to be spawned for each opened folder.

- **View Web Content in Folders.** If a folder contains Web-based content such as HTML files, the Desktop Update can display the content directly in the folder without launching an external browser. You can select the For All Folders with HTML Content option to have folders that contain HTML files exhibit this behavior. Alternatively, you can choose the Only for Folders Where I Select "As Web Page" (View Menu) option to view Web content.

- **Click Items as Follows.** This option allows users to establish how a folder item responds to mouse clicks. The user can select the Single-Click to Open an Item (Point to Select) option, which mimics Web behavior. Alternatively, the user can select the Double-Click to Open an Item (Single-Click to Select) option, which is the classic folder behavior. Additionally, if the single-click option is enabled, users can select the Underline Icon Titles Consistent with My Browser Settings option or the Underline Icon Titles Only When I Point at Them option.

By tweaking the customizations of the folder view, folders can take on the appearance of classic windows but still retain some of the functionality of the Desktop Update, as shown in Figure 5.18.

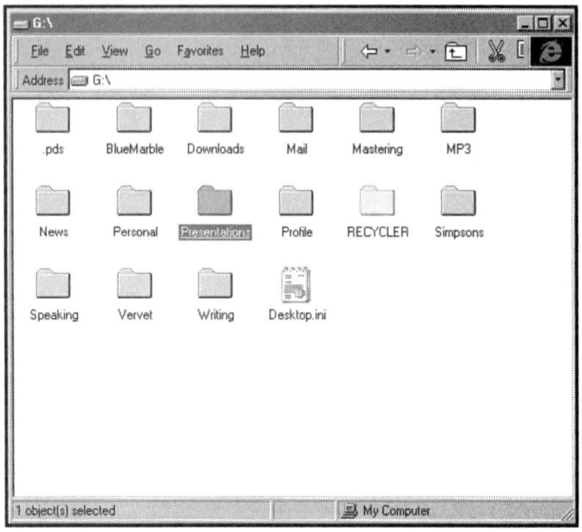

Figure 5.18

Customized folder views can retain the functionality of IE 4.0 with the look of traditional folders.

The next tab in the Folder Options Control Panel is the View tab, shown in Figure 5.19. This tab contains the customization settings for the folder elements to be displayed and those to be hidden. Table 5.2 lists the options that can be set in the View tab.

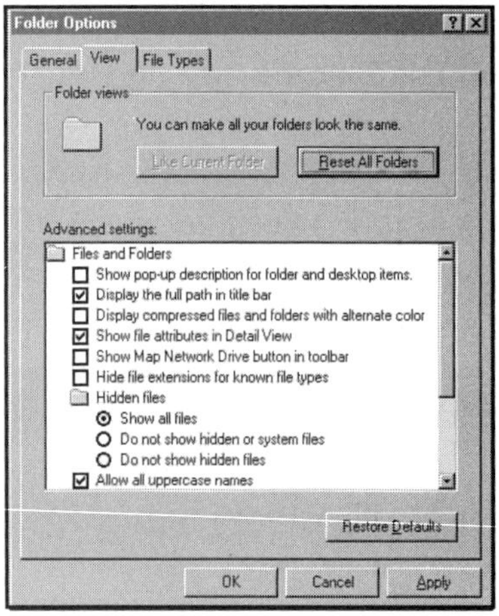

Figure 5.19

The View tab of the Folder Options Control Panel allows the user to customize which folder elements appear and which do not.

Table 5.2

Folder Options: Advanced Settings for Folder Views

Setting	Options
Files and Folders	Show pop-up description for folder and desktop items
	Display the full path in title bar
	Display compressed files and folders with alternate colors
	Show file attributes in Detail View
	Show Map Network Drive button in toolbar
	Hide file extensions for known file types
	Allow all uppercase names
	Remember each folder's view settings
Hidden Files	Show all files
	Do not show hidden or system files
	Do not show hidden files
Visual Settings	Hide icons when desktop is viewed as Web page
	Smooth edges of screen fonts
	Show window contents while dragging

The final tab in the Folder Options Control Panel is File Types. On this tab, you can specify which file extensions are associated with which applications. Because most of this association is automated by installation programs, there generally is no need for you to edit file types by hand.

By manipulating the settings for the Active Desktop and folder views, you can almost completely customize the user's environment. Of course, complete customization can lead to confusion, so it is best to customize conservatively. This is why many of the features support the classic look and feel of folders and the desktop users are accustomed to.

Customizing Active Channels

Objective

As is true with Active Desktop items, you cannot configure Active Channel subscriptions directly within the IEAK Wizard. Instead, you configure the settings for Active Channels from within the version of Internet Explorer installed on the machine running the IEAK Wizard. During the process of building a custom installation of Internet Explorer, the IEAK allows administrators to import channel settings from the IEAK Wizard, as shown in Figure 5.20.

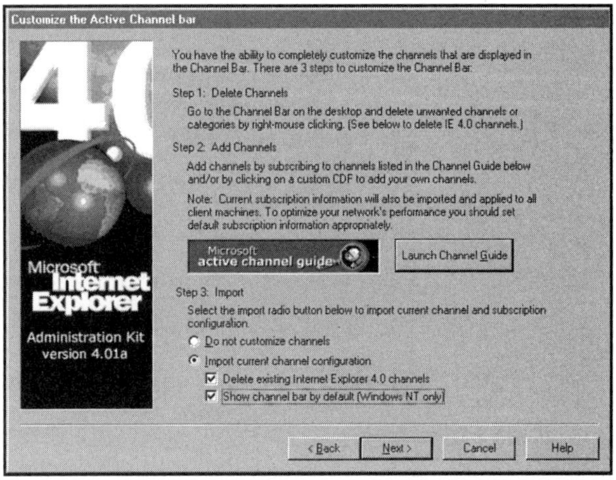

Figure 5.20

Importing Active Channel settings using the IEAK Wizard.

Because Active Channel settings are imported from the version of IE on the administrative machine, we'll talk about customizing Active Channels from within Internet Explorer.

Internet Explorer features support for two type of subscription mechanisms: site subscriptions and Active Channels. Site subscriptions are really just automatic caching of Web site pages so that the most current version is always on the user's machine. Active Channels provide more functionality. This section looks at Active Channels and how to customize the subscription specifications for channels and sites.

Active Channels are integrated into Internet Explorer by way of the Active Channel bar. The Active Channel bar lists channels preconfigured with Internet Explorer and channels added by user subscriptions. The channel bar is also available as an Active Desktop item (see Figure 5.21) or from within the IE browser (see Figure 5.22).

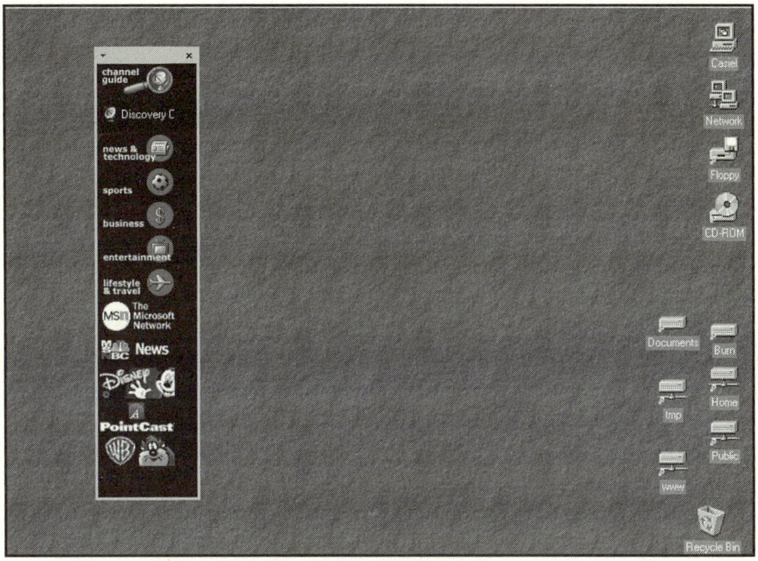

Figure 5.21

The Active Channel bar as an item on the Active Desktop.

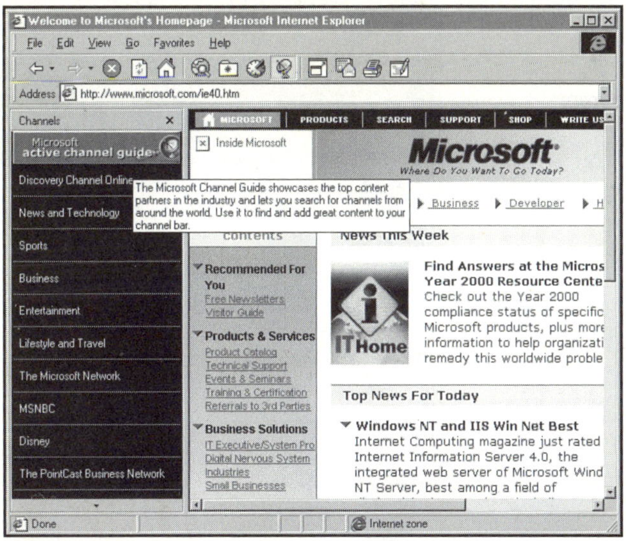

Figure 5.22

The Active Channel bar within the Internet Explorer browser.

The channels listed in the Active Channel bar are treated in a way similar to favorites. That is, the channels are files stored in a special folder that Internet Explorer scans to determine what to display in the Active Channel bar. The channels currently listed in the channel bar can be deleted (see Figure 5.23) by editing the list of favorites through the Organize Favorites option.

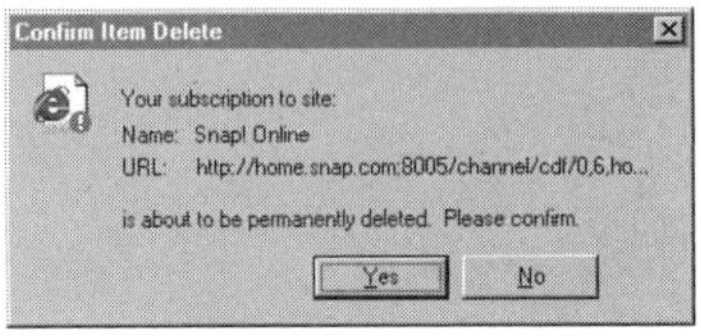

Figure 5.23

Removing channels is similar to removing favorites.

Adding channels is a bit different. When the user encounters a channel he or she wants to add, he or she can do so using the channel subscription mechanism provided by the channel's author. In addition to prestocking the Active Channel bar with channel content, Microsoft provides a Channel Guide that contains a number of channels to which users can subscribe with IE. The Channel Guide is located at `http://www.iechannelguide.com/guide/en/en_us.asp` and is shown in Figure 5.24.

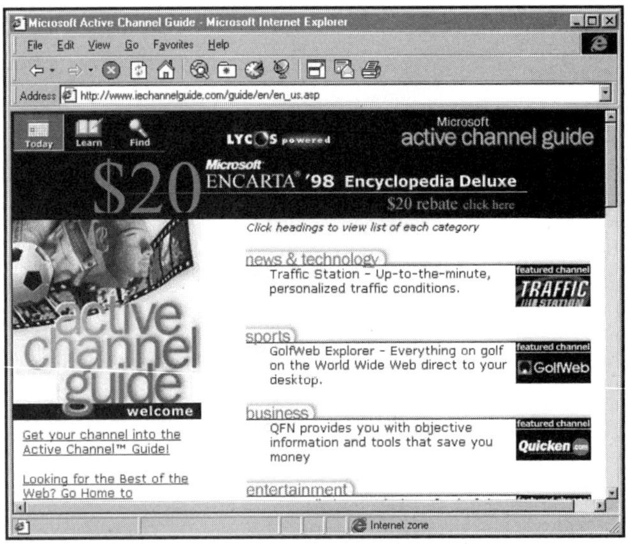

Figure 5.24

The Microsoft Active Channel Guide offers users different channels to choose from, organized by category.

The Active Channel Guide features an incredible number of channels to choose from. Administrators can also create their own channels using the Channel Definition Format (CDF) to create the channel file that points to Web-based content.

The Channel Guide features channel previews that allow users to see the type of content featured on a channel before they decide to subscribe to the channel. If the user decides he or she wants to subscribe to a channel, the Channels Listed in the Channel Guide feature is an easy subscription mechanism. The Add Active Channel button launches the Subscription Wizard so that the user can subscribe to the channel, as shown in Figure 5.25.

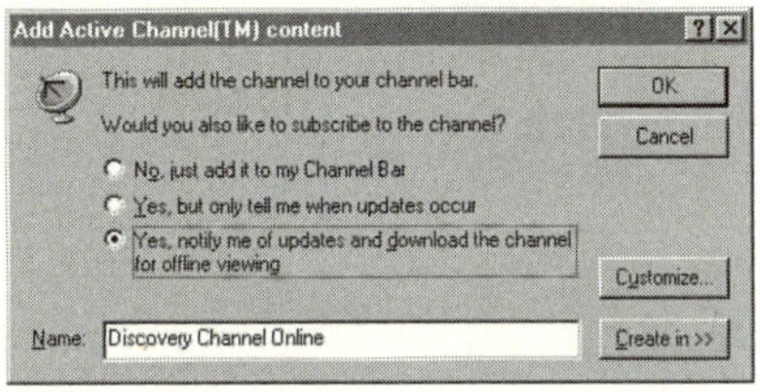

Figure 5.25

Add a channel subscription by clicking the Add Active Channel button.

The user is then prompted for information about how he or she wants to subscribe to the channel:

- **No, Just Add It to My Channel Bar.** This option simply adds a link to the channel in the user's Active Channel bar.
- **Yes, But Only Tell Me When Updates Occur.** This option adds the link and also notifies the user (through email or the channel bar) that the content of the channel has changed. The use can then load the channel and see the new content.
- **Yes, Notify Me of Updates and Download the Channel for Offline Viewing.** This option offers the most flexible subscription option. The channel is added to the channel bar, and the user is notified of updates. However, the channel content is also automatically downloaded to the user's computer so that he or she can view the channel content at any time to see the updated information.

Many Active Channels also feature Active Desktop components. It may be possible to add the channel as an Active Desktop item; the channel can also feature a screen saver. If this option exists, the subscription wizard presents it to the user, as shown in Figure 5.26.

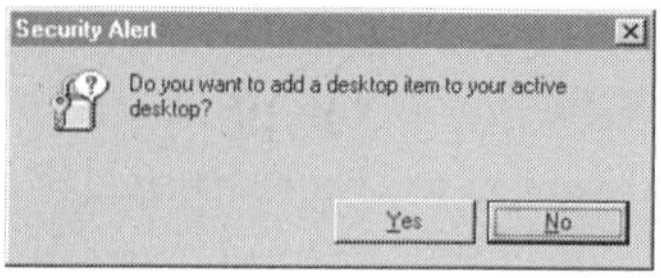

Figure 5.26

Some Active Channels feature Active Desktop items, such as screen savers.

Finally, the channel content is downloaded, and the subscription is complete, as shown in Figure 5.27. The user can now visit the channel at any time by selecting it from the Active Channel bar, either from the Active Desktop or through the IE browser.

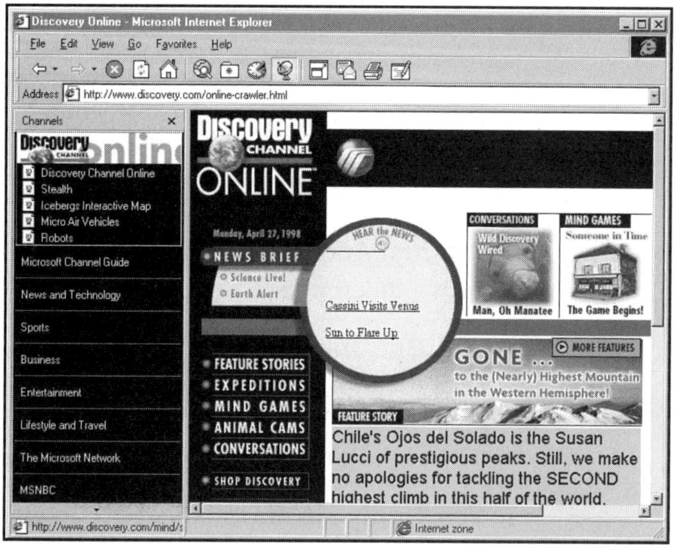

Figure 5.27

The final Active Channel, added to the channel bar, with content downloaded to the local machine.

Site Subscriptions

Another type of subscription is supported in Internet Explorer 4.0: Web site subscriptions.

A Web site subscription is simple: The user chooses to add a site to his or her favorites list. Instead of just creating a bookmark to the site, Internet Explorer also prompts the user with this question: `Would you also like to subscribe to this page?` The user can respond in one of three ways:

- No, Just Add the Page to My Favorites
- Yes, But Only Tell Me When This Page Is Updated

- Yes, Notify Me of Updates and Download the Page for Offline Viewing

These options, shown in Figure 5.28, are very similar to those for subscribing to a channel.

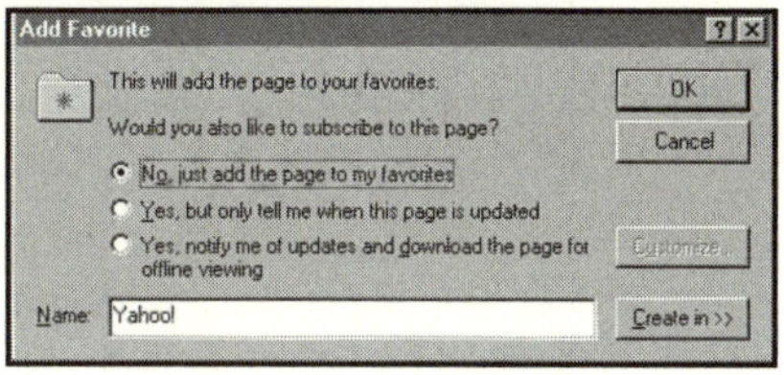

Figure 5.28

The Add Favorite Wizard allows users to subscribe to Web site content in a similar way to subscribing to a channel.

If the user chooses to add the site as a favorite, the site is added to the favorites list and the adventure ends there. However, if the user chooses one of the other options, more is in store.

The user can choose to add the site to the favorites list and be notified of updates. If this option is selected, Internet Explorer caches a copy of the site (the main page) and revisits it periodically to see whether the page has been updated. If it has, IE notifies the user of the new content.

If the user chooses the Subscribe to a Web Site and Download the Content for Online Viewing option, the site is cached and all the content, up to a specified number of levels (usually one or two), is downloaded to the user's machine. The user is then notified of the update and can view the new content at any time.

Scheduling Automatic Updates

Objective

Active Desktop components, site subscriptions, and Active Channels all share one common trait: the subscription schedule.

You've seen how you can add desktop items, Active Channels, and site subscriptions. Now let's look at the mechanism that alters the subscription settings for these elements.

In the Favorites menu of the Internet Explorer browser is the Manage Subscriptions option. This option takes you to the folder in which subscription files for any Active Desktop items, site subscriptions, and Active Channels are stored (see Figure 5.29).

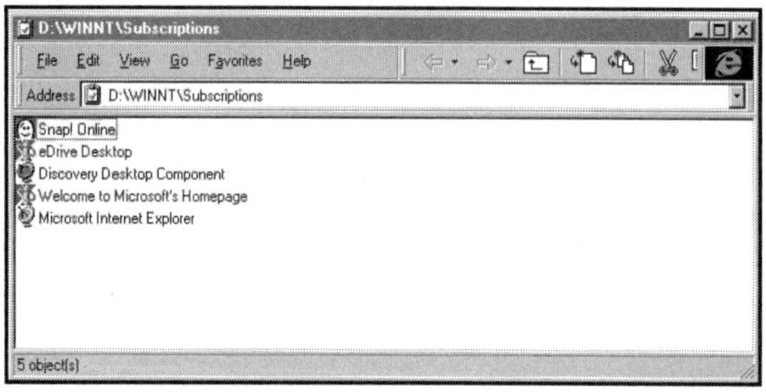

Figure 5.29

Managing subscriptions from Internet Explorer 4.0.

To modify the properties for an item, right-click the item and choose Properties, as shown in Figure 5.30.

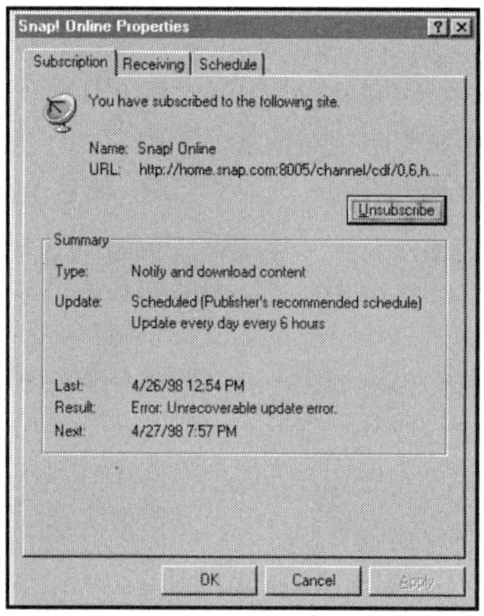

Figure 5.30

Editing the properties for active elements and Web sites within the subscription manager.

It the Properties dialog box looks familiar, it should. All three types of subscriptions make use of the same Properties dialog box, which was covered earlier in this chapter in the section "Editing Desktop Items." The major difference is that for some desktop items and Active Channels, there may be an option under the schedule for the publisher's recommended schedule. Because channel creators can specify an update schedule for their channels, this option sets the update to the schedule the channel developers have created.

Optimizing Components with the IEAK Profile Manager

Objective

As you have seen in previous chapters, the IEAK Profile Manager is a powerful tool for manipulating the settings for your customized installation of IE, after it has been created using the IEAK Wizard.

In previous sections, we examined many of the cosmetic features of the IEAK, without going into full detail about its functionality. This section covers the features of the IEAK Wizard that allow for the optimization and performance of Internet Explorer 4.0.

Let's start by looking at what the IEAK Profile Manager is capable of manipulating. Table 5.3 details all the settings that can be controlled with the Profile Manager.

Table 5.3

Complete List of Settings That Can Be Edited Using the IEAK Profile Manager

Setting	Elements	Options
Wizard Settings	Browser Title	Title Bar Text
		Toolbar Background Bitmap
	Support Page	Online Support Page URL
	Favorites	Favorite Folders
		Favorite Links
	Desktop Wallpaper	Wallpaper Bitmap
	User Agent	User Agent String
	Proxy Settings	Enable Proxy Servers
		Proxy Server Addresses
		Proxy Server Exceptions
	Start and Search Page	Home page URL Search Page URL

continues

Table 5.3 Continued

Setting	Elements	Options
	Import Channels	Import Custom Channels from IE
	Import Software Updates	Import Software Updates from IE
	Outlook Express	Incoming Mail Server
		Outgoing Mail Server
		Internet News Server
		Make Outlook Express the Default Mail Client
		Make Outlook Express the Default News Client
		Use Secure Password Authentication
	LDAP Settings	Friendly Name
		Directory Service
		Home Page
		Search Base
		Service Bitmap
		Check Names Against This Server When Sending Mail
		Authentication Type
	Outlook Express Customizations	InfoPane Settings Welcome Message HTML Path
		Welcome Message Sender
		Welcome Message Reply To
	Signature	Email Signature
		News Signature
	Specify Active Desktop Components	Import Active Desktop Settings from IE

Setting	Elements	Options
	My Computer and Control Panel Webview Customization	Path of My Computer Custom HTML File (`mycomp.htt`) Path of Control Panel Custom HTML File (`controlp.htt`)
	Automatic Browser Configuration	Enable Automatic Browser Configuration
		Autoconfigure URL
		Autoproxy URL
		Autoconfigure Interval
	Security Zones and Content Ratings	Customized Security Zones Customized Content Ratings
	Certificate Settings	Import Certificate Authorities
		Import Current Authenticode Security Information
System Policies and Restrictions	Microsoft Chat	Server List Default Server
		Default Chat Room
		Default Character
		Default Backdrop
		User Profile String
		Show Only Registered Rooms in List

continues

Table 5.3 Continued

Setting	Elements	Options
	Microsoft NetMeeting (Settings)	Prevent User from Sending Files Prevent User from Receiving Files
		Disable All Application Sharing Features
		Prevent User from Sharing the Clipboard
		Prevent User from Sharing MS-DOS Windows
		Prevent User from Sharing Explorer Windows
		Prevent User from Collaborating
		Disable the General Options Page
		Disable the My Information Options Page
		Disable the Calling Options Page
		Disable the Audio Options Page
		Disable the Video Options Page
		Disable the Protocols Options Page
		Prevent User from Answering Calls
		Prevent User from Using Audio Features
		Prevent User from Sending Video

Setting	Elements	Options
		Prevent User from Receiving Video
		Prevent User From Using Directory Services
		Default Directory Server
		Exchange Server Property
		Present User Information Category
		NetMeeting Homepage URL
		Limit Audio/Video Throughput
	Microsoft NetMeeting (Protocols)	Disable TCP/IP
		Disable Null Modem
	Internet Restrictions (General)	Disable Changing Home Page Settings
		Disable Changing Cache Settings
		Disable Changing History Settings
		Disable Changing Color Settings
		Disable Changing Link Color Settings
		Disable Changing Font Settings
		Disable Changing Language Settings
		Disable Changing Accessibility Settings

continues

Table 5.3 Continued

Setting	Elements	Options
	Internet Restrictions (Security)	Use Only Machine Settings for Security Zones Do Not Allow Users to Change Policies for Any Security Zone
		Do Not Allow Users to Add/ Delete Sites from a Security Zone
	Internet Restrictions (Content)	Disable Changing Ratings settings Disable Changing Certificate Settings
		Disable Changing Profile Assistant Settings
		Disable Changing Microsoft Wallet Settings
	Internet Restrictions (Connection)	Disable Calling Connection Wizard Disable Changing Connection Settings
		Disable Changing Proxy Settings
		Disable Changing Automatic Configuration Settings
	Internet Restrictions (Programs)	Disable Changing Messaging Settings Disable Changing Calendar and Contact Settings
		Disable Changing Checking if IE Is the Default Browser

Setting	Elements	Options
	Internet Restrictions (Advanced)	Disable Changing Settings on Advanced Tab
	Internet Restrictions (Code Download)	Path
	Internet Restrictions (User Profiles)	Disable Roaming Cache
	Internet Restrictions (Channels Settings)	Disable Channel UI
		Disable Adding and Subscribing to Channels
		Disable Editing Channel Properties and Channel Subscriptions
		Disable Removing Channels and Subscriptions to Channels
		Disable Adding Site Subscriptions
		Disable Removing Site Subscriptions
		Disable Channel Logging
		Disable Update Now and Update All for Channels and Subscriptions
		Disable All Scheduled Channel and Site Subscriptions
		Disable Unattended Dialing by Subscriptions
		Disable Password Caching for Channel and Site Subscriptions

continues

Table 5.3 Continued

Setting	Elements	Options
		Disable Downloading of Channel Subscription Content
		Disable Downloading of Site Subscription Content
		Disable Editing and Creating of Schedule Groups
	Internet Settings (Colors)	Background Color Text Color
		Link Color
		Visited Link Color
		Hover Color
	Internet Settings (Fonts)	Western Proportional Font Western Fixed Font
	Internet Settings (Languages)	Default Language Preference
	Internet Settings (Modem Settings)	Connection Type Enable Autodialing
		Number of Times to Attempt Connection
		Number of Seconds to Wait Between Attempts
		Connect Without User Intervention
		Disconnect If Idle
		Minutes to Wait Before Disconnecting
		Perform System Security Check Before Dialing

Setting	Elements	Options
	Internet Settings (Programs)	Program to Use for Calendar
		Program to Use for Contacts
		Program to Use for Internet Call
	Internet Settings (Advanced Settings — Browsing)	Disable Script Debugger
		Launch Channels in Full Screen Mode
		Launch Browser in Full Screen Mode
		Use Autocomplete
		Show Friendly URLs
		Enable Smooth Scrolling
		Enable Page Transitions
		Browse in a New Process
		Enable Page Hit Counting
		Enable Scheduled Subscription Updates
		Underline Links
	Internet Settings (Advanced Settings — Multimedia)	Show Pictures
		Play Animations
		Play Videos
		Play Sounds
		Smart Image Dithering

continues

Table 5.3 Continued

Setting	Elements	Options
	Internet Settings (Advanced Settings — Security)	Enable Profile Assistant Delete Saved Pages When Browser Closes Do Not Save Encrypted Pages to Disk Warn if Forms Submit Is Being Redirected Warn If Changing Between Secure and Insecure Mode Cookies
	Internet Settings (Advanced Settings — Java VM)	JIT Compiler Enabled Java Logging Enabled
	Internet Settings (Advanced Settings — Printing)	Print Background Colors and Images
	Internet Settings (Advanced Settings — Searching)	Autoscan Common Root Domains Search When URL Fails
	Internet Settings (Advanced Settings — Toolbars)	Show Font Button Small Icons
	Internet Settings (Advanced Settings — HTTP 1.1 Settings)	Use HTTP 1.1 Use HTTP 1.1 through Proxy Connections

Setting	Elements	Options
	Outlook Express (General Settings)	Put Mail and News in the Restricted Sites Zone
		Make Plain Text Message Composition the Default for Mail Messages
		Make HTML Message Composition the Default for News Posts
	Outlook Express (View Customization)	Turn on Outlook Bar
		Turn off Folder List
		Turn on Folder Bar
		Turn off Tip of the Day
	Web Desktop (Desktop)	Disable Active Desktop Do Not Allow Changes to Active Desktop
		Hide Internet Explorer Icon
		Hide Network Neighborhood Icon
		Hide All Items on Desktop
		Disable All Desktop Items
		Disable Adding Any Desktop Items
		Disable Deleting Any Desktop Items
		Disable Editing Any Desktop Items
		Disable Closing Any Desktop Items
		No HTML Wallpaper

continues

Table 5.3 Continued

Setting	Elements	Options
		Disable Changing Wallpaper
		Disable Dragging, Dropping and Closing All Toolbars
		Disable Resizing All Toolbars
	Web Desktop (Start Menu)	Remove Favorites Menu from Start Menu
		Remove Find Menu from Start Menu
		Remove Run Menu from Start Menu
		Remove the Active Desktop Item from the Settings Menu
		Disable Drag and Drop Context Menus on the Start Menu
		Remove the Folder Options Menu Item from the Settings Menu
		Remove Documents Menu from Start Menu
		Do Not Keep a History of Recently Opened Documents
		Clear History of Recently Opened Documents
		Disable Logoff
		Disable Shut Down Command
		Disable Changes to Printers and Control Panel Settings
		Disable Changes to Taskbar and Start Menu Settings
		Disable Context Menu for Taskbar

Setting	Elements	Options
		Hide Custom Programs Folders
		Hide Common Program Groups in Start Menu
	Web Desktop (Shell)	Enable Classic Shell Disable File Menu in Shell Folders
		Disable Context Menu in Shell Folders
		Only Allow Approved Shell Extensions
		Do Not Track Shell Shortcuts During Roaming
		Hide Floppy Drives in My Computer
		Disable Net Connections/ Disconnection
	Web Desktop (Printers)	Hide General and Details Tabs in Printer Properties
		Disable Deletion of Printers
		Disable Addition of Printers
	Web Desktop (System)	Run Only Specified Windows Applications
		Do Not Allow Computer to Restart in MS-DOS Mode
	Subscriptions	Maximum KB of Site Subscription
		Maximum KB of Channel Subscription
		Maximum Number of Site Subscriptions

continues

Table 5.3 Continued

Setting	Elements	Options
		Minimum Number of Minutes Between Scheduled Subscription Updates
		Beginning of Range in Which to Exclude Scheduled Subscription Updates. Measured in Minutes from Midnight.
		End of Range in Which to Exclude Scheduled Subscription Updates. Measured in Minutes from Midnight.
		Maximum Site Subscription Crawl Depth

As you can see, the functionality of the IEAK Profile Manger is extensive. However, a great deal of these settings are cosmetic or are functional settings that point the browser to server resources and the like. However, some settings specifically impact the performance of IE. These settings can be divided into two major areas:

- Internet settings
- Subscriptions

There are minor settings that affect the performance of some components, such as the settings for NetMeeting. However, these broader categories have an impact on the browser functionality, and deserve coverage of their own.

Internet Settings

The Internet settings policies determine how Internet Explorer treats information and sources it encounters on the Internet. Because connecting to sources over the Internet involves processing new information and downloading information from remote servers, this can have a profound impact on performance.

Within the Advanced Internet settings, the following settings most affect performance:

- Browsing
- Multimedia
- Java VM
- Searching

Advanced Settings: Browsing

Within the Internet Advanced settings there are three options that have the potential to seriously affect performance:

- **Enable Smooth Scrolling.** Internet Explorer features an enhancement to scrolling called *smooth scrolling*. This feature makes the graphics and text on a page scroll smoothly. However, smooth scrolling is processing intensive and may affect performance. If smooth scrolling is disabled, scrolling may appear jerky but performance is increased.
- **Enable Page Transitions.** Internet Explorer supports dynamic HTML, which allows content creators to use special effects, such as font and graphic manipulations. One of the set of effects can be used to create page transitions, such as scrolling, fades, and so on. The problem with page transitions is that they can slow down load times and rob the system of memory and processing power. For users who are concerned with performance and don't mind sacrificing the aesthetics of the transitions, disabling this feature can increase performance.
- **Browse in a New Process.** Internet Explorer is integrated into the Windows shell and is always running, allowing the user to browse the file system. When users launch the Internet Explorer Web browser, the process actually runs within Explorer. This arrangement increases performance. However, in some instances (especially with Windows NT), this arrangement can cause the shell to hang if Internet Explorer crashes. To avoid this crash, you can set Explorer to launch

in a separate process. Running Internet Explorer as a separate process may decrease performance but can help avoid crashes.

Advanced Settings: Multimedia

The multimedia settings control which multimedia elements are played by Internet Explorer. Content creators can include a variety of multimedia elements within Web pages, and these elements can sometimes adversely affect performance. Multimedia elements can be large and time consuming to download, and they are often processor intensive to display correctly. Here are some of the multimedia options you can disable to help increase performance:

- **Play Animations.** Animations, in the form of animated GIFs, are one of the most common multimedia features on Web pages today. Many sites—business sites included—make extensive use of animated GIFs for advertising. Unfortunately, these animated GIFs are usually configured to loop indefinitely, and many sites contain several animations. Animated GIFs use the processor to display; if the GIF loops, your processor is continually in use. When you add several GIFs to a page, this can quickly consume processor time. Disabling animated GIFs can dramatically increase performance when viewing pages with lots of animations.
- **Play Videos.** Adding video pages is a perfect way to showcase the new multimedia flexibility of the Web. Unfortunately, video files are quite large, and streaming video can consume a large amount of network bandwidth. Video also makes heavy use of the system processor for decoding during playback. Disabling video allows pages to load faster and frees system resources.
- **Play Sounds.** Sounds are a double-edged sword. In addition to increasing the load time of a Web page, they can also be just plain annoying. They can be unusually loud, inappropriate, or worse. Disabling sound in Internet Explorer can increase the load time of pages, free up processor time, and save users from embarrassment or annoyance.

Advanced Settings: Java VM

Java applets are not compiled into code specific to the platform on which they are running. This means that Java applets often suffer in performance compared to native-code applications. However, one performance enhancement can be enabled to help significantly increase the performance of Java within Internet Explorer. The JIT is the Just-in-Time compiler, a compiler that converts Java bytecode into a combination of bytecode and native methods the first time the application runs. This native code is then cached, so the second time the application runs, the native methods are already present. This process increases the performance of Java applets downloaded and run within Web pages.

Advanced Settings: Searching

To aid users in finding sites, Internet Explorer incorporates a feature called *autoscan common root domains.* This feature automatically searches through common domain names if the user accidentally leaves off the domain name (for example, `www.yahoo` instead of `www.yahoo.com`). IE tries the most common domains, such as `com`, `edu`, and so on. However, searching through domain names can decrease performance because IE cycles through the domains rather than just returning an error. Disabling this option can increase performance, although only very slightly.

Subscriptions

Because site subscription and channel subscription data is downloaded over the network and stored on local machines, subscriptions present two performance issues: disk storage space and network bandwidth. If you have a large number of subscriptions, or have subscriptions to large sites, the amount of data to be downloaded and stored can quickly become significant. Here are some of the settings you can use to manage resources tied to subscriptions:

- **Maximum KB of Site Subscriptions.** Disk space can be managed by establishing a maximum value of the content that can be downloaded, in kilobytes.
- **Maximum KB of Channel Subscriptions.** You can establish a maximum value for disk space consumed, in kilobytes, for channel subscriptions.
- **Maximum Number of Site Subscriptions.** Limiting the total number of site subscriptions can help limit the time and network bandwidth used for downloading and storing content.
- **Minimum Number of Minutes Between Scheduled Subscription Updates.** Specifying an interval to wait between scheduled updates can prevent runaway updates from consuming network resources and allow other network traffic an opportunity to make use of the machine's bandwidth.
- **Beginning of Range in Which to Exclude Scheduled Subscription Updates. Measured in Minutes from Midnight.**

  End of Range in Which to Exclude Scheduled Subscription Updates. Measured in Minutes from Midnight.

  These two options allow administrators to select a period of time during which site and channel subscriptions are not processed. These settings can be used to prevent IE from downloading new content automatically during times when the user is working with the machine. For example, preventing content updates during the business day allows the user to work without performance dropping because IE is downloading new content.
- **Maximum Site Subscription Crawl Depth.** This option specifies the number of levels of Web pages within a site that the automatic subscription mechanism will crawl to and download the content of. The problem with crawling too

deeply into a site is that the number of pages can increase exponentially. Suppose that there is a page with five links. Each of these linked pages contains three more links. If the crawl depth is set to 1, a total of six pages is downloaded: the initial page and the pages for the five links. If the crawl depth is changed to 2, the number of pages downloaded is 25: the initial page, the five first-level pages, and the pages from the next three links. If each page is 50KB, the difference between a crawl depth of 1 level and a crawl depth of 2 levels is 300KB versus 1.25MB. As you can see, keeping the crawl depth value low can reduce download times and the amount of disk space consumed by the content.

Optimizing Caching and Performance

Objective

The caching mechanism in Internet Explorer is how Internet Explorer keeps track of pages that have already been viewed. The idea behind the cache is simple: When a user visits a page, the information for the page is downloaded to the local machine and displayed in the browser. Those files are then stored locally, so that if the user goes back to that page in the same browser session, the information does not have to be redownloaded. Instead, the files are loaded from the local machine (in the cache). The result is a much faster display for the user.

The IE cache is also known as *temporary Internet files*, and there are a number of customizations you can make to tweak the performance of the cache. These settings can be accessed through the Internet Options dialog box, under the Temporary Internet Files settings, as shown in Figure 5.31.

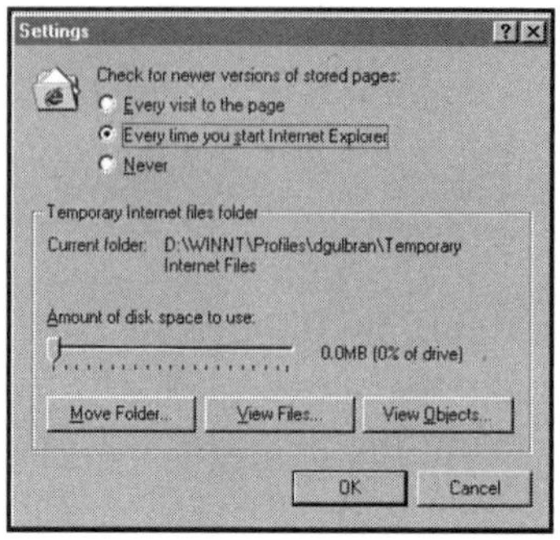

Figure 5.31

Altering the cache settings through the Temporary Internet Files setting in Internet Explorer 4.0.

The first group of settings controls how pages are pulled from the cache. Users can control how IE checks for newer versions of stored pages with the following options:

- **Every Visit to the Page.** If this option is selected, Internet Explorer does not make use of the cache. Instead, it always checks the network for a newer version of the page. This option ensures that the user always has the most recent content, but it may increase the network usage and lengthen the time spent waiting for downloads.

- **Every Time You Start Internet Explorer.** This option causes Internet Explorer to check for a new version of the page when IE is started. This can cause a slowdown of the initial load time, but decreases the time spent waiting for downloads.

- **Never.** The Never option causes Internet Explorer to never check for newer content. The cached version is always used. To obtain new content, the user must reload the page manually. This can cause the appearance of very fast page loading, but it can also result in very old data being used. Use this option with caution.

Finally, you can specify the amount of disk space to be used for storing cached files. The larger the amount of disk space, the more files that can be cached, and the faster pages appear to load. However, making the cache space too large can lead to users viewing data that is out of date.

Exercises

The following exercises are designed to give you some step-by-step, hands-on guidance for some of the tasks outlined in this chapter.

Exercise 5.1: Add a Desktop Item to the Active Desktop

In this exercise, you add an item to the Active Desktop. To do this, the Windows Desktop Update should be installed, and the View Desktop as Web Page option should be enabled.

1. Right-click the desktop and select Customize My Desktop. This action launches the Display Properties dialog box and selected the Web tab.
2. Make sure that the View My Active Desktop as a Web Page option is selected.
3. Click the New button to add a new Active Desktop item.
4. When prompted to visit the Active Desktop gallery, select Yes. This action launches IE and takes you to the Active Desktop Gallery, which lists available components.
5. Browse the gallery and select a desktop component item you want to add.
6. Click the selected item's Add to Active Desktop button.
7. Confirm that you want to add the item to your Active Desktop.
8. Internet Explorer downloads the component and adds it to the desktop. When the content is downloaded, the installation is complete.

Exercise 5.2: Subscribe to a New Active Channel

The following exercise covers the steps necessary to install an Active Channel from the Active Channel Gallery.

1. Launch Internet Explorer and activate the channel bar by clicking the channel bar icon.
2. Click the button for the Microsoft Channel Guide. This action displays the Microsoft Channel Guide in the browser portion of the IE window.
3. From the Channel Guide, select a channel you want to install. Note that you can preview the channel. When you find a channel you want to install, click the Add Active Channel Button to add the channel to the channel bar.
4. You are prompted to subscribe to the channel. Because we're going to subscribe to the full channel, select the Yes, Notify Me of Updates and Download the Channel for Offline Viewing option. Click OK to continue.
5. IE downloads the channel content and adds the channel icon to the Active Channel bar. When the download is complete, the channel is successfully added.

Review Questions

The review questions in this section can help you assess your understanding of the terms, concepts, and objectives covered in this chapter. These questions are written in the style of the questions presented on the MCSE exam and are an excellent way to prepare yourself for the material you will see on the exam. After you complete the review questions, you will find the answer to each question—along with an explanation of the answer—in the following section.

1. The Windows Desktop Update allows which of the following components to be configured with Internet Explorer? (Select all that apply.)

   A. Site subscriptions

   B. Active Desktop items

   C. Active Channels

   D. Web folder views

2. An administrator wants to add a custom news desktop item to his corporate installation of IE. To make the item a part of the install, he must (select all that apply):

   A. Use the IEAK Wizard's Add Desktop Item dialog box

   B. Use the IEAK Profile Manager's Add Desktop Item dialog box

   C. Configure the item in the IE version on the admininstrative machine

   D. Import the desktop settings with the IEAK Wizard or Profile Manger

3. The Microsoft Active Channel Gallery and Desktop Gallery contain:

   A. Downloadable items and channels

   B. Technical support information for the Windows Desktop Update

C. Help files for channels and items

D. Product information for the CDF and IE

4. Subscription settings can be altered to (select all that apply):

   A. Download updates without notifying the user of updates

   B. Suspend downloads during specified time periods

   C. Notify the user of updates only

   D. Download updates and notify the user

5. Default schedules are provided for which of the following sets of updates?

   A. Daily, Weekly, Monthly

   B. Weekly, Monthly, Annually

   C. Weekly, Biweekly, Monthly

   D. Hourly, Daily, Weekly

6. A user wants to install the Active Desktop but preserve his or her current Window 95 folder views. Which view setting should this user choose?

   A. Web Style

   B. Custom Style

   C. Classic Style

   D. Windows Style

7. From within Internet Explorer, how do users access Active Channels?

   A. The Windows Active Desktop

   B. The Microsoft Active Channel Gallery

   C. The Web folder view

   D. The Active Channel bar

8. What limitation should be placed on a single site subscription to decrease download time and to minimize the amount of disk space consumed for the download?

   A. Maximum site subscription size

   B. Levels of crawl depth

   C. Maximum number of site subscriptions

   D. The update schedule

9. Which of the following common Web page elements are frequent consumers of processor time and can be disabled with the Internet Settings Policy?

   A. MPEG movies

   B. ActiveX components

   C. Embedded documents

   D. Animated GIFs

10. Enabling which of the following Java VM settings will result in faster Java applet performance?

    A. Java logging

    B. The JIT compiler

    C. Protected scratch space

    D. Java applet scripting

11. John is preparing for a business trip during which he will not have online access. He would like to still access several pages of content on the road. Before leaving, he should select which of the following cache settings to check for updated content:

    A. Every Visit to the Page

    B. Only on Subscription Schedule

    C. Every Time You Start Internet Explorer

    D. Never

Review Answers

Now that you have completed the review questions, check your answers against those provided here. Explanations are provided for each answer so that you can see whether you arrived at the correct solution for the right reason, or so that you can see how your answer varied from the correct one.

1. **B and D** Both Active Desktop items and Web folder views require the installation of the Windows Desktop Update. If the update is installed, users can still disable these features; without the Windows Desktop Update, however, these features are not available at all.

2. **C and D** Settings for desktop items cannot be manipulated directly with any IEAK component. Instead, the settings are imported from the installed version of Internet Explorer on the machine the IEAK is installed on. Administrators therefore must configure items within IE and then import them with the IEAK Wizard or Profile Manager.

3. **A** The Microsoft galleries contain hundreds of components that can be installed in addition to privately developed items and channels.

4. **B, C, and D** Subscriptions cannot be configured to update without providing the user with some kind of notification.

5. **A** Subscriptions can easily be set to Daily, Weekly, or Monthly schedules. For other schedule types, a Custom schedule must be created.

6. **C** The Classic Style of folder views retains the same settings used in traditional Windows 95 installations.

7. **D** After a user subscribes to an Active Channel, the channel icon appears in the Active Channel bar, making the channel accessible through Internet Explorer.

8. **B** The number of levels traversed during a site subscription can seriously impact download times and disk space consumed. As the number of levels increases, download times and storage space increase almost exponentially.

9. **D** Looping animated GIFs are an extremely common element of many Web pages, often featured as online ads. However, GIFs use processor time to decode, and several animated GIFs on a page can adversely affect performance.

10. **B** The JIT (Just-in-Time) compiler for Java interprets incoming bytecode and, where appropriate, optimizes it for the platform by using native methods and caching those methods. The JIT compiler can increase the performance of applets dramatically.

11. **D** Setting the cache to never check for new updates means that the version of a page currently on the machine is always used. This option results in fast page display and permits disconnected viewing. However, it can also result in stale data.

Answers to Test Yourself Questions at Beginning of Chapter

The following answers are provided for the prechapter quiz at the beginning of this chapter. You can use these questions and answers to determine how familiar you may already be with this chapter's material. Each of the questions relates to a specific goal for the "Implementing and Supporting the Microsoft Internet Explorer Administration Kit for Microsoft Internet Explorer 4.0" MCSE exam. Each of the following answers references the section in this chapter that deals with the covered objective so that you can easily locate the material you may want to review or clarify.

1. The Active Desktop component is installed with the Windows Desktop Update, as are Web folder views. Administrators who want to use the Active Desktop must configure the Windows Desktop Update to be installed as well.

   Active Desktop items are not configured directly in the IEAK Wizard or the IEAK Profile Manager. Instead, their settings are imported from the version of IE installed on the administrative machine. Therefore, administrators must configure Active Desktop components from within Internet Explorer, and then import those settings to the custom build from the IEAK Wizard or Profile Manager.

Sections Referencing This Material:

- "Customizing Active Desktop Items"
- "Adding Desktop Items"
- "Deleting Desktop Items"
- "Editing Desktop Items"

2. With the Windows Desktop Update installed, folders can be manipulated to change the display properties. Here are the types of displays:

   - Web Style
   - Classic Style
   - Custom Style

   The Web Style results in local file system folders being viewed in a browser window, with files appearing as links. Files are selected by pointing and are activated with a single click.

   The Classic Style preserves the functionality of folders as found in Windows 95. Items are selected with single clicks and are activated with double clicks.

   Users can also choose a Custom view and mix and match features from the other styles to create customized folder viewing styles.

   Sections Referencing This Material:

   - "Customizing Active Desktop Items"
   - "Folder Options"

3. Active Channels allow users to subscribe over the Internet to content that is updated on a regular schedule. Channels can be configured by publishers to update the content of the

channel on a pre-set schedule, or the user can override the set schedule to create a custom update schedule.

Users also have the option of configuring how channel content is updated. The new content can either be downloaded automatically to the user's machine, so it is waiting for them the next time they access the channel, or they can choose to have an email notice sent to them when the channel has been updated. Users also may select both methods for updating content.

Active channels can be accessed through the Channel Bar from within Internet Explorer 4.0, or from the Channel Bar as a component on the Active Desktop. Administrators configure Active Channels for custom builds by customizing the Channel subscriptions from within Internet Explorer on the administrative machine, and then importing the channel settings using the IEAK Wizard or the IEAK Profile Manager.

Sections Referencing This Material:

- "Customizing Active Channels"
- "Site Subscriptions"

4. You can subscribe to Active Components, channels, and sites so that content is automatically updated. There are two options for updated content:

   - **User Notification Only.** With this option enabled, when IE detects that new content is available, it notifies the user that the element has been updated, but the user must manually view the element and update the data.
   - **Notify User and Download New Content.** With this option, the user is notified that the content has been updated, and the content is automatically downloaded to the user's machine. The user can then view the content at his or her leisure.

   Users can also customize the schedule for updating elements, either by using the schedule suggested by the item's creator or by specifying a new one.

Sections Referencing This Material:

- "Customizing Active Desktop Items"
- "Customizing Active Channels"
- "Site Subscriptions"

5. Many aspects of Internet Explorer have an impact on how fast pages load and are displayed. However, settings in the Internet Settings section of System Policies and Restrictions have the greatest impact. Settings found here include how elements are displayed in the browser window and when types of elements (such as multimedia files) are displayed. These settings can impact performance in a variety of ways.

   Sections Referencing This Material:

   - "Optimizing Components with the IEAK Profile Manager"
   - "Internet Settings"
   - "Advanced Settings: Browsing"
   - "Advanced Settings: Multimedia"

6. When Internet Explorer contacts a Web server to retrieve a page, the page is downloaded to the local machine where the files are stored as temporary Internet files. These files are then used by the browser to quickly redraw the page if the user revisits the page.

   As a result, instead of reconnecting to the server over the network, the page content is loaded almost instantly from the local hard drive. The default for caching with IE is to check the page in the cache against the network when IE is started. That means that the page is downloaded once, at most, during a browsing session. Caching can also be set to check the network every time a page is viewed (making performance slower but the data more current) or never to check (which is faster but can result in stale data).

   Section Referencing This Material:

   - "Optimizing Caching and Performance"

Chapter 6

Troubleshooting

In a perfect world, software applications would be bug free, and IS professionals could spend their valuable time developing new, better systems to increase productivity and lower costs. Our world is far from perfect. The reality of Information Systems has imposed many a hardship on users and administrators alike.

With a software application as robust and as complex as Internet Explorer, there are bound to be unforeseen issues that arise with some users. Sometimes, these problems are simple software conflicts or misconfigurations. Other times, there are complex hardware incompatibilities at work. Problems that arise from a straightforward installation of IE can be enough, but when administrators begin customizing different elements, problems can quickly compound.

So what is the solution? Never upgrade software? Lock users into old versions? Never add new features? Sure, most IS personnel have contemplated these options at some point, but realistically, we acknowledge the advancement of the craft. Fortunately, as software advances, so do the tools to deal with problems facing installation and operation. That's what this chapter is about: Troubleshooting the problems you can encounter with Internet Explorer and the IEAK. It covers the following objectives:

Objectives

- Diagnose and resolve the deployment failure of a preconfigured version of Internet Explorer 4.0.
- Diagnose and resolve problems related to the IEAK Wizard.
- Diagnose and resolve connection failures of Outlook Express.

continues

- Diagnose and resolve connection failures of NetMeeting.
- Diagnose and resolve failures of Webcasting. Types of Webcasting include:
  - Site subscriptions
  - Channels
  - Active Desktop items
- Diagnose and resolve failures of caching.
- Choose the appropriate tools for troubleshooting network connection failures. Tools for troubleshooting include:
  - IP configuration
  - Ping
  - `tracert`
  - Network Monitor
  - `nslookup`

STOP

Test Yourself! Before reading this chapter, test yourself to determine how much study time you will need to devote to this section.

The following prechapter quiz is designed to help you get a feel for how well you currently understand the material covered in this chapter. If you think you have a strong understanding of the objectives outlined in the previous list, try the quiz. Based on your score on this quiz, you may feel well-enough prepared to skip ahead to the Review Questions at the end of the chapter, or you may determine that you would like to study the chapter material more closely.

1. What log files are used by the Active Setup Wizard and the IE 4.0 installer? What type of information is contained in these files?
2. What are some common problems encountered with the IEAK Setup Wizard? How are those problems solved?
3. Most connectivity problems in Outlook Express are caused by what types of mistakes? Where can the most common Outlook errors be corrected?
4. What is a timeout error? How can it be resolved?
5. What are some of the most common problems with NetMeeting? How can these problems be resolved?
6. What is the most common problem responsible for subscription update failures? What are some steps to resolve the problem?
7. What is the purpose of periodically removing all the temporary Internet files?
8. What are Ping and `nslookup`? What types of problems do they identify? How are they used to diagnose problems?

The answers to this prechapter quiz are located at the end of this chapter. Score your answers against those provided to determine your course of study for this chapter.

Test Objectives Overview

The complexity of Internet Explorer is what gives the application the power users need to access information over networks from a variety of resources. The base browser, combined with additional components such as Outlook Express and NetMeeting, provide a powerful set of tools for users. They also make a difficult set of tools to manage for administrators.

Because of the interactions with components and the customizations administrators can make to Internet Explorer, there are also a number of diagnostics and troubleshooting areas that must be addressed for a successful deployment of Internet Explorer.

In this chapter, you will confront the issues of troubleshooting problems with the installation and operation of IE and the IEAK. We'll start off by looking at problems in the initial deployment of Internet Explorer. Users can face problems downloading the custom package and encounter more problems installing the package on their machines. We'll look at the most common types of failures, how to identify them, and how to solve them.

Of course, users aren't the only ones facing software issues. There are a number of problems that can arise with the installation and operation of the Internet Explorer Administration Kit itself, and we will take a look at these problems. Administrators need to know how to identify and solve problems with the IEAK in order to create the custom build of IE.

Because Internet Explorer is more than just a browser, we'll also look at some of the problems facing the installation and operation of components, specifically Outlook Express and NetMeeting. Both are valuable tools that contribute to the functionality of Internet Explorer. But neither contributes anything if it isn't working properly.

Some additional, complex issues can cause problems with Internet Explorer, including the configuration and operation of Webcasting. We'll look at the channel mechanisms and the problems that can result from subscriptions gone awry.

Finally, we will take a look at the underpinnings of Internet Explorer, where problems can seriously affect user interaction and performance and at the same time be very difficult to diagnose. Specifically, we will look at the internals and potential problems with Internet Explorer's cache, how those problems affect usage, and how they can be solved. And what would Internet Explorer be without network connectivity? You could certainly remove the "Internet" part of the label… So we will examine issues with network connectivity as well.

Here's a rundown of the specific topics covered in this chapter:

- Diagnosing and resolving the deployment failure of Internet Explorer 4.0
- Diagnosing and resolving problems related to the IEAK Wizard
- Diagnosing and resolving connection failures of Outlook Express
- Diagnosing and resolving connection failures of NetMeeting
- Diagnosing and resolving failures of Webcasting
- Diagnosing and resolving failures of caching
- Network troubleshooting

Diagnosing and Resolving the Deployment Failure of Internet Explorer 4.0

Microsoft has deliberately gone out of its way to make the installation of Internet Explorer simple and trouble free. The Active Setup Wizard can manage the download and installation of components so that users should not have to worry about errors.

And what a treat it would be if that were always the case. Unfortunately, the realities of Information Systems are that even in the best of planned installations, there is always the potential for problems. With adequate planning and careful construction of a custom installation, problems should be kept to a minimum. However, when trouble does occur, administrators have some tools at their disposal to diagnose and fix problems.

The first step the user takes in installing an Internet Explorer deployment is to run the Active Setup Wizard. Because the Active Setup Wizard must connect to the network, this is where most problems occur. Problems can also occur once the files for the installation have been downloaded. Files can be corrupted, or an error can occur during the download that slips by Active Setup but affects the installer. How can you diagnose these problems? Well, both the Active Setup Wizard and Internet Explorer keep log files that detail all aspects of the installation of IE, from the downloading of the configuration and Cabinet files to the final installation of program files. These files are listed here:

- `Active Setup Log.txt`
- `IE4 Setup Log.txt`

Each of these files contains valuable data for administrators who are troubleshooting IE deployments. These files are generally found in the Windows directory, for example `C:\Windows` or `C:\WINNT`.

The first file is `Active Setup Log.txt`, which contains logging details from the Active Setup Wizard. At each stage of the download process, the wizard logs status updates, such as this one:

```
Checking for previous version of Internet Explorer.
```

These updates indicate the task the wizard performed. Errors are also logged to the file, as in this example:

```
Error: No download site found for lang :EN: in download file.
```

This sort of error indicates that the wizard had trouble finding the correct file at the download site. With information like this in hand, the administrator can check the download URL in the IEAK Profile Manager to make sure that it is correct. If the URL is correct, the administrator can then check the site to make sure that the proper files are in the proper locations.

The Active Setup Log.txt file is quite extensive and detailed. Listing 6.1 shows an sample log file and the type of information it contains.

Listing 6.1

The Contents of Active Setup Log.txt

```
Logging information for IE4Setup.exe ...
Date:3/27/1998 (M/D/Y) Time:18:23:24
Command line:/S:"D:\TEMP\ie4setup.exe":
Checking for previous version of Internet Explorer.
Registry entry Software\Microsoft\Windows\CurrentVersion\
➥AppPaths\iexplore.exe found
AppPath entry :D:\PROGRA~1\Plus!\MICROS~1\iexplore.exe:
File Version :D:\PROGRA~1\Plus!\MICROS~1\iexplore.exe:
➥Version:4.72.2106.1
Default install path:D:\Program Files\Plus!\Microsoft Internet:
Checking for IE4 version.
File Version :D:\WINNT\System32\SHELL32.DLL: Version:4.72.2106.4
Currently Integrated Browser :1.
Integrated Browser choice :1.
Initialized OLE.
Language check. Shell32.dll:0x0409: Setup:0x0409:
On Welcome page.
On EULA page.
Version of ActiveX files.
File Version :D:\WINNT\System32\wininet.dll: Version:4.72.2106.5
File Version :D:\WINNT\System32\urlmon.dll: Version:4.72.2106.4
File Version :D:\WINNT\System32\shdocvw.dll: Version:4.72.2106.7
File Version :D:\WINNT\System32\shlwapi.dll: Version:4.72.2106.4
Version of trust files.
File Version :D:\WINNT\System32\Wintrust.dll:
➥Version:5.101.1700.1
File Version :D:\WINNT\System32\digsig.dll: Version:5.0.1541.64
File Version :D:\WINNT\System32\INSENG.DLL: Version:4.72.2106.1
```

continues

Listing 6.1 Continued

```
File Version :D:\WINNT\System32\JOBEXEC.DLL: Version:4.72.2106.1
Run setup command. File:D:\TEMP\IXP000.TMP\IE4Setup.inf:
➥Section:AXControl.Register:
RunSetupCommand returned :0:
On Setup Option page.
Setup Options :6:.
AskTrustQuestion from reg:0:
AskTrustQuestion :3:
Added Microsoft as trusted provider.
Write MS trust key.
Write MS trust key 1.
Write MS trust key 2.
On setup mode page.
Setup mode selected :2:
Locale from registry :7:
On Content Language Page
Date:3/27/1998 (M/D/Y) Time:18:23:33
Content selected :United States:
On setup install dir page.
Install dir :D:\Program Files\Plus!\Microsoft Internet:.
Install dir :D:\Program Files\Plus!\Microsoft Internet:.
On Install Location Page
Date:3/27/1998 (M/D/Y) Time:18:23:35
Download site URL: HTTP://WWW.MICROSOFT.COM/IE/IE401/DOWNLOAD/
➥RTW/x86/IE4SITES.DAT
g_lpInstallSiteMgr->Initialize :0:
Error: No download site found for lang :EN: in download file.
Download site URL: HTTP://WWW.MICROSOFT.COM/IE/IE401/DOWNLOAD/
➥RTW/x86/IE4SITES.DAT
g_lpInstallSiteMgr->Initialize :0:
Error: No download site found for lang :EN: in download file.
Download site URL: HTTP://WWW.MICROSOFT.COM/IE/IE401/DOWNLOAD/
➥RTW/x86/IE4SITES.DAT
g_lpInstallSiteMgr->Initialize :0:
Error: No download site found for lang :EN: in download file.
```

```
Error: Downloading site data file failed.
Run setup command. File:D:\TEMP\IXP000.TMP\IE4Setup.inf:
➥Section:IE4Setup.Failure:
RunSetupCommand returned :0:
Date:3/27/1998 (M/D/Y) Time:18:23:44
End of Logging.
```

As you glance through the file, you may notice that a number follows some of the instructions, as in this example:

```
On Setup Option page.
Setup Options :6:.
```

This number is a code that represents the status of the task being performed. In this example, the entry from the log indicates that the wizard was on the Setup Option page, and that the Setup Options returned a status code of `6`.

What does that mean? Because status code `6` is for decompressing files, we know that the Wizard was decompressing downloaded files. Each code number, `0` through `9`, has a different status indication. The details of the status codes are shown in Table 6.1.

Table 6.1

Active Setup Status Codes for Stages of IE Installation

Code	Status	Description
0	Initializing	Creating temp directories, checking disk space, and so on
1	Dependency	Checking all installation dependencies
2	Downloading	Downloading files from server
3	Copying	Copying files from the download directory to the temp install directory
4	Retrying	Retrying the download of files because of an error

continues

Table 6.1 Continued

Code	Status	Description
5	Checking Trust	Checking file permissions
6	Extracting Files	Decompressing files
7	Running Setup Program	Running an `.INF` or `.EXE` file
8	Finished	Installation complete
9	Download Finished	Download of files complete

In addition to these status codes, the log file can contain codes that indicate more specific errors. For example, if the setup process is canceled by the user, the log file contains the error code `8004004`. These error codes can indicate problems, and when used in conjunction with the status codes, they can paint a very detailed picture of the Active Setup Wizard's download process. Table 6.2 shows the more common error codes for the log, along with some code ranges.

Table 6.2

Common Error Codes Found in `Active Setup Log.txt`

Code	Description
`80100003`	Missing files from the download directory during the installation process
`800C005`	File or server not found
`800C00B`	Connection timed out
`8004004`	Setup canceled by user
`800b`*XXXX*	`800b` failures indicate a trust problem
`800C`*XXXX*	`800C` failures are urlmon failures

When the Active Setup Wizard finishes downloading the files for the installation, it launches the IE installer (which, incidentally, keeps a log file of its own: `IE4 Setup Log.txt`).

The IE4 Setup Log.txt file keeps extensive records of each step of the IE 4.0 installation process. Each step of the installation is divided into a Pass entry; the time at which each pass begins is also recorded. Here's an example of what a Pass entry might look like:

```
[12:19:34  Start of Pass: 14]
Overwriting file: 'D:\WINNT\EXTRACT.EXE'
Uncompressed copy file: 'C:\msdownld.tmp\ASE001.tmp\EXTRACT.EXE'
to: 'D:\WINNT\EXTRACT.EXE' Succeeded
Overwriting file: 'D:\Program Files\Plus!\
➥Microsoft Internet\IE4.DLL'
Cabinet file extracted: 'C:\msdownld.tmp\ASE001.tmp\ie4nt_5.CAB'
to: 'D:\WINNT\System32\' Succeeded
Cabinet file extracted: 'C:\msdownld.tmp\ASE001.tmp\ie4nt_5.CAB'
to: 'D:\WINNT\INF\' Succeeded
```

Notice that the time of the pass and the pass number are logged.

Each step performed in the pass is recorded. In this pass, two files were overwritten and two Cabinet files were extracted. When things go smoothly, this is the type of data contained in the IE4 Setup Log.txt file. When errors are generated for any reason, they are also listed here. Listing 6.2 shows a truncated IE Setup Log.txt file.

Note

The contents of the IE4 Setup Log.txt file, shown in Listing 6.2, have been truncated to give you an idea what to look for in the file. Because of the extensive nature of the logging that occurs, the actually size of the file can be several hundred kilobytes—quite large for a text file.

Listing 6.2

The (Truncated) Contents of an IE4 Setup Log.txt File

```
************************************************************

Microsoft Setup Log File Opened 02/27/98 12:19:18

Version number: 3.01.0.1622

Running under Windows NT.
```

continues

Listing 6.2 Continued

```
[12:19:18  Start of Pass: 0]
Command Line: /T ie40nt.stf  /S C:\msdownld.tmp\ASE001.tmp\ /QT /
➥g "D:\WINNT\IE4 Setup Log.Txt"
[12:19:18  Start of Pass: 1]
Floppy mode
Processing the header information of the file:
➥C:\msdownld.tmp\ASE001.tmp\ie40nt.stf
************************************************************
  Application name: IE4.DLL
  Application version: 4.72.2106.8(1033)
  Dialog caption base: Microsoft Internet Explorer 4.0
  Frame caption: Microsoft Internet Explorer 4.0 Setup
  Frame bitmap: ie4.dll, 102
  Modules: Themes, Desktop Theme Selector
  HLP file name: acmsetup.hlp
  INF file name: ie4.inf
  MSApps mode: local
[12:19:18  Start of Pass: 2]
 Object 1 - Setup is replacing an older version of Microsoft
Internet Explorer in the folder: D:\Program Files\Plus!\
➥Microsoft Internet\.
[12:19:18  Start of Pass: 6]
Phase = camfInitializeObject
Begin Custom Action: LogAndUpdatePhases
     Safe = 1
     CamfFriendlyName for jobexec: Initializing
End Custom Action: LogAndUpdatePhases
[12:19:31  Start of Pass: 13]
Phase = camfAddBillBoards
Begin Custom Action: LogAndUpdatePhases
     Safe = 0
     CamfFriendlyName for jobexec: Copying files
End Custom Action: LogAndUpdatePhases
```

```
Begin Custom Action: PreWizExec
     'D:\WINNT\System32\pstores.exe -remove' completed
➥successfully
End Custom Action: PreWizExec
Begin Custom Action: DelayedCopy
     MoveFile succeeded: D:\WINNT\System32\CRYPT32.DLL to
➥D:\WINNT\System32\IE4Setup\CRYPT32.DLL
     MoveFile succeeded: D:\WINNT\System32\MSOSS.DLL to
➥D:\WINNT\System32\IE4Setup\MSOSS.DLL
     MoveFile succeeded: D:\WINNT\System32\DIGSIG.DLL to
➥D:\WINNT\System32\IE4Setup\DIGSIG.DLL
End Custom Action: DelayedCopy
Begin Custom Action: DelayedCopy
     MoveFile succeeded: D:\WINNT\System32\MSNSSPC.DLL to
➥D:\WINNT\System32\IE4Setup\MSNSSPC.DLL
     File does not exist: D:\WINNT\System32\XENROLL.DLL
     MoveFile succeeded: D:\WINNT\System32\MSHTMLWB.DLL to
➥D:\WINNT\System32\IE4Setup\MSHTMLWB.DLL
     MoveFile succeeded: D:\Program Files\Plus!\
➥Microsoft Internet\IEXPLORE.EXE to
D:\WINNT\System32\IE4Setup\IEXPLORE.EXE
End Custom Action: DelayedCopy
[12:19:34  Start of Pass: 14]
Overwriting file: 'D:\WINNT\EXTRACT.EXE'
Uncompressed copy file: 'C:\msdownld.tmp\ASE001.tmp\EXTRACT.EXE'
➥to: 'D:\WINNT\EXTRACT.EXE' Succeeded
Overwriting file: 'D:\Program Files\Plus!\
➥Microsoft Internet\IE4.DLL'
Cabinet file extracted: 'C:\msdownld.tmp\ASE001.tmp\ie4nt_5.CAB'
➥to: 'D:\WINNT\System32\' Succeeded
Cabinet file extracted: 'C:\msdownld.tmp\ASE001.tmp\ie4nt_5.CAB'
➥to: 'D:\WINNT\INF\' Succeeded
[12:19:50  Start of Pass: 15]
Phase = camfDoNonVisualMods
```

continues

Listing 6.2 Continued

```
Begin Custom Action: LogAndUpdatePhases
     Safe = 0
     CamfFriendlyName for jobexec: Updating configuration
End Custom Action: LogAndUpdatePhases
Writing registry key value: key =
➥HKEY_LOCAL_MACHINE\Software\Microsoft\IE4\Setup;
 value name = SourcePath; value = C:\msdownld.tmp\ASE001.tmp\;
➥Succeeded.
Writing registry key value: key =
HKEY_LOCAL_MACHINE\Software\Microsoft\Windows\CurrentVersion\SharedDlls;
value name = D:\WINNT\System32\COMCAT.DLL; value = 2; Succeeded.
Begin Custom Action: DelayedCopy
     SwapFile succeeded: D:\Program Files\Plus!\
➥Microsoft Internet\IEXPLORE.EXE and
D:\WINNT\System32\IE4Setup\IEXPLORE.EXE
     SwapFile succeeded: D:\WINNT\System32\MSOSS.DLL and
➥D:\WINNT\System32\IE4Setup\MSOSS.DLL
     SwapFile succeeded: D:\WINNT\System32\CRYPT32.DLL and
➥D:\WINNT\System32\IE4Setup\CRYPT32.DLL
End Custom Action: DelayedCopy
Writing registry key value: key =
HKEY_LOCAL_MACHINE\Software\Microsoft\Windows\CurrentVersion\RunOnceEx\104;
 value name = 005; value =
➥D:\WINNT\System32\iemenu.ocx¦DllRegisterServer; Succeeded.
Creating registry key:
'HKEY_LOCAL_MACHINE\Software\Microsoft\Windows\CurrentVersion\RunOnceEx\101';
➥Succeeded.
Writing registry key value: key =
HKEY_LOCAL_MACHINE\Software\Microsoft\Windows\CurrentVersion\RunOnceEx\101;
 value name = 015; value =
➥D:\WINNT\System32\ielabel.ocx¦DllRegisterServer; Succeeded.
[12:20:01  Start of Pass: 16]
Phase = camfDoVisualMods
Begin Custom Action: LogAndUpdatePhases
     Safe = 0
End Custom Action: LogAndUpdatePhases
```

```
Begin Custom Action: Install128Schannel
     initcopy() called to rename D:\WINNT\System32\schnl128.dll
➥to D:\WINNT\System32\schannel.dll on next boot
End Custom Action: Install128Schannel
[12:20:03  Start of Pass: 17]
Phase = camfPostInstall
Begin Custom Action: LogAndUpdatePhases
     Safe = 0
End Custom Action: LogAndUpdatePhases
Begin Custom Action: WizExec
     'D:\WINNT\System32\WINHLP32.EXE -S WINDOWS.HLP' completed
➥successfully
End Custom Action: WizExec
Begin Custom Action: WizExec
     'D:\WINNT\System32\regsvr32.exe /s comcat.dll' completed
➥successfully
End Custom Action: WizExec
Begin Custom Action: EffectNoReboot
     IE4 success key written: 4.72.2106.8(1033)
     All Custom Actions completed successfully
End Custom Action: EffectNoReboot
Writing registry key value: key =
HKEY_LOCAL_MACHINE\Software\Microsoft\MS Setup (ACME)\
➥Table Files;
 value name = IE4.DLL@v4.72.2106.8(1033); value =
D:\Program Files\Plus!\Microsoft Internet\Setup\setup.stf;
➥Succeeded.
[12:20:08  Start of Pass: 18]
[12:20:08  Start of Pass: 19]
Phase = camfDtor
Begin Custom Action: LogAndUpdatePhases
     Safe = 0
End Custom Action: LogAndUpdatePhases
Microsoft Setup Log File Closed 02/27/98 12:20:08
```

By working with these two log files, administrators can get a very detailed picture of what is going on during the installation process. Administrators can then use that information to pinpoint problems with the installation process. If the problem is with a download, for example, administrators can begin checking their servers. If it is a disk space issue, administrators can check the user's machine.

There are no hard-and-fast rules about diagnosing problems using log files. The key is to pay attention to anything that looks out of place and to investigate it thoroughly. Diagnosing installation and deployment problems is a bit like being a detective. But with the aid of clues provided by the Active Setup log and the IE 4.0 Setup log, you should have a good start toward finding the answers.

Diagnosing and Resolving Problems Related to the IEAK Wizard

The IEAK Wizard is a pretty straightforward wizard-type application. Therefore, there isn't much that can go wrong. Assuming that you have downloaded and installed the wizard (which can be problematic if your network connectivity is sporadic), here are the three most common problems:

- Network connectivity
- IE 4.0 installation
- Customization codes

The following sections examine how each of these problems affects the IEAK Wizard and what you can do to resolve some of these issues.

Network Connectivity

The IEAK Wizard uses a connection to the Internet for the Automatic Version Synchronization (AVS) feature. This feature limits the use of the IEAK Wizard to machines that have an Internet connection. The problem results when you first try to run the IEAK Wizard. Because AVS cannot be disabled the first time you run the IEAK Wizard, the wizard must be able to connect to the Microsoft site to check the version of your components.

Therefore, you must have a working Internet connection in place the first time you run the IEAK Wizard. After that, you can disable the AVS feature, and you don't have to worry about the connection. If you are having trouble with the networking on your machine, you can use some troubleshooting tools to help you diagnose problems. These tools are covered in "Network Troubleshooting," later in this chapter.

IE 4.0 Installation

In addition to requiring a network connection, the IEAK Wizard also requires that a working installation of Internet Explorer 4.0 (with any necessary service packs) is installed on the administration machine. Several features of the IEAK Wizard rely on the installed version of IE, such as importing channel settings and Active Desktop settings.

If IE 4.0 is not installed on the administration machine, the IEAK Wizard might not run at all; but if it does, there will be other problems. Settings that rely on imported settings from IE 4.0 will not configure correctly, and any builds the IEAK Wizard creates will be incomplete. To solve these kinds of problems, simply install IE 4.0 on the same machine as the IEAK Wizard, and proceed from there.

Customization Codes

When you sign up for the IEAK and complete the questionnaires for license agreements, you are assigned a customization code that you are required to enter for the IEAK. The customization code is directly related to the license agreement you have signed and also configures the IEAK for your deployment role.

For example, if you sign a license to distribute your custom IE installation publicly, you are limited to an ISP or Content Developer role, and the customization code you are assigned will reflect this fact.

Of course, the potential problem is that not all features of the IEAK are available to all development roles. Although this may be perceived as a problem with the IEAK Wizard, it is actually a feature. By limiting you to the options covered by your license agreement, you are assured that you won't create a version that violates the agreement. Although you can apply for multiple licenses, be sure that you use the license that applies to the type of installation you want to create. If you do not, you might accidentally take advantage of features that place you in violation of your license agreement.

Diagnosing and Resolving Connection Failures of Outlook Express

The Outlook Express client with Internet Explorer relies heavily on network connectivity; without it, mail messages won't be delivered. Therefore, most of the issues surrounding troubleshooting with Outlook Express are related to the application's capability to connect to mail servers, news servers, or the network.

The five most common types of errors that users might encounter using Outlook Express are listed here:

- Timeouts
- Unable to send or receive email
- Cannot view newsgroups
- Can connect to some newsgroups, but not all
- Newsgroup connections

Most of the time, these errors are simple configuration problems that are straightforward to fix. But because you are dealing with services provided by remote servers, there is always a chance that the service problem is with the server, not the client. If, after troubleshooting the client, checking the client settings, and checking the machine's networking, a problem still persists, it is probably a good idea to check the server (mail or news) for problems as well.

The majority of the settings you should check when troubleshooting Outlook Express are found in the Internet Accounts dialog box (from the Tools menu, select Accounts). In this dialog box, you can view the account information used to check each type of server; you can even alter some of the settings each protocol uses to connect to the servers. The Internet Accounts dialog box is shown in Figure 6.1.

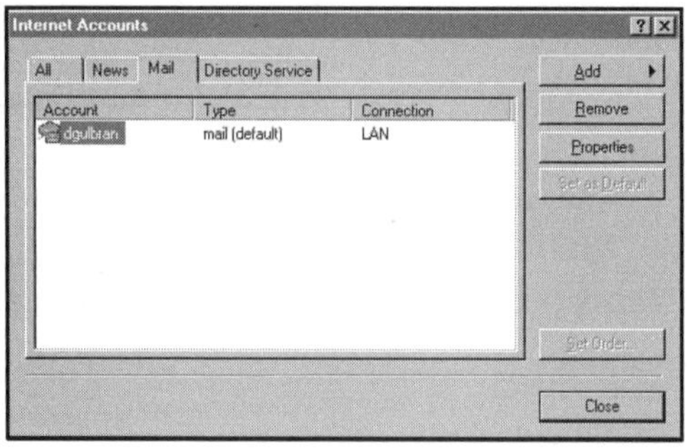

Figure 6.1

The Internet Accounts dialog box controls connectivity settings for various servers and accounts in Outlook Express.

By clicking a tab such as News or Mail, you can see the list of accounts created for that service. By selecting a listed account and clicking Properties, you can alter many of the connection properties, from general information to advanced.

Figure 6.2 shows the various Properties dialog boxes, which include these:

- General
- Servers
- Connection
- Security
- Advanced

Each of these pages in the Properties dialog box contains settings Outlook Express uses when connecting to servers. Incorrectly setting these properties frequently leads to connectivity problems.

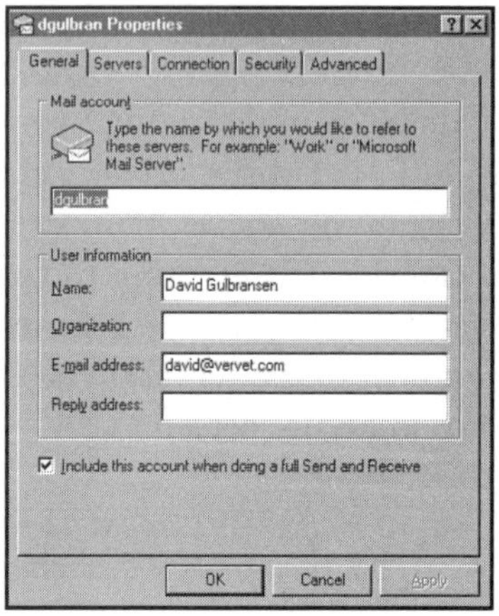

Figure 6.2

The account Properties dialog box for Outlook Express is used to manage account settings.

Now that you have an idea where the most crucial settings for Outlook Express are located, the following sections detail the most common errors and provide some steps you can take to solve them.

Timeout Errors

A timeout error is exactly what it sounds like. When the Outlook Express client attempts to connect to a server (either an email or a news server), there is a waiting period while the server responds. It's a bit like making a phone call; the person on the other end might not pick up immediately, and it's up to you to decide how long you are willing to let it ring before hanging up.

With mail and news servers, many factors can influence how long it takes the server to respond to requests. The first factor is server load. If many users attempt to read mail or send news at the same time, the server might get backlogged or bogged down with incoming requests and might take a while to respond. Response can also be slowed because of unusually high network traffic, which can delay the requests getting to and from the server and client.

So what recourse do you have in the face of server timeouts? Well, both the mail server settings and the news server settings include a Server Timeout parameter that allows you to specify how long the client should wait before returning an error.

Open the Account dialog box and select an account type, either mail or news, from the appropriate tab to select the account for that service. With the account selected, click the Properties button to see the connection properties for that service. Next, select the Advanced tab to display the advanced settings, which include the Server Timeout parameter as shown in Figure 6.3.

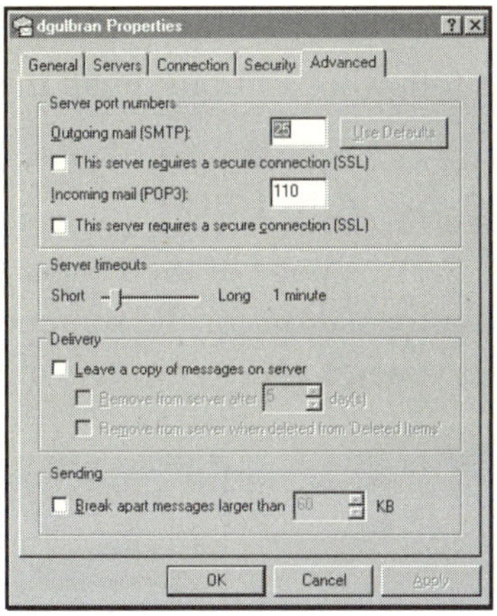

Figure 6.3

The Advanced server settings allow the user to increase the amount of time before server times out.

Under the Server Timeouts heading is a slider, which you can slide from the left value of 30 seconds to the right value of 5 minutes. The default value is 1 minute. By moving the slider to the right, you can increase the timeout value, and therefore make the client wait a little longer. In many cases, this action eliminates the problem. Of course, if the server is underpowered for the application, this action won't fix the problem. But in a majority of cases, simply bumping the timeout value up a notch or two eliminates timeout errors.

Unable to Send or Receive Email

If you cannot send or receive email using the Outlook Express client, the troubleshooting procedure is similar to the one outlined for server timeouts in the preceding section. Again, the place to start looking for trouble is in the Accounts dialog box. This time, start with the mail accounts and the Properties dialog box for the mail account.

In the case of email problems, there are three pages in the Properties dialog box that you will want to examine closely for problems:

- Servers
- Connection
- Advanced

The following sections detail these pages of the dialog box.

The Servers Page

The Servers page of the Properties dialog box shows the connection information for the servers to which Outlook Express connects to send and receive email (see Figure 6.4).

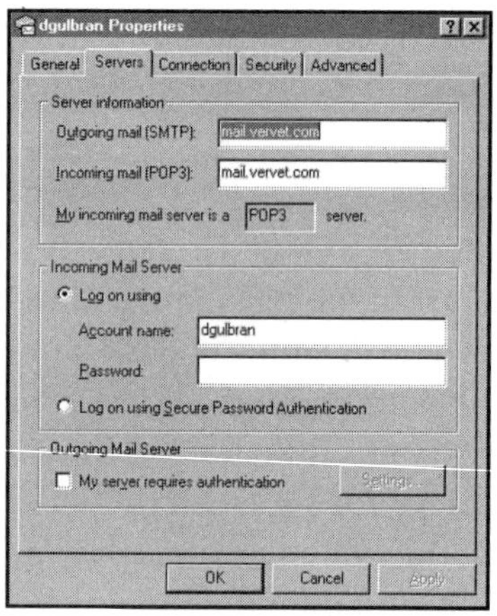

Figure 6.4

The Servers page of the Properties dialog box in Outlook Express is where server information is entered.

On this page, check the values of the following parameters:

- Outgoing Mail (SMTP)
- Incoming Mail (POP3)
- My Incoming Mail Server Is a ? Server

The Outgoing Mail setting must be set to the Fully Qualified Domain Name (FQDN) of the server your organization uses for outgoing email traffic. The same holds true for the Incoming Mail setting; it must reflect the value of your incoming server's FQDN. Finally, because Outlook Express supports two kinds of servers for incoming mail, POP3 and IMAP, you must also supply this information.

Finally, if either of the servers requires authentication, you must enter that information in the Incoming Mail Server and Outgoing Mail Server sections of this page.

The Connection Page

The next page of the Properties dialog box you must examine is the Connection page, as shown in Figure 6.5.

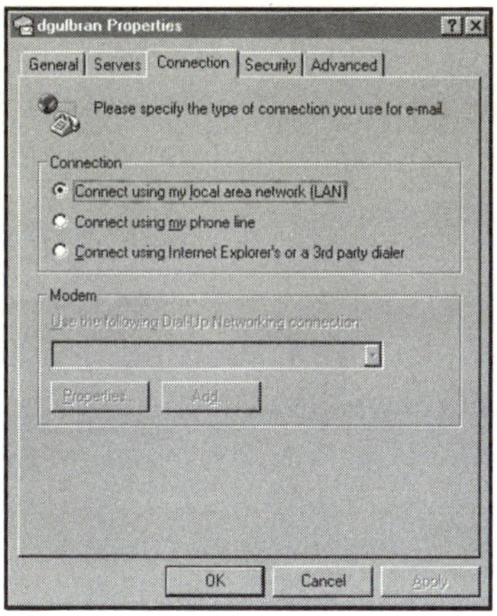

Figure 6.5

Use the Connection page of the Properties dialog box to correct configuration problems with network connectivity.

Double check to make sure that the correct connection type for your machine's connection to the Internet is selected. If it is not, change it. Because Outlook Express must connect to servers over the Internet to send and receive information, the connection must be solid and reliable (not to mention configured correctly).

The Advanced Page

Finally, you should also check the settings in the Advanced page of the Properties dialog box, as shown in Figure 6.6. The section to be concerned with here is the Server Port Numbers section.

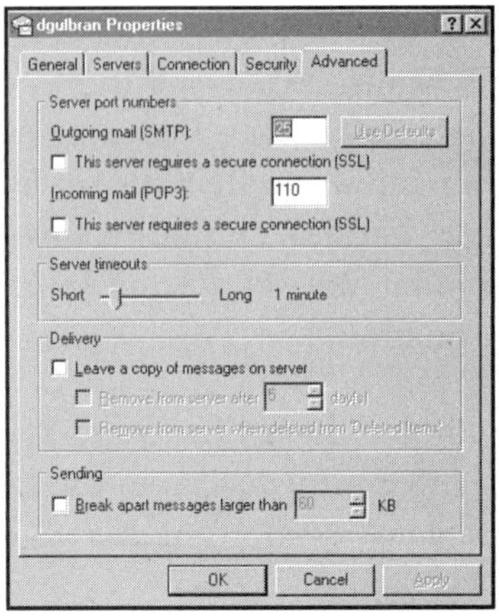

Figure 6.6

The Advanced page of the Properties dialog box contains additional information used by Outlook Express to correctly connect to the servers.

Specifically, the Outgoing SMTP port number should be `25` and the Incoming POP3 port number should be `110`, unless your organization has deliberately chosen other port numbers. You can also specify whether the connection must be a Secure Sockets Layer (SSL) connection. If these settings are configured incorrectly for your server, the Outlook Express client will have trouble connecting to the servers, and therefore have problems sending and receiving mail.

Again, these are the most connection common problems from the client end. It is always possible that there is a general problem with networking on the machine, or that the problem lies with the server. For more information and tools for diagnosing network problems, see "Network Troubleshooting," later in this chapter.

Cannot View Newsgroups

The procedure for connecting to a news server for newsgroups is similar to that for mail connections. To correctly post and read newsgroups, the server settings must be correct. Just as you did for mail server options in the preceding section, open the Accounts dialog box and select the account configured for your news service. You can use then access information in the tabbed dialog box.

If you are having trouble viewing newsgroups, select the news server from the Accounts dialog box and click Properties to view the Properties dialog box (see fig. 6.7).

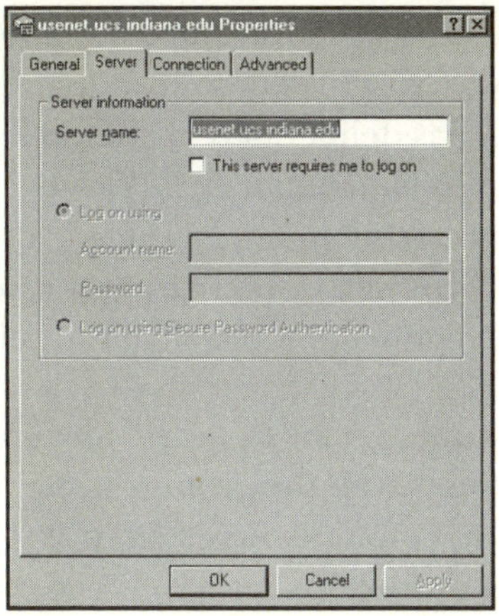

Figure 6.7

The Server page of the news server Properties dialog box.

The first step is to make sure that the server's Fully Qualified Domain Name is correctly entered for the Server Name field. If this is not the case, Outlook Express cannot connect. Similarly, if the server requires a logon account, select that option and specify the appropriate account name and password.

Next, just as with checking the mail configuration, check the Connections page to make sure that the network connectivity is configured correctly. Without correct network connectivity, news cannot be read or posted.

Finally, review the Advanced page of the Properties dialog box, as shown in Figure 6.8.

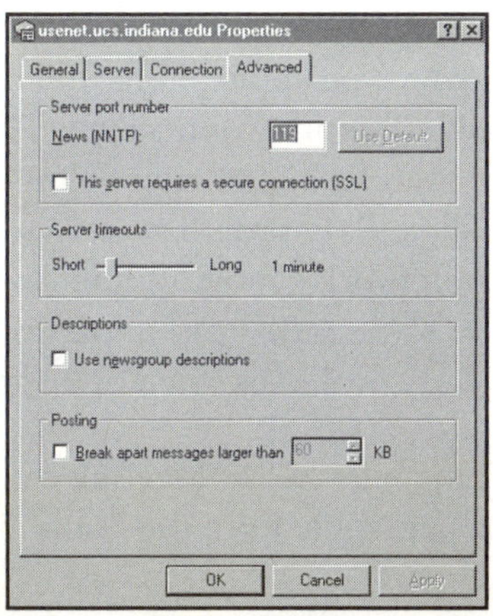

Figure 6.8

The Advanced page of the news server Properties dialog box contains settings for the server and server timeouts.

Just as you did for the mail server, check the port number for the news (NNTP) server. It should be port 119, unless your organization has deliberately chosen otherwise. Consider increasing the Server Timeouts value. Because there is so much news traffic on the Internet today, NNTP servers are often very overworked and underpowered. Increasing the Server Timeouts value can help with connection problems as well.

In some instances, users can connect to some groups on a server but not to all the groups. It may also happen that the user can connect to one server but not to another. More often than not, these problems are a result of incorrectly configured authentication. On the Server page of the Properties dialog box shown in Figure 6.7, make sure that the account name and password are correct. This is likely to eliminate the problem. If not, contact the administrator of the news server to troubleshoot from that angle.

Keep in mind that for mail, newsgroups, and most other network-based services, if the machine's network connection is faulty, server connection problems will abound in spite of correct configuration from within the client. Keep a close eye on network connectivity when diagnosing connection problems of any type.

Diagnosing and Resolving Connection Failures of NetMeeting

Although the functionality of NetMeeting is different from other Internet-type applications, the basic fundamentals still apply when troubleshooting connectivity. There is still the issue of making sure that the application is configured to connect to the correct server, and that you have selected the proper settings based on your network configuration. NetMeeting also has a number of other settings that can impact performance and appear to be connectivity problems when, in fact, they are not.

The settings for NetMeeting can be found in the Options dialog box, accessible from the Tools menu, as shown in Figure 6.9.

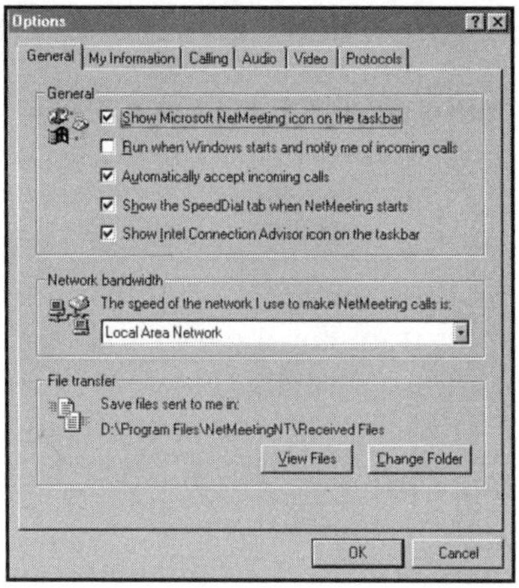

Figure 6.9

The Options dialog box contains all the settings regarding connectivity for NetMeeting.

In this dialog box, you can find the important settings for connectivity on the following pages:

- **General.** On this page, you should double-check the Network Bandwidth setting to make sure that it is set in accordance with your network connection. Doing so can impact the performance of conferencing features.
- **Calling.** On this page, the Directory settings are important. If you have configured NetMeeting to log in to a server automatically, you should make sure that indeed, the server is available. If the server is not, or if it is consistently overloaded, you may want to select a new server here.
- **Protocols.** On this page, you should make sure that the TCP/IP protocol is enabled. If it is not, NetMeeting will be unable to connect over the network.

At times, a performance problem or misconfiguration with NetMeeting can seem to be a connectivity problem. The two most common manifestations of this condition are problems with application sharing and with audio/video transmission.

Application Sharing Problems

Sharing applications is a powerful feature of NetMeeting. However, it also raises performance issues and can lead to some common misconceptions.

One problem is with commands on the File menu of the shared application. For the user sharing the application, the application functions normally. However, for the remote user, some functions of the File menu will be disabled (for example, the remote user cannot print or save the file).

The reason for this limitation is simple: Giving the remote user complete control over the application presents a serious security risk.

Another problem with application sharing is that if the user sharing the application has the window obscured by other applications, the remote user may not see all of the window. The solution in this case is to close any unnecessary applications and to minimize any applications that are not in use.

Audio Transmission Problems

There are generally two causes for problems concerning audio/video: miscalibration of the microphone settings or a physical connection problem with the user's audio/video equipment. In the case of the former, you can take a number of steps to make sure that the settings are correct.

The first step in diagnosing problems with audio levels is to run the Audio Tuning Wizard, found in the Tools menu. The Audio Tuning Wizard, shown in Figure 6.10, automatically walks users through the process of setting the microphone level correctly.

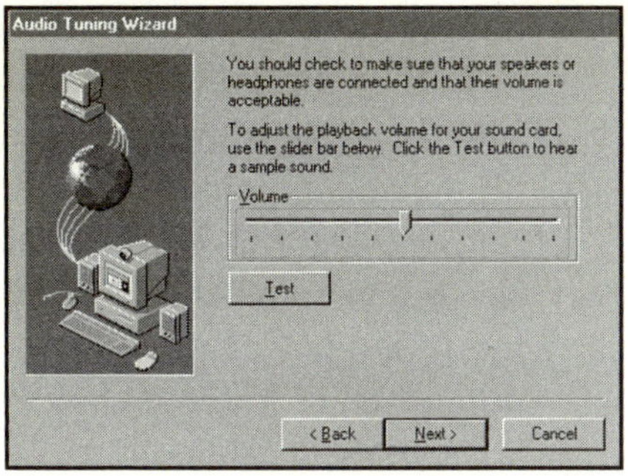

Figure 6.10

The Audio Tuning Wizard helps you set the level of microphones automatically.

Another option you can adjust to provide the best audio, and to ensure that users are heard, is found on the Audio page in the Options dialog box (see Figure 6.11). Here, users can adjust the way NetMeeting handles audio.

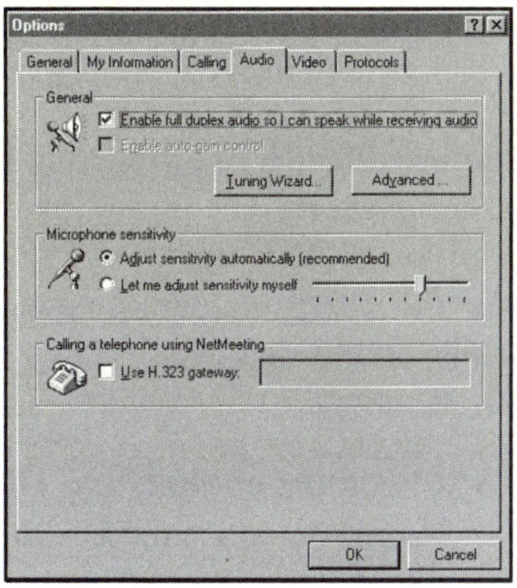

Figure 6.11

Adjusting the NetMeeting audio properties to ensure audio transmission.

On the Audio page of the Options dialog box, there are two categories of settings that have an impact on audio and how the user is heard:

- **General.** In this section of the dialog box, the user can choose the Enable Full Duplex Audio option, which allows users to send and receive audio simultaneously, as if they were talking on a telephone. Full duplexing decreases performance. Another option is the Auto-Gain Control, which automatically adjusts gain levels to compensate for abrupt changes in volume.

- **Microphone sensitivity.** Microphone sensitivity has a great impact on the ability of the user to be heard in a conference. The Adjust Sensitivity Automatically option allows the microphone to compensate for different speakers and to automatically adjust for varied levels of conversation. If the user chooses to adjust the sensitivity manually, he or she runs the risk of not having the microphone sensitive enough to pick up hushed or lowered conversation.

Other factors can also affect perceived performance. For example, in a multiperson conference, users can use audio/video features only with one other user. This is accomplished through the Switch Audio/Video Connection command, under the Tools menu. To be heard, the user must select the conference participant with whom he or she wants to talk using this option. If the user is not familiar with this feature, he or she might mistake the need to switch users for audio/video features malfunctioning.

Another category of problems that can affect NetMeeting is physical connections. The success of audio/video conferencing depends on good connections for microphones, speakers, and video cameras. The troubleshooting techniques for hardware are far too detailed and varied to cover here. However there are some general guidelines:

- **Check the connectors.** The first step in diagnosing hardware problems should be to double-check connections. If a microphone or speakers are not plugged in correctly, the transmission might be intermittent or fail completely. Double-check to make sure that everything is plugged in at the right port and that the connection is good. Performing this basic check can save you many headaches.

- **Try another application.** If you are having problems with audio and video performance, try the hardware in another application. If the devices work properly, you can link the problem to NetMeeting. However, if the devices still do not work in the other application, perhaps a hardware problem has developed.

- **Check the Windows system properties.** Because your sound card and video hardware should be installed through Windows, double-check the device properties using the System Control Panel and the Device Manager. Make sure that the devices are working properly and that there are no hardware conflicts.

For all the functionality that NetMeeting provides, it is a surprisingly trouble-free application. Although there are a number of hardware problems that can occur, if your hardware is in order, there is usually a good chance that NetMeeting will function without fault. However, when things do go wrong, you should now have some idea of where to look to make sure that things get back on track and meetings continue as scheduled.

Diagnosing and Resolving Failures of Webcasting

Webcasting, both in terms of channel subscriptions and Web site subscriptions, is subject to the same types of problems as other components of Internet Explorer. For example, if your machine is not connected to the Internet, the channel (or site) content cannot be downloaded during an update.

Here are the two big issues that affect Webcasting:

- Network connectivity
- Disk space

Network connectivity issues are similar to those found in other client applications. IE must have a working network connection to download updates. IE must also be able to reach the server on which the channel content or site content is located.

When errors are generated for subscription content, they are shown in the Subscription Manager, which can be found in the Favorites menu under Manage Subscriptions, as shown in Figure 6.12.

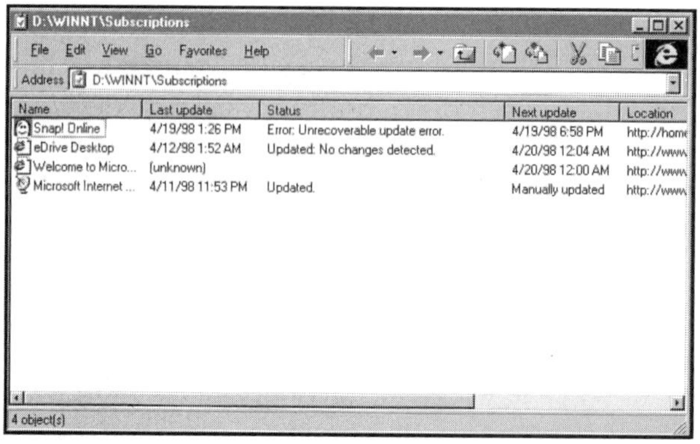

Figure 6.12

Subscription errors can be found in the Status field of the Subscription Manager.

If the error indicates that the update was not completed because the server could not be reached, networking trouble might be the culprit. Another issue might be disk space.

Keep in mind that if content is to be downloaded to the user's machine, the user's machine must have an adequate amount of disk space to handle the content. Because channel subscriptions or site subscriptions can get out of control and consume large amounts of disk space, administrators can take steps to limit the amount of disk space allocated to subscriptions; start with the System Policies and Restrictions settings available through the IEAK Wizard or Profile Manager.

Diagnosing and Resolving Failures of Caching

Although caching documents is a great way to increase the efficiency of viewing pages, there are times when caching documents can be detrimental. Occasionally, the caching mechanism has problems and incorrectly keeps loading a cached page. Additionally, the cache becomes less and less efficient as the cache becomes fuller. Although you can't do much to correct problems with the cache, there are a few things you can try.

First, to make sure that the cache functions optimally, set the amount of disk space consumed by the cache to a value between 5MB and 20MB. Allocating any more disk space than that will result in inefficient use of the cache.

You can also clear the cache of documents; access the Internet Options dialog box, as shown in Figure 6.13.

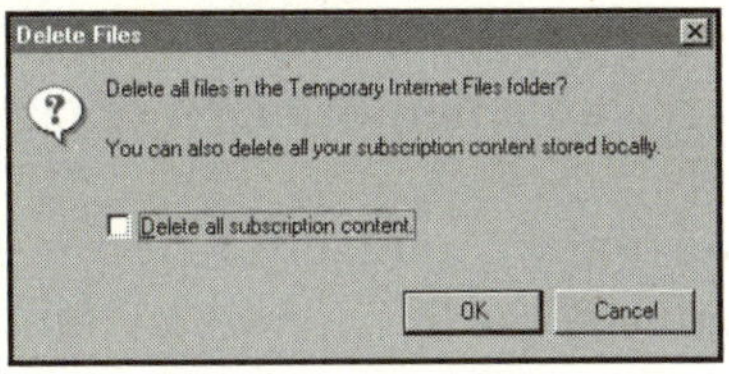

Figure 6.13

Clearing all the files, including subscriptions, from the cache can help eliminate caching problems.

Clearing the cache removes all the documents that have been stored in the cache; you can also clear subscription content. Clearing the cache results in all of the previously cached content being downloaded to the machine again. This approach can eliminate problems with pages not loading correctly and also ensures that the content of the pages is updated.

Network Troubleshooting

Because Internet Explorer is designed to work with the Internet and other network-based services, often problems you encounter with IE are not problems with the installation or performance of IE itself, but rather are problems with the network or the network configuration of the machine.

The following sections look at some of the tools you can use to diagnose networking problems. Most of these tools are available on multiple platforms, including Macintosh, Windows 95/NT, and UNIX. In the following sections, we use the specific syntax of the tools for Windows. Keep in mind that the syntax might vary for other platforms. However, the types of information each utility provides and the appropriate use of each tool are consistent across all platforms.

The `netstat` Command

At times, it will be useful to take a look in real time at what the machine is doing regarding networking connections. For example, what connections are being made? Where are they being made, and what types of protocols are involved? Answers to these questions can aid administrators in troubleshooting specific networking problems with a machine by helping the administrator see what networking is doing while IE 4.0 is running.

One of the commands that can provide administrators with information regarding network connections in real time is the `netstat` command. This command returns connection information for networking connections; it can deal with a variety of protocols including TCP/IP. The syntax for the `netstat` command is simple:

```
netstat
```

You can also use several command flags to display different information about network connections. Here are some of the more useful flags:

Flag	Description
`-a`	Displays all connections and listening ports
`-e`	Displays Ethernet statistics
`-n`	Displays addresses and port numbers in numerical form
`-p` *protocol*	Shows connections for the protocol specified (UDP, TCP, and so on)

The output from the `netstat` command looks something like this:

```
Active Connections
  Proto  Local Address     Foreign Address              State
  TCP    casiel:1025       localhost:1028               ESTABLISHED
  TCP    casiel:1028       localhost:1025               ESTABLISHED
  TCP    casiel:2562       members.tripod.com:80        ESTABLISHED
  TCP    casiel:3121       logic.vervet.com:nbsession   ESTABLISHED
  TCP    casiel:2101       209.1.224.15:80              ESTABLISHED
  TCP    casiel:3399       logic.vervet.com:telnet      ESTABLISHED
  TCP    casiel:1613       209.1.224.15:80              ESTABLISHED
  TCP    casiel:2127       209.1.224.15:80              ESTABLISHED
```

This output lists the protocol being used, the local address and port number, the foreign address and port number, and the state of the network connection.

You can use this information to help diagnose the types of connections being made on the machine and to determine if there are problems with a connection being made.

The Ping Utility

Another very useful—perhaps *the* most useful—network utility is Ping. Ping is a simple utility: It queries a remote host and then lets you know whether that host is available over the network. If the host is available, Ping also lets you know how long it took to reach it. You can think of the Ping utility as a computer sonar: Just as a submarine does, you *ping* a machine to see whether it is out there. Some sites, however, have disallowed Ping responses for security reasons; there might still be a few sites that are available but that are not Ping-able.

Because Ping can tell you whether a host is available, it can be used to make sure that you can connect to other machines. You can also use Ping to make sure that the server you are trying to contact is actually available. Or you can use it to see whether there is a lot of network congestion that is causing delays or timeouts.

The syntax for Ping is simple:

```
ping host
```

In this syntax, `host` is the IP number or domain name of the machine you are checking. The following example uses Ping on two different sites: `www.mcp.com` (an Internet site) and `www.vervet.com` (on my local network). Here are the results:

```
G:\>ping www.mcp.com
Pinging www.mcp.com [206.246.131.227] with 32 bytes of data:
Reply from 206.246.131.227: bytes=32 time=40ms TTL=249
Reply from 206.246.131.227: bytes=32 time=50ms TTL=249
Request timed out.
```

```
Reply from 206.246.131.227: bytes=32 time=40ms TTL=249
G:\>ping www.vervet.com
Pinging www.vervet.com [156.56.102.105] with 32 bytes of data:
Reply from 156.56.102.105: bytes=32 time<10ms TTL=255
Reply from 156.56.102.105: bytes=32 time<10ms TTL=255
Reply from 156.56.102.105: bytes=32 time<10ms TTL=255
```

For the first ping, you can see that the time required to return the ping was 40 milliseconds. The second ping, however, returned in less than 10 milliseconds! The difference, of course, is because the second machine is on my local network.

In the first ping, notice that there was a Request Timed Out statement, which lets us know that for some reason, the ping did not receive an answer before the specified timeout period. If you receive too many timeouts, it might be wise to increase your Server Timeout parameter in Internet Applications. Similarly, if a ping does not return anything, or times out completely, there might be a problem with your network connection. Try pinging other sites; if you can reach other sites, your network connection is probably okay, but the server/site you are trying to ping might be down.

Ping is quick and easy and is probably one of the first tools you should reach for if you are encountering network difficulty. A quick ping can tell you if the network is down, if your machine is having problems, or if the server is unreachable.

The `tracert` Command

In networking, there are a number of places where errors can occur in connectivity. Sometimes, there are problems with the client; sometimes, there are problems with the server. And of course, there can be problems with the Net itself—that is, problems with the route from the client to the server.

To help diagnose problems with network routes, you can trace the route that packets take from your machine to the other host machine. The syntax for the `tracert` command is simple:

```
tracert host
```

In this syntax, *host* is the domain name (or IP number) of the host you are trying to reach.

The output from `tracert` looks like this:

```
G:\>tracert www.mcp.com
Tracing route to www.mcp.com [206.246.131.227]
over a maximum of 30 hops:
 1 <10 ms <10 ms <10 ms  showers-gw102.ucs.indiana.edu
➥[156.56.102.254]
 2 <10 ms <10 ms   <10 ms  wcc-vbns-gw.ucs.indiana.edu
➥[129.79.5.10]
 3  10 ms  10 ms   <10 ms  IndyX-ATMFabric.OneCall.Net
➥[207.227.71.33]
 4  20 ms  10 ms    20 ms  core0-a0-ds3.chi1.nap.net
➥[207.227.0.173]
 5  40 ms    50 ms    30 ms  chi-f0.iquest.net [206.54.225.250]
 6  20 ms    20 ms    20 ms  204.180.50.9
 7  20 ms    20 ms    20 ms  www.mcp.com [206.246.131.227]
Trace complete.
```

The information provided here shows how long it takes for your packets to reach a host (in milliseconds) and the various machines (routers) that are passed along the way to your destination.

This information can be used to spot network hangups and to see whether something is causing network delays between your client and server. Because `tracert` shows the path your networking packets take over the Internet, it can be a useful tool for pointing out where network links are down. This information can then be passed on to your ISP to help troubleshoot larger network problems as well.

Network Monitor

The Microsoft Network Monitor is really a couple of tools rolled into one: the Network Monitor agent and the Network Monitor drivers. The Network Monitor agent is a service that runs under Windows 95 Networking to provide statistics on various network resources. The Network Monitor drivers actually interact with the machine's networking hardware to provide network statistics.

To take advantage of Network Monitor, administrators can use the System Management Server (SMS) from Microsoft to monitor multiple machines on a network—as long as those machines are running the Network Monitor agent. In addition to using the SMS, users can monitor statistics through the Windows 95 System Monitor.

There are really two steps to using Network Monitor to diagnose network problems:

1. Installing the Network Monitor agent and drivers.
2. Selecting the statistics to be monitored in the System Monitor and activating the System Monitor.

Because we can't really use any of the features of the Network Monitor until we install it, let's take a closer look at the installation process.

Installing the Network Monitor Agent and Drivers

To install the Network Monitor agent, you must download the installer from Microsoft. The Network Monitor can be obtained for download from this Microsoft site:

```
http://www.microsoft.com/windows/downloads/contents/admintools/
➥w95networkmonitor/default.asp
```

After the ZIP file has been downloaded, you must install the utility. The installation is not like a conventional software package. Instead, the Network Monitor must be installed like a networking service, through the Network Control Panel:

1. Download the Network Monitor from Microsoft and extract it into a directory on your hard drive.
2. Launch the Network Control Panel from the Start menu.
3. Select the Configuration page of the Network Control Panel and click the Add button.
4. In the Select Network Component Type dialog box, select Service and click Add, as shown in Figure 6.14.

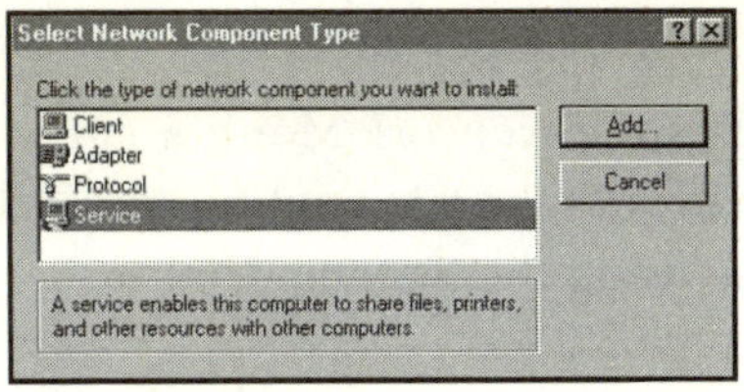

Figure 6.14

Installing a new networking service from the Network Control Panel.

5. Select Have Disk from the Select Network Service dialog box. When you are prompted to Install from Disk, enter the location of the directory to which you extracted the files.

6. Select the `netmon.inf` file from the Open dialog box and click OK.

7. From the Select Network Service dialog box, shown in Figure 6.15, select Microsoft Network Monitor Agent. Click OK to continue.

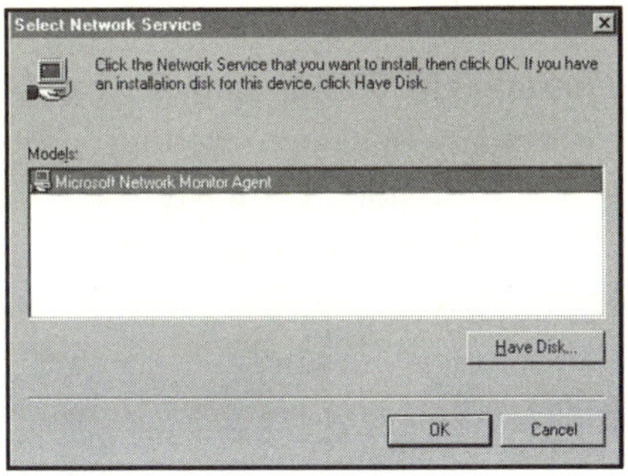

Figure 6.15

Installing the Network Monitor agent from the network.

8. The installer adds the Network Monitor driver to the list of network components that are installed. When the process is complete, you can exit the Network Control Panel by clicking OK.

9. You may be prompted to insert your Windows 95 CD-ROM so that some networking components can be copied from the disk. If you are prompted to do so, insert the CD. When the process is complete, you are prompted to restart your machine. After your machine has rebooted, you are ready to work with the Network Monitor.

Monitoring Performance with System Monitor

After the Network Monitor agent and drivers are installed, you are ready to take a look at the performance of your system's networking using the System Monitor.

The statistics gathered by the Network Monitor agent can be accessed through the Windows 95 System Monitor. The System Monitor can be installed from the Windows 95 Plus Pack (if it is not already installed on your machine). The System Monitor can be configured to monitor the following network items:

- Ethernet broadcast/second
- Ethernet bytes/second
- Ethernet frames/second
- Ethernet multicast/second

These performance statistics can be added to the System Monitor's charts by selecting the Add button and choosing the statistic you want to add, as shown in Figure 6.16.

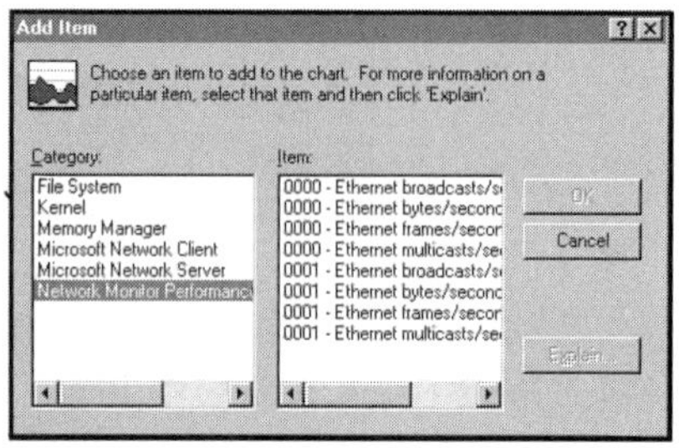

Figure 6.16

Selecting the Network Monitor agent statistics to be monitored in the System Monitor.

When you have selected the properties you want to monitor, those statistics show up in the System Monitor's charts, as shown in Figure 6.17.

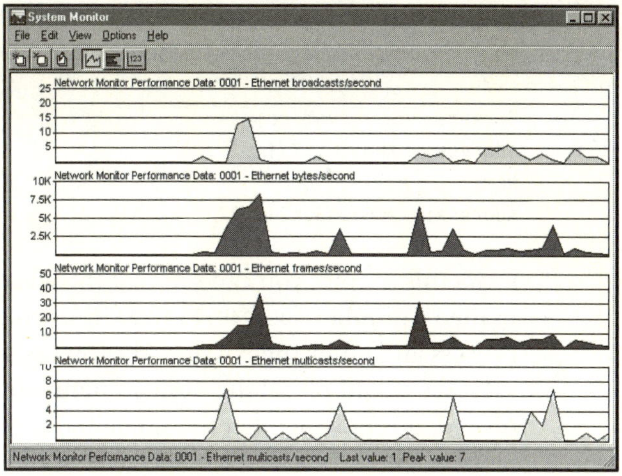

Figure 6.17

Monitoring Network Monitor agent statistics using the System Monitor tool with Windows 95.

You can use these charts to gauge how network performance is normally functioning and to see whether there are problems with the networking on a given machine.

The `nslookup` Utility

The `nslookup` utility is a command-line utility that allows users to check whether a domain name is being resolved correctly. The utility can also be used to look up a name for an IP number. The tool can be very useful if you are having trouble reaching a site, or if you are receiving a DNS error of some type.

> **Note**
>
> Although `nslookup` is a valuable tool, it is installed standard only on UNIX systems and Windows NT systems. Windows 95 users do not have `nslookup` installed on their systems by default.

The syntax for `nslookup` is simple:

```
nslookup www.mcp.com
```

This command performs a domain name lookup for the address `www.mcp.com`. The result returned looks something like this:

```
Server:  ns.vervet.com
Address:  198.88.18.1
Name:    www.mcp.com
Address:  206.246.131.227
```

From this output, you can see that the address correctly resolves to the IP number `206.246.131.227`. Likewise, you can reverse the process and enter the command **`nslookup 206.246.131.227`**; `nslookup` would reveal the domain name to us. If an error is returned, it is possible that the domain does not exist.

Similarly, if there is an error reaching a name server, for example, a DNS timeout error, there may be a configuration error for the DNS entries within Windows networking. The `nslookup` utility can be a valuable tool in determining whether an error in reaching sites is caused by a general networking error with the local machine's configuration or by a problem with the domain name itself.

Exercises

The following exercises are designed to step you through some of the processes outlined in this chapter. These exercises are based on manipulating the settings and using the tools discussed in this chapter for troubleshooting and problem resolution.

Exercise 6.1: Increasing Server Timeouts in Outlook Express

In this exercise, you will increase the server timeout levels for mail and news servers within the Outlook Express client.

1. Launch Outlook Express and select Accounts from the Tools menu.
2. In the Internet Accounts dialog box, select the News tab.
3. Select the listed news account and click the Properties button to open the news server's Properties dialog box.
4. In the news server's Properties dialog box, select the Advanced tab.
5. On the Advanced page, click the slider in the Server Timeouts section. Slide the selector to the right to increase the timeout value. Slide the selector until the timeout value is 2 minutes.
6. Click OK to exit the news server's Properties dialog box.
7. From the Internet Accounts dialog box, select the Mail tab to list the mail accounts configured.
8. Select the listed mail account and click the Properties button to open the mail server's Properties dialog box.
9. In the mail server's Properties dialog box, select the Advanced tab.
10. On the Advanced page, click the slider in the Server Timeouts section. Slide the selector to the right to increase the timeout value. Slide the selector until the timeout value is 2 minutes.

continues

Exercise 6.1: Continued

11. Click OK to exit the mail server's Properties dialog box.
12. Click Close to exit the Internet Accounts dialog box.

Exercise 6.2: Setting Microphone Levels in NetMeeting

In this exercise, you will run the Audio Settings Wizard to automatically calibrate the levels of the microphone.

1. Launch the NetMeeting client.
2. From the Tools menu, select the Audio Tuning Wizard.
3. After the wizard launches, click Next to continue.
4. Select the speed of your connection to the Internet. This value is used to help configure the amount of compression to use and to optimize audio settings. Click Next to continue.
5. Adjust your microphone to the physical position it will be in when you are conferencing. This step is important to help the wizard get an accurate level on the microphone.
6. Click the Start Recording button and read the paragraph displayed on the wizard screen. As you read, NetMeeting adjusts the levels to the volume and tone of your voice, so read in a normal, conversational tone.
7. When the wizard finishes adjusting the settings, you are notified that the process is complete. Click Finish to save the new audio settings.

Exercise 6.3: Clearing Temporary Internet Files

In this exercise, you will clear the Temporary Internet Files from within Internet Explorer to reset the caching mechanism.

1. Launch Internet Explorer.
2. From the View menu, select Internet Options.

3. In the Temporary Internet Files section of the Internet Options dialog box, click the Delete Files button.

4. When prompted for confirmation, click OK. At this point, you can also select the Delete All Subscription Content check box. If you have channel or site subscriptions, you should select this option.

5. When the process of deleting the temporary files is complete, click OK to exit the Internet Options dialog box.

Exercise 6.4: Pinging a Server for Connectivity

In this exercise, you will use the Ping utility to test the availability of a remote server. In this exercise, you will check for the availability of `www.mcp.com`. You can test for other servers simply by substituting the domain name of your server for `www.mcp.com`.

1. Launch an MS-DOS window to access the Ping command-line utility.

2. At the `C:\>` prompt, enter **`ping www.mcp.com`**.

   If the server is available, the response you see will resemble the following:

```
Pinging www.mcp.com [206.246.131.227] with 32 bytes of data:
Reply from 206.246.131.227: bytes=32 time=153ms TTL=250
Reply from 206.246.131.227: bytes=32 time=166ms TTL=250
Reply from 206.246.131.227: bytes=32 time=153ms TTL=250
Reply from 206.246.131.227: bytes=32 time=140ms TTL=250
```

   If the server is unavailable for some reason, the output will resemble the following:

```
Pinging www.mcp.com [206.246.131.227] with 32 bytes of data:
Request timed out.
Request timed out.
Request timed out.
Request timed out.
```

Review Questions

The review questions in this section can help you assess your understanding of the terms, concepts, and objectives covered in this chapter. These questions are written in the style of the questions presented on the MCSE exam and are an excellent way to prepare yourself for the material you will see on the exam. After you complete the review questions, you will find the answer to each question—along with an explanation of the answer—in the following section.

1. Which of the following files are log files generated when installing Internet Explorer 4.0? (Select all that apply.)

    A. `ActiveLog.txt`

    B. `Active Setup Log.txt`

    C. `IE4Inst.txt`

    D. `IE4 Setup Log.txt`

2. Your organization has an underpowered news server, and users frequently have trouble connecting. What server setting might help connectivity problems?

    A. Server Timeout

    B. Username/Password

    C. Proxy Settings

    D. Server Port

3. A user is having problems sending mail, but not receiving mail. What settings should be checked? (Select all that apply.)

    A. POP3 Server Address

    B. SMTP Server Address

    C. Server Port Number

    D. Server Timeout

4. Which of the following should be used first to diagnose problems with audio conferencing within the NetMeeting client?

   A. Conferencing Settings

   B. Audio/Video Bandwidth Restrictions

   C. Audio Connection Wizard

   D. Audio Tuning Wizard

5. A user cannot save files when using an application shared on another user's NetMeeting client. How can this problem be resolved?

   A. By adjusting the security zones

   B. By establishing a share

   C. Through the Options dialog box

   D. This is not a bug, it is a feature

6. Which of the following is required for Webcasting to function properly?

   A. Advanced caching configuration

   B. An Internet firewall

   C. A working network connection

   D. An Internet locator service

7. Which of the following can help eliminate problems with Web pages loading incorrect or outdated versions?

   A. Deleting temporary Internet files

   B. Unsubscribing to Web sites

   C. Adjusting server timeout settings

   D. Checking proxy server settings

8. Which of the following are three command-line utilities that can be used to diagnose network problems?

   A. `ipstat, ping, traceroute`

   B. `ping, traceroute, dnslookup`

   C. `tcpstat, ping, traceroute`

   D. `ping, tracert, nslookup`

Review Answers

Now that you have completed the review questions, check your answers against those provided here. Explanations are provided for each answer so that you can see whether you arrived at the correct solution for the right reason, or so that you can see how your answer varied from the correct one.

1. **B and D** `Active Setup Log.txt` and `IE4 Setup Log.txt` are the log files created by the Active Setup Wizard and the IE 4.0 installer. Both files contain status information and error codes that can diagnose deployment problems.

2. **A** Servers that are overloaded may take more time to respond to client requests. As a result, increasing the Server Timeout parameter can help prevent clients from timing out and generating errors before the server has a chance to respond.

3. **B and C** Because the client is receiving mail, the network connection must be okay. Outgoing mail is handled by the SMTP server, so you should double-check the SMTP server address and port number.

4. **D** The Audio Tuning Wizard should be used first to check audio problems, after all the physical audio connections have been verified.

5. **D** Remote users engaged in application sharing with NetMeeting are prohibited from using some features on the File menu (for example, they cannot print or save files). This is

to protect the security of the file system of the user hosting the application.

6. **C** Webcasting requires a working network connection to the Internet or an intranet so that it can connect to the server's hosting channel or the site content to be downloaded.

7. **A** Deleting temporary Internet files forces IE to reload the pages, refreshing the data in the cache, and updating the content for the user.

8. **D** The `ping`, `tracert`, and `nslookup` command-line utilities can be used to see whether a host is available, to verify correct routing, and to test domain name resolution.

Answers to Test Yourself Questions at Beginning of Chapter

The following answers are provided for the prechapter quiz at the beginning of this chapter. You can use these questions and answers to determine how well you may already be familiar with this chapter's material. Each of the questions relates to a specific goal of the "Implementing and Supporting the Microsoft Internet Explorer Administration Kit for Microsoft Internet Explorer 4.0" MCSE exam. Each of the following answers references the section in this chapter that deals with the covered objective so that you can easily locate the material you may want to review or clarify.

1. The Active Setup Wizard creates a log file called `Active Setup Log.txt`. The IE 4.0 installer creates a file called `IE4 Installer Log.txt`. Both of these files record status messages at each step of the installation process. The log files also contain status messages and error codes generated during the installation, so that administrators can make sure that each step went smoothly. If an error is recorded, administrators can examine the error and the stage at which it occurred to determine what went wrong.

Section Referencing This Material:

- "Diagnosing and Resolving the Deployment Failure of Internet Explorer 4.0"

2. The most common errors with the IEAK Wizard are related to incorrect customization codes, Internet connectivity, and Internet Explorer 4.0 installation.

   To build a custom version of IE, administrators need a customization code. The code determines the deployment role that can be used and also what features are enabled. Using the incorrect code can cause some features of the IEAK Wizard to be unavailable and can result in a custom build that violates the license agreement.

   The IEAK Wizard also requires a connection to the Internet for Automatic Version Synchronization and the valid IE 4.0 installation on the administrative machine. If these two elements are missing, the IEAK Wizard may not run; if the wizard does run, it may create an incomplete custom build.

   Section Referencing This Material:

   - "Diagnosing and Resolving Problems Related to the IEAK Wizard"

3. The majority of problems with Outlook Express connectivity are related to network problems or incorrect server configuration information.

   Troubleshooting Outlook Express involves first checking all the server configuration information to make sure that the client is correctly configured for your organization's servers. If the configuration is correct, the network connectivity for the machine should also be evaluated for problems.

   Section Referencing This Material:

   - "Diagnosing and Resolving Connection Failures of Outlook Express"

4. A timeout error can result from many causes, such as server overload, network congestion, and so on. The error is reported when the client attempts to connect to a server but is unable to make contact within a specified amount of time.

   If a client is receiving excessive server timeout errors, the timeout interval can be increased from the server's Options dialog box.

   Sections Referencing This Material:

   - "Diagnosing and Resolving Connection Failures of Outlook Express"
   - "Timeout Errors"

5. NetMeeting's most common problems are related to the network and hardware. If all hardware connections are good, and the audio/video hardware is working properly (as determined by testing in other applications), the next step is to diagnose network connectivity.

   Section Referencing This Material:

   - "Diagnosing and Resolving Connection Failures of NetMeeting"

6. Subscription updates are most often affected by two problems: network connectivity and disk space.

   Administrators can configure the amount of disk space that can be consumed by subscriptions using the System Policies and Restrictions mechanism, and they can remove subscription content by clearing the temporary Internet files.

   Because network connectivity is required to download updates, a valid Internet connection is necessary to correctly download content updates. Network connectivity can be diagnosed using tools such as Ping, `nslookup`, and `netstat`. Problems with networking can sometimes be resolved using the Network Control Panel.

Section Referencing This Material:

- "Diagnosing and Resolving Connection Failures of Webcasting"

7. Clearing all the temporary Internet files resets the cache for Internet Explorer 4.0. If the cache is full or experiencing problems, resetting the cache can help users obtain updated documents.

   Section Referencing This Material:

   - "Diagnosing and Resolving Connection Failures of Caching"

8. Ping and `nslookup` are both network diagnostic tools. The Ping utility queries a remote host to see whether the host is available. The `nslookup` command is used to see whether DNS servers are correctly resolving domain names into IP numbers.

   The syntax of Ping is `ping` *`hostname`* where the *`hostname`* is a Fully Qualified Domain Name. If the host is reachable, Ping returns a time value; if the host is unreachable, Ping returns a timeout error.

   The syntax of `nslookup` is `nslookup` *`hostname`* where the *`hostname`* is a Fully Qualified Domain Name. If the name is resolving correctly, `nslookup` returns an IP number; if the domain name is not able to resolve, `nslookup` returns an error.

   Both of these utilities can test the network connectivity of the local machine and also reveal hosts that might be temporarily unavailable.

   Section Referencing This Material:

   - "Network Troubleshooting"

Appendix A

Overview of the Certification Process

You must pass rigorous certification exams to become a Microsoft Certified Professional. These certification exams provide a valid and reliable measure of your technical proficiency and expertise. The closed-book exams are developed in consultation with computer industry professionals who have on-the-job experience with Microsoft products. These exams are conducted by an independent organization—Sylvan Prometric—at more than 1,200 authorized Prometric Testing Centers around the world.

Currently, Microsoft offers six types of certification, based on specific areas of expertise:

- **Microsoft Certified Professional (MCP).** Qualified to provide installation, configuration, and support for users of at least one Microsoft desktop operating system, such as Windows NT Workstation. In addition, candidates can take elective exams to develop areas of specialization. MCP is considered the initial or first level of expertise leading to a premium certification.

- **Microsoft Certified Professional+Internet (MCP+Internet).** Qualified to plan security, install and configure server products, manage server resources, extend service to run CGI scripts or ISAPI scripts, monitor and analyze performance, and troubleshoot problems.

- **Microsoft Certified Systems Engineer (MCSE).** Qualified to effectively plan, implement, maintain, and support information systems with Microsoft Windows NT and other Microsoft advanced systems and workgroup products, such as Microsoft Office and Microsoft BackOffice. MCSE is a second level of expertise.

- **Microsoft Certified Systems Engineer+Internet (MCSE+Internet).** Qualified in the core MCSE areas, as well as qualified to enhance, deploy, and manage sophisticated intranet and Internet solutions that include a browser, proxy server, host servers, database, and messaging and commerce components. In addition, an MCSE+Internet-certified professional can manage and analyze Web sites.

- **Microsoft Certified Solution Developer (MCSD).** Qualified to design and develop custom business solutions by using Microsoft development tools, technologies, and platforms, including Microsoft Office and Microsoft BackOffice. MCSD is a second level of expertise.

- **Microsoft Certified Trainer (MCT).** Instructionally and technically qualified by Microsoft to deliver Microsoft Education courses at Microsoft-authorized sites. An MCT must be employed by a Microsoft Solution Provider Authorized Technical Education Center or a Microsoft Authorized Academic Training site.

Note

For up-to-date information about each type of certification, visit the Microsoft Training and Certification World Wide Web site at `http://www.microsoft.com/train_cert`. You must have an Internet account and a WWW browser to access this information. You also can call the following sources:

- Microsoft Certified Professional Program: 800-636-7544
- Sylvan Prometric Testing Centers: 800-755-EXAM
- Microsoft Online Institute (MOLI): 800-449-9333

How to Become a Microsoft Certified Professional (MCP)

Becoming an MCP requires you to pass one operating system exam. The following list shows the names and exam numbers of all the operating systems from which you can choose to qualify for your MCP certification:

- Implementing and Supporting Microsoft Windows 95, #70-063*
- Implementing and Supporting Microsoft Windows 95, #70-064
- Implementing and Supporting Microsoft Windows NT Workstation 4.02, #70-073
- Implementing and Supporting Microsoft Windows NT Workstation 3.51, #70-042
- Implementing and Supporting Microsoft Windows NT Server 4.0, #70-067
- Implementing and Supporting Microsoft Windows NT Server 3.51, #70-043
- Microsoft Windows for Workgroups 3.11-Desktop, #70-048*
- Microsoft Windows 3.1, #70-030*
- Microsoft Windows Architecture I, #70-160
- Microsoft Windows Architecture II, #70-161

Note

Exams marked with an asterisk (*) are scheduled to be retired. Check the Microsoft Training and Certification World Wide Web site at `http://www.microsoft.com/train_cert` for details.

How to Become a Microsoft Certified Professional+Internet (MCP+Internet)

Becoming an MCP with a specialty in Internet technology requires you to pass the following three exams:

- Internetworking Microsoft TCP/IP on Microsoft Windows NT 4.0, #70-059
- Implementing and Supporting Microsoft Windows NT Server 4.0, #70-067
- Implementing and Supporting Microsoft Internet Information Server 3.0 and Microsoft Index Server 1.1, #70-077

  or

  Implementing and Supporting Microsoft Internet Information Server 4.0, #70-087

How to Become a Microsoft Certified Systems Engineer (MCSE)

MCSE candidates must pass four operating system exams and two elective exams. The MCSE certification path is divided into two tracks: the Windows NT 3.51 track and the Windows NT 4.0 track.

> The exams included in this software product span the core requirements for the Windows NT 4.0 track only.

The following lists show the core requirements (four operating system exams) for both the Windows NT 3.51 and 4.0 tracks, and the elective courses (two exams) you can choose from for either track.

The four Windows NT 3.51 Track Core Requirements for MCSE certification are as follows:

- Implementing and Supporting Microsoft Windows NT Server 3.51, #70-043
- Implementing and Supporting Microsoft Windows NT Workstation 3.51, #70-042
- Networking Essentials, #70-058
- Microsoft Windows 3.1, #70-030*

  or

  Microsoft Windows for Workgroups 3.11, #70-048*

  or

  Implementing and Supporting Microsoft Windows 95, #70-063*

  or

  Implementing and Supporting Microsoft Windows 95, #70-064

The four Windows NT 4.0 Track Core Requirements for MCSE certification are as follows:

- Implementing and Supporting Microsoft Windows NT Server 4.0, #70-067
- Implementing and Supporting Microsoft Windows NT Server 4.0 in the Enterprise, #70-068
- Networking Essentials, #70-058
- Microsoft Windows 3.1, #70-030*

  or

  Microsoft Windows for Workgroups 3.11, #70-048*

or

Implementing and Supporting Microsoft Windows 95, #70-063*

or

Implementing and Supporting Microsoft Windows 95, #70-064

or

Implementing and Supporting Microsoft Windows NT Workstation 4.0, #70-073

For either the Windows NT 3.51 or the 4.0 track, you must pass two of the following elective exams for MCSE certification:

- Implementing and Supporting Microsoft SNA Server 3.0, #70-013

  or

  Implementing and Supporting Microsoft SNA Server 4.0, #70-085

- Implementing and Supporting Microsoft Systems Management Server 1.0, #70-014*

  or

  Implementing and Supporting Microsoft Systems Management Server 1.2, #70-018

  or

  Implementing and Supporting Microsoft Systems Management Server 1.2, #70-086

- Microsoft SQL Server 4.2 Database Implementation, #70-021

  or

  Implementing a Database Design on Microsoft SQL Server 6.5, #70-027 *or*

Implementing a Database Design on Microsoft SQL Server 7.0, #70-029

- Microsoft SQL Server 4.2 Database Administration for Microsoft Windows NT, #70-022

  or

  System Administration for Microsoft SQL Server 6.5, #70-026

  or

  System Administration for Microsoft SQL Server 7.0, #70-028

- Microsoft Mail for PC Networks 3.2-Enterprise, #70-037

- Internetworking with Microsoft TCP/IP on Microsoft Windows NT (3.5-3.51), #70-053

  or

  Internetworking with Microsoft TCP/IP on Microsoft Windows NT 4.0, #70-059

- Implementing and Supporting Microsoft Exchange Server 4.0, #70-075*

  or

  Implementing and Supporting Microsoft Exchange Server 5.0, #70-076

  or

  Implementing and Supporting Microsoft Exchange Server 5.5, #70-081

- Implementing and Supporting Microsoft Internet Information Server 3.0 and Microsoft Index Server 1.1, #70-077

  or

  Implementing and Supporting Microsoft Internet Information Server 4.0, #70-087

- Implementing and Supporting Microsoft Internet Explorer 4.0 by Using the Internet Explorer Resource Kit, #70-079

How to Become a Microsoft Certified Systems Engineer+Internet (MCSE+Internet)

MCSE+Internet candidates must pass seven operating system exams and two elective exams.

The following lists show the core requirements and the elective courses (two exams). The seven MCSE+Internet core exams required for certification are as follows:

- Networking Essentials, #70-058
- Internetworking with Microsoft TCP/IP on Microsoft Windows NT 4.0, #70-059
- Implementing and Supporting Microsoft Windows 95, #70-063

  or

  Implementing and Supporting Microsoft Windows NT Workstation 4.0, #70-073
- Implementing and Supporting Microsoft Windows NT Server 4.0, #70-067
- Implementing and Supporting Microsoft Windows NT Server 4.0 in the Enterprise, #70-068
- Implementing and Supporting Microsoft Internet Information Server 3.0 and Microsoft Index Server 1.1, #70-077

  or

  Implementing and Supporting Microsoft Internet Information Server 4.0, #70-087

- Implementing and Supporting Microsoft Internet Explorer 4.0 by Using the Internet Explorer Resource Kit, #70-079

You must also pass two of the following elective exams:

- System Administration for Microsoft SQL Server 6.5, #70-026
- Implementing a Database Design on Microsoft SQL Server 6.5, #70-027
- Implementing and Supporting Microsoft Exchange Server 5.0, #70-076

  or

  Implementing and Supporting Microsoft Exchange Server 5.5, #70-081
- Implementing and Supporting Microsoft Proxy Server 1.0, #70-078

  or

  Implementing and Supporting Microsoft Proxy Server 2.0, #70-088

How to Become a Microsoft Certified Solution Developer (MCSD)

MCSD candidates must pass two core technology exams and two elective exams. The following lists show the required technology exams, plus the elective exams that apply toward obtaining the MCSD.

You must pass the following two core technology exams to qualify for MCSD certification:

- Microsoft Windows Architecture I, #70-160
- Microsoft Windows Architecture II, #70-161

You must also pass two of the following elective exams to become an MCSD:

- Microsoft SQL Server 4.2 Database Implementation, #70-021

  or

  Implementing a Database Design on Microsoft SQL Server 6.5, #70-027

  or

  Implementing a Database Design on Microsoft SQL Server 7.0, #70-029

- Developing Applications with C++ Using the Microsoft Foundation Class Library, #70-024

- Microsoft Visual Basic 3.0 for Windows-Application Development, #70-050

  or

  Programming with Microsoft Visual Basic 4.0, #70-065

  or

  Developing Applications with Microsoft Visual Basic 5.0, #70-165

- Microsoft Access 2.0 for Windows-Application Development, #70-051

  or

  Microsoft Access for Windows 95 and the Microsoft Access Development Toolkit, #70-069

- Developing Applications with Microsoft Excel 5.0 Using Visual Basic for Applications, #70-052

- Programming in Microsoft Visual FoxPro 3.0 for Windows, #70-054

- Implementing OLE in Microsoft Foundation Class Applications, #70-025

How to Become a Microsoft Certified Trainer (MCT)

To understand the requirements and process for becoming a Microsoft Certified Trainer (MCT), you must obtain the Microsoft Certified Trainer Guide document (`MCTGUIDE.DOC`) from the following WWW site:

`http://www.microsoft.com/train_cert/download.htm`

On this page, click the hyperlink `MCT GUIDE (mctguide.doc) (117K)`. If your WWW browser can display DOC files (Word for Windows native file format), the MCT Guide appears in the browser window. Otherwise, you must download it and open it in Word for Windows or Windows 95 WordPad. The MCT Guide explains in detail the following four-step process to becoming an MCT:

1. Complete and mail a Microsoft Certified Trainer application to Microsoft. You must include proof of your skills for presenting instructional material. The options for doing so are described in the MCT Guide.

2. Obtain and study the Microsoft Trainer Kit for the Microsoft Official Curricula (MOC) course(s) for which you want to be certified. Microsoft Trainer Kits can be ordered by calling 800-688-0496 in North America. Other regions should review the MCT Guide for information about how to order a Trainer Kit.

3. Pass the Microsoft certification exam for the product for which you want to be certified to teach.

4. Attend the Microsoft Official Curriculum (MOC) course for the course for which you want to be certified. This must be done so that you understand how the course is structured, how labs are completed, and how the course flows.

Caution

> You should consider the preceding steps as a general overview of the MCT certification process. The precise steps you must take are described in detail in the `MCTGUIDE.DOC` file on the WWW site mentioned earlier. Do not misconstrue the preceding steps as the actual process you have to follow.

If you are interested in becoming an MCT, you can receive more information by visiting the Microsoft Certified Training (MCT) WWW site at `http://www.microsoft.com/train_cert/mctint.htm`; alternatively, call 800-688-0496.

Appendix B

Study Tips

Self study involves any method you employ to learn a given topic. The most popular kind of self study is third-party books, such as the one you hold in your hand. Before you begin to study for a certification exam, you should know exactly what Microsoft expects you to learn.

Pay close attention to the objectives posted for the exam. The entire set of objectives is listed in the introduction of this book. The relevant subset of objectives also appears at the beginning of each chapter. The objectives can always be found on Microsoft's WWW site at `http://www.microsoft.com/train_cert`. Also notice that the beginning of the book includes a handy tear-out card with an objective matrix that lists all objectives and the page you can turn to for information about that objective.

Another thing to think about is this: Humans vary in their learning styles. Some people are visual learners, others are textual, and still others learn best from aural sources. However, certain basic principles of learning apply to everyone. For example, students who take notes during lectures have better recall on exam day—even if they didn't study the notes later—because they encoded the information as well as decoded it: They processed it in a deeper, more active fashion than those who simply listened to the lecture.

You should use the study techniques you know work for you but also take advantage of more general principles of learning. For example, if you are a visual learner, pay special attention to the figures provided in this book. Also, create your own visual cues by doing things such as diagramming processes and relationships.

A general principle of learning you can take advantage of has to do with studying the organization and the details of information separately. Cognitive learning research has demonstrated that if you attempt to focus on learning the organization of the information and then focus on learning the specific details, you will retain the information better than if you attempt to take in all the information at once. Use your study materials to prepare a detailed outline of the material on the exam. Study the outline first by learning the organization of the material. Then in your next pass through the outline, focus on memorizing and understanding the details. Trying to do both at once only leads to the two types of information interfering with your overall learning.

Finally, follow common-sense practices in your studying. These basic sorts of studying strategies are listed here:

- Study in bright light to reduce fatigue and depression.
- Establish a regular study schedule and stick as close to it as possible.
- Turn off all forms of distraction, including radios and televisions. Alternatively, try studying in a quiet room.
- Always study in the same place so that your materials are always readily at hand.
- Take short (approximately 15-minute) breaks every two to three hours or so. Studies have proven that your brain assimilates information better when you take rest periods.

Pre-Testing Yourself

Before taking the actual exam, verify that you are ready to do so by testing yourself many times in a variety of ways. This book includes questions at the beginning and end of each chapter. The accompanying CD-ROM contains an electronic test engine that emulates the actual Microsoft exam and enables you to test your knowledge of the subject areas. Use this tool repeatedly until you are consistently scoring in the 90 percent range (or better).

Note

You realize, of course, that you can't start studying five days before the exam begins. You have to give yourself plenty of time to read, practice, and test yourself several times.

We believe the New Riders' TestPrep electronic testing engine is the best test-preparation tool on the market, unparalleled by most other engines. TestPrep is described in detail in Appendix D, "All About TestPrep."

Hints and Tips for Doing Your Best on the Exam

When you take the actual exam, be prepared. Arrive early and be ready to show two forms of identification. Expect wordy questions. Although you have 90 minutes to take the exam, there are at least 50 questions you must answer. This gives you a little more than one minute to answer each question. Although this may sound like ample time for each question, remember that many of the questions can involve lengthy word problems, exhibits that must be referred to, and, more recently, simulations. Your 90 minutes of exam time can be consumed very quickly.

It has been estimated that approximately 85 percent of the candidates taking their first Microsoft exam fail it. It is not so much that they are unprepared and lack the knowledge they need. It is more the case that they don't know what to expect and are immediately intimidated by the wordiness of the questions and the ambiguity they feel is implied in the answers.

Things to Watch For

When you take the exam, read very carefully! Make sure that you understand what the question requires and take notice of the number of correct choices you have to make. Remember that some questions require you to select a single correct answer; other questions have more than one correct answer. Radio buttons next to the answer choices indicate that the answers are mutually exclusive—there is but one correct answer. On the other hand, check boxes indicate that the answers are not mutually exclusive—there are multiple correct answers.

Read the questions fully. With lengthy questions, the last sentence often dramatically changes the scenario. When you take the exam, you are given pencils and two sheets of paper. If you are uncertain about what the question requires, map out the scenario on the paper until it is clear in your mind. You must turn in the scrap paper at the end of the exam.

Choosing the Right Answer

Adopt a strategy for evaluating possible answers. Eliminate those answers that are impossible or implausible. Carefully evaluate those answers that remain. Be careful: Some answers are true statements as they stand on their own, but in the context of the question, do not makes sense as correct answers. The answers must match or relate to the question before they can serve as correct choices.

Marking Answers for Return

You can mark questions on the actual exam and refer back to them later. If you encounter a wordy question that will take a long time to read and decipher, mark it and return to it when you have completed the rest of the exam. This strategy prevents you from wasting time on the question and running out of time on the exam—only 90 minutes are allotted for the exam, and the exam ends when those 90 minutes expire, whether or not you are finished.

Changing Answers

The rule of thumb for changing answers is *don't*! If you have read the question carefully and completely, and you felt like you knew the right answer, you probably did. Don't second-guess yourself! If, however, as you check your answers, one answer stands out as clearly marked incorrectly, of course you should change it. But if you are at all unsure, go with your first impression.

Attaching Notes to Test Questions

At the conclusion of the exam, before the grading takes place, you are given the opportunity to attach a message to any question. If you feel that a question was too ambiguous or tested knowledge you don't need to know to work with the product, take this opportunity to state your case. It is unheard of for Microsoft to change a test score as a result of an attached message. However, it never hurts to try—and it helps to vent your frustration before you blow the proverbial 50-amp fuse.

Good luck!

Appendix C

What's on the CD-ROM

This appendix is a brief rundown of what you'll find on the CD-ROM that comes with this book. For a more detailed description of the newly developed TestPrep test engine, exclusive to New Riders Publishing, please see Appendix D, "All About TestPrep."

TestPrep

TestPrep is a new test engine developed exclusively for New Riders Publishing. We believe it is the best test engine available because it closely emulates the actual Microsoft exam. TestPrep also enables you to check your score by category, which helps you determine the topics you need to study further. Before running the TestPrep software, be sure to read `CDROM.hlp` (in the root directory of the CD-ROM) for late-breaking news on TestPrep features. For a complete description of the benefits of TestPrep, refer to Appendix D.

Exclusive Electronic Version of Text

Also contained on the CD-ROM is an electronic version of this book. You can use this electronic book to help you search for terms or areas you want to study. The electronic version comes complete with all figures as they appear in the printed version of the book.

Copyright Information and Disclaimer

Appendix D

All About TestPrep

The TestPrep software included on the CD-ROM accompanying this book enables you to test your knowledge of Internet Explorer 4 and the Administration Kit in a manner similar to that employed by the actual Microsoft exam. TestPrep actually includes three applications: Practice Exams, Study Cards, and Flash Cards. Practice Exams provides you with simulated multiple-choice tests. Study Cards provides the same sorts of questions (but enable you to control the number and types of questions) and gives immediate feedback to you. This format enables you to learn from your testing and control the topics on which you want to be tested. Flash Cards provides this same sort of feedback and enables the same sort of control but requires short answers or essay answers to questions; you are not prompted with multiple-choice selections or cued about the number of correct answers to provide.

Although you can maximize the size of the TestPrep applications, by default they run in smaller mode so that you can refer to your Internet Explorer desktop while answering questions. TestPrep uses a unique randomization process to ensure that each time you run the programs, you are presented with a different sequence of questions. This randomization enhances your learning and helps prevent you from merely memorizing the expected answers over time without reading the question each and every time.

Question Presentation

TestPrep Practice Exams and Study Cards emulate the actual Microsoft exam "Implementing and Supporting Microsoft Internet Explorer 4.0 by Using the Microsoft Internet Explorer Administration Kit" (#70-079). In this format, radio (circle) buttons are used to signify only one correct choice; check boxes (squares) are used to indicate multiple correct answers. Whenever more than one answer is correct, the number you should select is given in the wording of the question.

Scoring

The TestPrep Practice Exam Score Report uses the same number of correct questions required to pass the exam and the same time limit as the "Implementing and Supporting Microsoft Internet Explorer 4.0 by Using the Microsoft Internet Explorer Administration Kit" exam.

Index

A

B - C

D

J - K - L

M

N

O

P

R

S

T

MCSE Training Guide: Core Exams (BUNDLE)

New Riders Development ISBN: 1-56205-821-5 $149.99 US/$208.95 CDN 3000 pp.

This bundle covers all four core exams for only $149.99. CD-ROM's TestPrep software hyperlinks test questions to book's text immediately: readers can find complete explanations for any study question. The *only* study materials you need to pass *all* core exams, and it's approved by Microsoft.

Covers: Certification—MCSE

MCSE Training Guide: Internet Information Server 4

Emmett Dulaney, MCSE ISBN: 1-56205-823-1 $49.99 US/$70.95 CDN 500 pp.

IIS 4 is covered by objective; each objective is broken down into manageable chunks and explained so that readers can easily study and find what they need to know for that objective. Following each chapter is a series of review questions that relate to the chapter. The New Riders test engine completes the package by including practice exam questions in a format very similar to that of the actual certification exam. Offers insider tips and information from a distinguished MCSE.

Covers: Certification—MCSE, MCSE+I, MCP

MCSE Training Guide: Windows 95 70-64 Exam

Ed Tetz, MCSE ISBN: 1-56205-880-0 $49.99 US/$71.95 CDN 864 pp.

Utilizing the successful Training Guide approach, this book covers the *new* Windows 95 core exam: Exam #70-64—Implementing and Supporting Windows 95 (Exam 70-63 was retired April 98). Study test questions and practice taking the exam with the exclusive TestPrep test engine on the CD-ROM. Approved by Microsoft as Microsoft Certified Professional study material.

Covers: Certification—MCP, MCSE, MCSE+I

MCP+I Training Guide: Internet Exams

Emmett Dulaney, MCSE ISBN: 1-56205-879-7 $99.99 US/$143.95 CDN 1584 pp.

MCP+I Training Guide: Internet Exams instructs exam takers on the details they need to pass each of the exams leading to the popular new Internet certification in an efficient, effective manner. This comprehensive book covers each of the three exams: Internetworking with Microsoft TCP/IP on Microsoft Windows NT 4.0 (70-059), Implementing and Supporting Microsoft Windows NT Server 4.0 (70-067), and Implementing and Supporting Microsoft Internet Information Server 4 (70-087). Our exclusive TestPrep test engine software provides the realistic simulation of the exams and allows users to link back to chapters in an electronic version of the book to review incorrect responses. Each exam section is organized by the Microsoft exam objectives.

Covers: Certification—MCP+I, MCSE+I, MCP

MCSE Training Guide: TCP/IP

Anthony Tilke, et al.   ISBN: 1-56205-747-2
$49.99 US/$70.95 CDN   670 pp.

MCSE Training Guide: TCP/IP is the most comprehensive, cost-effective, and efficient way to pass the Internetworking Microsoft TCP/IP on Microsoft Windows NT 4.0 (Exam 70-59) elective. Organized in a concise, easy-to-read manner, this book is the only study material readers will need to pass one of the most popular and challenging MCSE electives! Written by a professional team of Microsoft Certified Systems Engineers and Microsoft Certified Trainers. Includes practice test questions, lists, table, notes, tips, and tricks to completely prepare users for the exams. CD-ROM contains TestPrep test engine software: a realistic simulation of the actual exams. It enables users to link back to chapters in an electronic version of the book for review of incorrect responses. Each exam section is organized by the Microsoft exam objectives.

Covers: Certification—MCSE, MCSE+I, MCP+I, MCP

MCSE Training Guide: SQL Server 6.5 Administration

Brad McGehee, et al.   ISBN: 1-56205-726-X $49.99 US/$70.95 CDN   704 pp.

MCSE Training Guide: SQL Server Administration provides users with all of the latest information they need to pass this popular exam and covers all the intricacies of SQL Server 6.5. Utilizing the knowledge of MCSDs, MCSEs, and MCTs, this book contains all the insider tips, notes, and strategies readers need to take a step closer to becoming an MCSE. The book contains test questions, lists, tables, notes, tips, and tricks to completely prepare readers for the exam. It's organized in a concise, easy-to-read manner to give users the most valuable information efficiently. It contains complete coverage of the Exam 70-26 objectives. Provides readers with more than just exam basics—offers extra information on the technology itself! Hundreds of practice test questions and hands-on lab exercises allow readers to apply what they've learned—right away! CD-ROM features TestPrep test simulator, with practice questions, study cards and flash cards features, and links to electronic copy of the entire book.

Covers: Certification—MCSE, MCSE+I, MCP

MCSE Training Guide: SQL Server 6.5 Design & Implementation

Sean Baird, MCSE, et al.   ISBN: 1-56205-830-4 $49.99 US/$70.95 CDN   553 pp.

MCSE Training Guide: SQL Server 6.5 Design & Implementation provides users with all of the latest information they need to pass this popular exam and covers all the intricacies of SQL Server 6.5. Utilizing the knowledge of MCSDs, MCSEs, and MCTs, this book contains all the insider tips, notes, and strategies readers need to take a step closer to becoming an MCSE or MCSD. The book contains test questions, lists, tables, notes, tips, and tricks to completely prepare readers for the exam. It's organized in a concise, easy-to-read manner to give users the most valuable information efficiently. *MCSE Training Guide: SQL Server 6.5 Design & Implementation* contains complete coverage of Exam 70-027. Hundreds of practice test questions and hands-on lab exercises allow readers to apply what they've learned—right away! CD-ROM features TestPrep test simulator, with practice questions, study cards and flash cards features, and links to electronic copy of the entire book.

Covers: Certification—MCSE, MCSE+I, MCSD, MCP

REGISTRATION CARD

MCSE Training Guide: Internet Explorer 4

Name ______________________ Title ______________________

Company ______________________ Type of business ______________________

Address ______________________ E-mail ______________________

City/State/ZIP ______________________

Have you used these types of books before? ☐ yes ☐ no

If yes, which ones? ______________________

____

How many computer books do you purchase each year? ☐ 1–5 ☐ 6 or more

How did you learn about this book? ______________________

Where did you purchase this book? ______________________

Which applications do you currently use? ______________________

____

Which computer magazines do you subscribe to? ______________________

____

What trade shows do you attend? ______________________

____

Comments: ______________________

____

____

Would you like to be placed on our preferred mailing list? ☐ yes ☐ no

☐ **I would like to see my name in print!** You may use my name and quote me in future New Riders products and promotions. My daytime phone number is: ______________________

New Riders Publishing 201 West 103rd Street ◆ Indianapolis, Indiana 46290 USA

Fax to **317-581-4663**

Fold Here

NO POSTAGE
NECESSARY
IF MAILED
IN THE
UNITED STATES

BUSINESS REPLY MAIL

FIRST-CLASS MAIL PERMIT NO. 9918 INDIANAPOLIS IN

POSTAGE WILL BE PAID BY THE ADDRESSEE

NEW RIDERS PUBLISHING
201 W 103RD ST
INDIANAPOLIS IN 46290-9058

Licensing Agreement

By opening this package, you are agreeing to be bound by the following agreement:

Some of the software included with this product may be copyrighted, in which case all rights are reserved by the respective copyright holder. You are licensed to use software copyrighted by the Publisher and its licensors on a single computer. You may copy and/or modify the software as needed to facilitate your use of it on a single computer. Making copies of the software for any other purpose is a violation of United States copyright laws.

This software is sold as is without warranty of any kind, either expressed or implied, including but not limited to the implied warranties of merchantability and fitness for a particular purpose. Neither the publisher nor its dealers or distributors assumes any liability for any alleged or actual damages arising from the use of this program. (Some states do not allow for the exclusion of implied warranties, so the exclusion may not apply to you.)